The economics of imperfect competition

This book takes a new approach to traditional price theory and to the analysis of imperfect competition. It represents a breakthrough in the development of a "new" microeconomic theory. Increasingly, it has been recognized that the perfectly competitive paradigm is inappropriate to the explanation of pricing behavior in many "real life" markets characterized by a significant separation between producers and consumers. The spatial perspective adopted by the authors provides a natural separation of markets, but provides as well a powerful analogy for apparently nonspatial issues such as product differentiation, pricing over time, problems of storage and transportation, and the economics of intraindustry trade and of the multinational enterprise.

A major concern of *The Economics of Imperfect Competition: A Spatial Approach* is to make these analogies explicit by applying this spatial analysis to a wide variety of nonspatial problems. In addition, the analysis and results presented in this book are shown to carry significant policy implications with respect, for example, to the Robinson-Patman legislation, antimerger policies, and antidumping legislation. In particular, the authors have addressed issues that are of increasing concern to specialists, researchers, policy makers, and students in the areas of price theory, industrial organization, international trade, and regional and urban economics.

Dr. Melvin L. Greenhut is currently Abell Professor of Liberal Arts and Distinguished Professor of Economics at Texas A & M University as well as Visiting Distinguished Professor of Economics at the University of Oklahoma. He is the author of ten books and over sixty articles published in academic journals. Dr. George Norman is currently Tyler Professor of Economics and Chairman of the Department of Economics at the University of Leicester. He specializes in spatial, industrial, and regional economics. He is the author of four books and is published widely in academic journals. Dr. Chao-shun Hung is an Assistant Professor of Economics at Florida Atlantic University. In addition to spatial economic pricing, his fields of specialization include industrial, regional, and international economics.

The economics of imperfect competition

A spatial approach

Melvin L. Greenhut
Texas A&M University

George Norman
University of Leicester

Chao-shun Hung
Florida Atlantic University

The right of the
University of Cambridge
to print and sell
all manner of books
was granted by
Henry VIII in 1534.
The University has printed
and published continuously
since 1584.

CAMBRIDGE UNIVERSITY PRESS

Cambridge
London   New York   New Rochelle
Melbourne   Sydney

Published by the Press Syndicate of the University of Cambridge
The Pitt Building, Trumpington Street, Cambridge CB2 1RP
32 East 57th Street, New York, NY 10022, USA
10 Stamford Road, Oakleigh, Melbourne 3166, Australia

First published 1987

Printed in Canada

Library of Congress Cataloging-in-Publication Data
Greenhut, Melvin L.
The economics of imperfect competition.
Bibliography: p.
1. Competition, Imperfect.   2. Space in economics.
3. Price policy.   I. Norman, George, 1946–
II. Hung, Chao-shun, 1942–   .   III. Title.
HB238.G74   1987   338.6′048   86–11707

British Library Cataloguing in Publication Data
The economics of imperfect competition :
a spatial approach.
1. Competition, Imperfect
I. Greenhut, M. L.   II. Norman, George
III. Hung, Chao-shun
338.6′048   HB238

ISBN 0 521 30552 7 hard covers
ISBN 0 521 31564 6 paperback

Contents

Part II. Discriminatory pricing

x   **Contents**

Figures and tables

Figures

Tables

Preface

Microeconomic theory has undergone a quiet revolution in recent years. In particular, developments in the economics of imperfect competition and in what by some has been termed "new industrial organization" are responses to the deficiencies of the competitive paradigm in explaining the workings of modern economic markets. These developments take explicit account of the fact that individual buyers and sellers are not atomistic. The actions of any one economic agent will have noticeable effects on the economic environment for other agents and so can be expected to call forth reactions. The nature of these expected reactions, or "conjectural variations," will be of vital importance to price setting and efficiency in imperfectly competitive markets.

A central feature of the analysis to be presented in this book is the power that individual sellers have to set prices. This power rests in the ability of the seller to assign its customers to separate markets. In other words, an alternative subtitle to this book could have been "the economics of differentiated markets." What is needed is a convenient, powerful, and yet realistic analogy for market separation.

It has become apparent that "space" or "distance" can provide such an analogy. A spatial framework opens up entirely new ways of viewing long-standing problems in microeconomics. For example, the pricing of services and, more generally, of differentiated products and the pricing of electric power, amusement park privileges, and many other products, even though not distance-related per se, can be analyzed from a spatial perspective. Nor should it be thought that we address purely theoretical issues. Firms in private-enterprise nations have been increasingly subjected to legislation improperly rooted on a perfectly competitive paradigm. The recognition of market differentiation brings with it the need to develop significant insights into oligopoly market structures. Simply put, the spatial framework provides policymakers with a more adequate foundation on which to base legislative judgments.

We shall show that modern firms can be expected to price heterogeneously over the differentiated markets they serve. If reasoned statements are to be made explaining why this heterogeneity exists, and how it might change over time, a general theoretical framework is needed. This framework is readily formulated on the presumption that firms sell to spatially separated and distinct markets, each typically subject to different demands and competitive influences.

"Space" and "distance," in other words, are merely labels for a variety of economic phenomena. As noted earlier, one illustration relates to product differentiation, where individual product variants can be viewed as if located along a spectrum of consumer desires, with each variant having a well-defined "market area." The spatial framework allows investigation of the effects of new product variants and comparisons of product varieties in a number of different market structures. As another example, it is well recognized that demands for many products and services are limited not only by the price of the good or the fee that is charged but also by other costs of acquisition, such as waiting time or storage costs. This is particularly true in evaluating service activities, including private medical-care alternatives. The spatial analogy then sheds new light on the positive relation between fees and the number of medical practitioners.

Analysis of the impacts of mergers and antitrust regulation is made more tractable and realistic once the imperfectly competitive environment of firms is taken into account. Similarly, the efficiency and welfare implications of such topics as the bundling of goods (so-called tying contracts), bank charges on checking accounts, wage discrimination by sex and education, quantity discounts, and nonlinear price schedules charged by telephone companies are amenable to spatial analysis.

The reader of this book will find that the spatial framework sheds light on a number of important international trade issues. Tariff barriers have many of the properties of transport costs, but it will emerge that an ad valorem tax acts somewhat differently than a specific tax. International-trade theorists are becoming particularly concerned with two phenomena that do not fit easily into "traditional" theories: the emergence of the multinational enterprise and the increasing proportion of trade flow that is accounted for by intraindustry trade. Spatial microeconomic analysis provides insights into why companies and industries change orientation from chiefly export-based operations to strict emphasis on local markets, or even dealing in both markets, with intraindustry trade going both ways.

The topics indicated earlier by no means compose a complete list of the applications discussed in this book. We also hope that readers will identify applications that have never occurred to us or to others who have specialized in spatial microeconomics. Indeed, we would venture to suggest that the applications are limited only by imagination.

One final comment is worth making in this preface. The very concept of an economic space requires rejection of many of the principles derived in the theory of perfect competition. This book must, accordingly, center part of its attention on the following question: If perfect competition does not (cannot) characterize an economy of differentiated markets, then what is left of microeconomic theory? Perhaps most important, the reader will find that the long-existing intrinsic contradiction – between a macroeconomics based on aggregating business investment and foreign-sector activities along with the consumer and government sectors, and a microeconomics predicated on individual atomistic firms behaving as robots – will no longer apply to a microeconomics founded on both time and space. In a nutshell, the fundamental objective of this book is much deeper than simply recording the basic framework of *spatial* microeconomic analysis.

The authors owe an intellectual debt to far too many of their fellow economists for them to be named individually. Many of Dr. Greenhut's former students have contributed directly and indirectly to improving our exposition. In particular, we would like to thank Bruce Benson for his advice on the later chapters. Our colleagues in Texas, Leicester, and Florida have all provided unstinting advice and support, and our families have borne uncomplainingly the pressures that writing a book of this type inevitably imposes.

November 30, 1985

Melvin Greenhut
George Norman
Chao-shun Hung

CHAPTER 1

Introduction

The past decade has seen rapidly developing interest in the economic implications of imperfect competition. It is increasingly being recognized that we must depart from the competitive paradigm in which all economic agents are assumed to be price takers and in which there is no strategic interaction between economic agents. Rather, we should, as economists, be developing theories that recognize the importance and prevalence of imperfect competition and take explicit account of the power that individual buyers and sellers may have to control, or at least exert substantial influence over, particular markets.

The economics of imperfect competition does, of course, have a long history, as evidenced by the contributions of such eminent economists as Cournot, Edgeworth, and Chamberlin. Nevertheless, it is fair to say that only in recent years have the seeds sown by these economists begun to bear fruit.

Growth has been rapid. In the past few years there has been what is approaching an avalanche of research on imperfect competition, both within the context of "standard" microeconomic theory and under the wider umbrella of theories of market organization or industrial organization. The central focus of this research is on the concepts of the market and the firm and on the implications for resource allocation of alternative market structures. Explicit account is taken of the power that economic agents, such as firms, have to acquire and exercise market power and of the strategic interactions between economic agents.

It is now time to take stock and, in particular, to ask if it is possible to unify this rapidly expanding body of theory. Thus, although the analysis to be presented in this book can be viewed as part of the wider theory of industrial organization, it should be seen in a more fundamental sense as providing a general set of tools that can be brought to bear on the problems inherent in the economics of imperfect competition.

It should not be thought that only theoretical issues will be addressed in the following chapters. Firms and economic agents are generally subject to increasing degrees of legislative control. In particular, controls apply or guidelines have been set with respect to industrial pricing policies, international pricing arrangements, and company mergers. The Robinson-

Patman legislation in the United States constrains the pricing behavior of firms within that economy. The United Kingdom Price Commission argued strongly (prior to its abolition) that particular systems of discriminatory prices should be broken down (Norman 1981a). Antidumping legislation imposes constraints on the pricing policies of firms selling in international markets. Antimonopoly and antimerger legislation constrains the activities of firms when those activities lead to "excessive" market power.

This legislation is rooted in economic principles derived from classical competitive economics, but the legislation is applied almost by definition to imperfectly competitive markets. It is necessary, therefore, that the methodological foundations of this legislation be examined: It will emerge from this examination that much of the legislation should be re-evaluated.

1.1   Imperfect competition and "space": some introductory remarks

"Imperfect competition" is a very broad and imprecise term. It embraces market structures ranging from monopolistic competition, through oligopoly, to monopoly. Nevertheless, there is one distinguishing property common to all imperfectly competitive markets, no matter their type: Sellers in such markets have some power to choose price. In contrast to the competitive paradigm in which any price above the ruling market price leads to a complete loss of market share, the manager of the imperfectly competitive firm has some flexibility to choose between, for example, high price/low quantity and low price/high quantity.

Two minimum conditions are necessary for the exercise of such market power. First, there must exist some criterion on the basis of which consumers can be assigned to separated markets. Second, the individual firms must be capable of exercising at least local monopoly power over one or a group of these separate consumer markets.

The most natural criterion for the separation of consumers and of individual consumer markets is a spatial criterion. Households exist, purchase, and consume in a spatial setting. Firms produce at particular locations and sell in a series of spatially separated markets. Transport costs and the general frictions of distance (information loss, inconvenience, etc.) are important parts of their economic environment. They have to choose production locations, the markets in which they will attempt to sell their products, and the prices they will charge for those products. At the same time, these firms are likely to face a diversity of competitive conditions in their various markets: In some markets a given firm may be a near-monopolist, while simultaneously being subject to fierce competitive pressures in other markets.

In other words, firms and households exist and make decisions in a spatial economic environment. As a result, this book can be read in a relatively narrow sense as being "about" spatial economics and spatial pricing. A much stronger reason, however, underlies our use of the spatial theme and the foregoing statement that "space" is the most natural criterion for the separation of consumer markets in the context of imperfect competition. It is clear that "space" and "distance" are merely labels for a wide variety of other important economic phenomena: Tariff costs, waiting time, storage costs, and product differentiation are four obvious examples. When we talk of the consumer's location in a spatial sense, we can equally talk of the country in which the consumer is located, the time of day, month, or year at which the consumer would prefer to purchase the commodity, or the consumer's most preferred product variety, in the sense of Lancaster (1979). When we refer to the producer's location, we can equally consider the country in which the product is produced, the time of day, month, or year at which it is produced, or the product variety actually manufactured by the producer. In place of transport costs, we can substitute tariff barriers, waiting time or storage time, or the utility loss consequent upon the consumer being offered a product other than the most preferred product.

"Space," in other words, provides the unification referred to earlier. It provides us with a simple and convenient language with which we can approach and interpret many of the current problems in imperfect competition.

1.2   Price policy and imperfect (or spatial) competition

Once we approach the analysis of imperfect competition from a spatial perspective, several important issues are brought into focus, particularly as regards pricing policies of imperfectly competitive firms. Significant differences arise between classical competitive price theory and imperfectly competitive price theory – differences that are supported by extensive empirical evidence. See, for example, Phlips (1983) for an excellent discussion of empirical pricing practices.

The work of authors such as Greenhut (1956), Greenhut, Greenhut, and Kelly (1977), Capozza and Van Order (1978), and Benson (1980a) shows that increases in pressures of competition may well lead to higher prices than those resulting under monopoly conditions. Moreover, these authors have shown that comparative statics can appear to be perverse in a world of imperfect competition. Capozza and Van Order (1978) indicate that increases in fixed costs, marginal costs, or transport costs can result in effects opposite to those that occur in perfectly competitive markets. In addition, the aforementioned writers indicate that if firms selling in a series of separated markets adopt the nondiscriminatory pricing policy to which legislators appear to be committed, competitive entry may well lead to a general *increase* in prices.

Just what is meant by nondiscriminatory pricing has been defined very clearly by Phlips (1983, p. 6). A pricing policy is defined to be nondiscriminatory when two varieties of a product are sold by the same seller to two different buyers at the same *net* price, the net price being the price paid by the buyer corrected for the cost associated with product differentiation. Phlips has in mind very broad concepts of product variety and product differentiation. Transport of a commodity from one place to another, storage from one time to another, making products available at particular times, as well as "conventional" variations in packaging, design, and so forth, all constitute types of product differentiation. It follows, for example, that the only nondiscriminatory *spatial* pricing policy is the f.o.b. pricing policy under which all consumers pay exactly the same (mill) price at the factory gates and then pay full transport costs to their own consuming locations.

We shall have much more to say about nondiscriminatory pricing policies later, and in particular we shall call into question the revealed preference of legislators for such pricing policies. It is not beyond the bounds of possibility that this preference rests on the naive, perfectly competitive ideal that firms should price at marginal cost! More fundamentally, consequent upon the work of Singer (1937) and Hoover (1937), the principle that a firm in an imperfectly competitive environment should, or would, adopt a nondiscriminatory pricing policy has been called into question. Classical microeconomic theory indicates that a firm *may discriminate* in price provided that (1) it controls the means by which its overall market is separated into a number of distinct submarkets and (2) elasticity of demand varies between submarkets. We have already seen that under imperfect competition, markets are naturally separable, whether by the costs of distance, storage, waiting time, or product variety. This separation is controlled by the firm provided that the firm controls the transport facilities or storage facilities, can identify the consumer's preferred time of consumption, or can identify the consumer's preferred product variety. All that is necessary, therefore, is that condition (2) hold.

It is easiest to consider condition (2) in the context of spatial competition: We shall show in later chapters how the remarks that follow can be interpreted in terms of other types of market separation. Even if all consumers in all markets exhibit identical demand curves for a particular commodity, distance costs have the effect of generating varying demand elasticities between spatially separated markets. In other words, in the absence of institutional or legislative constraints, price discrimination would naturally characterize the spatial economy.

More fundamentally, standard microeconomic theory confines the discussion of price discrimination to monopolistic market structures: The idea that competition might lead a firm to discriminate between markets simply is not considered. In contrast, recent theoretical analysis of spatial pricing policies generates the conclusion that *profit-maximizing spatial competitors will price-discriminate*. Indeed, it was shown in the work of Greenhut and Ohta (1975a), Greenhut and Greenhut (1975, 1977), and Norman (1981b) that the degree of spatial price discrimination *tends to increase as competitive forces increase*, a result subsequently empirically supported in several nations by the findings of Greenhut (1981).

Price discrimination in response to the demand factors noted earlier will give rise to a reasonably well ordered pattern of spatial prices. A further feature of spatial economics, however, is the recognition that there are forces *intrinsic to spatial competition* such that a firm is likely to face widely varying competitive pressure in the markets it serves. Prices across these markets need bear little relation to the distances from the firm to its markets (Norman 1986), while being a totally rational response to the firm's economic environment. Spatial price theory thus uncovers reasons for price differentials in different markets that go beyond average production-cost differentials, essentially the only basic justification for differential net prices allowed by statutes such as the Robinson-Patman Act. In a broad sense, spatial price theory views a statute of the Robinson-Patman type as a complete rejection of maximum-profit/free-enterprise goals.

As we have indicated, this discussion can be extended beyond the simple spatial separation of markets. Modern industrial societies contain many firms that sell their products in a number of distinct markets. For example, there are conglomerates that operate in several "industries" and multiple-product firms that produce a range of differentiated products, each product differentiate being aimed at a more or less distinct set of consumers (e.g., motor-car manufacturers produce compact, medium-size, and large cars). The more heterogeneous the competitive forces operating in particular "markets," the less likely is it that prices across markets will be in any definable way related to the costs of serving those markets. In certain markets, the firm, whether it be a conglomerate or multiproduct firm, will be able to earn some degree of monopoly rent, while in others it will be forced to meet the competitive price.

One area in which it might be expected that classical microeconomics would embrace the spatial dimension is in the analysis of international trade. Even here, however, the principles of spatial economics and imperfect competition are sadly neglected. In particular, antidumping legislation is justified by policymakers at least in part on the basis of a classical (spaceless) economic theory that conceives of the dumping of goods in foreign markets at lower prices than in domestic markets as a discriminatory (artificial) sales device. Imperfect competition, however, leads to the view that what is seen as dumping, either within or between countries, is a natural way of pricing in response to a heterogeneous competitive environment.

1.3   Market demand and pricing policy

We have seen that market separation is central to imperfect competition. This implies that a distinction must be drawn between the net price received by the seller and the full price actually incurred by the consumer. Once we allow for product differentiation by means of factors such as transport costs, storage costs, waiting time, or utility loss, the firm proposing to sell its product to a number of consumers must distinguish between the (gross) demand for a good on the part of each consumer and the effective (net) demand that the seller actually perceives.

The importance of this distinction can be highlighted by contrasting spatial and spaceless aggregate demand. Consider a very simple case in which there are N identical consumers for each of whom individual (gross) demand is a simple linear function of price:

$$q = \frac{a}{b} - \frac{p}{b} \quad (a, b > 0) \tag{1.1}$$

or, in indirect form,

$$p = a - bq \tag{1.1'}$$

In classical economics, distance is ignored – effectively, transport costs are zero. As a result, identical (gross) demands for a good on the part of buyers also imply identical effective (net) demands. Aggregate (market) demand is obtained simply by multiplying individual demand by the number of buyers:

$$Q = Nq = \frac{N}{b}(a - p) \tag{1.2}$$

or, in inverse form,

$$p = a - \frac{b}{N}Q \tag{1.2'}$$

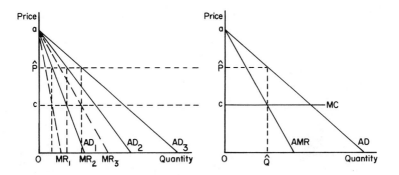

Figure 1.1. Spaceless aggregate demand and profit maximization.

Thus, with linear individual demands, aggregate demand is also linear, the process of aggregation merely leading to a rotation of the individual demand function as in Figure 1.1 (left).

Total revenue in this simple world is $R = pQ$. Assume that marginal cost is constant at c per unit. Profits are maximized when marginal revenue (MR) equals marginal cost (MC), from which it follows that the profit-maximizing price and output are (Figure 1.1, left)

$$\hat{P} = \frac{a}{2} + \frac{c}{2}; \qquad \hat{Q} = \frac{N}{2b}(a - c) \tag{1.3}$$

Note that the profit-maximizing price in this spaceless world is independent of the number of consumers. Rotation of the individual demand functions as in Figure 1.1 is such that *aggregate demand has the same elasticity as individual demand at any given price*[1] and so leaves the profit-maximizing price unaltered.

Now consider a space economy in which there are positive transport costs, and assume that the seller adopts an f.o.b. pricing policy. Then, as was noted earlier, a distinction must be drawn between the individual buyer's gross demand [equation (1.1)] and the effective net demand perceived by the seller. The full price (the delivered price) to a buyer located r distance units from the seller is made up of the mill price, m, plus the freight cost, tr, where t is a constant freight rate and r the number of distance units from seller to buyer: That is to say, price at distance r is $p(r) = m + tr$.

Assume that the N potential consumers are located in three spatially distinct markets at distances 0, r_1, and r_2 from the seller, with $N/3$ consumers at each location. Because delivered price in market i is $m + tr_i$, individual demand in market i is

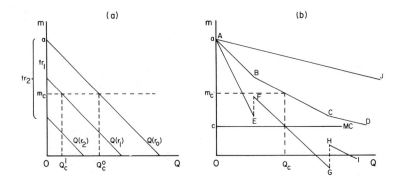

Figure 1.2. Spatial aggregate demand and profit maximization.

$$q(r_i) = (a - m - tr_i)/b \qquad (1.4)$$

and, in indirect form,

$$m = a - tr_i - bq(r_i) \qquad (1.4')$$

Comparison of (1.4′) and (1.1′) indicates that the effective individual demand curve is subjected to a downward shift under the impact of distance costs. Total demand in market i is

$$Q(r_i) = \frac{N}{3}(a - m - tr_i)/b \qquad (1.5)$$

These total demand curves are illustrated in Figure 1.2(a). Horizontal aggregation of the three (net) demand curves establishes aggregate demand in the three markets *at any mill price* as in Figure 1.2(b) – the demand curve *ABCD*. The associated marginal-revenue curve (MR) is *AEFGHI*; the breaks in this MR curve occur at corners of the aggregate demand curve. [The spaceless aggregate demand curve *AJ* is also illustrated in Figure 1.2(b).]

Given a marginal cost (MC) of c, the seller maximizes profit by setting MR = MC. It will produce a total output of Q_c at mill price m_c, of which Q_c^0 is supplied to market 0, and Q_c^1 to market 1. Note that nothing is supplied to market 2, because mill price m_c is greater than the maximum (net of transport cost) price consumers in market 2 are willing to pay.

The corners in the aggregate demand function *ABCD* arise because attention has been confined to a finite number of markets. The aggregate spatial demand curve (and MR curve) will become more smoothly convex the greater the number of spatially separated markets in which the firm sells its product.

This can be easily demonstrated. Assume that consumers are evenly distributed at density D over a line market, with the producer, again for simplicity, located at one end of that market. Individual demand from consumers located distance r from the seller is[2]

$$q(r) = (a - m_L - tr)/b \tag{1.6}$$

and aggregate demand in a market of length R is

$$Q_L(R) = D \int_0^R q(r)\, dr = \frac{DR}{b}\left(a - m_L - \frac{1}{2}tR\right) \tag{1.7}$$

The maximum distance over which the firm can sell its product is the distance R^* at which demand falls to zero. In other words, R^* is given by

$$(a - m_L - tR^*)/b = 0 \Rightarrow R^* = (a - m_L)/t \tag{1.8}$$

Substituting this value of R^* in (1.7) gives the aggregate demand function

$$Q_L(R^*) = \frac{D}{2bt}(a - m_L)^2 \tag{1.9}$$

or, in indirect form,

$$m_L = a - \left(\frac{2bt}{D}Q_L\right)^{1/2} \tag{1.9'}$$

This demand curve is illustrated in Figure 1.3. As is to be expected from the discussion of Figure 1.2, it is convex to the origin despite the fact that individual demand is linear.

Equation (1.9') can be used to identify optimal f.o.b. price/quantity decisions in the line market. Setting MR = MC gives (see Mathematical Appendix)

$$\hat{Q}_L = \frac{2D}{9bt}(a - c)^2 \tag{1.10}$$

Substituting this value into (1.9') and recalling (1.3), the following optimal f.o.b. mill prices are obtained:

$$\hat{m}_S = \frac{a}{2} + \frac{c}{2} \quad \text{(spaceless monopolists)}$$
$$\hat{m}_L = \frac{a}{3} + \frac{2c}{3} \quad \text{(spatial line monopolists)} \tag{1.11}$$

Because $a > c$ (a is the highest delivered price consumers are willing to pay for the product), it follows that

$$\hat{m}_L < \hat{m}_S \tag{1.12}$$

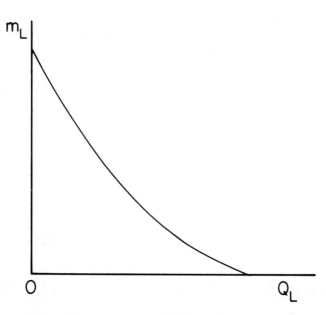

Figure 1.3. Aggregate spatial demand.

The spaceless monopolist charges a higher mill price than the spatial monopolist.

An intuitive reason can be advanced for this result. The spaceless monopolist faces a known number of consumers, but the spatial monopolist, by cutting mill price, can increase the market area over which he sells and thus can increase the number of consumers supplied. There is a trade-off that can then be made between loss of revenue from existing consumers, consequent upon a reduction in mill price, and additional revenue that will arise from the new consumers who are supplied as a result of the increase in market radius.

1.4   Discriminatory pricing: an introduction

The analysis of Section 1.3 assumes that the firm adopts a nondiscriminatory pricing policy: in a spatial context, an f.o.b. pricing policy. It will emerge in later chapters of this book, however, and is clear from the work of Phlips (1983), that price discrimination is prevalent. We defined in Section 1.2 just what is meant by price discimination. *Spatial* price discrimination can then be interpreted in either of two (effectively equivalent) ways. It occurs either as freight absorption by the seller or, equiva-

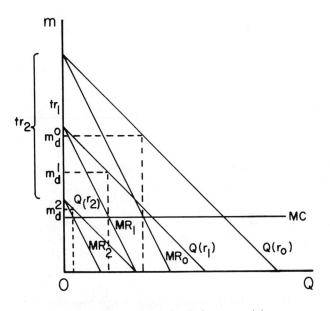

Figure 1.4. Optimal discriminatory pricing.

lently, as the seller charging different f.o.b. mill prices to buyers at different locations.

As a simple prelude to our later discussion, note that in Figure 1.2(a) the net market demand curves for the spatially separated markets have different elasticities at any given mill price, one of the necessary conditions for price discrimination to be profit-maximizing. That figure is repeated as Figure 1.4, where now we also introduce the marginal-revenue curve MR_i at each selling location.

Given the assumption of constant marginal production costs, cost conditions in any one market are unaffected by the amount supplied to any other market. Aggregate profit maximization is achieved, therefore, by setting $MR_i = MC$ *at each market point*, that is, by maximizing profit at each market point. This is illustrated in Figure 1.4 using the same marginal-cost curve as for Figure 1.2. Several points emerge from Figure 1.4. First, it should be obvious that spatial price discrimination is actually occurring, because the optimal mill prices in markets 0, 1, and 2 are m_d^0, m_d^1, and m_d^2, respectively, and these are not equal.[3] Second, it can be seen by comparing Figures 1.2(a) and 1.4 that the discriminatory mill price is higher in market 0 than is the f.o.b. mill price (and so the quantity supplied is lower), but market 2 is supplied under the discriminatory scheme, whereas it was not in the f.o.b. scheme.[4]

Finally, the discriminatory mill prices bear a strong relationship to each other. Given linear individual demand functions, these mill prices are such that (see Mathematical Appendix)

$$m_d^1 = m_d^0 - \tfrac{1}{2}tr_1; \qquad m_d^2 = m_d^0 - \tfrac{1}{2}tr_2 \qquad (1.13)$$

In other words, optimal mill price to a particular selling point is reduced by one-half the amount of transport costs to that point. The seller is absorbing 50 percent of transport costs to each selling location.

1.5   The generality of a spatial approach to imperfect competition: an example

Our primary intention in this book is to shed light on the nature and implications of imperfect competition, and we hope that even the very brief hints contained in this introductory chapter are sufficient to convince the reader that "space" provides a useful analogy for this purpose. The spatial labels are capable of being reinterpreted in a wide variety of ways. They provide us with an important set of tools and open up new avenues for viewing some of the most important problems in modern microeconomics and industrial organization.

For those who are not yet fully convinced that when we talk of "space" we are, in effect, talking of a much wider range of economic phenomena in our imperfectly competitive world, a simple application of the use of spatial economics to analyze a nonspatial problem may be helpful.[5]

Consider the market for a service such as private health care. It has been noted by various researchers that the fees charged by physicians tend to increase with the number of physicians in a particular catchment area. Can a simple explanation be suggested for this apparently paradoxical result? The full price paid by a particular patient is a combination of the physician's fee *plus* the patient's waiting time (for an appointment and in the waiting room). This price can be written

$$p(\gamma, n) = n + w\gamma \qquad (1.14)$$

where n is the fee, w is the unit price of customer-supplied time (e.g., the wage rate), and γ is the actual time willingly supplied by the patient. Note the similarity between this price and an f.o.b. price. By analogy, n is equivalent to the mill price, w to the transport cost, and γ to the distance from the supplier.

Patients can be ordered in terms of the time they are willing to wait for an appointment, determined in part by commuting time and by the opportunity cost they attribute to their waiting time. There will be some maximum time T (analogous to the market radius R) that patients will be

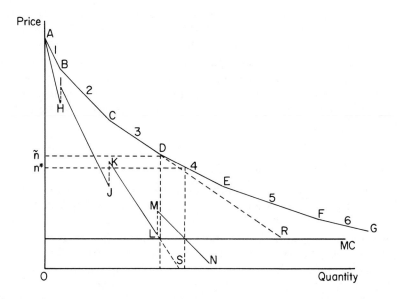

Figure 1.5. Pricing of physicians' services.

required to supply, determined largely by the number of physicians in a given catchment area. Assume that current market conditions are such that the potential patients for a particular physician are grouped in six "markets" determined by waiting times $\gamma_1, \gamma_2, \gamma_3, \ldots, \gamma_6$. Aggregate demand is $ABCDEFG$ in Figure 1.5, with marginal revenue $AHIJKLMN$. If marginal cost is MC, the physician will supply patients with waiting times up to γ_4 ($T = \gamma_4$) and charge a fee of n^*.

Now let additional physicians enter the catchment area. This will serve to reduce the waiting time that patients are required to supply. In other words, entry of new physicians will reduce the maximum waiting time T. Assume that our physician loses the potential patients in markets 4, 5, and 6; these patients can now switch to another physician offering a shorter waiting time. The aggregate demand curve is now $ABCDR$, with marginal revenue $AHIJKLS$.

With marginal cost of MC, the physician's fee has increased to $\tilde{n}$. In other words, entry of additional physicians has led to an increase in physicians' fees – the seemingly paradoxical empirical regularity with which we started.

Many other nonspatial examples will be suggested in the following chapters. We shall, for example, provide a drastically different understanding of what antitrust policy should be. We explain (account for) the correspondences in the price policies of manufacturing firms and the pricing techniques of public utilities, the bundling of goods, the use of quantity discounts, the advantages of multinational enterprises, the dumping of goods and reverse dumping patterns (within regions of countries and between countries), the creation of multiple product lines, and the reasons for changing competitive conjectural variations over time. These and other business practices and relationships are readily evaluated by use of a spatial analogy.

1.6   Plan of the book

Recent research concerning imperfect competition and, in particular, the pricing strategies that are likely to be used by firms in imperfectly competitive markets has developed along two main lines: One has been concerned with the optimal pricing policy of the profit-maximizing firm; the other has dealt with the implications for the firm's pricing behavior of restrictions on optimal pricing. Under the first approach, a firm is free of institutional constraints and has complete information. It is therefore able to choose the pricing policy that will maximize its profits. This form of price policy will generally result in some form of price discrimination. Under the second approach, institutional constraints or limitations on information in the market space cause the firm to adopt either a mill-price policy or a special variant of price discrimination, namely, uniform delivered pricing.

Institutional constraints and information limitations are important elements in the real world of economic space. The first part of this book, therefore, will focus attention on the nondiscriminatory (f.o.b.) mill-price policy, the second part will deal with a firm's discriminatory price policy, and the third part will determine the equilibrium properties of the imperfectly competitive (space) economy.

Analysis of f.o.b. pricing stresses the impact on a firm's pricing policy of (1) the price conjectural variations of the entrepreneur and (2) the underlying demand conditions that exist over the firm's market space. Analysis of general price discrimination and the special discriminatory form known as uniform delivered pricing centers on the relation between demand conditions and price discrimination, a comparison of output and welfare effects under all alternative price policies, and the impacts of competitive entry on the pricing policy of the firm. The third part of this book focuses attention on the locations and market areas of firms under the alternative price policies. It establishes the imperfectly competitive counterpart to the classical perfectly competitive long-run equilibrium conditions.

A few statements about organization and style of writing may be useful. In particular, because the subject matter and approach of this book will be new for many readers, selected mathematical details are provided in Mathematical Appendixes at the ends of chapters. This is done chiefly to facilitate reading for those who prefer to "track down" final results, as well as to introduce these readers to the mathematical approaches that are most often used is this branch of microeconomic theory. It is worth emphasizing that we presume knowledge of not much more than elementary calculus in the mathematical exposition. Throughout this book we shall intersperse important theoretical conclusions with examples drawn from the world around us, examples that, as we noted earlier, will not necessarily reflect the subject of economic space per se.

Mathematical appendix

Optimal f.o.b. mill price: Total revenue is $m_L Q_L$. Marginal revenue is, from equation (1.9′),

$$\mathrm{MR}_L = a - \frac{3}{2}\left(\frac{2bt}{D}Q_L\right)^{1/2} \tag{A1.1}$$

Setting $\mathrm{MR}_L = c$ gives equation (1.10).

Optimal discriminatory price: Total revenue from consumers at a distance r from the producer is [from (1.1)]

$$\mathrm{TR}(r) = p(r)q(r) = (a - bq(r))q(r) \tag{A1.2}$$

Total cost is

$$\mathrm{TC}(r) = (c + tr)q(r) \tag{A1.3}$$

Equating marginal revenue with marginal cost,

$$a - 2bq(r) = c + tr$$

$$\Rightarrow \qquad q(r) = (a - c - tr)/2b$$

$$\Rightarrow \qquad p(r) = a - bq(r) = \tfrac{1}{2}(a + c) + \tfrac{1}{2}tr \tag{A1.4}$$

In terms of mill prices,

$$m_d(r) = p(r) - tr = \tfrac{1}{2}(a + c) - \tfrac{1}{2}tr$$

$$= m_d(0) - \tfrac{1}{2}tr \tag{A1.5}$$

Nondiscriminatory pricing

A general theory of imperfect competition and nondiscriminatory pricing: the short run

It was noted in Chapter 1 that profit maximization and imperfect competition generally imply a discriminatory pricing policy. Why, therefore, do we feel it necessary to devote Part I of this book to nondiscriminatory pricing? Several reasons can be advanced to justify this approach. First, nondiscriminatory pricing is the pricing policy preferred by policymakers. Whether for this or other reasons, it is also a pricing policy used by more than 29 percent of businesses in a recent empirical analysis of spatial pricing (see Chapter 14). If we are to comment sensibly on policy, we must first understand the preferred option of policymakers.

Second, there are many cases in which delivery is taken by consumers at the factory gates, at the retail outlet, or by carriers under the control of the buyer. In such cases the sellers will find it difficult, if not impossible, to discriminate between buyers, because they will be unlikely to have the information that will allow them to assign buyers to separate markets. Nondiscriminatory (f.o.b.) pricing is effectively the only feasible pricing policy.

Third, when we move outside the purely spatial setting and use "space" as an analogue for other economic phenomena, f.o.b. pricing will often be the appropriate pricing system. It has already been shown that that is the case with "full-price" models that include waiting time. It is also the case, as will be shown in Chapter 5, when spatial models are applied to analysis of product differentiation.

As has been indicated, f.o.b. pricing is a pricing policy that has gained favor among policymakers and those who advise governments. It is effectively the form of spatial pricing preferred by proponents of the Robinson-Patman Act in the United States, and the only form of spatial pricing that avoids the criticisms of cross-subsidization made by the Price Commission in the United Kingdom (Norman 1981a). In an international context, departure from f.o.b. pricing leaves exporters open to accusations of dumping in foreign markets.

Is it not surprising, therefore, that there has been extensive examination of the properties of f.o.b. pricing schemes. What is surprising is the controversy to which this examination has given rise. In particular, many of the well-known and accepted properties of the classical nonspatial paradigm have been shown to hold only under special conditions once analysis is conducted in an imperfectly competitive, nondiscriminatory environment.

Two examples illustrate this controversy and will set the scene for the remainder of this chapter. Contrary to classical economic theory, in which a monopolist is conceived to charge a higher price than a competitive firm, some forms of spatial competition will generate a higher price than that charged by a spatial monopolist (Greenhut 1956; Greenhut, Hwang, and Ohta 1975). Second, the price effects of spatial competition depend crucially on how a spatial firm anticipates rival reactions to its own change in price. In other words, the outcome of the competitive process, both in terms of price *levels* and in terms of the impact on prices of changes in the economic environment, depends on the conjectural variations held by a firm regarding the reactions of its rivals (Capozza and Van Order 1978).

Although many conjectural variations can be envisaged, three have entered the folklore of spatial economics:

1. *Löschian competition,* under which the firm presumes that its rivals will react identically to any proposed price change.
2. *Hotelling-Smithies (H-S) competition,* under which the firm presumes that its rivals will not react to a proposed price change.
3. *Greenhut-Ohta (G-O) competition,* under which the firm anticipates its price on the market boundary to be constrained to a known, fixed value.

Students of oligopoly theory will note that the Hotelling-Smithies assumption is equivalent to the Bertrand-Nash assumption in the "traditional" analysis of oligopoly. Thus, whenever reference is made to H-S competition, this is equivalent to a Bertrand-Nash solution.

With respect to prive *levels*, Löschian competition will lead to market prices higher than those charged by a monopolist. H-S competition, in contrast, results in market prices that may be higher or lower than those of the spatial monopolist (for reasons to be discussed in detail later), whereas G-O competition leads to the lowest competitive prices.

With respect to the impact on prices of changes in the economic environment (costs, consumer density, etc.), apparently perverse results vis-à-vis classical economic theory obtain only when rival firms react analogously or identically, as in the case of Löschian competition. More specifically, H-S competitive assumptions, in particular circumstances, lead to the following, and G-O competitive assumptions always lead to the following:

1. As transport costs and/or fixed costs approach zero, nonspatial perfect competition results, and the firm's price approaches marginal costs.
2. Rises in fixed costs, marginal costs, and transport cost all lead to the classical-theory increase in price.
3. As more firms enter the industry, the increased competition lowers price.
4. Price falls in the long run as population density increases.

Löschian competition, on the other hand, leads to results violating those of nonspatial competitive theory:

1. As transport costs and/or fixed costs approach zero, price will approach the nonspatial monopoly price.
2. As fixed costs and transport costs rise, price *falls*, whereas an increase in marginal cost leads to ambiguous results.
3. As firms enter and thus competition increases, price increases.
4. Price increases as population density increases.

It has been argued by Capozza and Van Order (1978) that the spatial firm typically will not expect rival firms to react to its actions, because each firm constitutes only a small proportion of the total competition in the market. Thus, what generally prevails over economic space is the H-S result, and these authors conclude that the perverse effects vis-à-vis classical competitive theory need not cause great alarm.

Whether or not H-S competition is "more reasonable" than Löschian competition is open to question, because in many cases spatial competition takes place between "few" rather than "many" firms. Nor should it be thought that the effects of entry on spatial prices are determined solely by the competitive assumptions. The relationship between monopoly and competitive prices, the effects on price of competitive entry, and the effects on price of changes in costs are also crucially affected by the precise form of the individual demand curve (Benson 1980a; Ohta 1980). The perverse results under the Löschian assumption arise only if individual demand is not "very convex" in a manner that will be made clear in subsequent discussion in this chapter.

Many other elements of the debate will emerge later. What should be clear is that this controversy is of considerable importance, because it brings into question many of the fundamental principles of pricing under alternative market structures. Analysis in this chapter concentrates on price determination in the short run. In the following three chapters, the theory is extended to the long-run (zero-profit) equilibrium state, and the implications for both spatial and nonspatial markets are demonstrated.

2.1   The basic spatial model

In order to investigate in detail the connections between alternative forms of spatial competition (or conjectural variations), the shapes of the individual demand curves, and the resulting market prices, we use a model defined by a number of basic assumptions that will characterize much of our subsequent analysis:

> *Assumption 1:* Each producer is located at a point on an unbounded line market.[1]
> *Assumption 2:* All producers produce a homogeneous product.
> *Assumption 3:* Producers are local monopolists. When firms are in competition, there is no market overlap; consumers buy from the firm offering the lowest price.
> *Assumption 4:* Consumers are continuously distributed over the market at uniform density D.
> *Assumption 5:* Individual demand functions are identical for all consumers and have negative slopes in the relevant domain.
> *Assumption 6:* The freight rate is linearly proportional to distance and quantity transported.

Certain of these assumptions will be relaxed in later chapters. In particular, spatial competition will be considered in cases in which firms' market areas overlap (thus relaxing Assumption 3) and in cases in which consumers are unevenly distributed (thus relaxing Assumption 4).

Individual demand is assumed to be given by the general functional form

$$q(r) = f(p(r)) \quad (f' < 0) \tag{2.1}$$

and price $p(r)$ is given by the f.o.b. mill pricing policy:

$$p(r) = m + tr \tag{2.2}$$

In order to relate this discussion to the profit-maximizing decision of the spatial firm, the firm's production costs must be specified. The assumed cost structure is that common to much of spatial analysis. Total production costs are

$$C(Q) = F + cQ \tag{2.3}$$

where F is fixed costs, c is (constant) marginal costs, and Q is total output. Thus, production is assumed to be characterized by economies of scale.

2.2   Elasticity and the fundamental pricing equation

We are now in a position to derive the fundamental pricing equation that applies with f.o.b. pricing. It should be emphasized that no judgment is made at this stage as to whether the firm is a spatial monopolist or spatial competitor, nor about the nature of the competitive process.

Aggregate spatial demand at mill price m over a market with radius R is

$$Q(R, m) = 2D \int_0^R f(m + tr) \, dr \qquad (2.4)$$

Because the firm is assumed to apply an f.o.b. pricing policy, all transport costs are paid by the consumers. The net price received by the firm from *each* consumer is therefore the mill price m, while production cost on each unit of output is c. Profit for the firm is

$$\pi(R, m) = (m - c) Q(R, m) - F \qquad (2.5)$$

The first-order condition for the profit-maximizing choice of mill price is then

$$\frac{d\pi(R, m)}{dm} = (m - c)\frac{dQ}{dm} + Q = 0 \qquad (2.6)$$

Under an f.o.b. pricing policy, the appropriate decision variable for the firm is the mill price, m, because once that has been specified, delivered prices are determined by equation (2.2). In addition, the price *actually received* by the firm is delivered price net of transport costs (i.e., the mill price). Hence, elasticity of demand, which will be shown to be crucial to the profit-maximizing pricing decision, should be considered with respect to *mill price* rather than with respect to delivered price.

The elasticity of aggregate demand with respect to mill price is[2]

$$e(R, m) = -\frac{m}{Q}\frac{dQ}{dm} = -\frac{m \int_0^R f'(m + tr) \, dr}{\int_0^R f(m + tr) \, dr} - m\frac{\partial R}{\partial m}\frac{f(m + tR)}{\int_0^R f(m + tr) \, dr} \qquad (2.7)$$

Reorganizing (2.6) and applying (2.7) gives the *fundamental pricing equation* for *any* aggregate demand function $Q(R, m)$:

$$m^*\left(1 - \frac{1}{e(R, m^*)}\right) = c \qquad (2.8)$$

The less (more) elastic is aggregate demand $Q(R, m)$, the higher (lower) will be the f.o.b. mill price m^* that satisfies the fundamental pricing equation.

This discussion allows little to be said about f.o.b. prices in a spatial world unless more specific comments can be made about the determinants of the aggregate demand elasticity $e(R, m)$. Let us go back, therefore, to the individual demand function (2.1).

The elasticity of individual demand with respect to mill price is given in the usual way by[3]

$$\epsilon(r,m) = -\frac{m}{f}\frac{df}{dm} = -m\frac{f'(m+tr)}{f(m+tr)} \tag{2.9}$$

In other words, elasticity of individual demand with respect to mill price is a function of distance (and thus transport costs) from the producer. The precise behavior of $\epsilon(r,m)$ will be determined by the behavior of the ratio $f'(m+tr)/f(m+tr)$.

Now consider the elasticity of aggregate demand – equation (2.7). This can be rewritten

$$e(R,m) = \int_0^R \frac{-mf'(m+tr)}{f(m+tr)}\frac{f(m+tr)}{Q(R,m)}\,dr + v_i mw(R) \tag{2.7'}$$

where

$$v_i = -\partial R/\partial m$$

$$w(R) = f(m+tR)\Big/\int_0^R f(m+tr)\,dr$$

Now define a weighting function $w(r)$:

$$w(r) = f(m+tr)\Big/\int_0^R f(m+tr)\,dr \tag{2.10}$$

Note that

$$\int_0^R w(r)\,dr = 1 \tag{2.11}$$

Substituting (2.9) and (2.11) in (2.7') gives a much simpler equation for aggregate demand elasticity:

$$e(r,m) = \int_0^R \epsilon(r,m)w(r)\,dr + v_i mw(R) \tag{2.12}$$

Ignore the final term in equation (2.12) for the moment; we shall return to this term later and consider its significance. Then, as might be expected, *the elasticity of aggregate spatial demand is a weighted average of the elasticities of the individual spatial demand functions,* with weights given by $w(r)$. The weights $w(r)$ appeal to intuition: The weight applied to the individual demand elasticity of consumers distance r from the seller is just the proportion of total demand taken by these consumers [see equation (2.10)]. Note that because $f(m+tr)$ is monotonic decreasing with respect to distance r, then $w(r)$ is also monotonic decreasing with respect to r.

The aggregate demand elasticity, and thus the optimal f.o.b. price, will be determined in large part by the behavior of the individual demand elasticity $\epsilon(r, m)$. We now turn briefly to a consideration of the behavior of this latter elasticity.

2.3   A seeming digression: negative exponential demand

From Stevens and Rydell (1966) we have the following definitions:

> *Definition 1:* Demand curve $f[p(r)]$ is a negative exponential if and only if $f''[p(r)] = \{f'[p(r)]\}^2/f[p(r)]$ for all $p(r)$.
>
> *Definition 2:* Demand curve $f[p(r)]$ is less convex than a negative exponential if and only if $f''[p(r)] < \{f'[p(r)]\}^2/f[p(r)]$ for all $p(r)$.
>
> *Definition 3:* Demand curve $f[p(r)]$ is more convex than a negative exponential if and only if $f''[p(r)] > \{f'[p(r)]\}^2/f[p(r)]$ for all $p(r)$.

One weakness of this classification should be noted. Because the second-derivative conditions apply to all delivered prices, the classification is neither exhaustive nor mutually exclusive. Some demand curves clearly do not fit any of these definitions, whereas others can fit more than one of the categories. On the other hand, the classifications are sufficiently general to capture the most generally used demand functions.

The negative-exponential demand function is

$$f(p(r)) = ae^{-bp(r)} \tag{2.13}$$

where a and b are positive constants.[4] This function can be related to a particular individual inverse demand function often used in spatial analysis, $p = \alpha - (\beta/x)q^x$, which in direct form is given by

$$q = \left(\frac{x}{\beta}(\alpha - p)\right)^{1/x} \quad (x \neq 0) \tag{2.14}$$

The demand function (2.14) is more convex than a negative exponential for $x < 0$ and less convex than a negative exponential for $x > 0$ (see Mathematical Appendix). Economists have in the past used the linear demand curve as the basis for comparing demand convexities. In the analysis that follows, it will be shown that the negative-exponential demand curve is the more appropriate dividing line. Demand curves less convex than a negative exponential include mildly convex, linear $(x = 1)$, and concave demand curves. As a consequence, the assumption of linear demand that is often necessary to facilitate mathematical analysis is not, in fact, a special case. Qualitative results that hold for the linear case will also hold for a wide range of convex and concave demand functions.

2.4   Elasticity revisited

The reason for using the convex, negative-exponential demand curve as a departure point is that this particular form of demand curve has the analytically revealing property of making $-f'[p(r)]/f[p(r)]$ a constant with respect to $p(r)$. It will emerge later that this property has important implications for the elasticity of the individual spatial demand function in the marketplace and thus for the profit-maximizing pricing decision.

Recall equation (2.9). It can be seen from this equation that individual demand elasticity will vary with distance r in a manner determined by the ratio $f'(m+tr)/f(m+tr)$. Specifically,

$$\frac{d}{dr}\epsilon(r,m) = m\frac{d}{dr}\frac{f'(m+tr)}{-f(m+tr)} \tag{2.15}$$

Now,[5]

$$\frac{d}{dr}\left(-\frac{f'(m+tr)}{f(m+tr)}\right) = \frac{t\{-f(p(r))f''(p(r))+(f'(p(r)))^2\}}{(f(p(r)))^2} \tag{2.16}$$

The following lemma follows immediately:

Lemma 1: If the individual demand function is less (more) convex than a negative exponential, the elasticity of the individual demand function with respect to mill price will be a monotonically increasing (decreasing) function of distance r, that is, $\partial\epsilon(r,m)/\partial r > 0$ $[\partial\epsilon(r,m)/\partial r < 0]$. If the individual demand function is a negative exponential, the elasticity of the individual demand function will be constant with respect to r, that is, $\partial\epsilon(r,m)/\partial r = 0$.

The proof follows immediately from equation (2.16) and Definitions 1–3.

2.5   Spatial monopoly

The single-plant spatial monopolist employing an f.o.b. pricing policy will always sell to that market boundary at which demand falls to zero, that is, to market radius R_M at which $f(m+tR_M)=0$.

Applying this to equation (2.12), and noting that $f(m+tR_M)=0$ implies that $w(R_M)=0$, gives the spatial monopolist's aggregate demand elasticity:

$$e(R_M,m) = \int_0^{R_M} \epsilon(r,m)w(r)\,dr \tag{2.17}$$

where $w(r) = f(m+tr)/\int_0^{R_M} f(m+tr)\,dr$, and hence, to restate (2.11),

$$\int_0^{R_M} w(r)\,dr = 1 \tag{2.18}$$

It follows, therefore, that *the elasticity of the spatial monopolist's demand function is a weighted average of the elasticities of the individual spatial demand functions,* with weights given by $w(r)$.

Spatial and spaceless monopoly pricing can now be compared. The elasticity of the spaceless, or basic, individual demand function can be written as

$$e_B(m) = e(0, m) = \int_0^{R_M} \epsilon(0, m) w(r) \, dr \qquad (2.19)$$

Thus,

$$e_M(R_M, m) - e_B(m) = \int_0^{R_M} (\epsilon(r, m) - \epsilon(0, m)) w(r) \, dr \qquad (2.20)$$

From Lemma 1, $\epsilon(r, m) > \epsilon(0, m)$ for all r if individual demand is less convex than a negative exponential, and $\epsilon(r, m) < \epsilon(0, m)$ if individual demand is more convex than a negative exponential. The following theorem holds.[6]

Theorem 1: If the individual demand function is less (more) convex than a negative exponential, the spatial monopolist's aggregate demand function with respect to mill price will be more (less) elastic than the spaceless monopolist's demand function. If the individual demand function is a negative exponential, the spatial monopolist's aggregate demand function will have the same elasticity as the spaceless monopoly demand.

The discussion of the fundamental pricing equation then gives the following corollary.

Corollary 1: If individual demand is less (more) convex than a negative exponential, the spatial monopoly price will be lower (higher) than the spaceless monopoly price. If individual demand is a negative exponential, the spatial monopoly market demand will have the same elasticity as the spaceless monopoly market demand, and the spatial monopoly price will equal the spaceless monopoly price.

2.6   Spatial competition and aggregate demand elasticity

The essential difference between spatial monopoly and spatial competition is that whereas the spatial monopolist perceives no constraint on its market area other than that imposed by the form of the individual demand function, the spatial competitor's market area is constrained by its neighbors. In Figure 2.1, at mill price m^* a monopolist located at 0 will sell to all consumers up to market radius R_M. If, on the other hand, the firm at 0 is subject to competition from a firm located at $0'$, its market radius will be constrained to R.

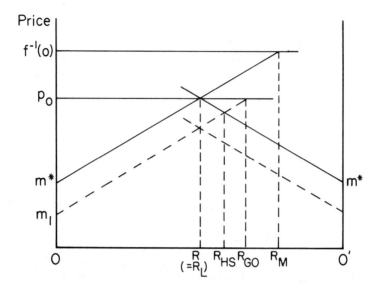

Figure 2.1. Alternative competition models and expected market radii.

Thus, although an f.o.b. pricing system does lead to each firm having a local (or regional) monopoly, this does *not* mean that the firm is free of competitive pressures. Firms share common boundaries and thus are directly affected by spatial competition. Nor should it be thought that these competitive pressures are in some sense unimportant, occurring as they do at the market boundaries. Each firm's pricing policy with respect to *all* consumers is affected by competition from neighboring firms.

The effect of such spatial competition on pricing policy is, given the individual demand function, crucially dependent on the belief the spatial competitor holds concerning its rivals' reactions to a change in price, that is, dependent on the conjectural variations the spatial competitors attribute to each other.

The analysis that follows concentrates initially on the three price conjectural variations specified earlier: Löschian competition, Hotelling-Smithies competition, and Greenhut-Ohta competition. The differences in these three competition assumptions lie essentially in the resulting differences in the short-run expected (or ex ante) market radii. A Löschian firm's short-run expected market area is the same as the constrained market radius, whereas the H-S and G-O expected and constrained market radii of the firm are different. The spatial competitor located at 0 *believes* that if it cuts its mill price from m^* to m_1 (Figure 2.1), its competitors will react in such a way that its market radius will be (1) R_L under Löschian competition (i.e., unchanged) or (2) R_{HS} (R_{GO}) under H-S (G-O) competition.

This discussion can be used to derive the elasticity of aggregate demand *in a market of known radius R* under the three competitive assumptions. Recall equation (2.12), repeated here for ease of reference:

$$e_i(R, m) = \int_0^R \epsilon(r, m) w(r) \, dr + v_i m w(R) \qquad (2.21)$$

where $v_i = -\partial R / \partial m$.

A much stronger interpretation of v_i can now be given. This is, in fact, a conjectural variation. It is the increase in market radius that a spatial competitor expects will follow any reduction in mill price. Referring to Figure 2.1, note that[7]

1. $v_i = 0$ for Löschian competition,
2. $v_i = 1/2t$ for H-S competition,
3. $v_i = 1/t$ for G-O competition.

It follows, therefore, that

$$e_L(R, m) = \int_0^R \epsilon(r, m) w(r) \, dr \qquad (2.22a)$$

$$e_{HS}(R, m) = \int_0^R \epsilon(r, m) w(r) \, dr + m w(R)/2t \qquad (2.22b)$$

$$e_{GO}(R, m) = \int_0^R \epsilon(r, m) w(r) \, dr + m w(R)/t \qquad (2.22c)$$

Thus, in a market of known radius R,

$$\epsilon_L(R, m) < \epsilon_{HS}(R, m) < \epsilon_{GO}(R, m) \qquad (2.23)$$

and mill prices are such that

$$m_L(R) > m_{HS}(R) > m_{GO}(R) \qquad (2.24)$$

In other words, *within a given constrained market, the Löschian competitor will adopt the highest prices, followed by the H-S competitor, then the G-O competitor.*

The structure of equations (2.22) is such that we can extend the analysis to cover totally general price conjectural variations. Elasticity of aggregate demand in a market of radius R is

$$e_i(R, m) = e_L(R, m) + v_i m w(R) \qquad (2.22d)$$

where v_i is the price conjectural variation. This gives the following general result.

Theorem 2: In a market of known radius, the elasticity of demand is an increasing function and the mill price a decreasing function of the conjectural variations held by spatial competitors about the expected increase in market radius that will follow a reduction in mill price.

2.7   Demand effect and competition effect under free entry

It is worth stressing that Theorem 2 is a short-run result, referring as it does to relative prices within a market of known radius. In other words, no matter the conjectural variations held by the spatial competitors, all firms are assumed to have identical market areas and thus aggregate the same set of individual demand functions. As a result, the differences in relative prices noted in Theorem 2 do not arise from differences either in individual demand or in the consumers that enter aggregate demand. In this short-run equilibrium, differences in relative prices between, for example, Löschian, H-S, and G-O firms arise solely because these firms have different conjectural variations, that is, hold different beliefs about the responses of competitors to a change in price.

A more intuitive interpretation of these results may impart further insight into the factors underlying spatial pricing behavior under an f.o.b. pricing system. The spatial competitor faces two forces in determining its pricing behavior: (1) the demand effect, related to the basic demand convexities, and (2) the competition effect, related to the price conjectural variations of spatial competitors.

Because the Löschian firm believes that price changes will be exactly matched by its competitors, it believes that its market area is fixed. Such a firm, therefore, *always prices as does the spatial monopolist within its own market area.* The demand effect is the only factor determining a Löschian firm's price.

On the other hand, both the demand and competition effects determine an H-S or G-O firm's price. Such a firm recognizes that its pricing policy will affect demand within its market area, but also believes that the market area will change. What this means is that the H-S (or G-O) firm reacts not according to the actual demand curve but according to a more elastic imagined (or expected) curve.

In this sense, the competition effect and its associated imagined aggregate demand curve bear a commonality with the entry effects in spaceless monopolistic competition. Suppose initially, as shown in Figure 2.2, that the equilibrium (mill) price is m^* for a firm's aggregate demand curve DD', and the corresponding output is q^*. If the firm's price is changed and its manager believes that all other competing firms will follow suit, the manager will expect some increase in sales from the price reduction

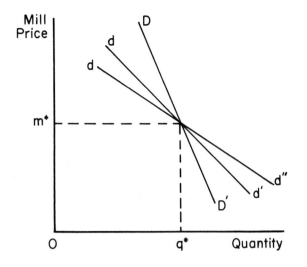

Figure 2.2. Actual demand and imagined demand.

as a result of the demand effect noted earlier. This manager follows the demand curve DD'.

Now consider a manager who assumes that other competing firms' prices will be held constant. This manager will expect an increase in sales following a price reduction, not merely from the price change but also from an increase in the firm's market radius. Thus, the firm is following a more elastic imagined curve such as dd'. Finally, consider the G-O competitor. A manager with G-O beliefs expects an even greater increase in market radius as a result of a reduction in mill price – an even greater competition effect. This manager is effectively following the even more elastic imagined demand curve dd''.

For a discussion of this imagined demand curve in a spaceless context, see, for example, Chamberlin (1933), Needham (1978, pp. 56–7), and Ferguson and Maurice (1978, pp. 288–97); the imagined demand curve in a spatial context was noted by Ohta (1980).

2.8   Effect of entry on competitive prices

It is now possible to examine the price effects of competitive entry under the various competitive assumptions. Entry implies a smaller market area for the spatial competitor and thus will affect the aggregate demand elasticity as described by equations (2.22).

2.8.1   *Löschian competition*

It is easy to show (see Mathematical Appendix) that

$$\frac{de_L(R,m)}{dR} = \int_0^R (\epsilon(r,m) - \epsilon(R,m)) w_R(r)\, dr \qquad (2.25)$$

where $w_R(r) = \partial w(r)/\partial R < 0$. Lemma 1 and equation (2.25) give the following.

Theorem 3: If the individual demand function is less (more) convex than a negative exponential, competitive entry will reduce the Löschian firm's market radius and reduce (increase) the elasticity of the firm's demand function with respect to mill price. If the individual demand function is a negative exponential, demand elasticity will be unaffected by competitive entry.

To prove this theorem, note that if the individual demand function is less convex than a negative exponential, $\partial \epsilon(r,m)/\partial r > 0$; hence, $\epsilon(r,m) < \epsilon(R,m)$ for all r. Further, $w_R(r) < 0$. Hence, $\partial e_L(R,m)/\partial R > 0$. Similarly for other demand elasticities.

What is the intuition behind this result? We know that for the Löschian firm, aggregate demand elasticity is a weighted average of the individual spatial demand elasticities (because the conjectural variation v_i is zero). Now consider an individual demand function that is less convex than a negative exponential. Then individual demand elasticity increases with distance from the firm. Competitive entry in such circumstances takes away those consumers with the highest individual demand elasticities and thus reduces aggregate demand elasticity.

Conclusion 1: If the individual demand function is less (more) convex than a negative exponential, competitive entry will raise (lower) the Löschian firm's mill price. If the individual demand function is a negative exponential, competitive entry will not affect mill price.

Proof merely requires application of the fundamental pricing equation.

Corollary 1: If the individual demand function is less (more) convex than a negative exponential, the spatial monopolist's aggregate demand function will be more (less) elastic with respect to mill price than that of the Löschian competitor, which in turn will be more (less) elastic than the individual (basic) demand function:

$$f'' \lesseqgtr (f')^2/f \Rightarrow e_M \gtreqless e_L \gtreqless e_B$$

Proof comes from noting that market area for the spatial monopolist is always greater than for the Löschian competitor, and from noting that individual spaceless demand elasticity is always at the lower or upper end of the range of individual *spatial* demand elasticities.

Corollary 2: If the individual demand function is less (more) convex than a negative exponential, then mill prices will be, in ascending (descending) order: (a) spatial monopoly, (b) Löschian competition, (c) spaceless monopoly. Mill prices will be identical if the individual demand function is a negative exponential.

Proof again merely requires application of the fundamental pricing equation.

A likely application of the findings to this point may be suggested here. Consider a spatial monopolist on a sparsely populated section of the beach at Coney Island, where the monopolist sells a variety of foods (chiefly, hamburgers and hot dogs) and soft drinks to sunbathers willing to walk the hot sands to his site. Because he needs to attract customers from an extensive area if he is to make sufficient sales to cover his costs, the prices charged must be low. Now insert a competitor located a comparatively short distance away. Classical, spaceless analysis would imply that prices should fall. The discussion in this chapter indicates, however, that the effect of the new entrant on price cannot be specified a priori. Price may rise, fall, or remain unaltered, depending on the precise form of the individual demand functions. What can be said is that such small-scale entry may well be expected to lead to an increase in prices.

Return now to the original case of the beach monopolist, except let the population density be great, as it typically is all over Coney Island. The effect of this is that the market area necessary to generate sufficient sales is so small that walking distances are negligible. The (effectively spaceless) monopolist's price will generally be found to be the highest, and competition can be expected to lower price.

2.8.2 H-S and G-O competition

Matters are not quite as straightforward under H-S and G-O competitive assumptions, because, as can be seen from equations (2.22b) and (2.22c), demand elasticity under both H-S and G-O competition consists of two elements. The first element is the demand effect on Löschian elasticity, and the second element is the competition effect, uniquely related to non-Löschian competitive assumptions.

Entry will cause the magnitude of the first element, $e_L(R, m)$, to increase, decrease, or remain constant, depending on whether individual demand is more or less convex than a negative exponential or is of the negative-exponential form. The second term, on the other hand, unambiguously increases as entry takes place: A decrease in R decreases the denominator and increases the numerator of the term $w(R)$ in (2.22b) and (2.22c). In the limit, the denominator approaches zero, and the second term approaches infinity. Therefore, though entry may lower, raise, or keep constant a spatial competitor's aggregate demand elasticity according to the demand effect, the competition effect unambiguously results in an increase in aggregate demand elasticity.

It follows that if the individual demand function is more convex than a negative exponential, or is a negative exponential, then the demand effect and competition effect will reinforce each other. Competitive entry will increase aggregate demand elasticity under H-S and G-O competitive assumptions. On the other hand, if the individual demand function is less convex than a negative exponential, the demand effect and competition effect will work in opposite directions. Whether aggregate demand elasticity increases or decreases with competitive entry then depends on the relative magnitudes of the two effects.

The intuition behind these conclusions can be seen from Figure 2.1. The competition effect operates at the market boundary, whereas the demand effect operates within that boundary. As entry takes place, the market boundary contracts, and the competition effect becomes proportionately more important. Eventually, the competition effect will dominate and outweigh the demand effect. Competitive entry can be expected at some point to increase aggregate demand elasticity even if individual demand is less convex than a negative exponential.

The foregoing analysis indicates that, contrary to the case of Löschian competition, in which price following entry may rise or fall or remain unchanged depending on the shape of the basic demand curve, the H-S price (and G-O price) can eventually be expected to fall regardless of the shape of individual demand. To summarize:

Conclusion 2: If the individual demand is a negative exponential, or is more convex than a negative exponential, the H-S price (and the G-O price) will unambiguously fall following entry. If individual demand is less convex than a negative exponential, the price effect of entry will depend on the level of entry. It can be expected that substantial entry will eventually lower the price.

This conclusion can in fact be made even stronger. It can be shown (see Mathematical Appendix) that aggregate demand elasticity under G-O competition is a monotonic increasing function of market radius, *no matter the convexity of the individual demand function.* As a result, competitive entry will *always* result in a fall in price under G-O competition.

A likely application of these findings regarding H-S and G-O competition may be suggested here. Return to a section of Coney Island with a moderate density of sun worshippers. Dot the beach with many rival hamburger and hot dog stands, such that the representative seller's market space has been sharply reduced from its monopoly size. Now it can be easily demonstrated, but should be sufficiently obvious without proof, that if each new entrant locates at a point half the distance from the representative firm's site to the prior market periphery, that entrant will capture the same proportion of sales of the representative seller as was the case for the previous distant entry of a rival firm. However, an easy inroad on sales carries a significantly greater impact on profits. This follows because profits have already been squeezed. The last buyers lost to a rival will have had relatively greater demands, *ceteris paribus*, than those lost in the past. A greater willingness to cut prices by older firms can thus be conjectured, and with it significantly greater (hoped for) inroads on the market space of the new entrant. It is doubtful that a price-increase effect could arise in this case no matter how *concave* (i.e., very much less convex) the individual demand curves are. With significant entry, price falls, as predicted by the H-S or G-O model.

2.9   Concluding remarks

The foregoing analysis indicates that the price effects of competitive entry and changes in the cost or demand conditions are crucially dependent on the shape of the individual demand functions and on the nature of competitive forces – in particular, on the way in which a firm believes its rivals will react to a proposed price change.

Where firms exist in a strongly competitive spatial environment – the "normal" case of the H-S model, and the constrained conditions that define the G-O model – price changes are consistent with classical, spaceless models. On the other hand, if competitive forces are weaker, or if the firm acts as a monopolist within a defined market area – the Löschian case – the price changes may be opposite to those suggested by classical theories. It would appear, therefore, that knowledge of a firm's spatial competitive environment is a crucial prerequisite to any analysis of pricing as market conditions change.

Mathematical appendix

Curvature of negative-exponential demand: From equation (2.13),

$$f' = abe^{-bp(r)}; \qquad f'' = ab^2 e^{-bp(r)} \tag{A2.1}$$

Hence,

$$(f')^2 = a^2 b^2 e^{-2bp(r)} \tag{A2.2}$$

$$ff'' = ae^{-bp(r)} ab^2 e^{-bp(r)} = a^2 b^2 e^{-2bp(r)} = (f')^2 \tag{A2.3}$$

Curvature of demand function (2.14): From equation (2.14),

$$f' = \frac{1}{x}\left(-\frac{x}{\beta}\right)\left(\frac{x}{\beta}(\alpha-p)\right)^{1/x-1} = -\frac{1}{\beta}\left(\frac{x}{\beta}(\alpha-p)\right)^{1/x-1} \tag{A2.4}$$

$$f'' = -\frac{1}{\beta}\left(\frac{1}{x}-1\right)\left(-\frac{x}{\beta}\right)\left(\frac{x}{\beta}(\alpha-p)\right)^{1/x-2} = \frac{1}{\beta^2}(1-x)\left(\frac{x}{\beta}(\alpha-p)\right)^{1/x-2} \tag{A2.5}$$

Hence,

$$\frac{(f')^2}{f} = \frac{\frac{1}{\beta^2}\left(\frac{x}{\beta}(\alpha-p)\right)^{2/x-2}}{\left(\frac{x}{\beta}(\alpha-p)\right)^{1/x}} = \frac{1}{\beta^2}\left(\frac{x}{\beta}(\alpha-p)\right)^{1/x-2} \tag{A2.6}$$

Comparison of (A2.5) and (A2.6) indicates that

$$f'' \gtrless (f')^2/f \quad \text{as} \quad 1-x \gtrless 1 \quad \text{or} \quad x \lessgtr 0 \tag{A2.7}$$

Löschian demand elasticity: Aggregate demand elasticity under Löschian competition is given by equation (2.22a). We differentiate using the Leibniz formula to give

$$de_L(R,m)/dR = \int_0^R \epsilon(r,m)w_R(r)\,dr + \epsilon(R,m)w(R) \tag{A2.8}$$

where $w_R(r) = \partial w(r)/\partial R < 0$. We now differentiate equation (2.11):

$$\int_0^R w_R(r)\,dr + w(R) = 0 \tag{A2.9}$$

Substituting in (A2.8) and rearranging gives equation (2.25).

Elasticity under G-O competition: Recall that aggregate demand elasticity is given by

$$e_i(R,m) = -\frac{m\int_0^R f'(m+tr)\,dr}{\int_0^R f(m+tr)\,dr} + mv_i\frac{f(m+tR)}{\int_0^R f(m+tr)\,dr} \tag{A2.10}$$

Consider $\int_0^R f'(m+tr)\,dr$, and change the variable of integration. Let

$$m+tr = y : r=0 \Rightarrow y=m; \; r=R \Rightarrow y=m+tR; \; dr = \frac{1}{t}\,dy$$

Hence,

$$\int_0^R f'(m+tr)\,dr = \int_m^{m+tR} f'(y)\frac{1}{t}\,dy = \frac{1}{t}\int_m^{m+tR} f'(y)\,dy$$

$$= \frac{1}{t}(f(m+tR)-f(m))$$

Substitute in (A2.10):

$$e_i(R, m) = -\frac{m}{t} \frac{\{f(m+tR) - f(m)\}}{\int_0^R f(m+tr)\, dr} + m v_i \frac{f(m+tR)}{\int_0^R f(m+tr)\, dr}$$

$$= \frac{m}{\int_0^R f(m+tr)\, dr} \left\{ -\frac{1}{t} f(m+tR) + \frac{1}{t} f(m) + v_i f(m+tR) \right\}$$

Hence,

$$e_i(R, m) = \frac{m}{\int_0^R f(m+tr)\, dr} \left\{ \frac{1}{t} f(m) - \left(\frac{1}{t} - v_i\right) f(m+tR) \right\} \tag{A2.11}$$

Under G-O competition, $v_i = 1/t$. Hence,

$$e_{GO}(R, m) = mf(m) \bigg/ \left(t \int_0^R f(m+tr)\, dr \right) \tag{A2.12}$$

and

$$\frac{de_{GO}(R, m)}{dR} < 0 \quad \text{for all } R \tag{A2.13}$$

A reduction in market radius *always* increases G-O elasticity and thus *always* reduces the G-O mill price.

A general theory of imperfect competition and nondiscriminatory pricing: the long run

The discussion in Chapter 2 assumed a known fixed market area. As a result, the price effects of competitive entry and the relative magnitudes of prices under varying competitive and demand conditions outlined in Chapter 2 are essentially short-run in nature. They do not help identify the relative magnitudes of long-run equilibrium (zero-profit) nondiscriminatory prices, because there is no reason to believe that long-run equilibrium market radii will be the same under alternative competitive assumptions. If, for example, the long-run equilibrium market radius under Löschian competition is "sufficiently small" with respect to H-S and G-O competition, and individual demand is more convex than a negative exponential, it might be that the long-run equilibrium mill price under Löschian competition will be lower than under the alternative competitive assumptions.

3.1   Long-run equilibrium prices

Before long-run equilibrium prices can be compared, it is necessary to define what is meant by equilibrium in a spatial market. The definition used is based on classical, spaceless concepts. A market is defined to be in equilibrium when no firm currently in the market wishes to exit the market and no potential entrant wishes to enter. This definition is generally taken to mean that all existing firms are making just normal profits, and no potential entrant believes that it can achieve at least this profit level. Other possibilities can be considered, particularly within the spatial framework. For example, it might be the case that existing firms are making above-normal profits, but the market remains in equilibrium because a potential entrant cannot secure a sufficiently large market share to allow it to break even.[1]

Our feeling is that these alternative assumptions introduce undue complications to the analysis at this stage, while leaving the basic conclusions unaltered. We shall therefore assume that long-run equilibrium is characterized by a situation in which each firm is making just normal profit.

Conventionally, normal profit is considered to be a cost of production – a wage paid to the entrepreneur that is just sufficient to encourage him to continue in his current occupation. Thus, a spatial firm will be considered to be earning normal profit if market radius and mill price are such that the profit function $\Pi(R, m)$ [see Chapter 2, equation (2.5)] is just equal to zero. This allows us to derive what Capozza and Van Order refer to as the zero-profit locus (ZPL). Maintaining the demand, cost, and market-structure assumptions of Chapter 2, the ZPL is given by the implicit equation

$$\Pi(R, m) : 2D(m-c) \int_0^R f(m+tr)\, dr - F = 0 \tag{3.1}$$

where F and c are fixed and marginal costs, respectively.

By definition, the slope of an implicit equation such as (3.1) is given by

$$\frac{dm}{dR} = -\frac{\partial \Pi(R, m)/\partial R}{\partial \Pi(R, m)/\partial m} \tag{3.2}$$

Evaluating the partial derivatives of (3.2) gives

$$\frac{dm}{dR} = -\frac{(m-c)f(m+tR)}{(m-c)\int_0^R f'(m+tr)\, dr + \int_0^R f(m+tr)\, dr} \tag{3.2'}$$

The numerator of (3.2′) is always positive, given, of course, that R is less than the monopolist's market radius. Consider, however, the denominator. Because the Löschian competitor prices as a monopolist within his given market area, the profit-maximizing mill price for a given market radius R is just equivalent to the Löschian mill price and is obtained from the equation $\partial \Pi(R, m)/\partial m = 0$. Thus, *at the Löschian market price for a market of radius R,* the denominator of (3.2′) is zero, and *the slope of the ZPL is infinity.*[2]

Assume that the long-run (zero-profit) Löschian equilibrium is characterized by mill price m_L^* and market radius R_L^* in Figure 3.1. Now consider profit under H-S and G-O competition at the same market radius R_L^*. Ohta (1980) has shown that in a market of given size, Löschian competition provides the greatest profits, followed by H-S competition, with G-O competition offering the least profit. Intuitively, both H-S and G-O competitors price on erroneous beliefs regarding their competitors' actions, and so depart from the profit-maximizing (Löschian) pricing strategy. The H-S competitor is less optimistic about the increased market share that will come from a reduction in mill price than is the G-O competitor (recall Figure 2.1 and the firms' conjectural variations). Consequently, the H-S competitor departs less from the Löschian pricing policy than does the G-O competitor, and thereby suffers a smaller reduction in profit.

More generally, because m_L^* is the profit-maximizing mill price at market radius R_L^*, any departure from this mill price will lead to negative

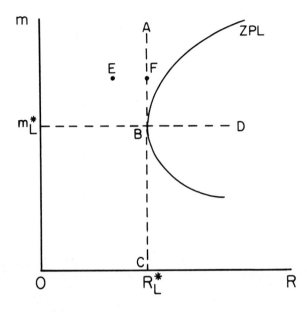

Figure 3.1. The ZPL.

profits. The ZPL through (R_L^*, m_L^*) must, therefore, lie to the right or left of ABC in Figure 3.1.

Next, note that $\partial\Pi(R, m)/\partial R > 0$ if, as we would expect, the long-run competitive market radius is less than the monopolist's market radius. The ZPL must, therefore, pass below (and above) BD in Figure 3.1 and must lie to the right of ABC.[3]

We can now add the pricing equation under the three competitive assumptions. The discussion of equations (2.23) and (2.24) indicated that no matter the convexity of the individual demand function, the Löschian pricing equation lies everywhere above the H-S pricing equation, which lies everywhere above the G-O pricing equation. This is illustrated in Figure 3.2,[4] in which the pricing equations are the curves m_L, m_{HS}, and m_{GO}. Optimal mill price occurs at the intersection of the ZPL and the appropriate pricing equation and leads to the following fundamental conclusion:

Conclusion 1: No matter the convexity of the individual demand function, the ranking of long-run equilibrium f.o.b. mill prices will be, from highest to lowest: (a) Löschian price, (b) H-S price, (c) G-O price.

Whether the long-run equilibrium competitive prices are higher or lower than the spatial monopolist's price depends on the convexity of the individual demand function and, for less convex demand functions, on the strength of the competition effect. The following conclusion can be stated.

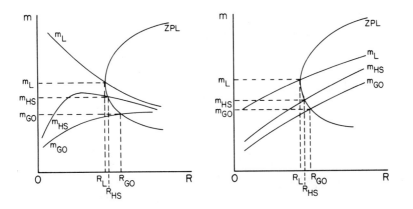

Figure 3.2. Long-run zero-profit equilibrium prices. Left: less convex than a negative exponential. Right: more convex than a negative exponential.

Conclusion 2: If the individual demand function is more convex than a negative exponential, the ranking of long-run equilibrium prices will be, from highest to lowest: (a) spatial monopoly, (b) Löschian price, (c) H-S price, (d) G-O price. If the individual demand function is less convex than a negative exponential, and if competition is "strong," the ranking will be from highest to lowest: (a) Löschian price, (b) spatial monopoly, (c) H-S price, (d) G-O price.

This discussion has been confined to a comparison of Löschian, H-S, and G-O prices. The reasoning underlying Theorem 2 in Chapter 2 [see equation (2.22d)] can be used, however, to state a rather more general conclusion.

Conclusion 3: No matter the convexity of the individual demand function, the long-run equilibrium price will be lower the greater the increase in market area that the spatial competitor *expects* as a consequence of a reduction in mill price.

Proof comes from recognizing that the greater is the expected increase in market area (the conjectural variation $\partial R / \partial m$), the greater is the imagined elasticity of demand [from equation (2.22d)], and so the lower will lie the pricing equation in the (R, m) plane of Figure 3.2.

3.2   Comparative-statics effects of changes in fixed costs, transport costs, and consumer density

The effects of competitive entry noted in Chapter 2 and the discussion in Section 3.1 in this chapter can be used to analyze the effects on long-run

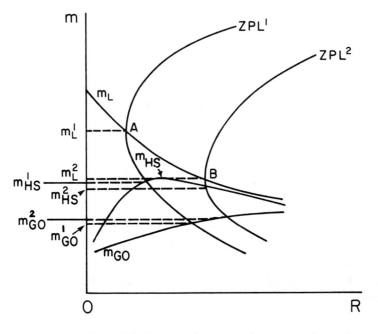

Figure 3.3. Comparative statics: less convex demand.

equilibrium competitive prices of changes in some of the underlying market conditions. Given an initial zero-profit equilibrium, as fixed costs (or transport costs) increase, existing firms will be subject to losses, exit will occur, and the remaining firms' market areas will expand. An increase in consumer density will have the opposite effect: Greater density will result in short-run profits for existing firms, entry will occur, and market areas will become smaller.

These effects are illustrated in Figure 3.3 in the case in which individual demand is less convex than a negative exponential (e.g., for linear individual demand).[5] Assume an initial long-run equilibrium with zero-profit locus ZPL^1. Now assume that fixed costs increase or consumer density falls. At the existing equilibrium (e.g., point A under Löschian competition), all firms will be suffering losses. Firms will leave the industry until equilibrium is restored on the new zero-profit locus ZPL^2 (e.g., at point B under Löschian competition).

Unambiguous results are immediately obtained with regard to the effects on the Löschian firm's price of changes in fixed costs, transport costs, and consumer densities. Specifically, if individual demand is less (more) convex than a negative exponential, the Löschian price will fall (rise) following an increase in fixed costs or transport costs. On the other hand, if individual demand is a negative exponential, changes in fixed costs or transport costs will leave the Löschian price unchanged.

A higher consumer density will result in a higher (lower) Löschian price if individual demand is less (more) convex than a negative exponential. If, in contrast, individual demand is a negative exponential, an increase in density will not affect the Löschian price.

Analogously, if individual demand is a negative exponential, or is more convex than a negative exponential, the H-S (and G-O) price will rise following an increase in fixed costs or transport costs or a decrease in consumer density. If, on the other hand, individual demand is less convex than a negative exponential, the H-S price effect will depend on the initial zero-profit market radius and the extent to which fixed costs, transport costs, and consumer density change. If the initial market radius is "close to" the spatial monopolist's market radius, and if there is a relatively small change in fixed costs, transport costs, or consumer density, the demand effect will dominate. On the other hand, the smaller the initial market radius, or the greater the change in costs or density, the more likely is it that the competition effect will outweigh the demand effect. Thus, it can be asserted that as fixed costs or transport costs decrease or consumer density increases, the H-S price will eventually decrease regardless of the demand convexity. (Note that the G-O price falls regardless of the demand convexity.) In other words, H-S (and G-O) competition possesses the appealing properties of nonspatial competitive theory when competition is substantial or when a significant change in market conditions occurs. These results are summarized in Table 3.1.

3.3   An application: pricing in the service industry with different entry conditions[6]

The discussion in Chapter 2 and in Sections 3.1 and 3.2 of this chapter might be considered somewhat abstract. There is considerable value, therefore, in indicating how the essence of this spatial oligopoly theory can be applied in real-world markets. In order to emphasize the generality of the "spatial" label, the application presented in this section refers only peripherally to "space" and "distance costs."

We examine pricing in two sets of service industries differentiated by the extent to which entry to the industry is restricted or relatively free. As an example of a service industry with restricted entry we use the medical-services market. The long period of education and training and the license restrictions operated by the professional associations create barriers to entry to the profession. Alternatively, some readers may prefer

Table 3.1. *Price effects of spatial competition under alternative demand conditions*

Parameter change	Löschian competition			H-S (and G-O) competition		
	$f'' > \dfrac{(f')^2}{f}$ (more convex than a negative exponential)	$f'' = \dfrac{(f')^2}{f}$ (a negative exponential)	$f'' < \dfrac{(f')^2}{f}$ (less convex than a negative exponential)	$f'' > \dfrac{(f')^2}{f}$ (more convex than a negative exponential)	$f'' = \dfrac{(f')^2}{f}$ (a negative exponential)	$f'' < \dfrac{(f')^2}{f}$ (less convex than a negative exponential)
Increase in fixed costs	Up	No change	Down	Up	Up	Up[a]
Decrease in density	Up	No change	Down	Up	Up	Up[a]
Increase in transport cost per unit distance	Up	No change	Down	Up	Up	Up[a]
Entry of new firms	Down	No change	Up	Down	Down	Down[a]

[a] These directional changes relate for H-S competition to the price effects of substantial changes in fixed or transport costs, and consumer density, or to situations where competition is "strong" and market areas "small."

to view this industry as one in which fixed costs of entry are high. On either interpretation, pricing behavior can be expected to take place in the context of a market structure containing a "small" number of rival oligopolists. A change in price by any one practitioner can be expected to have a noticeable effect on rival practitioners and thus induce a price reaction on the part of those rivals.

In contrast, other service industries can be envisaged into which entry is relatively free because the costs of entry are low: plumbing, television, general household maintenance, and the like. This market structure will contain "many" oligopolists, each of whom views himself as being comparatively unimportant.

Why have we chosen this example? As has been noted several times in the context of traditional microeconomic theory, the entry of new firms into a competitive market is always expected to lower the price of the product being exchanged. However, in the health-care industry, several empirical investigations have uncovered an apparently "perverse" relation: As the number of health-care providers increases, the price of the health-care service (the fee) increases. A significant, positive relation between fees and health-care provider density (e.g., physicians per capita) has been reported by Newhouse (1970), Fuchs and Kramer (1972), and Dyckman (1978). Indeed, Pauly and Satterthwaite (1980) have asserted that "the zero order correlation between physicians per capita and various measures of physician fees tends invariably to be positive." Therefore, the available empirical evidence implies that entry of additional health-care providers would raise rather than lower the price of the service.

As would be expected, these empirical results relate to a number of studies that have examined the fees charged in the health-care markets. Some authors, such as Feldstein (1970) and Fuchs and Kramer (1972), attempted to explain the observed price behavior by assuming health-care providers to be price takers. Others, including Frech and Ginsburg (1975), who considered insurance effects, used monopolistic models to indicate how health-care providers react to exogenous changes; however, they were unable to explain how an increase in the number of providers would impact on price.

Most notable, however, have been the studies in which the researchers abandoned neoclassical theory and turned instead to "targeted income/demand creation" to explain the behavior of prices in this market. The idea that a service provider would be able to create demand was first introduced formally by Newhouse (1970). This idea was expanded by Evans, Parish, and Sully (1973), Evans (1974), Green (1978), Fuchs (1978), and Dyckman (1978). In its simplest form, the notion is that health-care providers have some "target income." If the number of providers increases, each individual provider can prevent a decline in income by advising a patient to consume additional health-care services (e.g., more diagnostic tests). In this way, the providers are able to "create demand," and they can increase the fee charged by pricing along the new demand curve.

Anderson, House, and Ormiston (1981) examined theoretically the concept of supplier-induced demand. As they demonstrated, a model using supplier-induced demand can indeed explain the empirically obtained positive relation between the density of health-care providers and fees. However, such a model would also yield additional predictions that do not appear to be borne out empirically. For example, supplier-induced demand would also imply that physicians would strive to increase their numbers. Such a prediction certainly does not coincide with the long-standing view that organized medicine has attempted to limit entry into the profession. Furthermore, some recent empirical evidence provided by Pauly and Satterthwaite (1981) has called into question the validity of "targeted income/demand creation."

Our opinion is that the supplier-induced demand approach is unsatisfactory. In addition, analysis of f.o.b. pricing can be used to reconcile the existing empirical evidence with traditional microeconomic theory.

Given the policy implications of "targeted income/demand creation," many authors have been searching for such a reconciliation. An "increasing-monopoly" theory, in which an increase in the number of sellers of a "reputation" good or service would make search more costly and thereby increase price, was first proposed by Satterthwaite (1979) and subsequently expanded by Pauly and Satterthwaite (1980, 1981). Much closer to the analysis to be presented later is the "full-price" model proposed by Anderson and Ormiston (1983). Indeed, our analysis is based on the full-price notion of DeVany (1976), DeVany and Saving (1977), and Saving (1982).

Our use of health-care markets as an example permits us to set the stage for the manner in which we employ the f.o.b. pricing model. First, no assumptions are made about the location of the service-providing firms (e.g., physicians' offices). Either spatially concentrated or dispersed markets are possible. Neither is it required that customers (patients) go to the nearest provider. Although the analysis is simplified by conceiving of a uniform fee for a particular service, differentiated services (or skills of the providers) are within the scope of the model. Such differentiation would simply generate a set of fee differentials, but would not affect the primary concern of the analysis: the impact on fees of the entry of new providers. In other words, the reader can visualize any number of alternative circumstances: large or small cities, medical complexes, service providers located next door to one another or at great distances, and providers with varying skills. Quite simply, the f.o.b. spatial pricing model is employed precisely because its framework readily encompasses not only the direct fee paid but also the other costs borne by the consumer in the form of travel time, waiting time, and time in service.

3.3.1   The model with restricted entry

In the preceding discussion we concentrated on the health-care industry, because that is where a "perverse" relation was discovered. However, it should be noted that the model is more general. Accordingly, simply consider a service industry. As has been demonstrated by DeVany and associates (1983), customer-supplied time (time in service, waiting time, and commuting time) is a principal cost in service industries, and a change in any time component impacts consumer demand.[7] Hence, the full price is defined as

$$\Pi = p(\gamma, n) = n + w\gamma \qquad (3.3)$$

where n is the nominal fee, w is the value of customer-supplied time, and γ is the amount of time supplied by the customer. In this formulation, the amount of consumer-supplied time, γ, clearly depends on the arrival rate of customers. However, it also depends on the service capacity of the firm (DeVany et al. 1983). Hence, the firm can alter its full price, p, via changes in either the nominal fee charged, n, or the amount of customer-supplied time required, γ.

The reader should begin to see the connection between this formulation and the concept of delivered price in spatial economics. Compare equation (3.3) with equation (2.2). By analogy, Π would be delivered price, where n would be mill price, w would be transport cost per unit of distance, and γ would be distance.

With respect to the consumers, some additional assumptions are necessary, again analogous to those in spatial economics:

1. All consumers have identical demand functions.
2. All consumers have the same value of time; so, for simplicity, consider w equal to unity.
3. The consumer's basic demand is a function of the full price. That is,

$$q(\gamma, n) = f(\Pi) = f(p(\gamma, n)) \quad (f' < 0) \qquad (3.4)$$

It is intrinsic to this model that the amount of time consumers will be willing to provide depends in part on the consumers' opportunity cost of time. This might appear, at first glance, to contradict the assumption of homogeneous demand, but actually it does not. To appreciate this statement, note that the assumption of homogeneous demand is employed in order to identify systematically the forces that produce different results in the market. Spatial price theory provides a unique framework for this systematic analysis. In particular, our model encompasses the situation in which two individuals can have identical tastes, incomes, and desires for the service (e.g., health care), can be situated at the same location (or, if you prefer, in the same household), and also can frequent the same service provider (e.g., physician), but yet can have substantially different costs of time. So $w\gamma$ varies among individuals with otherwise identical demands, because the opportunity costs of time will differ. The term $w\gamma$ is, accordingly, a counterpart to distance; see Phlips (1983).

It follows that the elasticity of the individual demand curve with respect to the nominal fee is given by

$$\epsilon(\gamma, n) = -n\frac{f'(p(\gamma, n))}{f(p(\gamma, n))} = -n\frac{f'}{f} \tag{3.5}$$

We can now use our discussion of the negative-exponential demand function (see Chapter 2) to state

$$\frac{\partial \epsilon(\gamma, n)}{\partial \gamma} \lesseqqgtr 0 \quad \text{as} \quad f'' \gtreqqless \frac{(f')^2}{f} \tag{3.6}$$

In order to analyze the effects of competitive entry on fees, however, we know from Chapter 2 that some assumption is needed with respect to the way a particular firm believes its competitors will react to a change in the former's nominal fee (i.e., the firm's *price conjectural variation*).

Because it appears reasonable to claim that entry to the medical-services industry is restricted, we propose that in the medical-services industry there are so few rivals in the market that each is aware of (and hence will react to) any rival's change in price. This type of behavior, as we have seen, is characterized by Löschian competition.

Consider this paradigm in the context of our full-price model. In the short-run equilibrium there will exist some "limit time," Γ, for each of the competitors in the service industry. Analogous to the spatial concept of market radius, the prevailing limit time gives the maximum amount of customer-supplied time *actually required* from the customers of a particular competitor. Suppose that only one firm lowered its nominal fee. Obviously, customers would be willing to wait or commute longer; so the limit time for this firm would rise. However, under Löschian competition, no one firm can reduce its nominal fee unilaterally. If one firm reduces its nominal fee, all firms will reduce the fee. Hence, although customers would be *willing* to provide more customer-supplied time in response to a lower nominal fee, there will be no change in the amount of time *actually required*. With no change in the number of service providers (as well as no change in the distribution of consumers and the service capacities of the firms), a change in the nominal fee by all of the firms will have no effect on the prevailing limit time, because firms will be unable to capture each other's customers. That is, $\partial \Gamma / \partial n = 0$.

The aggregate demand function for any given medical-service provider is given by

$$Q(\Gamma, n) = D \int_0^\Gamma f(n + \gamma) \, d\gamma \tag{3.7}$$

and the elasticity of aggregate demand with respect to the nominal fee is

$$e(\Gamma, n) = n \int_0^\Gamma f'(n+\gamma) \, d\gamma \bigg/ \int_0^\Gamma f(n+\gamma) \, d\gamma - n \frac{\partial \Gamma}{\partial n} \frac{f(n+\Gamma)}{\int_0^\Gamma f(n+\gamma) \, d\gamma} \qquad (3.8)$$

Under Löschian competition, the second term in the right-hand expression is zero, because $\partial \Gamma / \partial n = 0$. Hence, for Löschian competition, we can rewrite (3.8) as

$$e_{\mathrm{L}}(\Gamma, n) = \int_0^\Gamma \epsilon(\gamma, n) w(\gamma, \Gamma) \, d\gamma \qquad (3.9)$$

where $w(\gamma, \Gamma)$ is a weighting function directly analogous to the weighting function $w(r)$ specified in equation (2.10):

$$w(\gamma, \Gamma) = f(n+\gamma) \bigg/ \int_0^\Gamma f(n+\gamma) \, d\gamma > 0 \qquad (3.10)$$

and

$$\int_0^\Gamma w(\gamma, \Gamma) \, d\gamma = 1 \qquad (3.11)$$

The connection between equations (3.9) and (2.22a) is direct. As a result, the analysis in Chapter 2 can be used to write

$$\frac{de_{\mathrm{L}}(\Gamma, n)}{d\Gamma} = \int_0^\Gamma (\epsilon(\gamma, n) - \epsilon(\Gamma, n)) w_\Gamma(\gamma, \Gamma) \, d\gamma \qquad (3.12)$$

where $w_\Gamma(\gamma, \Gamma) < 0$. The analysis in Chapter 2, particularly Theorem 3, can also be used to turn to our primary objective: determination of the impact of entry on the nominal fees charged by the competitive firms. With entry, customer-supplied time will be reduced, and the elasticity of the aggregate demand curve is thereby affected.[8] If the basic demand function is less convex than a negative exponential, the entry of new firms will result in a less elastic aggregate demand curve; so nominal fees will rise. More generally, with the entry of new firms, the behavior of the nominal fee, n, can be characterized as follows:[9]

$$n \text{ will remain unchanged as} \quad f'' \lesseqqgtr \frac{(f')^2}{f} \quad \begin{matrix} \text{rise} \\ \\ \text{fall} \end{matrix}$$

Hence, it is not necessary to appeal to "demand creation" or some form of market failure in order to reconcile the empirically observed positive relation between nominal fees and service provider density. If one considers full price – including time costs to the consumer – the initially surprising relation can be seen to be a natural outcome of a not particularly restrictive set of demand conditions and conjectural variations.[10]

3.3.2   *A caveat: unrestricted large-scale entry*

To this point it has been assumed that entry to the market is sufficiently restricted to justify the assumption that each competitor holds Löschian conjectural variations. In service industries characterized by much freer entry, in contrast, each firm can be expected to be "small" relative to market size. The pricing behavior of any one firm will therefore have a negligible impact on its competitors. Following the reasoning of Capozza and Van Order (1978), it would appear more likely that such firms will hold something akin to H-S conjectural variations.

Once again, the analysis in Chapter 2 can be applied in a direct way. The competitor in our service market is subject to two special price-behavior determinants: (1) the demand effect associated with the basic demand convexity

$$-n\int_0^\Gamma f'(n+\gamma)\,d\gamma \bigg/ \int_0^\Gamma f(n+\gamma)\,d\gamma \tag{3.13}$$

and (2) the competition effect stemming from the price conjectural variations of competitors.

$$-n(\partial\Gamma/\partial n)\,f(n+\Gamma) \bigg/ \int_0^\Gamma f(n+\gamma)\,d\gamma \tag{3.14}$$

As has been noted, the Löschian decisionmaker believes that price changes will be matched exactly by competitors; so the firm's market space is believed to be fixed, and the decisionmaker always prices as does the spatial monopolist within his own trading space. This means that the demand effect is the only factor determining the Löschian firm's price.

However, both the demand and competition effects apply under conjectural variations such as H-S or G-O. In the H-S case, the decisionmaker assumes that his competitors are sufficiently unaffected by a reduction in his nominal fee as to leave their own nominal fees unchanged; so a projected price reduction would be expected to extend the firm's trading space with respect to rivals. More specifically, with respect to limit time and fees, we have $\partial\Gamma/\partial n = -\frac{1}{2}w$. In effect, the price cutter is able to substitute slightly greater Γ for n. Were we to consider the market space of the typical physician, this effect might well be small; however, it is nonetheless reflected in (3.14). The result is that the H-S elasticity exceeds the Löschian elasticity, $e_{\mathrm{HS}}(\Gamma,n) > e_{\mathrm{L}}(\Gamma,n)$.

On the other hand, G-O conjectural variation entails a constant delivered price (full price) over all border-zone areas (a paradigm that may be somewhat inapplicable to medical services, but quite applicable to other activities in which services are priced over zones). The expected trading-space extension resulting from a conjectured price reduction by the subject firm under this paradigm would be greater than that projected under H-S competition (i.e., $\partial\Gamma/\partial n = -1w$). The conjectured negativity of $\partial\Gamma/\partial n$ and the (increasing) negativity of the weighting function $[f(n+\gamma)/\int_0^\Gamma f(n+\gamma)\,d\gamma]$ as competition increases imply $e_{GO}(\Gamma, n) > e_{HS}(\Gamma, n) > e_L(\Gamma, n)$. Hence, the relation of the nominal fees under these three paradigms is $n_L > n_{HS} > n_{GO}$, as in Chapter 2. It is again clear that the H-S and G-O firms react according to an imagined (expected) demand curve that is more elastic than the actual demand curve viewed by the Löschian firm.

More important, the effect of competitive entry on nominal fees under H-S and G-O conjectural variations is likely to be somewhat different from the effect that characterizes Löschian competition. Under the initial price conjectural variations, aggregate demand elasticity may rise, remain unchanged, or fall as a result of the impact of competitive entry on the demand effect of equation (3.13). The precise effect will be determined by the degree of convexity of the individual demand function, as in equation (3.12). But we know that competitive entry will *always* increase aggregate demand elasticity under the competition effect in equation (3.14), regardless of the shape of the individual demand function. Furthermore, because the denominator of (3.14) tends toward zero as Γ falls, the competition effect will eventually outweigh any offsetting demand effect. Intuitively, the demand effect applies within the firm's market space, whereas the competition effect operates toward the market boundary. The smaller the market radius, the proportionately greater will be the competition effect. Indeed, under the G-O price conjectural variation, it was shown in Chapter 2 that the increasing elasticity effect of the competition term in equation (3.14) *always* outweighs the demand effect, thereby invariably producing lower prices with entry.

Thus, if the individual demand function is less convex than a negative exponential and the degree of entry is modest (as is possible, and even likely, in the medical services), entry will lead to an increase in nominal fees. However, for service industries with multiple-firm, low-cost entry, we can expect a change in conjectural variations toward H-S (or G-O) competition: Each firm considers itself to have no noticeable effect on its rivals. In these circumstances, competitive entry can be expected to lead eventually (immediately) to a reduction in nominal prices (fees). Classical microeconomic theory may explain nominal prices in service industries subject to multiple-firm entry, but it does not apply – in its traditional form – to other service industries.

3.3.3   Summary

We began with some empirical evidence from the literature on medical services. A positive relation has been found to exist between nominal fees charged and the density of the providers of the service. Interpreting this to mean that entry of new firms raises, rather than lowers, price in a competitive market, much research has been devoted to nontraditional models of behavior, particularly in the health-care markets.

We have proposed as an alternative that the appropriate analytical tools to be applied are those contained in an extended neoclassical microeconomic theory. It can then be readily demonstrated that the apparently perverse price movements are consistent with theoretical expectations. Only four prime requirements need be fulfilled:

1. Demand is determined by full price rather than only the nominal fee.
2. Löschian competition prevails.
3. The individual demand functions are less convex than a negative exponential (and thus include linear demand functions).
4. Entry occurs on a modest level.

We would suggest that these requirements are much easier to accept than resorting to the idea of supplier-induced demand.

It has further been observed that different demand conditions and different conjectural variations generate contrasting price effects. In particular, it has been shown that under Löschian competition *and* less convex demand curves, the effect of entry in the medical profession is to raise fees. But how can our mathematical results be explained?

Following Greenhut's emphasis (1956) on the demand factor in location economics and, for example, Benson (1980b), an intuitive justification can be provided for this somewhat counterintuitive result. Were we to exclude time costs and concentrate only on nominal fees, it is apparent that entry into a competitive market would shift the supply curve out and reduce the fee charged. Considering full price, the entry of new firms would again increase supply. However, the difference results from the fact that the entry of new firms also affects the demand curve. As firms enter the market, the amount of customer-supplied time is reduced; so there is also a change in demand elasticities. Herein lies one of the primary differences between a spaceless analysis and one in a spatial world (or, in our case, between analyses of nominal and full prices): Events that will affect either supply or demand in a spaceless (nominal-price) world will affect both supply and demand in a spatial (full-price) world.

Note that this analysis does not suggest that the full price of the service will rise. If the foregoing requirements 1–4 are met, entry will raise the nominal fee but will lower the time-cost component; the impact on full price is indeterminate. If the individual demand functions are more convex than or identical with a negative exponential, or, alternatively, if H-S or G-O competition arises (exists) and entry is sufficient, both the nominal fee and the full price will decline.

3.4   F.o.b. prices vis-à-vis uniform prices: tying contracts

A major concern of many researchers in their analysis of f.o.b. mill pricing is to compare this pricing form with another commonly used form of pricing: uniform pricing. F.o.b. pricing involves charging buyers the full cost of shipment from the seller's site to that of the buyer. In effect, the seller turns the good over to the buyer at the transport carrier's terminal. Uniform pricing, on the other hand, involves a fixed price regardless of distances involved. Buyers everywhere pay the same (total) price. Because a uniform delivered price is one variant of discriminatory pricing, we shall wait until later in the book to present a formal comparison of these price forms. For the moment we shall content ourselves with a generalized nontechnical discussion to show in an intuitive way how the spatial properties of these two pricing systems apply to nonspatial economics.

Many nonspatial aspects can, in fact, be envisaged. All that needs to be recognized is that a firm supplying a product ancillary to which is either some additional product or service is, in effect, supplying a good that is subject to additional (differential) costs to buyers. The firm can offer the variable (differential) characteristic at an explicit price per unit, acting as if it is selling two complementary products (the f.o.b. case), or it can offer the two as a package, bundling the variable (or differential) characteristic with the main product (the uniform-price case). For instance, fastidious consumers who are heavy users of a product require more of its services than others in a given span of time. Intensity of use governs judgments of whether or not the product's performance matches its cost. Whether a seller prices separately or bundles the variable determines its profits and economic welfare.

As a further example, Phlips (1983) aptly points out that the service attached to a money market or checking account depends partly on the number of drafts *and* also on possible overdrafts; basic custom helps determine whether or not unlimited checking at one price is offered. Another variant that might be mentioned here is the typical sale of a television set, where a service contract may be included at a fixed price, or repairs paid for separately. Charging for information services by telephone companies is another example. Monopoly power suffices to enable bundling (i.e., uniform pricing) or may even encourage separate (f.o.b.) sales. Conceptually, perfect competition would be required for separate charges.

It follows that additional costs for nonbundled products are just like waiting costs, commuting-time costs, and service-time costs. Similar to decreases in bank charges for extra drafts as a result of more intensive competition from a greater number of rivals, so will GM's charges for Mr. Goodwrench's repairs decrease (including decreases in waiting, service, and delivery times) under conditions of greater competition from Chrysler. In effect, all of these prices are analogous to spatial prices. Even such attempts as A. B. Dick's tying of ink and paper to their office machines correspond to a manufacturer whose own carriers are required for delivery of the product. Whether the price set is *fixed for all* or includes variable features per consumer is analogous to the comparison of uniform delivered and f.o.b. pricing in spatial economics. Thus, the extent of entry and the type of competition between firms, along with statutory and judicial acceptance or rejection of a certain practice, help determine price levels and changes in prices over time.

3.5   Concluding remarks

F.o.b. pricing is crucially affected in the space economy by both the nature of the competitive forces and the underlying demand conditions. In comparing spaceless and spatial monopolistic pricing, a crucial distinction must be drawn between the basic (gross) demand function and the spatial (aggregate) demand function. The elasticities of these two functions with respect to the net (mill) price vary in a well-ordered manner relative to the convexity of the basic demand function. As a result, the spatial monopolist will, in general, choose a net price different from that chosen by the spaceless monopolist.

Whether competitive prices are higher or lower than the spatial monopoly price also depends on the demand conditions and the nature of competitive forces. If individual demand is relatively convex (more convex than a negative exponential) or if competitive forces are strong and the firm is not a Löschian competitor, the competitive price can be expected to be lower than the spatial monopolist's price.

Turning to the perverse results noted by Capozza and Van Order, it has now been shown that they occur only when the basic demand function is less convex than a negative exponential, and then only under Löschian competition or, shall we say, typically when competitive forces are relatively weak. No matter what the convexity of the basic demand function, Löschian competition generates the highest competitive prices. Further, whether in the short run or long run, the competitive price is lower when the belief (conjectural variation) held by the spatial competitor is that it will gain an increase in market radius following a reduction in its mill price.

The sharp conflicts between spaceless and spatial microeconomics noted by Capozza and Van Order would appear to have been resolved, or to characterize what might be considered to be a relatively narrow set of market conditions. This is not to say that spatial and spaceless microeconomics are, after all, in some sense "the same." The resolution of the apparent conflict centers on demand conditions and the nature of competitive processes. Explicit recognition of the spatial dimension introduces a richness and diversity of actions open to the spatial firm that do not naturally characterize the spaceless firm. Even long-run equilibria within their spatial setting are crucially dependent on short-run (often erroneous) expectations. In addition, the conclusions of our spatial analysis are capable of shedding light on apparently perverse price movements in seemingly nonspatial markets.

We shall have more to say about the long-run equilibrium state in later chapters. Now, however, we turn our attention to other special applications of our analysis, after which we shall consider spatial price discrimination: the spatial firm's behavior when it is *not constrained* to an f.o.b. pricing policy.

Mathematical appendix

Shape of the pricing equations: The fundamental pricing equation, from Chapter 2, is

$$P_i(R, m) : m\left(1 - \frac{1}{e_i(R, m)}\right) - c = 0 \qquad (A3.1)$$

The slope of this equation is

$$\left.\frac{dm}{dR}\right|_{P_i} = -\frac{\partial P_i/\partial R}{\partial P_i/\partial m} \qquad (A3.2)$$

Because the individual demand functions are assumed to be well-behaved, $\partial P_i/\partial m > 0$. Hence,

$$\left.\frac{dm}{dR}\right|_{P_i} \gtreqless 0 \quad \text{as} \quad \frac{\partial P_i}{\partial R} \lesseqgtr 0 \qquad (A3.3)$$

From (A3.1),

$$\frac{\partial P_i}{\partial R} = \frac{m\partial e_i(R, m)/\partial R}{(e_i(R, m))^2} \qquad (A3.4)$$

Hence,

$$\left.\frac{dm}{dR}\right|_{P_i} \gtreqless 0 \quad \text{as} \quad \frac{\partial e_i(R, m)}{\partial R} \lesseqgtr 0$$

The analysis of Chapter 2 gives

$$\frac{\partial e_i(R, m)}{\partial R} = \int_0^R [\epsilon(r, m) - \epsilon(R, m)] w_R(r)\, dr + v_i m w_R(R) \qquad (A3.5)$$

The second term is nonpositive. Two cases then arise:

Demand is more convex than a negative exponential: Chapter 2 gives $\epsilon(r, m) > \epsilon(R, m)$. Also, $w_R(r) < 0$. Hence, (A3.5) is negative, and the slope of the price equation is positive.

Demand is less convex than a negative exponential: Now $\epsilon(r, m) < \epsilon(R, m)$. The first term of (A3.5) is positive, and the second negative; the sign of (A3.5) is ambiguous. A change in variable (see Chapter 2 Mathematical Appendix) allows elasticity of aggregate demand to be rewritten

$$e_i(R, m) = \frac{m}{\int_0^R f(m+tr)\, dr} \left\{ \frac{1}{t} f(m) - \left(\frac{1}{t} - \nu_i\right) f(m+tR) \right\} \qquad (A3.6)$$

Under G-O competition, $\nu_i = 1/t$; hence,

$$e_{GO}(R, m) = mf(m) \Big/ \int_0^R f(m+tr)\, dr \qquad (A3.7)$$

and the G-O pricing equation is upward-sloping, because

$$\frac{\partial e_{GO}(R, m)}{\partial R} < 0$$

Under Löschian competition, $\nu_i = 0$, and the analysis in Chapter 2 gives

$$\frac{\partial e_L(R, m)}{\partial R} > 0$$

Hence, the Löschian pricing equation is always downward-sloping.
   Now assume $0 < \nu_i < 1/t$. Then

$$\frac{\partial e_i(R, m)}{\partial R}$$

$$= \frac{m}{(\int_0^R f(m+tr)\, dr)^2} \left[\left\{ -t \int_0^R f(m+tr)\, dr \left(\frac{1}{t} - \nu_i\right) f'(m+tR) \right\} \right.$$

$$\left. + \left\{ -\left[\frac{1}{t} f(m) - \left(\frac{1}{t} - \nu_i\right) f(m+tR)\right] f(m+tR) \right\} \right]$$

$$\qquad (A3.8)$$

The first term in braces in (A3.8) is positive, and the second negative. But $\int_0^R f(m+tR)\, dr \to 0$ as $R \to 0$; hence, as $R \to 0$ the first term tends to zero. Thus, for "small" R, the second term dominates, and $\partial e_i(R, m)/\partial R < 0$. As R increases, $f(m+tR) \to 0$, and the second term tends to zero. Thus, for "large" R, the first term dominates, and $\partial e_i(R, m)/\partial R > 0$. Hence, with less convex individual demand and $\nu_L < \nu_i < \nu_{GO}$, the pricing equation is initially upward-sloping and subsequently downward-sloping.

CHAPTER 4

Nondiscriminatory prices, economic development, and merger policies

The discussion in Chapters 2 and 3 has deliberately been kept abstract in order to allow derivation of general results. We recognize, however, that for many readers intuition is considerably aided if specific examples are presented to illustrate the general conclusions. Section 4.1 in this chapter provides such an illustration using two specific functional forms as examples of demand functions that are less convex or more convex than a negative exponential. Section 4.2 applies this discussion and the results of the analysis in Chapters 2 and 3 to demonstrate how prices can be expected to change in an expanding (developing) economy. Finally, it is shown in Section 4.3 that the antitrust perspective of the spatial price theorist differs quite radically from those of other microeconomic theorists. Readers with limited time who are also most concerned with pure theory may omit this chapter. Its basic intention is to discuss f.o.b. pricing and cite applications in addition to those in Chapters 2 and 3.

4.1 Examples of less and more convex demand functions

The specific individual demand function used is that already discussed briefly in Chapter 2. In inverse form, it is given by

$$p(r) = m + tr = \alpha - \frac{\beta}{x}q(r)^x \quad (\alpha, \beta > 0; \ x \neq 0) \tag{4.1}$$

This demand function encompasses a wide range of special cases.[1] Specifically, if $x = 1$, the demand function (4.1) reduces to a linear function and corresponds to the demand function used in the model of Capozza and Van Order (1979). More generally, this demand function is more convex than a negative exponential if $x < 0$, and less convex than a negative exponential if $x > 0$.[2] In other words, the degree of convexity (or concavity) of the individual demand function is determined by the exponent x.

Some further comments are necessary on the demand function (4.1). First, x must be restricted to $-1 < x < \infty$ if a determinate solution is to be obtained.[3] Second, the interpretation of the demand parameter α varies with the value of x. When $x > 0$, α is the maximum price consumers are

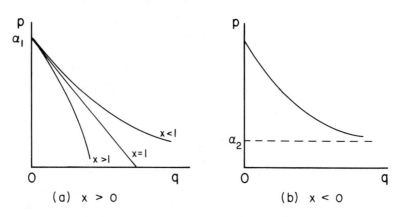

Figure 4.1. Alternative demand functions: $p = \alpha - (\beta/x)q^x$.

willing to pay for the product, but when $x < 0$, α is a lower limit on price. This is illustrated in Figure 4.1. Rather than evaluating the optimal non-discriminatory (f.o.b.) prices for all values of x, we follow Greenhut and associates (1977) and Benson (1980a) by restricting investigation to two specific alternative demand conditions, namely, $x = 1$ to represent all cases of $x > 0$ (less convex than a negative exponential) and $x = -\frac{1}{2}$ to represent all cases of $-1 < x < 0$ (more convex than a negative exponential).

To obtain aggregate market demand, rewrite (4.1) in direct form:

$$q(r) = \left(\frac{x}{\beta} (\alpha - tr - m) \right)^{1/x} \tag{4.2}$$

Then

$$q(r) = \frac{1}{\beta} (\alpha - tr - m) \qquad \text{if } x = 1 \tag{4.3a}$$

$$q(r) = \left(-\frac{1}{2\beta} (\alpha - tr - m) \right)^{-2} \qquad \text{if } x = -1/2 \tag{4.3b}$$

Aggregate spatial demand is obtained by integrating the individual demand functions (4.3) over the firm's market area to obtain

$$Q_p = 2D \int_0^R \frac{1}{\beta} (\alpha - tr - m) \, dr = \frac{2DR}{\beta} \left(\alpha - m - \frac{tR}{2} \right) \qquad \text{if } x = 1 \tag{4.4a}$$

$$Q_n = 2D \int_0^R \left(-\frac{1}{2\beta} (\alpha - tr - m) \right)^{-2} dr$$

$$= \frac{8\beta^2 D}{t} \left(\frac{1}{m - \alpha} - \frac{1}{m - \alpha + tR} \right) \qquad \text{if } x = -\frac{1}{2} \tag{4.4b}$$

where Q_p represents the aggregation of demand curves with positive exponents (i.e., $x > 0$), Q_n denotes the aggregation of the demand curves with negative exponents,[4] and R denotes the radius of the firm's market area.

Given the production-cost function specified in equation (2.3), the firm's profits are given by

$$\Pi = (m-c)Q - F \tag{4.5}$$

Combining (4.4) and (4.5) gives

$$\Pi_p = \frac{2DR}{\beta}(m-c)\left(\alpha - m - \frac{tR}{2}\right) - F \tag{4.6a}$$

$$\Pi_n = \frac{8\beta^2 D}{t}\left(\frac{1}{m-\alpha} - \frac{1}{m-\alpha+tR}\right)(m-c) - F \tag{4.6b}$$

Differentiating equations (4.6) with respect to mill price establishes the profit-maximizing pricing equations from the conditions

$$\frac{d\Pi_p}{dm} = \frac{2DR}{\beta}\left(\alpha - 2m - \frac{tR}{2} + c\right) + \frac{2D}{\beta}(m-c)(\alpha - m - tR)\frac{\partial R}{\partial m} = 0 \tag{4.7a}$$

$$\frac{d\Pi_n}{dm} = \frac{8\beta^2 DR((c-\alpha)tR + (c-\alpha)^2 - (m-c)^2)}{(m-\alpha)^2(m-\alpha+tR)^2} + \frac{8\beta^2 D(m-c)}{(m-\alpha+tR)^2}\frac{\partial R}{\partial m} = 0 \tag{4.7b}$$

4.1.1 Alternative competitive models[5]

Consider first the Löschian model. Then $\partial R/\partial m = 0$, and (4.7) becomes

$$m_p^L = \frac{1}{2}(\alpha + c) - \frac{tR}{4} \tag{4.8a}$$

$$m_n^L = c + ((c-\alpha)tR + (c-\alpha)^2)^{1/2} \tag{4.8b}$$

On the other hand, in the H-S model, $\partial R/\partial m = -1/2t$, and (4.7) gives

$$m_p^{HS} = c + \frac{2tR(\alpha - m_p^{HS} - tR/2)}{(\alpha - m_p^{HS} + tR)} \tag{4.9a}$$

$$m_n^{HS} = c + \frac{2tR((c-\alpha)tR + (c-\alpha)^2 - (m_n^{HS} - c)^2)}{(m_n^{HS} - \alpha)^2} \tag{4.9b}$$

One point is worth noting. For equations (4.8b) and (4.9b) to give profit-maximizing values for m_n, it is necessary that $c - \alpha > 0$ (i.e., that marginal

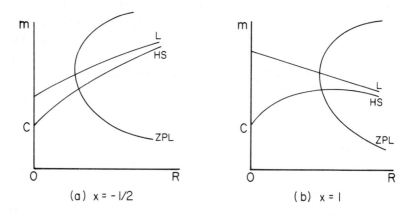

Figure 4.2. Price determination.

costs exceed the lowest price consumers offer for the product). To see why this constraint is necessary, consider Figure 4.1(b). If $\alpha > c > 0$, then there is nothing to prevent the firm from setting mill price $m_n = \alpha$ and selling an infinite amount (with infinite profit) at the seller's location.

Note also that the precise forms of equations (4.8) and (4.9) are determined by the assumption of a linear market rather than a plane market. In a plane market, (4.8a) would have been (see Mathematical Appendix)

$$m_p^L = \frac{1}{2}(\alpha + c) - \frac{tR}{3} \tag{4.10}$$

and the term $tR/2$ in (4.9a) would have been replaced by $2tR/3$. The reason for the differences between equations (4.9a) and (4.10) is easily explained. Under an f.o.b. pricing system, the firm is trading off mill price against market radius. The lower the mill price, the greater the market radius the firm can serve. If the market area is a plane rather than a line, a reduction in mill price will give access to proportionately more consumers. As a result, the mill price charged in a plane market will be lower than that charged in a line market. Effectively, the firm is willing to absorb additional total freight costs in a plane market, a result that will be shown later to be of some importance in the explanation of price movements in a developing economy.

Returning to equations (4.6), (4.8), and (4.9), the ZPL from equation (4.6b) and the price equations (4.8b) and (4.9b) are illustrated in the (R, m) plane of Figure 4.2(a). In contrast, Figure 4.2(b) illustrates the pricing equations (4.8a) and (4.9a). As is to be expected from the general analysis in Chapters 2 and 3, the perverse price movements generated by the Löschian model, and in certain circumstances by the H-S model, when demand is linear disappear when individual demand is "very" convex: An increase in consumer density, or a reduction in fixed costs or transport costs, will result in a leftward shift of the ZPL in Figure 4.2.

4.1.2   Spatial and nonspatial prices viewed in the classical demand-curve diagram

Why should it be that a firm's pricing policy in a world of imperfect competition is so sensitive to the nature of the individual demand function, a sensitivity that would appear to be fundamental to imperfect competition? The reason comes very simply from the fundamental pricing equation derived in Chapter 2:

$$m^*\left(1 - \frac{1}{e(R, m^*)}\right) = c \tag{4.11}$$

where $e(R, m^*)$ is the elasticity of the aggregate demand function in the total market R. The more elastic is aggregate demand, the lower will be the profit-maximizing discriminatory price.

Second, a distinction must be made between individual *gross* demand and individual *net* demand.[6] Returning once more to the spatial analogy, even though individual gross demand functions may be identical, in which case spaceless aggregate demand is the summation of these identical gross demands, spatial aggregate demand is obtained by the summation of *varying* net demands. This distinction relates in turn to the distinction between the price received by the firm and the price paid by consumers. In a spaceless world these are identical, but in a spatial world they differ by the amount paid for transportation.

Our preliminary discussion in Chapter 1 indicated that this difference between the firm's receipts and the consumer's expenditure is not confined to a spatial world. Storage and inventory costs and even production bottlenecks due to delays in receiving purchased raw materials carry similar differential effects and are therefore tractable using techniques developed in spatial price theory. Similarly, in full-price models that include factors such as waiting time, a distinction must be drawn between the price (fee) received by the seller and the full price paid by the consumer. It will also be shown in the next chapter that in a world of differentiated products, a distinction should be drawn between the price received by a seller of a particular product variant and the full price consumers of that variant are paying.

Returning to the demand function (4.1), it is easy to show (Greenhut et al. 1977; Benson 1980a) that *when transport costs are subtracted from*

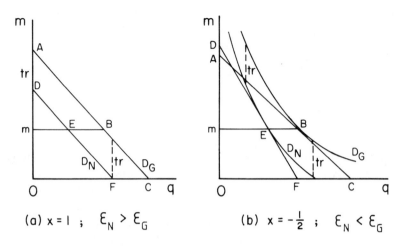

(a) $x = 1$; $\varepsilon_N > \varepsilon_G$ (b) $x = -\frac{1}{2}$; $\varepsilon_N < \varepsilon_G$

Figure 4.3. Net and gross demand elasticities.

the gross demands to obtain the net demands, *elasticity at a given (mill) price increases with distance from the seller if $x > 0$, but falls when $x < 0$.* To see this analytically, rewrite the individual demand function (4.1) as

$$m = (\alpha - tr) - \frac{\beta}{x}q(r)^x \qquad (4.12)$$

For each consumer at distance r from the seller, demand elasticity with respect to the mill price is then

$$\epsilon(r, m) = \frac{dq(r)}{dm}\frac{m}{q(r)} = \frac{m}{\beta q(r)^x} \qquad (4.13)$$

Differentiate with respect to r to obtain

$$\frac{\partial \epsilon(r, m)}{\partial r} = \frac{mtx}{(x(\alpha - m - tr))^2} \lessgtr 0 \quad \text{as } x \lessgtr 0 \qquad (4.14)$$

because the denominator is positive. The distant buyer's demand is less (more) elastic with respect to the mill price as $x < 0$ $(x > 0)$.

This conclusion can also be illustrated diagrammatically. Simple microeconomic principles indicate that the elasticity at price m of a linear demand curve such as D_G in Figure 4.3(a) is given by the ratio BC/AB. Similarly, for a nonlinear demand curve such as D_G in Figure 4.3(b), elasticity at price m is given by the ratio BC/AB, where ABC is the tangent to D_G at price m. Introduction of transport costs is equivalent to a downward shift of the demand function D_G. Thus, the net demand curve, D_N, for consumers at distance r from the firm is given in Figure 4.3 by

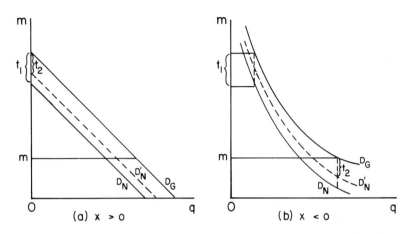

Figure 4.4. Shifts in net demand due to a fall in t.

shifting the gross demand curve down *throughout its range* by the amount tr. If the elasticities of net spatial demands and gross (spaceless) demands are denoted by ϵ_N and ϵ_G, respectively, it follows from Figure 4.3 that

$$\epsilon_G = BC/AB; \qquad \epsilon_N = EF/DE \qquad (4.15)$$

and that

$$\epsilon_N > \epsilon_G \quad \text{if } x = 1; \qquad \epsilon_N < \epsilon_G \quad \text{if } x = -\tfrac{1}{2} \qquad (4.16)$$

As a result, if individual gross demands have positive exponents (i.e., $x > 0$), elasticity of spatial aggregate demand increases at any mill price as more distant consumers are added, because individual net demands with increasing elasticities are being added to aggregate demand. On the other hand, elasticity of aggregate demand falls at any mill price as more distant consumers are added when individual gross demands have negative exponents (i.e., $x < 0$), because decreasing elasticities are added in forming the seller's aggregate spatial demand curve.

4.1.3   *Shifts in net demand due to changes in transport costs*

As illustrated in Figure 4.4, a fall in transport costs is represented by an upward shift in the net demand curves (i.e., from D_N to D_N'). In the case of demand curves with positive exponents, this implies that the elasticity of net demand for consumers *at each point* in the market space will decrease. The resulting aggregate demand is less elastic, and the price effect is upward. The only offsetting influence in this case is the competition effect (see Chapter 2) given that the conjectural variation $\partial R/\partial m$ is nonzero.

Table 4.1. *Effects on price in Benson's model*

Parameter increased	Löschian competition		H-S competition	
	$x = 1$ (CVO)	$x = -\frac{1}{2}$	$x = 1$ (CVO)	$x = -\frac{1}{2}$
Demand density	+	−	∓	−
Fixed costs	−	+	±	+
Transport costs per unit of distance	−	+	±	+
Entry of new firms	+	−	∓	−

If the gross demands have negative exponents, a fall in the transport rate will increase the elasticity of *each* individual (net) demand curve in the seller's space. Thus, the aggregate demand becomes more elastic, and the price effect is downward.

4.1.4 Changes in consumer density and fixed costs

The pricing equations (4.8) and (4.9) and the elasticity of aggregate demand are independent of consumer density (and, of course, of fixed costs). Effectively, an increase in consumer density merely leads to a *rotation* of the individual and thus aggregate demand functions around their price intercepts. This can be seen as a change in β [see equation (4.2)], which does not affect the elasticity of individual or aggregate demand: It can be seen from equations (4.8) and (4.9) that f.o.b. mill-pricing equations are independent of β. However, an increase in consumer density or a decrease in fixed costs increases profit [see equations (4.6)], thus leading to a leftward movement in the ZPL in Figure 4.2 and to a change in the zero-profit f.o.b. mill price.

4.1.5 Summary

The basic findings regarding the effects of changes in various parameters of the model are summarized in Table 4.1; note that for $x = 1$, the price effects are just those identified by Capozza and Van Order (CVO).

4.2 Prices in a developing economy (newly formed industries)[7]

It is possible to use the analysis of this and previous chapters to interpret price movements in an advancing economy as an inevitable consequence of the growth and scattering of its population. In the interest of brevity, the discussion assumes that the basic demand function (4.2) has a positive exponent. This assumption is not particularly restrictive in that it encompasses linear, concave, and *some* convex demand functions, but the reader may wish to rework the analysis on the assumption that individual demand is "very" convex.

The elements of our theoretical analysis on which we concentrate in this application are (1) the impact on price of changes in market radius, and (2) the impact on price that arises when we move from a linear market to a two-dimensional plane market.

Economic development implies that there will be decreasing numbers of desirable home sites at established residential places. People then migrate from existing centers, and the mill prices of firms located there will tend to fall. This lowering of mill prices both maximizes entrepreneurial profits and keeps the migrants within the seller's market area.

In the transitional stage toward a fully developed economy, people generally move to outlying regions by following the waterways and other natural transport routes. A linear type of scattering results, in which the principles of freight absorption and falling prices outlined in Chapter 2 apply. Given a linear type of spatial dispersion, the more distant regions are relatively unimportant, thus causing only a small amount of freight absorption and therefore a small reduction in mill price.

As population pressures continue and improvements in transportation methods arise, people will tend to disperse from the major transport nodes. Their attempts to find more *Lebensraum* make each outlying ring relatively more important than in the case of linear dispersion. The market area increasingly takes on the characteristics of a plane market rather than a series of linear markets. Thus, the amount of freight absorption is increased by manufacturers seeking prices that offer greater profits through access to greater numbers of consumers. And through this increase in the amount of freight absorption, net mill prices continue to fall.

Oddly enough, a paradoxical situation exists within each type of migration, whether linear or otherwise: For after people have reached the remote extremities of a country's land surface, future movements must be confined to places between the extremities, the amount of freight absorption will fall, and prices will rise. This fact is patently due to the relative increase in importance of buyers situated nearest to the seller's plant. The filling up of areas causes a slightly higher net mill price and leads to contraction in the sales radius of the firm. A similar effect occurs when rivals enter the market and locate at distant locations.

The natural underlying movement of prices in a space economy is therefore spasmodic. As people move outward to a given extremity, prices fall. As people fill up the area between the old center and the extremity, prices rise. As people move outward from this extremity to still more distant points, prices fall, and so on. It follows that the natural force of population on the efforts of entrepreneurs to find the profit-maximizing net mill price and sales radius is such that movements to uninhabited areas cause prices to fall, and filling up of these areas causes prices to rise. The greater the number of people in an economy, the smaller is the sales radius of the firm, and the more often will rivals (or branch plants) appear in outlying regions. A natural tendency for industrial decentralization and its surprising by-product, higher net mill prices, therefore exists after all frontiers have been reached.

The foregoing remarks have concentrated on discussion of population changes (number and movement) and comparatively small entry. A similar appraisal of the impact of improvement in transportation on prices and sales radii may be mentioned. Briefly, the lowering of freight rates as a result of technological development results in a decrease in the amount of freight absorption, because in effect the economy approaches the spaceless economy, with the result that aggregate demands become smoother; in turn, net mill prices rise even while the sales radius of the firm is extended.[8] Thus, technological improvements in transportation, which lead to a cut in rates, accrue in large part to the benefit of the entrepreneur. This gain is partially at the expense of those consumers situated near to the seller's plant.[9]

It is important to note with respect to f.o.b. prices that it does not matter if several firms are located at the same place (the production center) or if they locate at a distance. The main implication of increased numbers is the possibility that price lies closer to competitive levels than what would prevail if there were only one firm in the market; they tend to promote the H-S or G-O model; a priori, it suffices that a nondiscriminatory f.o.b. mill-price system is followed and that demand is not strongly convex to lead to the general principles established earlier.

The impacts on f.o.b. prices of negatively sloping or positively increasing marginal costs should be mentioned briefly. Under the general demand case used here, each extension in sales radius causes a more elastic demand curve, a rightward shifting of the marginal-revenue curve, and an intersection between it and marginal costs at a point farther removed from the origin than was originally the case. If marginal costs are decreasing, net mill price will fall as the seller extends its market area. Indeed, it might further be pointed out that here, as in the prior cases, the decrease in net mill price caused by the expansion in market is, in a practical sense, greater than in the nonspatial case. But an unusual exception does exist when marginal costs decrease very rapidly. In such a case, the greater magnitude of nonspatial demand may lead to intersection of falling marginal values at a very extended point, leaving the same or a lower total price received by the seller.

In somewhat similar manner, increasing marginal costs generate a lower net mill price than that derived in nonspatial models. This follows because each market-area extension yields a total effective demand curve in spatial models that is lower than the corresponding demand curve derived in nonspatial models. The intersection of marginal values leads to a relatively lower net mill price in the economics of space than in traditional dimensionless economics. Of course, in this particular case of increasing marginal costs, unlike the others, extension of sales radius may cause an absolute increase in net mill price. It proves to be an exception in this regard, but not relative to the findings with models that abstract from space.

It follows that the outlined theory of economic history is not limited to assumptions of negatively sloping *straight-line* demand curves or constant marginal-cost curves. It is much broader than that. It defines the relative underlying trend of net mill prices in an expanding spatial economy, as compared with the impact on price of new consumers in nonspatial economics. In fact, if it were not for the significant exception of rapidly increasing marginal costs or the possibility that demands *could be* more convex than the negative exponential, we would be tempted to hold that the hypothesis of absolute falling net mill prices in a developing free-entry spatial economy is not only a particular theory but also a very general explanation of prices.

A spatial perspective allows us to shed light on some further elements of economic history and economic development.[10] In *Industry and Trade,* Alfred Marshall described an important rule of market areas:

improvements in the mechanism or organisation of transport, which increase the distance over which trade can be carried at a given expense, are *prima facie* likely to increase in the square of that ratio the area over which the trade can be conducted profitably. [1923, p. 27]

This rule was stated as *Lardner's law of squares in transport* in honor of the Irish engineer-economist Dionysius Lardner (1793–1859). The law assumes that firms are supplying circular market areas. It is set out in Lardner's book *Railway Economy* as follows:

Any improvement in transport which will double its speed will double the radius of [the] circle; an improvement which will treble its speed will increase the radius in a threefold proportion. Now, as the actual area or quantity of soil included with such a radius is augmented, not in the simple ratio of the radius itself, but in the proportion of its square, it follows that a double speed will give a fourth-fold area of supply, a triple speed a ninefold area of supply, and so on. How great the advantages are, which in this case attend increased speed, are abundantly apparent. [1850, p. 35]

Marshall considered this law to be "epoch-making." He used it as an important element of the relation between industry and trade and in particular indicated that Lardner's law:

applies fairly well to a trading port in close touch with an archipelago or river delta studded with rich markets [and] has had much to do with the brilliant careers of Athens, Alexandria, Byzantium, Marseilles, and Venice; of the Hanseatic League, and of Holland. [1923], p. 28]

Lardner's law can also be seen to underpin explanations of the rise of major industrial cities such as Manchester in the United Kingdom and Pittsburgh in the United States. Improvements in the speed and efficiency of transport allowed producers in those cities to supply an ever-increasing hinterland.

4.3   Antitrust merger policy[11]

In the United States today, few topics are as hotly debated, both politically and in the context of the new industrial economics, as that involving corporate takeovers and government antimerger policies. Indeed, American newspapers and TV networks appear to revel in spreading paranoia concerning the dominance of (control by) a few merging pirates of industry, emphasizing the need for countervailing power, advocating breaking up conglomerates, and so forth. From the level of the uninformed to that of the supposed expert, emotion bordering on hysteria can be seen as discussions on the subject periodically degenerate into arguments as bitter as those involving religion and politics.

It is our belief that a spatial approach leads to a vastly different perspective on merger policy than that typically taken by legislators and economists in the United States. Section 7 of the Clayton Act, as amended by the Celler-Kefauver Act of 1950, prohibits a merger "where in any line of commerce in any section of the country the effect of such acquisition may be substantially to lessen competition, or tend to create a monopoly." The U.S. Department of Justice must define the appropriate "line of commerce" and delineate the relevant "section of the country" when attempting to demonstrate that a merger challenged under Section 7 substantially lessens competition. Designation of both the line of commerce and the section of the country is especially crucial because of the Justice Department's use of concentration ratios and market shares as the measures of the competitive impact of merger. An inappropriate designation of either the line of commerce or the market is tantamount to an inaccurate estimate of the competitive impact.

A critical factor in defining the relevant geographic market under the traditional approach adopted by the Justice Department is that the requisite rivalry involve competition between firms for the same customers. This occurs when two or more firms are located within the same service area. Is such a restrictive definition of competition necessary? In a spatial economy it is easy to show that it is not. Spatially separate competitive firms *need not compete for all of the same customers.* But they do compete for those located at all service-area boundary points, and this form of spatial competition is sufficient to result in transmission of price changes over extensive geographic spaces. Effectively, individual market areas are linked in a form of chain. Hence, competitive geographic market areas tend to be *larger* than those designated by Justice Department methods, as well as by the methods proposed by Elzinga and Hogarty (1973) and Shrieves (1978). The implication is that mergers of firms in a particular service area may not eliminate or reduce competition. Competition exists only so long as firms share common market boundaries.

It has been noted that the impact of a change in one firm's competitive position varies in alternative spatial contexts. The basic idea is that lower prices are not transmitted by profit-maximizing firms *throughout the market.* Instead, any improvement in one firm's competitive position that enables it to reduce its price and thus expand into a neighboring service area could elicit increases in the prices of adjacent firms. Lower prices are transferred throughout the market only when the individual spatial demand is the relatively more convex curve. The argument that competition must be preserved in order to derive a lower general price level becomes much weaker in the context of extensive competitive market spaces. It would hold true if and only if it could be shown that there would be more plant sites (smaller firms producing efficiently) if no merged (large) firms existed.

Additional conditions deserve consideration with respect to the price effects stemming from a merger of spatially separated firms:

1. It has been argued by some analysts that a greater possibility of collusive pricing exists if a market becomes more concentrated. However, laws against collusive pricing should stand or fall on their own. If free entry is preserved, any extra profits resulting from merger can be expected to attract new firms over the landscape.
2. There may be price changes if there are economies or diseconomies of scale resulting from the formation of multiunit firms.[12] If economies of scale exist for the two merging firms, their prices will fall rather than rise, a condition that promotes productive efficiency, and consumers will be better off.[13]

3. There is a demand effect. Because multiunit firms may offer more branch (plant) locations (supply points), consumers may prefer multiunit firms to single-unit firms. Thus, consumers may be willing to pay a premium to do business with a multiunit firm. This will alter a merged firm's marginal revenue, and its price will rise. However, the price increase is associated with changing demand conditions due to the greater benefits that consumers derive from the reduction in transport cost that itself is attributable to the increase in concentration per se.

4. There is an impact on allocative efficiency. Perhaps a firm has discovered a technological improvement, or perhaps some input is relatively abundant at its location. Mergers often result in spatial transfers of technology, with inputs moving from relatively abundant areas to relatively scarce areas. The result is that some prices will fall, whereas others may rise. Resource allocation is generally improved. Theoretically, the net effect of the foregoing interacting forces is unclear. However, empirical evidence for one industry, the banking industry, "suggests that the effect of MBHC affiliation has resulted in some instances in lower interest charges on loans" (Drum 1976, p. 10). The same can be said for branching systems (Horvitz and Shull 1964). We can, however, generalize beyond the banking industry, as in the following.

5. Because competitive geographic market areas tend to be larger than those designated by Justice Department methods, a merger between, say, firms A and C located at extreme points along a line market, with at least one rival, firm B, in between, need not violate the classical "invisible hand." For that matter, merger between firm A and the adjacent firm B need not eliminate cost-saving price effects between A and B, nor the transmission process to C and other firms in the economy. The fact that even between firms A and B, each unit (whether merged or not) prices as a monopolist within its trading space implies that cost changes for A or B that affect profit-maximizing f.o.b. mill prices will be transmitted to other markets as described earlier. (Incidentally, to the extent that manufacturing firms typically discriminate in price,[14] the same price effect can be shown to apply. Thus, our emphasis to this point in the book on f.o.b. mill pricing is actually fully general.)

6. It matters not where the merged firms are located unless the whole landscape contains no (or virtually no) competitive boundary points. And even in the latter case, the constraint to be applied should center on Section 2 of the Sherman Act, distinct from the

Celler Act and the restricted geographic market concept that has stemmed from it.

7. What about the often-used cliché that mergers should be disallowed in general unless substantial cost savings are shown to result? Is it not the case that those who advocate applying this constraint really are asking if any merger should ever be allowed? Spatial price theory proposes as its answer that empirically observed transitive spillover effects will take place only so long as competition prevails in *some* areas adjacent to those of firms *A* and *C*. It follows that regulatory authorities should make sure that new entry will occur whenever possible and determine the type of demand curves so as to anticipate new distant-entry price effects and the impacts of changes in cost.

To sum up, we propose simply that merger of firms should be allowed *provided* that competition will still exist over the economic landscape or that competitive entry of new units will remain likely at any location, *nearby or distant*. It is particularly the case that if demand were relatively convex, the price effects of lower cost or *distant* entry would be downward. We propose finally the thought that mergers in a spatial economy should be evaluated in the context of spatial microeconomic theory, not the classical spaceless theory that has characterized microeconomics in the past.

4.4 Concluding remarks

The heart of the pricing-competition relationships in a space economy lies in the difference between spaceless gross demands and spatial net demands. As set forth by Greenhut and associates (1977):

A gross demand of constant elasticity equal to 1, for example, implies that the percentage decline in quantity demanded always equals the percentage increase in total price (including transportation costs). But from the standpoint of a producer who is netting less than the total price (since the total includes transportation costs), a percentage increase in net price does not yield the corresponding percentage increase in total price, nor does it therefore reduce quantity demanded by 1 per cent. The percentage change in quantity demanded relative to net price is not even constant. The problem boils down, in other words, to the fact that economists tend to think in terms of equating price received with price paid. But consumers virtually always incur buying costs in addition to the price paid to the seller for his product, and producers are accordingly subject to demand elasticity that relates to the (net) market price, not the total price. [p. 244]

Mathematical appendix

Optimal nondiscriminatory price in a planar market: Aggregate demand in the plane market is

$$Q_p = D \int_0^{2\pi} \int_0^R \frac{1}{\beta} (\alpha - tr - m) r \, dr \, d\theta$$

$$= \frac{D}{\beta} \int_0^{2\pi} \left(\frac{\alpha R^2}{2} - \frac{tR^3}{3} - \frac{mR^2}{2} \right) d\theta$$

$$= \frac{2\pi DR^2}{\beta} \left(\frac{\alpha}{2} - \frac{tR}{3} - \frac{m}{2} \right) \tag{A4.1}$$

Profit is, from (4.5),

$$\Pi_p = \frac{2\pi DR^2}{\beta} (m - c) \left(\frac{\alpha}{2} - \frac{tR}{3} - \frac{m}{2} \right) - F \tag{A4.2}$$

Löschian conjectures give $\partial R / \partial m = 0$. Thus, the profit maximizing Löschian mill price is such that

$$\frac{\partial \Pi_p}{\partial m} = \frac{2\pi DR^2}{\beta} \left(\frac{\alpha}{2} - \frac{tR}{3} - m + \frac{c}{2} \right) = 0 \tag{A4.3}$$

Simplifying and reorganizing gives (4.10).

CHAPTER 5

Product differentiation: a spatial f.o.b. perspective

The use of spatial models to analyze product differentiation has a long intellectual pedigree. Hotelling (1929) indicated that the analysis of location choice (which we shall discuss in more detail in Part III) could equally be applied to the choice of product variety. Chamberlin (1933) was concerned directly with the implications that product differentiation holds for the competitive process and recognized the strong connections between product differentiation and location choice.

It was only with the pioneering work of Lancaster (1966, 1979), however, that this early work came to full fruition. The essence of Lancaster's new theory of consumption is the suggestion that consumers' preferences do not relate to final products, as such, but rather to the *characteristics* embodied in those final products.[1] Rather than buying a motor car, the consumer is buying some combination of body style, speed, gasoline consumption, reliability, and so forth. In buying a radio, the consumer is buying some combination of weight or bulkiness and sensitivity.

The traditional approach to consumption theory is set in a commodity space of P dimensions, where P is the total number of commodities available to consumers. Each consumer is supposed to derive utility from consumption of a commodity bundle $x = (x_1, x_2, \ldots, x_P)$, where x_i is consumption of commodity i. Lancaster's consumption theory, in contrast, assumes that there is a characteristic space of S dimensions, where S is the total number of characteristics possessed by the P products noted earlier. Each consumer derives utility from consumption of a characteristic bundle $z = (z_1, z_2, \ldots, z_S)$, where z_j is consumption of characteristic j. Each dimension in characteristic space relates to a particular characteristic: taste, color, speed, social standing, and so forth.

It is very rarely the case that consumers can purchase characteristics directly, because these are embodied in varying proportions in commodities. Thus, for example, a motor car combines characteristics such as speed, comfort, social standing, and mobility. More generally, each commodity is represented in characteristic space by a vector $c_i = (c_{i1}, c_{i2}, \ldots, c_{iS})$, where c_{ij} is the amount of characteristic j possessed by one unit of commodity i.

This leads to some problems in the characteristics approach (Friedman 1983, chap. 4). In certain cases consumption is *combinable*. If this is so, a commodity bundle x will give the consumer $x_1 c_{11} + x_2 c_{21} + \cdots + x_p c_{p1}$ units of characteristic 1, and in general,

$$z = \sum_{i=1}^{P} x_i c_i \qquad (5.1)$$

is the characteristics bundle consumed from purchase of the commodity bundle x.

Food items are good examples of combinable consumption. Four steaks contain four times the nutrition of one steak, and the total nutrition of a meal is obtained by adding the nutrients in all the food items consumed.

Noncombinable consumption can also arise, however, relating in the main to indivisibility problems. One motor car gives a certain amount of speed and mobility, but three motor cars do not give three times as much speed and mobility.

There is no easy way to solve the problems that noncombinable consumption generates. One approach often adopted is to divide commodities into types or groups related to their characteristics and then assume that each consumer buys only one version of a particular type of good. This is not a particularly good solution, but it appears to be the best that is available at the moment. It is, therefore, the approach adopted in the remainder of this chapter.

In essence, it is assumed that each commodity can be defined by a series of measurable and observable characteristics, each of which enters into the consumer's utility function. That such characteristics do actually exist is quite clear from the basic philosophy of market research and advertising. Examples of the characteristics offered by particular commodities can be drawn from *Consumer Reports* in the United States and *Which?* in the United Kingdom.

5.1   A simple model of product differentiation

The model to be presented in this section is based on the work of Salant (1980). Consider an economy consisting of two industries. The first industry produces a differentiated product with defined characteristics, and the second industry produces a homogeneous product. None of the characteristics embodied in the differentiated product is supplied by the homogeneous product.

In representing the differentiated product in characteristic space, it is assumed that each product variant occupies a unique position in a single-dimensional space. This assumption will be satisfied if each product variant differs in terms of only one characteristic (e.g., degree of blueness, alcoholic content) or if each product contains two related characteristics in well-defined proportions; see Friedman (1983, pp. 81–3) for a more detailed discussion.

Production in the differentiated-product industry is assumed to be characterized by economies of scale over at least some range of output. If that were not the case – if, for example, there were increasing or constant average costs throughout the range of output – an optimum configuration would contain infinite numbers of firms *and* brands of the differentiated product, one at each point ("location") in the characteristic space.

The economies-of-scale assumption, by contrast, allows us to state that equilibrium in a bounded market will contain a finite number, say n, of firms in the differentiated-product industry, where n is to be determined by the model. Fortunately, this assumption is not at all restrictive: There are at least some economies of scale in most industries (Pratten 1971).

For consumers, it is assumed that consumption of the differentiated good is noncombinable. Consumers also have available the homogeneous product of the second industry. This product has been termed an "outside good" by some authors (Salop 1979; Salant 1980). Assume that the outside good is produced under perfectly competitive conditions. Then it is available at a known, parametric price and can be used as numeraire. Consumers' known, fixed incomes are measured, therefore, in terms of endowments of the outside good.

Assume for simplicity that by appropriate scaling of characteristics the one-dimensional characteristic space can be represented by the [0, 1] line. Each producer in the differentiated-product industry is assumed to produce only one product variant. Thus, producer i is defined by the location of product i on the [0, 1] line: $0 \le i \le 1$. The index i, in other words, refers both to the product i and to producer i. Total output of producer i (and of product i) is q_i.

The "location" of consumers in the characteristic space is defined by each consumer's most preferred product variant. Thus, consumer j is represented by the index $j \in [0, 1]$, where j is the product variant that consumer j would buy if all varieties in the characteristic space [0, 1] were available at identical prices. The amount of product brand i bought by consumer j from producer i is q_{ij}, the quantity of the outside good consumed by j is denoted x_j, and R_j is his income measured in terms of the outside good.

Because there is a finite number of producers in the differentiated-product industry, very few consumers will actually be able to buy their most preferred product variety; in general, consumers will buy a product variety that differs to some degree from the most preferred. Denote the "distance" between product i and desired variety j for consumer j as $\delta_{ij} = |i - j|$. Then δ_{ij} represents a loss of utility for consumer j consequent upon his consumption of product i. It follows that the utility of consumer j is determined by x_j, q_{ij}, and δ_{ij}. In other words, the satisfaction obtained from the commodity bundle (x_j, q_{ij}) is given by the utility function $u_j(x_j, q_{ij}, \delta_{ij})$.

It is assumed that consumers aim to maximize utility. Each consumer must therefore solve a two-stage maximization problem. Denote the set of producers $\{1, 2, \ldots, i, \ldots, n\}$ by I, and assume that they charge prices $p_1, p_2, \ldots, p_i, \ldots, p_n$. Because the outside good is numeraire, its price is taken as unity.

The first stage for the consumer is to identify the optimal quantity of the differentiated product i he will buy, given that he does in fact choose to buy this particular product. In other words, the consumer must first solve the problem

$$\max_{q_{ij}} u_j(x_j, q_{ij}, \delta_{ij}) \quad \text{for all } i \in I \tag{5.2}$$

subject to the budget constraint

$$x_j + p_i q_{ij} = R_j \tag{5.3}$$

(Recall that because consumption is noncombinable, the consumer will purchase only one variety of the differentiated product.)

Solution of the system (5.2) and (5.3) will give, *for each product i,* the consumption bundle (x_j^i, q_{ij}^*). In the second stage, the consumer compares the consumption bundles $\{(x_j^1, q_{1j}^*), (x_j^2, q_{2j}^*), \ldots, (x_j^i, q_{ij}^*), \ldots, (x_j^n, q_{nj}^*)\}$ and chooses the one giving the highest utility.

To illustrate this two-stage process, note that the first stage – maximization of (5.2) subject to (5.3) – generates an indirect utility function $v_i(j, p_i)$, where $v_i(j, p_j)$ is the maximum utility that consumer j can derive from consumption of product i. This maximum utility is a function of the consumer's location (j), the producer's location (i), and the producer's price (p_i).

The indirect utility functions for three products r, s, and t are illustrated in Figure 5.1(a), where the curve v_r is the indirect utility function for a firm located at r and producing product variety r. Similarly for v_s and v_t. Suppose that all consumers have identical incomes and utility functions (except for differences in most preferred variety). Then each indirect utility function achieves its maximum at the appropriate firm's "location": The maximum utility obtainable by consumers of product i is greatest for consumers whose most preferred variety is i.

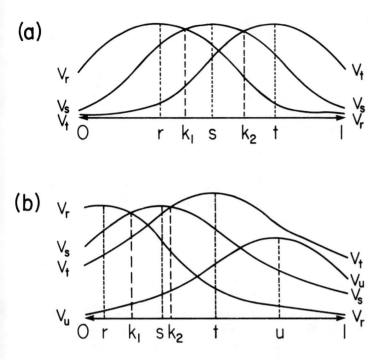

Figure 5.1. Indirect utility functions in the Salant model.

The indirect utility functions in Figure 5.1(a) are drawn on the further assumption that all three producers charge identical prices; hence they achieve their maxima at the same height. An alternative case is illustrated in Figure 5.1(b). Now four firms, r, s, t, and u, are represented and are assumed to charge different prices (it is still assumed that consumers have identical tastes and incomes). It can be seen that firm t is charging the lowest price, because the maximum of v_t is greater than for the other indirect utility functions, and that firm u is charging the highest price.

It is also possible to identify from Figure 5.1 just how market share is determined for each firm in the differentiated-product industry – the second stage of the consumer's maximization problem. In Figure 5.1(a), consumers in the region $[0, k_1)$ obtain greater utility from consumption of differentiated product r than from consumption of either differentiated product s or t. They will, therefore, buy product r. Similarly, consumers in (k_1, k_2) buy product s, and consumers in $(k_2, 1]$ buy product t. Consumers at k_1 are indifferent between products r and s, and those at k_2 are indifferent between products s and t.

Table 5.1. *Analogy between space and product differentiation*

Space	Product differentiation
Geographic space	Characteristic space
Consumer location	Preferred consumer variety i
Producer location	Product variant j
Transport cost	Loss of utility δ_{ij}

In Figure 5.1(b), product r will be bought by consumers in $[0, k_1)$, product s by consumers in (k_1, k_2), and product t by consumers in $(k_2, 1]$. Product u, on the other hand, will not be bought by any consumer; its price is so high that even consumers whose most preferred variety is u will actually buy product t.

The analogy between product differentiation and spatial analysis should now be clear. Some of the main elements of that analogy are summarized for convenience in Table 5.1.

Two further elements of this analogy can be identified. Corresponding to the concept of delivered price in spatial analysis, there is a full-price notion in product differentiation consisting of a combination of money price p_i and utility loss δ_{ij}. The concept of a market boundary in spatial analysis is equivalent to the consumer location (e.g., k_1), where consumers are indifferent between purchasing differentiated product r or s.

5.2   Equilibrium in a differentiated-product industry

Salop (1979) uses a model that has much in common with the one discussed earlier to investigate some of the properties of market equilibrium in differentiated-product markets. Again there are assumed to be two industries, one producing a differentiated product and the other a homogeneous outside good, but now the market is assumed to be the unit circumference of a circle, as in Figure 5.2, in order to avoid "corner" problems that arise with firms located at or near the ends of finite line markets. There are L consumers, each of whom has a most preferred brand specification j such that consumers are evenly spread over the market. Because the market has unit circumference, the point density of consumers is also L. Each consumer is assumed to purchase either one unit or none of the differentiated commodity, determined by preferences, prices, and the distribution of brands in characteristic space. All remaining income is spent on the outside good, which can therefore be taken as numeraire.

Assume that there are n brands of the differentiated commodity available at prices p_i and locations $i \in \{1, 2, \ldots, i, \ldots, n\} = I$ and that brand i

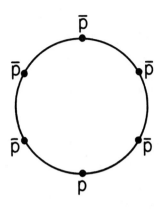

Figure 5.2. The circular market.

is valued by consumers with most preferred variety j according to a preference function $U(i, j)$. Then the two-stage maximization problem discussed in Section 5.1 indicates that a consumer with most preferred variety j will purchase one unit of the product brand i that maximizes surplus of utility over price across all brands, *provided* this surplus is greater than the surplus obtained from consumption of the outside good.

Suppose that consumption of the outside good generates surplus $\bar{s}$. Then a consumer with most preferred brand j will purchase one unit of the differentiated product i satisfying

$$\max_i [U(i, j) - p_i] \geq \bar{s} \tag{5.4}$$

This can be put into the transport-cost framework of Chapters 2–4 if preferences are given by

$$U(i, j) = u - c|i - j| = u - c\delta_{ij} \tag{5.5}$$

Equation (5.4) can now be written

$$\max_i [(u - \bar{s}) - p_i - c\delta_{ij}] \geq 0 \tag{5.6}$$

Using this formulation, the effective delivered price is $p_i + c\delta_{ij}$, and the effective reservation price is

$$v = u - \bar{s} > 0 \tag{5.7}$$

Consumers with most preferred variety j will consider purchasing the differentiated brand i only if the effective delivered price is less than the reservation price v and will then actually buy i only if i maximizes $U(i, j)$.

It should be noted in passing that this approach is directly analogous to the analysis of f.o.b. pricing in Chapters 2 through 4. Consumers of

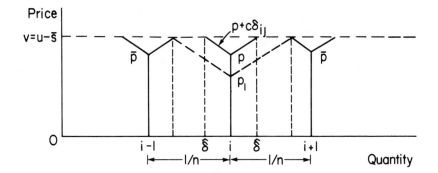

Figure 5.3. The monopoly market.

differentiated product i are paying the mill price p_i plus the loss of surplus $c\delta_{ij}$, which "looks like" transport costs with transport-cost rate c and distance δ_{ij}. The full price $p_i + c\delta_{ij}$ is equivalent to an f.o.b. mill price plus transport costs.

5.2.1   The demand curve

Now consider the perceived demand curve for a representative brand of the differentiated product. Let the representative brand be sold at price p, and suppose that its nearest competitors are located at distance $1/n$ and charge price $\bar{p}$, as in Figure 5.3. The perceived demand curve for the representative brand then has a number of distant regions, as follows.

If price p is greater than p_1 in Figure 5.3, there is effectively no competition from neighboring brands. The representative brand is bought by all consumers whose "distance" from the representative brand is such that the net surplus in (5.6) is nonnegative. Denote this maximum distance by $\hat{\delta}$. Then $\hat{\delta}$ is given by

$$p + c\hat{\delta} = u - \bar{s} = v \tag{5.8}$$

from which

$$\hat{\delta} = (v - p)/c \tag{5.9}$$

Note again the analogy with spatial analysis and f.o.b. pricing. In a space economy, if the maximum price consumers are willing to pay is p^0, the mill price charged is m, transport costs are t, and an f.o.b. pricing system is applied, then a monopolist will supply a market area with maximum radius $\hat{r}$ given by

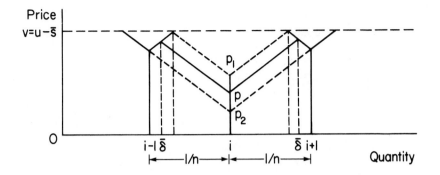

Figure 5.4. The competitive market.

$$\hat{r} = (p^0 - m)/t \tag{5.10}$$

With L consumers evenly spread over the circular market, and because the representative brand is sold to consumers within distance $\hat{\delta}$ on each side of the firm, the monopoly demand for the representative brand is

$$q^m = 2L(v - p)/c \tag{5.11}$$

Recall that each consumer is assumed to purchase just one unit of the differentiated product.

Now consider the case in which p is less than p_1, as in Figure 5.4. Consumers will buy that brand of differentiated product offering the greatest net surplus. With competing brands at distance $1/n$ on either side, each priced at $\bar{p}$, the representative brand will be bought by all consumers within distance δ given by

$$v - p - c\delta \geq v - c\left(\frac{1}{n} - \delta\right) - \bar{p} \tag{5.12}$$

Let $\bar{\delta}$ be the value for which (5.12) holds with equality. Then

$$\bar{\delta} = (\bar{p} + c/n - p)/2c \tag{5.13}$$

and the representative brand's competitive market demand is $q^c = 2L\bar{\delta}$; that is,

$$q^c = L(\bar{p} + c/n - p)/c \tag{5.14}$$

It is now possible to put monopoly demand and competitive demand together in a single demand function, as in Figure 5.5. At price $p = v$, sales of the representative brand will be zero. As price is reduced below v, demand will increase, as indicated in Figure 5.3, in accordance with

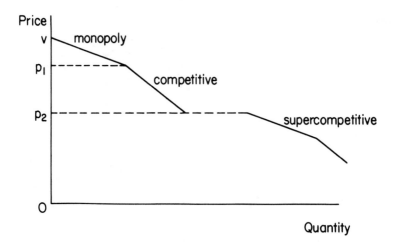

Figure 5.5. A typical demand curve.

the monopoly equation (5.11). Once price has fallen to p_1, continued price reductions will lead to further increases in demand, but now according to the competitive equation (5.14). The market of the representative brand overlaps those of its neighbors at prices below p_1. The demand function for the representative brand is therefore kinked at price p_1 (determination of price p_1 will be discussed in more detail later).

At a still lower price, even those consumers whose most preferred brand is the neighbor's brand will be induced to switch to the representative brand, as was noted with respect to brand u in Figure 5.1(b). In Figure 5.4, if the representative brand is priced below p_2, the representative firm will capture the entire market of its neighbors. The price p_2 is given by

$$p_2 = \bar{p} - c/n \tag{5.15}$$

and the representative firm's demand function has a discontinuity at p_2 from its "predatory" pricing.

The slopes sl(D) of the monopoly and competitive regions of the demand curve illustrated in Figure 5.5 are easily obtained from equations (5.11) and (5.14). Differentiating these equations gives

$$\mathrm{sl}(D^m) = \frac{dp}{dq^m} = -c/2L \tag{5.16}$$

$$\mathrm{sl}(D^c) = dp/dq^c = -c/L \tag{5.17}$$

Note that these slopes are independent of the prices and locations of neighboring firms.

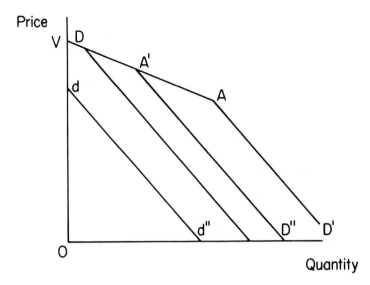

Figure 5.6. A family of demand curves.

It follows from (5.16) and (5.17) that demand is *more* elastic in the monopoly region than in the competitive region. This may appear surprising in the context of traditional (spaceless) microeconomic analysis, but it is perfectly reasonable in the differentiated-product (spatial) context of this analysis. A monopolist will capture more new consumers from a reduction in price than will a firm subject to competition from neighboring firms.

The price p_1 is determined by the price at which the representative brand's market just touches those of its neighbors. This price is most easily determined by noting that $q^m = q^c$ at the kink in the demand function. Equating (5.11) and (5.14) gives

$$p_1 = 2v - \bar{p} - c/n \tag{5.18}$$

It follows from (5.18) that there will be a family of demand curves for the representative brand, determined by the prices and locations of neighboring brands.

Such a family is illustrated in Figure 5.6 (excluding the supercompetitive regions). Suppose that neighboring firms lower their prices or are located nearer to the representative brand (n rises, and $1/n$ falls). Then price p_1 will increase, and the demand curve for the representative brand will move to the left (e.g., from DAD' to $DA'D''$). As indicated in Figure 5.6, price $\bar{p}$ can be sufficiently low that the monopoly region disappears altogether – demand curve dd''.

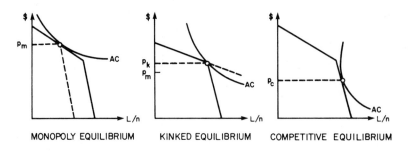

Figure 5.7. Market equilibrium.

5.2.2   *Market equilibrium*

The family of demand curves can be used to derive the zero-profit equilibrium. Assume that total production costs are identical for all brands of the differentiated product and are given for the representative brand by

$$C = F + mq \qquad\qquad (5.19)$$

where F is fixed production costs, and m is marginal production costs. This is a function used extensively in Chapters 2–4, and it captures the economies of scale that are assumed to exist.

A symmetric zero-profit equilibrium (SZPE) exists (Salop 1979) in which all brands are equally spaced and are sold for identical prices p, and in which each producer just breaks even. Three possibilities arise, as illustrated in Figure 5.7, where monopoly, kinked, and competitive equilibrium prices are denoted by subscripts m, k, and c, respectively.

In the monopoly equilibrium of Figure 5.7(a), there may well be some consumers who do not buy any differentiated commodity: In Figure 5.3, consumers just to the left of $\hat{\delta}$ buy only the outside commodity. Each producer is free to price as a monopolist constrained only by the outside commodity. At the kinked equilibrium, markets just touch. It follows, as illustrated in Figure 5.7(b), that the kinked equilibrium price p_k will be greater than the monopoly price p_m. In the competitive equilibrium of Figure 5.7(c) there is some potential market overlap. The competitive price may, however, be greater or less than the monopoly price; the precise outcome will be determined by demand and technology.

Just how this market equilibrium is arrived at is illustrated in Figure 5.8 for the competitive case. Assume an initial market configuration with demand curve DAD'. Then each firm in the market will be earning supernormal profits: The optimal price–quantity pair (not shown) will be such that price will exceed average cost. New firms will enter the market, and

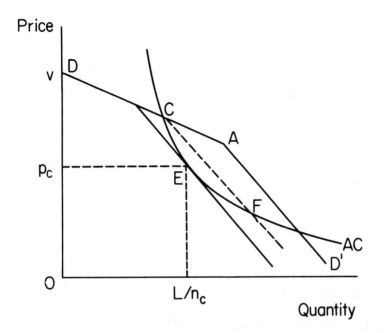

Figure 5.8. Determination of competitive equilibrium.

additional differentiated products will be introduced, moving the demand curve to the left (recall Figure 5.6). The final equilibrium is achieved, as in the Chamberlin model of monopolistic competition, when the demand curve just touches the average-cost curve:[2] point E, price p_c, and number of brands n_c.

The SZPE satisfies two conditions: marginal revenue less than or equal to marginal cost, and price equal to average cost,

$$p + q\frac{dp}{dq} \le m \tag{5.20}$$

$$p = m + F/q \tag{5.21}$$

Assume that the equilibrium has no gaps. Then, if the differentiated-product industry contains n viable firms (brands), sales of each in the SZPE will be

$$q = L/n \tag{5.22}$$

The slope dp/dq of the demand function is given by equation (5.16) or (5.17). Substituting (5.16), (5.21), and (5.22) into (5.20) gives the monopoly price and *maximum* number of brands:[3]

$$p_m = m + c/2n_m \qquad (5.23)$$

$$n_m = \frac{1}{\sqrt{2}} \sqrt{cL/F} \qquad (5.24)$$

The competitive equilibrium is characterized by equation (5.17), rather than (5.16), and is given by

$$p_c = m + c/n_c \qquad (5.25)$$

$$n_c = \sqrt{cL/F} \qquad (5.26)$$

The kinked equilibrium lies between these values. Salop shows that this equilibrium is given by

$$p_k = v - c/n_k \qquad (5.27)$$

Substituting (5.27) and (5.22) in (5.21) gives

$$\frac{F}{L} n_k + c/n_k = v - m \qquad (5.28)$$

The monopoly equilibrium requires the stringent condition that the average-cost curve be tangent to the demand curve somewhere on the monopoly region of the demand curve. This, in turn, requires $v - m = \sqrt{2cF/L}$, a very restrictive condition that can be assumed not to arise.

The competitive equilibrium occurs when[4]

$$v - m \geq \tfrac{3}{2} \sqrt{cF/L} \Rightarrow \text{competitive}; \qquad (5.29)$$

and the kinked equilibrium occurs when

$$\sqrt{2cF/L} \leq v - m \leq \tfrac{3}{2} \sqrt{cF/L} \Rightarrow \text{kinked} \qquad (5.30)$$

5.2.3   Comparative statics

Comparative statics in the competitive case are best analyzed by first solving (5.25) and (5.26). Substituting (5.26) into (5.25) gives

$$p_c = m + \sqrt{cF/L} \qquad (5.25')$$

$$n_c = \sqrt{cL/F} \qquad (5.26')$$

The comparative statics are then as traditional analysis would predict. An increase in fixed costs increases price and reduces product variety. An increase in marginal costs is fully reflected in an increase in prices and so leaves product variety unaltered. The market equilibrium is, however, unaffected by changes in the reservation price v: An increase in v raises the monopoly portion of the demand curve, but leaves unaffected the tangency with the average-cost curve.[5]

By contrast, many of the comparative statics are perverse for the kinked equilibrium. These are best illlustrated diagrammatically. An increase in fixed or marginal costs moves the average-cost curve outward, as in Figure 5.9(a), and changes equilibrium from E to E'. Price *falls*, as does equilibrium variety.

Intuitively, cost increases reduce the equilibrium number of brands, allowing the remaining brands to further exploit scale economies. This is a very striking result. If the increase in costs is interpreted as an excise tax levied on the industry, then the incidence of that tax is negative at the kinked equilibrium. In terms of consumer welfare, the lower price is offset by the decline in variety, of course. [Salop, p. 149].

An increase in reservation price (v) raises price and variety: the move from E to E'' in Figure 5.9(a). On the other hand, an increase in market size (L) or a reduction in the value of product differentiation (c) increases brand variety *but also* increases price: the move from E to E' in Figure 5.9(b).

5.3   Some extensions

The basic Salop model of Section 5.2 can be extended in a number of ways.

5.3.1   *Alternative competitive reactions*

An important assumption underlying the derivation of the demand curve in Figure 5.5 is the Bertrand-Nash (or Hotelling-Smithies) assumption that neighboring firms do not react to a reduction in price of the representative brand, even when their market areas overlap. Now consider the outcome if this behavioral assumption is replaced by the Löschian assumption that neighbors will exactly match any price cuts by the representative firm in order to retain their existing consumers.

Under the Löschian assumption, once price has been reduced to p_1 (Figure 5.4), any further price cut will be exactly matched. Because each consumer is assumed to buy only one unit of the differentiated product, it follows that price reductions below p_1 will lead to no increase in sales. The supercompetitive region of the demand curve will also disappear, leading to the family of demand curves in Figure 5.10. Demand is perfectly inelastic once the representative brand's price is reduced to the point at which its market touches those of its neighbors.

It follows, of course, that the kinked equilibrium is the most likely equilibrium, because the average-cost curve cannot be expected to be vertical (see Figure 5.10). Note further, therefore, that with Löschian reactions,

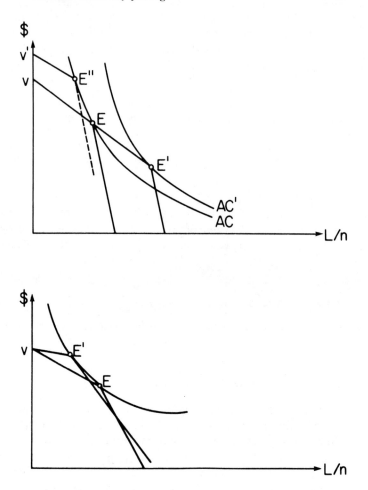

Figure 5.9. Comparative statics: kinked equilibrium.

the comparative statics of changes in market conditions will be perverse in "traditional" terms: They will be just as discussed in Section 5.2.3.

A less extreme case can be imagined in which price reactions lie somewhere between Bertrand-Nash (Hotelling-Smithies) and Löschian. The demand curve will then lie somewhere between DAD_{HS} and DAD_L in Figure 5.11. Clearly, the stronger the price reactions of neighboring firms, the nearer will the demand curve lie to the Löschian curve DAD_L, and the more likely it is that a kinked equilibrium will emerge.

Figure 5.11 also indicates that a stronger price reaction on the part of neighbors will lead to a higher price, but also more product variety, as

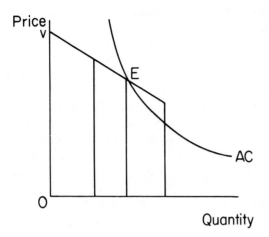

Figure 5.10. Demand curve: Löschian reaction.

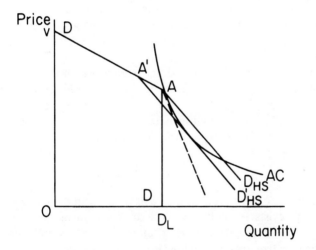

Figure 5.11. Alternative price reactions.

compared with the Bertrand-Nash case; equilibrium in the latter case is at *E*. The reader will note the very strong similarity between these results and those that emerged in Chapter 3 in the comparison of Löschian competition and Hotelling-Smithies competition in spatial markets.

What about the G-O model in the context of product differentiation? The original conception of the G-O model was that of a distant firm practicing stepped-up zonal prices. The outcome was that sufficient competitive inroads could be made by a price cutter (and a new firm) to yield classical (nonperverse) price effects (e.g., prices falling with entry). As viewed somewhat differently by Capozza and Van Order (CVO), it would be as if a firm that was located at a distance raised its mill price in response to a price cutter.

In the product-differentiation analogue of the G-O model, the rival firm can be expected to ignore the price cutter over the relevant characteristic space, because the price cutter is considered to be unimportant in the market. Alternatively, following the CVO interpretation *precisely*, the rival firm will increase its price: We now have the rival firm seeking to differentiate its product further, possibly in deference to conspicuous-consumption interests. On either view, the characteristic space of the "representative" price cutter will increase substantially, and the kink in its demand curve will disappear. The spatial/product-differentiation analogy thus appears complete.

It is, however, the case that whereas in the strictly spatial model the entry price-cutting effect can be expected to lead to price cutting over the entire landscape, the conspicuous-consumption analogy required for the product-differentiation case entails such product heterogeneity as to virtually establish separate goods (i.e., separate monopoly worlds over the price ranges where the goods are no longer competitive). To this extent, the final long-run results would appear to differ from those for the spatial model, except for the likelihood of new entry taking place and decreasing product differentiation resulting. Underlying the G-O market is a feeling of the unimportance of the individual firm and the belief that price cutting will not elicit price reactions from firms at a distance.

5.3.2   *Collusion*

Once equilibrium has been achieved on the basis of Bertrand-Nash reactions, the possibility exists for collusion between those firms that now populate the market. A tacit entry-deterring collusive (EDC) equilibrium can be derived as the outcome of a two-stage process (MacLeod, Norman, and Thisse 1984). The first stage identifies the SZPE as defined by Salop. In the second stage, those firms in the SZPE can move from the Bertrand-Nash price thus identified [equation (5.25)] to the optimal Löschian price (p_L^*) for that market area, as illustrated in Figure 5.12: from equilibrium at E to equilibrium at E^*.

Each firm earns excess profit in the EDC equilibrium, leading to the threat of entry by new firms. There is, of course, the possibility common to all collusive agreements that some members of the collusion will try

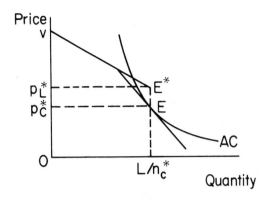

Figure 5.12. A collusive equilibrium.

to cheat on their neighbors, but there are available rational and credible reactions on the part of the incumbents that will deter entry and prevent cheating and thus maintain the EDC equilibrium (MacLeod et al. 1984).

5.3.3 Elastic individual demand

One of the limitations of many recent analyses of product differentiation is the assumption that each consumer buys exactly one unit of the differentiated commodity (if, of course, the differentiated commodity is bought at all). It is, however, a very simple matter to relax this assumption and consider the case of rather more elastic individual demand.

As an example, suppose that consumer j has a linear demand function for the product of the differentiated industry:

$$q_{ij} = \max[a - b(p_i + c\delta_{ij}), 0] \qquad (5.31)$$

This demand function will arise, for example, if the individual utility function is of the form (Lovell 1970)

$$U = (a/b - c\delta_{ij})q_{ij} - q_{ij}^2/2b + x_j \qquad (5.32)$$

and is maximized subject to the budget constraint

$$R_j = p_i q_{ij} + x_j \qquad (5.33)$$

where x_j denotes consumption of the outside good.[6]

Using Salop's approach, monopoly demand is given by (see Mathematical Appendix)

$$q^m = 2L \int_0^\delta \{a - b(p + c\delta)\} \, d\delta = \frac{bL}{c}\left(\frac{a}{b} - p\right)^2 \qquad (5.34)$$

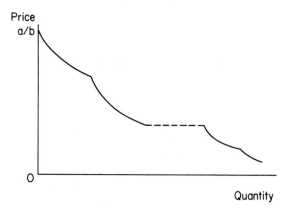

Figure 5.13. A typical demand curve: elastic demand.

where now a/b is the reservation price, equivalent to v in Section 5.2. Competitive demand is

$$q^c = 2L \int_0^{\bar{\delta}} \{a - b(p + c\delta)\}\, d\delta$$

$$= \frac{bL}{c} \left\{ \left(\frac{a}{b} - c \right) \left(\bar{p} + \frac{c}{n} - p \right) - \frac{1}{4} \left(\bar{p} + \frac{c}{n} - p \right)^2 \right\} \tag{5.35}$$

These two sections of the representative brand's demand curve are illustrated in Figure 5.13. Note that the main distinction between this demand curve and that in Figure 5.5 is that various segments of the demand curve are now convex to the origin (recall the discussion of aggregate spatial demand in Chapters 2 and 3).

Precisely the same analysis as presented in Section 5.2 can now be used. It is also possible to apply the analysis of Chapter 3 directly. Zero-profit equilibrium in the differentiated-product industry will be symmetric in price and locations of the firms in the industry – using the same arguments as applied by Salop in deriving his SZPE. The zero-profit condition for the representative firm is therefore given by

$$\Pi(\bar{\delta}, p): 2L(p - m) \int_0^{\bar{\delta}} f(p + c\delta)\, d\delta - F = 0 \tag{5.36}$$

Compare this equation with equation (3.1), repeated here for convenience:

$$\Pi(R, m): 2D(m - c) \int_0^R f(m + tr)\, dr - F = 0 \tag{5.37}$$

There is a notational change such that $L \equiv D$, the m of (5.36) is equivalent to the c of (5.37), and the p of (5.36) is equivalent to the m of (5.37). Thus, the two equations are identical in structure. The analogy developed in Table 5.1 applies: Where R is the market boundary of the spatial competitor, $\bar{\delta}$ is the consumer location at which consumers are indifferent between buying the representative brand and a neighboring brand; where tr is transport cost, $c\delta$ is the loss of utility consequent upon purchasing other than the most preferred brand; where r is distance in geographic space, δ is distance in characteristic space.

It follows that the analysis of Chapter 3, and, indeed, of Chapter 2, can be applied directly. The nature of the zero-profit competitive equilibrium in the differentiated-product industry can be analyzed using the zero-profit-locus approach developed by Capozza and Van Order (see the Appendix to this chapter).

5.3.4 *Other extensions: strategic behavior, advertising*

Many other extensions of the Salop model can be envisaged, as evidenced by the proliferation of analyses of product differentiation.[7] Two such extensions will be considered briefly in this section.

The analysis of Section 5.2 is based on the assumption that long-run equilibrium is characterized by zero profits. It has been suggested, however, (Eaton and Lipsey 1975) that firms may be able to behave more strategically and ensure long-run supernormal profits even in the face of threats of competitive entry.

The Eaton-Lipsey analysis is considered in some detail in Part III of this book. A simple intuitive explanation can, however, be given at this stage (Prescott and Visscher 1977). Suppose that firms enter the market sequentially. Then each new firm will choose a location with respect to its nearest neighbor such that no new entrant will wish to enter in the interval between the two firms. As a result, firms are more widely spaced than in the SZPE and thus earn supernormal profits. But no new entrant is able to enter the market, because there is no location for this firm's brand that will allow the firm to break even.

With such strategic behavior, it is, of course, the case that there will be fewer brands than in the SZPE. Salop indicates that in his model there will be half the number of brands as in the SZPE equilibrium.

The other extension that can be considered is to introduce advertising to the analysis – a natural extension in the context of product differentiation. There are several ways in which advertising can work. For example, it may work to increase the reservation price of the differentiated product, in which case the comparative-statics analysis of Section 5.2 can be applied in a reasonably straightforward fashion.

A rather more interesting approach is adopted by Grossman and Shapiro (1984). They assume that advertising informs consumers of the *existence* of particular differentiated brands. A consumer will consider buying a brand only if she has seen that brand advertised.

The representative firm's demand curve is then given by

$$q^c(p, \phi) = L_1\phi_1 + L_2\phi_2 + \cdots + L_n\phi_n \tag{5.38}$$

where L_1 is the number of consumers for whom, with complete information, the representative brand is the most preferred brand, L_2 is the number of consumers for whom, with complete information, the representative brand is the second most preferred brand (consumers who, if fully informed, would buy the immediately neighboring brand), and, in general, L_i is the number of consumers for whom the representative brand is the ith most preferred brand; ϕ_1 is the proportion of consumers in L_1 who have seen an ad for the representative brand, ϕ_2 is the proportion of consumers in L_2 who have seen an ad for the representative brand but *not* for their more preferred brand, and, in general, ϕ_i is the proportion of consumers in L_i who have seen an ad for the representative brand but *not* for any of their more preferred brands.

Grossman and Shapiro investigate oligopoly equilibrium and monopolistically competitive equilibrium for their "with-advertising" model. They show that with an oligopoly equilibrium, an increase in the number of brands leads to a reduction in advertising intensity. An increase in the importance to consumers of product differentiation (the parameter c of Section 5.2) increases advertising intensity. If advertising costs increase, markups rise, as does product diversity, but the effects on profits are ambiguous.

With monopolistic competition, increases in costs increase advertising intensity, because firms are forced to exit, increasing the value to the remaining firms of additional advertising. Advertising itself raises prices but has an ambiguous effect on product diversity: Whereas additional advertising will increase profits in the oligopoly equilibrium, it will lead to more product diversity in the monopolistically competitive equilibrium.

5.4   Conclusions

There is a very close analogy between models of spatial competition with f.o.b. pricing and models of product differentiation based on commodity characteristics. The Lancaster theory of consumption, in which consumers are assumed to derive utility from the consumption of characteristics embodied in commodities rather than from the commodities themselves, lends special relevance to spatial forms of analysis. As a result, it is possible to return to Chapters 2-4 and, by using the analogy detailed in Table 5.1, reinterpret these early chapters as an analysis of product differentiation rather than of spatial (f.o.b.) pricing.

Appendix: equivalence of the Salop and Capozza-Van Order analyses

Product differentiation is analyzed in Chapter 5 following the approach developed by Salop, and spatial competition is analyzed in Chapters 2 and 3 following the approach developed by Capozza and Van Order (CVO). This appendix shows that these two approaches are equivalent.

Zero-profit equilibrium in the Salop model requires [equation (5.36)]

$$\Pi(\bar{\delta}, p) : 2L(p-m) \int_0^{\bar{\delta}} f(p+c\delta) \, d\delta - F = 0 \tag{A5.1}$$

and in the CVO model requires [equation (3.1)]

$$\Pi(R, m) : 2D(m-c) \int_0^R f(m+tr) \, dr - F = 0 \tag{A5.2}$$

It was shown in Table 5.1 that there is a direct equivalence across these two equations, as in Table 5A.1.

The optimal pricing equation in the CVO model is [Chapter 3, Mathematical Appendix, equation (A3.1)]

$$P_i(R, m) : m\left(1 - \frac{1}{e_i(R, m)}\right) - c = 0 \tag{A5.3}$$

Substituting from Table 5A.1 gives the corresponding equation for the Salop model:

$$P_i(\bar{\delta}, p) : p\left(1 - \frac{1}{e_i(\bar{\delta}, p)}\right) - m = 0 \tag{A5.4}$$

where $e_i(\bar{\delta}, p)$ is the elasticity of the aggregate demand function $q(\bar{\delta}, p)$ with respect to p, and $q(\bar{\delta}, p)$ is given by

$$q(\bar{\delta}, p) = 2L \int_0^{\bar{\delta}} f(p+c\delta) \, d\delta \tag{A5.5}$$

All we need do, therefore, to use the CVO approach to analyze product differentiation is to relabel Figure 3.2 as in Figure 5A.1 (this assumes,

Table 5A.1. *Salop-CVO equivalence*

Equation (A.5.1) (Salop)	Equation (A.5.2) (CVO)
L	D
p	m
m	c
$\bar{\delta}$	R
c	t
δ	r
F	F

of course, and as we would expect, that equilibrium occurs in Salop's competitive region, i.e., that firms compete for consumers at the market boundaries). By the same token, we can use the Salop approach to analyze spatial competition by relabeling Figure 5.8, 5.11, or 5.13.

Mathematical appendix

Monopoly demand with elastic demand curve: Aggregate demand is

$$q^m = 2L \int_0^{\hat{\delta}} \{a - b(p + c\delta)\} \, d\delta$$

$$= 2L \left[a\delta - bp\delta - \frac{bc}{2}\delta^2 \right] \Big|_0^{\hat{\delta}} \tag{A5.6}$$

$$q^m = 2L \left[(a - bp)\hat{\delta} - \frac{bc}{2}\hat{\delta}^2 \right]$$

Now $\hat{\delta}$ is given by

$$p + c\delta = a/b$$

defined as the market distance at which price equals the reservation price a/b, and

$$\hat{\delta} = (a - bp)/bc \tag{A5.7}$$

Substituting in (A5.6) gives

$$q^m = \frac{bL}{c} \left(\frac{a}{b} - p \right)^2 \tag{A5.8}$$

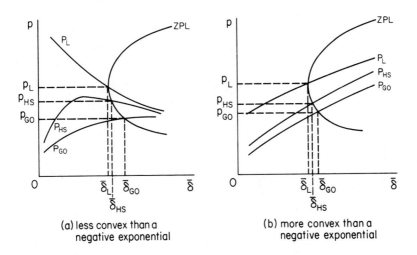

(a) less convex than a
negative exponential

(b) more convex than a
negative exponential

Figure 5A.1. Long-run zero-profit equilibrium: product differentiation.

Competitive demand with elastic demand: Distance $\bar{\delta}$ is given by

$$p + c\bar{\delta} = \bar{p} + c\left(\frac{1}{n} - \bar{\delta}\right)$$

Hence,

$$\bar{\delta} = (\bar{p} + c/n - p)/2c \qquad (A5.9)$$

Aggregate demand is

$$q^c = 2L \int_0^{\bar{\delta}} \{a - b(p + c\delta)\} \, d\delta = 2L\left[(a - bp)\bar{\delta} - \frac{c}{2}\bar{\delta}^2\right] \qquad (A5.10)$$

Substitute (A5.9) in (A5.10) to give equation (5.35).

PART II

Discriminatory pricing

CHAPTER 6

Discriminatory pricing and alternative demand conditions

The analysis in Part I covers most of what can be said about nondiscriminatory pricing in isolation. Indeed, we should now call into question the implicit assumption that this form of pricing would be adopted by a profit-maximizing entrepreneur operating in an imperfectly competitive world. We emphasized in Chapter 1 that a central property of imperfect competition is the segmentation of consumers into separated markets. It was noted in our discussion in Part I that this segmentation of consumers gives rise to a distinction between the full price paid by consumers and the net price received by producers. Further, the economic phenomenon underlying market segmentation – whether this be transport costs, waiting time, storage costs, or product characteristics – may well lead to individual demand functions with differing elasticities in the separate selling locations. So long as the producer controls this economic phenomenon, therefore (i.e., so long as the producer controls the means of transport, storage, or product differentiation), the conditions are satisfied that microeconomic theory predicts will lead to price discrimination. We now turn to an examination of the form such price discrimination will take and the effects on price discrimination of demand and competitive conditions.

Once more we concentrate initially on the spatial analogy. The pioneering work of Hoover (1937) and Singer (1937), refined and extended by, for example, Greenhut and Ohta (1972, 1975a), indicates that a spatial monopolist free of institutional constraints will generally depart from the nondiscriminatory f.o.b. pricing rule. Only if demand is of a very special form (which turns out, as will be shown in this chapter, to be the negative exponential) or only if transport is under the control of the consumer or an independent carrier (a possibility considered in detail in Chapter 8) will the monopolist *choose* f.o.b. pricing.

What about the firm subject to spatial competition? Attention is confined in this chapter and in Chapter 7 to situations in which competition occurs solely at the market boundaries (this assumption also characterizes Chapters 1–5). Each competitive firm is effectively a local monopolist in that there is no market overlap. In these circumstances, intuition should suggest that if a competitive firm is not subject to an arbitrary (perhaps institutional) constraint that it adopt f.o.b. pricing, and subject to the same caveats as apply to the monopolist, the firm will move to a discriminatory pricing scheme, because this will improve its profitability.

6.1   Price discrimination

We should first indicate what we mean by price discrimination. This is not an easy question to resolve. As Phlips (1983, p. 5) points out, "the more one thinks about price discrimination, the harder it is to define." The most acceptable definition of price discrimination is, in our view, just that provided by Phlips:

Price discrimination should be defined as implying that two varieties of commodity are sold (by the same seller) to two different buyers at different *net* prices, the net price being the price (paid by the buyer) corrected for the cost associated with the product differentiation. [1983, p. 6]

As Phlips points out, once price discrimination is defined in this clear way, it is likely to be a rather ubiquitous phenomenon: "Discrimination might be as common in the marketplace as it is rare in the economics textbooks" (1983, p. 7).

The simplest way of putting Phlips's definition into a spatial context is to use the characteristics approach to consumption discussed in Chapter 5. An important characteristic of an otherwise homogeneous product is the location at which it can be purchased. Transporting a commodity from one location to another is therefore one form of product differentiation.[1] It leads to the possibility of a particular form of price discrimination between spatially separated consumers termed *spatial price discrimination*.

Given Phlips's definition, spatial price discrimination can be seen in one of two (equivalent) ways. On the one hand, the manager of a firm supplying a number of spatial markets can be considered to choose a series of *delivered prices* at which his product will be supplied to the various markets. Spatial price discrimination exists when the difference in delivered prices between any pair of markets is not equal to the difference in transport costs incurred by the firm in supplying those markets.

Alternatively, the manager of the firm can be considered to choose a series of *mill prices* at which his product will be supplied to the various spatial markets. Consumers in a particular market pay the mill price appropriate to that market plus transport costs incurred by the firm in supplying that market. Spatial price discrimination arises when mill prices vary across markets.

It should be emphasized that there is no a priori presumption about the direction of spatial price discrimination. Discrimination may be in favor of more distant consumers, in which case delivered price will not increase by the full extent of transport costs, implying that more distant consumers will pay lower mill prices than proximate consumers. Or discrimination may be in favor of proximate consumers, with delivered prices increasing by more than the amount of transport costs, and so more distant consumers will pay higher mill prices than proximate consumers.

In the former case, the firm is effectively *absorbing* some element of freight costs to more distant consumers.[2] In the latter case, "phantom freight" is being charged to more distant consumers.[3]

6.2   A model of spatial competition

The model underlying the analysis in this chapter is similar in many respects to that used in previous chapters. It may, however, be useful to record the basic assumptions of the model:

Assumption 1: There is a single homogeneous commodity that is produced by all firms.

Assumption 2: The cost function is the same for all firms; it exhibits economies of scale and is characterized by constant marginal costs and fixed costs:

$$C = F + cX \tag{6.1}$$

where X is output, C is production cost, F is fixed cost, and c is marginal cost.

Assumption 3: Transport costs are linear in distance and weight and equal to t per unit per unit distance.

Assumption 4: Consumers are evenly distributed over a one-dimensional market at uniform density D.

Assumption 5: Consumers are identical and have individual inverse demand functions of the form

$$p(r) = g(q(r)); \qquad g' < 0 \tag{6.2}$$

where $q(r)$ is the amount bought by each consumer at distance r from the supplier at delivered price $p(r)$.

Assumption 6: Consumers buy from the firm offering the lowest delivered price. Spatial price discrimination is allowed.

Assumption 7: Each firm is a local monopolist; that is, firms do not share locations, and there is no market overlap.

Assumption 2 is critical. Given constant marginal production costs, production and pricing decisions with respect to a consumer at location r_i are independent of production and pricing decisions with respect to a consumer at location r_j so long as the producer's delivered pricing policy does not allow profitable retrading between consumers.[4,5]

In other words, the independence of pricing and production decisions between selling locations implies a market-point-by-market-point solution and further implies that the extent of the firm's market area is, except for production-cost effects, irrelevant. Löschian, H-S, G-O, and other *conjectural variations* are inapplicable to the case of price discrimination derived from profit maximization at each market point. (It will be seen in Chapter 7 that they are applicable to the uniform-delivered-price-schedule type of spatial price discrimination, and in later chapters they will be shown to be relevant to more heterogeneous forms of spatial competition.) Rather, discriminatory pricing requires emphasis on the demand and competitive conditions *in each market* of the firm's entire market space. This chapter chiefly concentrates on the impacts of demand conditions on the firm's discriminatory price. Later chapters will center attention on competitive impacts.

6.3 Optimal discriminatory pricing

Given that Assumption 2 holds, global profit maximization is achieved by maximizing profit at each consumer location, that is, by identifying the price/quantity decisions at each location that are such that marginal cost (MC) equals marginal revenue (MR). This gives rise to a very simple spatial pricing rule, illustrated in Figure 6.1 for two consumer locations r_1 and r_2 (Norman 1983b). The change in delivered price with a change in transport costs is given by

$$\frac{\Delta p(r)}{\Delta(tr)} = \frac{\Delta p(r)}{\Delta q(r)} \frac{\Delta q(r)}{\Delta MR(r)} \frac{\Delta MR(r)}{\Delta MC(r)} \frac{\Delta MC(r)}{\Delta(tr)} \tag{6.3}$$

Because profit maximization requires that for each market

$$MC(r) = MR(r)$$

and because marginal cost changes solely in response to a change in transport costs, it follows that $\Delta MR(r)/\Delta MC(r) = 1$, and $\Delta MC(r)/\Delta(tr) = 1$. Thus, as $\Delta tr \to 0$,

$$\frac{dp(r)}{d(tr)} = \frac{dp(r)}{dq(r)} \bigg/ \frac{dMR(r)}{dq(r)} = \frac{dg(q(r))}{dq(r)} \bigg/ \frac{dMR(r)}{dq(r)} \tag{6.4}$$

In other words:

Proposition 1: The slope of the optimal discriminatory delivered-price schedule (DPS) is given by the ratio of the slope of the inverse demand function to the slope of the marginal-revenue function.[6]

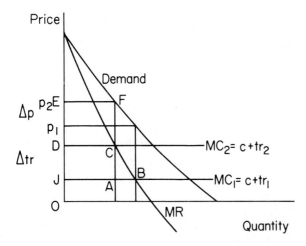

Figure 6.1. Local profit maximization.

Consider the general inverse demand function (6.2). Its slope is $g'[q(r)]$, and the slope of the associated marginal-revenue function is

$$2g'[q(r)] + q(r)g''[q(r)]$$

Hence, the slope of the optimal discriminatory DPS is

$$\frac{dp(r)}{d(tr)} = g'(q(r))/\{2g'(q(r)) + q(r)g''(q(r))\} \tag{6.5}$$

What about delivered prices? Mill prices are related to delivered prices through the equation $p(r) = m(r) + tr$, where $m(r)$ is the mill price to consumers at distance r from the producer. Thus,

$$\frac{dm(r)}{d(tr)} = \frac{dp(r)}{d(tr)} - 1 \tag{6.6}$$

Substitute from equation (6.5) in (6.6) to give

$$\frac{dm(r)}{d(tr)} = -\left\{\frac{g'(q(r)) + q(r)g''(q(r))}{2g'(q(r)) + q(r)g''(q(r))}\right\} \tag{6.7}$$

in terms of the inverse demand function. This can be expressed in a more familiar form if we work instead with the *direct* demand function. Let this demand function be

$$q(r) = f(p(r)); \quad f' < 0, \ f(p(r)) = g^{-1}(p(r)) \tag{6.8}$$

Using the inverse-function rule of differential calculus[7] gives

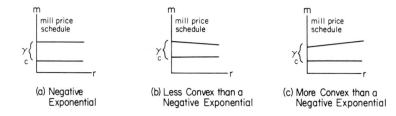

Figure 6.2. Optimal mill-price schedules under alternative demand conditions.

$$\frac{dm(r)}{d(tr)} = -\left\{\frac{[f'(p(r))]^2 - f(p(r))f''(p(r))}{2[f'(p(r))]^2 - f(p(r))f''(p(r))}\right\} \tag{6.9}$$

Standard microeconomic analysis indicates that the denominator of the right-hand side of (6.9) is positive so long as marginal revenue is downward-sloping – the second-order condition necessary for profit maximization. Thus, the sign of (6.9) is determined by the numerator. In particular,

$$\frac{dm(r)}{d(tr)} \gtreqless 0 \quad \text{as} \quad \frac{(f')^2}{f} \lesseqgtr f'' \tag{6.10}$$

But this is just the condition used in Chapters 2 and 3 to distinguish between more and less convex individual demand functions. In other words:

Proposition 2: Within a given market area, a spatial competitor will price-discriminate against distant consumers [i.e., $dm(r)/d(tr) > 0$] if the basic demand is more convex than a negative exponential [i.e., $f'' > f'^2/f$]. It will price-discriminate against more proximate consumers [i.e., $dm(r)/d(tr) < 0$] if the basic demand is less convex than a negative exponential [i.e., $f'' < f'^2/f$]. A constant mill-price schedule will result, and thus no price discrimination will result [i.e., $dm(r)/d(tr) = 0$], if the basic demand is a negative exponential [i.e., $f'' = f'^2/f$].

These relations correspond to the Greenhut and Ohta (1975c) propositions based on Hoover's pioneering research (1937) in this area. They are illustrated in Figure 6.2 for mill prices and Figure 6.3 for delivered prices.

As in the f.o.b. case, we see the importance of the negative-exponential demand function as a dividing line. Only if demand is of this form will the firm *choose* f.o.b. pricing even when allowed a discriminatory DPS.

Equation (6.5) gives some indication of just how much freight will be absorbed by the firm – in other words, how discriminatory the profit-

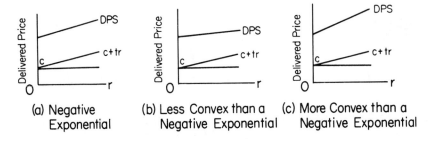

Figure 6.3. Optimal DPS under alternative demand conditions.

maximizing pricing policy will be. Using equation (6.9) it is possible to be more precise regarding the degree and direction of price discrimination. Clearly, the degree of price discrimination is conditional on the convexity of the individual demand function. If this demand function is linear, so that the second derivative f'' equals zero, (6.9) reduces to

$$\frac{dm(r)}{d(tr)} = -\frac{1}{2} \tag{6.11}$$

Thus, the rate of change in mill price with respect to distance[8] is $(-t/2)$; the firm absorbs 50 percent of freight costs. If the basic demand is convex (i.e., $f'' > 0$), it can be shown that less than half of the freight is absorbed. If the basic demand is concave (i.e., $f'' < 0$), more than half of the freight will be absorbed.[9]

Is it possible that the firm would absorb the entire freight? Total freight absorption is equivalent to a uniform pricing policy, that is, to a pricing policy which is such that

$$p(r) = m(r) + tr = \bar{m} \tag{6.12}$$

from which it follows that

$$\frac{dm(r)}{d(tr)} = -1 \tag{6.13}$$

Substituting (6.13) in (6.9) indicates that

$$p(r) = \bar{m} \quad \text{if and only if} \quad f' = \frac{df(p(r))}{dp(r)} = 0 \tag{6.14}$$

Equation (6.14) is satisfied only by a perfectly inelastic demand curve.

Corollary 1: Uniform delivered pricing as a special type of price discrimination in which complete freight is absorbed will occur only if the demand

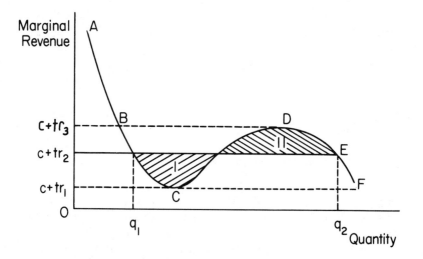

Figure 6.4. Nonmonotonic marginal revenue.

curve is perfectly inelastic. In such a case the firm's profit-maximizing mill price is infinity, leading to an indeterminate solution.

An implication of Figures 6.2 and 6.3 and, indeed of the discussion throughout this chapter, is that delivered price will increase with distance from the plant. In other words, the manager of the firm will never adopt a pricing policy that is of "predatory" form, with delivered price *lower* in distant markets than in (some or all) more proximate markets. That this implication is justified follows from Corollary 2 (Norman 1983b):

Corollary 2: In any economy characterized by the foregoing Assumptions 1–7, predatory pricing cannot be profit-maximizing.

To see why this is so, note that if the marginal-revenue curve is monotonic decreasing, the average-revenue curve (the inverse demand curve) is also monotonic decreasing. Hence, the ratio in (6.4) is always positive, and predatory pricing is excluded for all demand functions which are such that marginal revenue is a monotonic decreasing function of quantity.

Now consider a marginal-revenue curve such as that illustrated in Figure 6.4 (i.e., an MR curve that increases over part of its range).[10] The producer will never choose to operate on the upward-sloping part of the MR curve (the region CD); Profit will be increased by operating on ABC or DEF. For consumers "proximate" to the firm (e.g., those within distance r_1), the firm will treat DEF as the relevant marginal-revenue curve. Similarly, if $r = r_3$ (i.e., for more distant consumers), the firm will switch to ABC (and in this case choose point B).

The switch between *DEF* and *ABC* will occur at that market location for which the area I in Figure 6.4 just equals area II. When this switch occurs, delivered price increases. Hence, even if the MR curve does have an upward-sloping segment, predatory pricing will not arise.

Given the market structure defined by Assumptions 1–7, the crucial property on which this fourth proposition is based is that all consumers have identical local demand functions. Only if the assumed market structure is amended is it likely that local price cutting, or predatory pricing, will be profit-maximizing.

One obvious change would be to drop Assumption 5, but even then predatory pricing would emerge only if demand elasticity *at any given price* were "significantly" greater for consumers more distant from the firm. On the other hand, given the assumption of identical individual demands, predatory pricing is likely to emerge only if some of the assumptions regarding market structure and the nature of competitive forces are changed. In particular, alternative versions of Assumption 7 and the implicit assumptions regarding competitive responses of rival firms will yield market overlap and what could appear to be predatory pricing.

Changed assumptions of this type will provide the basis for the discussions in subsequent chapters. It will be shown, for example, that if allowance is made for market overlap and the potential of competitive entry, a heterogeneous DPS is likely to emerge, exhibiting price cutting in particular "very competitive" markets. In a similar context, Greenhut and Greenhut (1977) identify demand curves that generate what *appears* to be predatory pricing.

The discussion thus far has concentrated on the *slope* of the discriminatory delivered-price schedule. We now turn to a consideration of the *level* of delivered prices the discriminating firm will choose. This is done by deriving the *fundamental pricing equation* for discriminatory pricing analogous to that derived in Chapter 2 for f.o.b. pricing.

As was noted earlier, aggregate profit in the model defined in Section 6.2 is maximized by maximizing profit at each selling location. Profit from consumers distance r from the firm (gross of fixed costs) is

$$\Pi(r) = D(p(r) - c - tr) f(p(r)) \tag{6.15}$$

Maximizing with respect to price $p(r)$ gives the familiar fundamental pricing equation (see Mathematical Appendix):

$$p(r)\left[1 - \frac{1}{\epsilon(r)}\right] = c + tr \tag{6.16}$$

This equation bears a strong resemblance to that derived for f.o.b. pricing (Chapter 2) and should also be familiar to students of classical, spaceless economics. The left side is marginal revenue from sales to each consumer at selling location r, and the right side is the marginal cost of supplying that consumer. It follows from equation (6.16) that the optimal pattern of discriminatory delivered prices is determined by the behavior of the demand elasticity $\epsilon(r)$, that is, as has been emphasized earlier, by the precise form of the individual demand function.

It may be useful in closing this section to illustrate how the various results derived earlier can be applied in a particular case. Consider the GGK (Greenhut, Greenhut, and Kelly 1977) inverse demand function discussed in Chapter 4:

$$p(r) = a - \frac{b}{x}q(r)^x \quad (x > -1; \ x \neq 0) \tag{6.17}$$

Applying Proposition 1 (see Mathematical Appendix), it follows that the slope of the delivered-price schedule is[11]

$$\frac{dp(r)}{d(tr)} = \frac{-bq(r)^{x-1}}{-b(1+x)q(r)^{x-1}} = \frac{1}{1+x} \quad (x > -1; \ x \neq 0) \tag{6.18}$$

When $x = 0$, the demand function equivalent to (6.17) is just the negative exponential function [recall the discussion in previous chapters, and see Greenhut and Greenhut (1977)]:

$$q(r) = ae^{-bp(r)} \tag{6.19}$$

Applying Proposition 1, the slope of the optimal discriminatory DPS for the negative-exponential demand function is (see Mathematical Appendix)

$$\frac{dp(r)}{d(tr)} = 1 \tag{6.20}$$

Elasticity of demand for function (6.17) is (Mathematical Appendix)

$$\epsilon(r) = \frac{p(r)}{x(a - p(r))} \quad (x \neq 0) \tag{6.21}$$

and optimal delivered prices are

$$p(r) = \frac{ax + c}{1 + x} + \frac{tr}{1 + x} \quad (-1 < x; \ x \neq 0) \tag{6.22}$$

For the negative-exponential demand function, elasticity of demand is (Mathematical Appendix)

$$\epsilon(r) = bp(r) \tag{6.23}$$

and delivered prices are

$$p(r) = \frac{1}{b} + c + tr \tag{6.24}$$

an f.o.b. pricing scheme with mill price $1/b + c$.

6.4   Product differentiation revisited

We shall show in subsequent chapters how the foregoing analysis can be applied to an analysis of price discrimination over time and between countries (or states) by absorption, respectively, of storage costs and tariffs (or local taxes). What might not be so clear is how this analysis generalizes to the pricing of differentiated products of the type discussed in Chapter 5.

For price discrimination to be possible with respect to a particular consumer in the Lancastrian world of Chapter 5, two conditions must be satisfied. First, the producer must be able to identify the consumer's most preferred commodity characteristics (his "location"). Second, the producer must be able to control the supply of these characteristics to the consumer (control the "transportation" of the product).

A simple example will serve to illustrate the circumstances in which we might expect both of these conditions to be satisfied. Assume that the purchasers of a particular automobile vary only in regard to the type of radio they would like fitted, ranging from consumers who prefer to travel in silence to those who desire full quadraphonic sound. The producer may decide to produce only the basic product and allow consumers to fit their desired radios, in which case we have the equivalent of nondiscriminatory (f.o.b.) pricing. Alternatively, the producer can offer a radio as an "optional extra" and ask the consumer to specify the radio he would like fitted. There is no reason to believe in this latter case that the additional charge levied by the producer to fit a particular radio need reflect the full cost of that radio. Price discrimination is feasible and is likely to occur.

This example can be extended to the case in which the producer makes available a range of products – as is typically the case in motor-car manufacture – differentiated by engine size, quality of finish, and the range of equipment that is considered "standard." Again, price discrimination is likely, as is evident from one typical example: A major motor-car manufacturer in the United Kingdom produces, as part of a total range of sixty-two cars, two models that are identical in all respects other than those listed in Table 6.1. All of the extra features standard on model B can be obtained as factory-fitted options on model A at the prices (in December 1984) listed in Table 6.1.

Upgrading model A costs an additional £842-19, whereas buying model B incurs an additional cost of only £774-90. Further, because the *only* features differentiating these two models are the optional extras (and, of course, the letters painted on the tailgate giving the model name), there are no lost economies of scale if model A is bought in preference to model B.

Many other examples of price discrimination by bundling of characteristics can be found (Phlips 1983). For example, one of the authors, in

Table 6.1. *Pricing of product characteristics (December 1984)*

Additional features standard on model B	Price of feature (£)
Stereo radio/cassette	129-57
Seat height adjustment	24-92
Alloy wheels and low-profile tires	198-09
Tilting/sliding sunroof	290-28
Central door-locking	199-33
Total price of additional features	842-19
Actual price difference: model B − model A	774-90

traveling to the United States in 1985, had to choose between purchasing his London–Boston return flight from one of the major carriers or from one of the new, cheaper minor carriers. The price charged by the major carrier was $100 greater, but it allowed the traveler to purchase eight further flights within the United States for an additional $120: The author actually chose return flights from Boston to New York, Boston to St. Louis, St. Louis to Houston, and St. Louis to Los Angeles!

This latter example is, in fact, an example of price discrimination by means of an entry charge: To qualify for the additional flights within the United States, the traveler has to purchase a transatlantic flight from the same carrier. This can be extended, as we shall see in a later chapter, to prices charged for entry to amusement parks and the subsequent charges made for the rides available in the park. Similarly, producers of products such as photocopiers or typewriters or microcomputers may tie users in to the use of particular additional products (e.g., paper or typewriter ribbons or software) and may then charge discriminatory prices on the bundled products.

In summary, wherever we refer in the following chapters to "the market r" or "consumers in market r," this can be taken as referring either to a separate spatial market or to a market differentiated in a more general sense from other markets (and subsets of consumers) that the firm might consider supplying.

6.5   Conclusions

It has been shown that in the short run the optimal discriminatory pricing pattern depends on the underlying basic demand conditions in the market space. The major conclusions can then be summarized as follows:

1. The slope of the delivered-price schedule is given by the ratio of the slope of the inverse demand function to the slope of the marginal-revenue function, and this for *any* inverse demand function.
2. The source of price discrimination lies in the basic demand conditions. If the basic demand function is less (more) convex than a negative exponential, discrimination will be against the more proximate (distant) consumers, *ceteris paribus*. The degree of price discrimination (e.g., the amount of freight absorption) also depends on the shape of the underlying demand curves. Linear demand curves will give rise to 50 percent freight absorption over the market space. Convex demand curves give rise to less than 50 percent freight absorption and will lead to phantom freight being charged if demand is more convex than a negative exponential. Concave demand curves give rise to more than 50 percent freight absorption.
3. If the basic demand curve is the negative exponential, the optimal pricing policy is the nondiscriminatory (f.o.b.) pricing policy.
4. Uniform delivered pricing, which involves complete freight absorption, will not take place unless the basic demand function is perfectly inelastic, but that would lead to an infinite price at every consumer location.

Mathematical appendix

The fundamental pricing equation: From (6.15), the first-order condition for profit maximization is

$$f'(p(r))(p(r)-c-tr)+f(p(r))=0 \tag{A6.1}$$

where $f'[p(r)]=df[p(r)]/dp(r)$. Elasticity of demand with respect to delivered price $p(r)$ is

$$\epsilon(r)=-p(r)f'(p(r))/f(p(r)) \tag{A6.2}$$

Reorganizing (A6.1) and substituting (A6.2) gives (6.16).

Slope of DPS with the GGK demand function: From equation (6.17), the slope of the inverse demand function is

$$dp(r)/dq(r)=-bq(r)^{x-1} \tag{A6.3}$$

Total revenue is $p(r)q(r)$, and marginal revenue is

$$MR(r)=p(r)+q(r)dp(r)/dq(r)=a-b\left(\frac{1+x}{x}\right)q(r)^x \tag{A6.4}$$

The slope of the marginal-revenue function is

$$dMR(r)/dq(r) = -b(1+x)q(r)^{x-1} \qquad (A6.5)$$

Divide (A6.3) by (A6.5) to give equation (6.18).

Slope of the DPS with negative-exponential demand: The demand function (6.19) can be written in inverse form as

$$p(r) = \frac{\ln(a)}{b} - \frac{\ln(q(r))}{b} = \alpha - \beta \ln(q(r)) \qquad (A6.6)$$

where $\alpha = \ln(a)/b$, and $\beta = 1/b$.

$$dp(r)/dq(r) = -\beta/q(r) \qquad (A6.7)$$

Total revenue is $\alpha q(r) - \beta q(r) \ln[q(r)]$, and marginal revenue is

$$MR(r) = \alpha - \beta \ln(q(r)) - \beta q(r)/q(r)$$

$$= \alpha - \beta - \beta \ln(q(r)) \qquad (A6.8)$$

The slope of $MR(r)$ is

$$dMR(r)/dq(r) = -\beta/q(r) \qquad (A6.9)$$

Dividing (A6.7) by (A6.9) gives equation (6.20).

Elasticity of GGK demand: Elasticity of demand can be written

$$\epsilon(r) = -\frac{dq(r)}{dp(r)} \frac{p(r)}{q(r)} = -\frac{p(r)}{q(r)} \bigg/ \frac{dp(r)}{dq(r)} \qquad (A6.10)$$

From equation (A6.3), this gives

$$\epsilon(r) = -p(r)/\{q(r)[-bq(r)^{x-1}]\} = p(r)/bq(r)^x \qquad (A6.11)$$

From equation (6.17), $bq(r)^x = x[a - p(r)]$. Hence,

$$\epsilon(r) = p(r)/x(a - p(r)) \qquad (A6.12)$$

Elasticity of negative-exponential demand: From (6.19), $dq(r)/dp(r) = -abe^{-bp(r)}$. Substituting this and (6.19) in (A6.10) gives

$$\epsilon(r) = -\left(-abe^{-bp(r)} \frac{p(r)}{ae^{-bp(r)}}\right) = bp(r) \qquad (A6.13)$$

CHAPTER 7

Alternative pricing policies

The discussion of nondiscriminatory and discriminatory pricing has been based on a relatively simple view of the way in which competitive forces work. Such competition has been assumed to occur solely at the market boundary, with the result that each individual firm can act as a monopolist within that boundary. The shape of the firm's optimal delivered-price schedule, therefore, helps to characterize a monopolist.

Quite clearly, many more complex forms of competition than this relatively simple form can be envisaged: Markets may overlap, the firm may face some constraint on the maximum price it can charge, price may be chosen in an environment in which the firm is facing the threat of entry by competitive producers. In addition, there is the possibility that a competitor free of any institutional constraints will adopt a pricing policy somewhat different from that which would be adopted by a profit-maximizing monopolist or nondiscriminating competitor.

These questions provide the focus of Chapters 8 through 10. As a preliminary to this discussion, the present chapter compares three commonly used "real-world" pricing policies – f.o.b. mill pricing, uniform pricing, and the optimal discriminatory pricing of the form discussed in Chapter 6. This comparison is presented in section 7.1 on the assumption that the competitor is operating in a *fixed* market area. Output, profit, and some of the welfare implications of these pricing policies are compared.

The interested reader may consider whether or not the results of this comparison hold if the firm has a significant degree of monopoly power. Rather than break into the discussion of Section 7.1, Mathematical Appendix I to this chapter gives an analogous comparison on the assumption that the producer is a monopolist.

One point that is stressed in Section 7.1 is that a discriminatory pricing policy is at least as likely to be adopted by a firm operating in an oligopolistic or monopolistically competitive market as it is to be adopted by a pure monopolist. It is also shown that a uniform-delivered-pricing policy cannot be rejected as a possible pricing policy. Section 7.2, therefore, analyzes the competitive equilibria for the uniform-delivered-pricing system and illustrates the comparative statics of these equilibria.

7.1   Comparison of alternative pricing policies: the f.o.b. mill schedule, the uniform schedule, and a discriminatory price schedule

7.1.1   *Prices and profits*

The model employed throughout this section is the one specified in previous chapters. In order to keep the technical problems within manageable bounds, the model is simplified by assuming that the individual inverse demand function is linear and is given by

$$p(r) = a - bq(r) \quad (a, b > 0) \tag{7.1}$$

Under an f.o.b. pricing policy, the firm sets a mill price m, and transport costs are paid by the consumers. With a uniform-delivered-price policy the firm charges all consumers the same delivered price regardless of the delivery cost on the product. Under a more diverse form of spatial price discrimination, consumers at different distances from the firm are quoted different mill and delivered prices. This means that the mill price paid by a consumer will be some function $m(r)$ of the distance r from the firm to the consumer.[1] More formally, delivered price under these three pricing policies is given by[2]

$$p_f(r) = m_f + tr \qquad \text{(f.o.b. mill pricing)} \tag{7.2a}$$

$$p_u(r) = m_u = \text{constant} \qquad \text{(uniform pricing)} \tag{7.2b}$$

$$p_d(r) = m(r) + tr \qquad \text{(optimal discriminatory pricing)} \tag{7.2c}$$

Profit in the firm's constrained[3] market area R is given by

$$\Pi = 2D \int_0^R (p(r) - c - tr)(a/b - p(r)/b) \, dr - F \tag{7.3}$$

where $p(r)$ is given by equations (7.2). Substituting from equations (7.2) gives the profit equations:

$$\Pi_f = 2D \int_0^R (m_f - c)(a/b - (m_f + tr)/b) \, dr - F$$

$$= \frac{2D(m_f - c)}{b} \left(aR - m_f R - \frac{1}{2} tR^2 \right) - F \tag{7.4a}$$

$$\Pi_u = 2D \int_0^R (m_u - c - tr)(a/b - m_u/b) \, dr - F$$

$$= \frac{2D(a - m_u)}{b} \left(m_u R - cR - \frac{1}{2} tR^2 \right) - F \tag{7.4b}$$

$$\Pi_d = 2D \int_0^R (m(r) - c)(a/b - (m(r) + tr)/b) \, dr - F \qquad (7.4c)$$

To establish the optimal f.o.b. mill price and uniform price, differentiate equations (7.4a) and (7.4b) with respect to m_f and m_u and set the derivatives to zero. This gives the optimal competitive f.o.b. mill price and uniform price for the market area R:[4]

$$m_f = \frac{a}{2} + \frac{c}{2} - \frac{tR}{4} \qquad (7.5a)$$

$$m_u = \frac{a}{2} + \frac{c}{2} + \frac{tR}{4} \qquad (7.5b)$$

The optimal f.o.b. mill price or uniform price is not independent of the market area R: The greater is R, the lower will be the optimal f.o.b. mill price and the greater will be the optimal uniform price.

This f.o.b. mill-price result is, of course, merely a restatement of the analysis in Chapters 2 and 4. Under uniform pricing, slightly different considerations apply. Effectively, all freight costs are being absorbed by the seller. As a result, a larger market area increases the freight costs imposed on the seller and thus leads the seller to increase the uniform price.

To identify the optimal discriminatory pricing policy, advantage is taken of the assumption that marginal production costs are constant: With this assumption, aggregate profit is maximized in any market area R simply by choosing the pricing policy that maximizes profit at each selling point in R. From equations (7.2c) and (7.3), profit at each selling point (gross of fixed costs) is given by

$$\Pi_d(m, r) = D(m(r) - c)(a/b - (m(r) + tr)/b) \qquad (7.6)$$

Differentiating with respect to $m(r)$ gives the optimal discriminatory price:

$$m(r) = \frac{a}{2} + \frac{c}{2} - \frac{tr}{2} \qquad (7.7)$$

Note that the pricing policy (7.7) is independent of market radius R. It is the pricing policy identified in Chapter 6 in the case of linear demand, with the producer absorbing 50 percent of transport costs to each selling point.

7.1.2 Welfare effects

Delivered prices under the three alternative pricing policies are, from equations (7.2), (7.5), and (7.7),

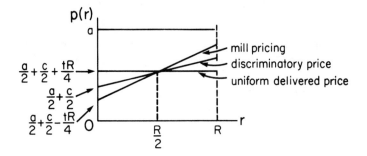

Figure 7.1. A spatial competitor's alternative pricing policies in the competitive equilibrium under the linear demand assumption.

$$p_f(r) = \frac{a}{2} + \frac{c}{2} - \frac{tR}{4} + tr \qquad (7.8a)$$

$$p_u(r) = \frac{a}{2} + \frac{c}{2} + \frac{tR}{4} \qquad (7.8b)$$

$$p_d(r) = \frac{a}{2} + \frac{c}{2} + \frac{tr}{2} \qquad (7.8c)$$

These price equations are illustrated in Figure 7.1. The following relations are established with regard to relative delivered prices under the three pricing policies:

$$p_f(r) \gtreqless p_d(r) \gtreqless p_u(r) \quad \text{according as } r \gtreqless R/2 \qquad (7.9)$$

The general price level is not invariably lower under discriminatory pricing than mill pricing or uniform delivered pricing. Thus, no distinctive welfare comparisons can be made under the alternative price policies in terms of delivered prices. It can be asserted only that relative to the f.o.b. mill price, a general discriminatory policy and the uniform-delivered-price policy impose a welfare loss on nearby consumers – consumers in the region $(0, R/2)$ – but result in a welfare gain for consumers in the region $(R/2, R)$.

What about total output under the alternative price policies given the fixed market area R? Total output is given by

$$Q^R = 2D \int_0^R q(r)\, dr = 2D \int_0^R (a/b - p(r)/b)\, dr \qquad (7.10)$$

Substituting from (7.8) gives

$$Q_f^R = \frac{DR}{b}\left(a-c-\frac{tR}{2}\right) \tag{7.11a}$$

$$Q_u^R = \frac{DR}{b}\left(a-c-\frac{tR}{2}\right) \tag{7.11b}$$

$$Q_d^R = \frac{DR}{b}\left(a-c-\frac{tR}{2}\right) \tag{7.11c}$$

Total outputs are identical under the alternative price policies. The larger demand from distant consumers attracted by the lower discriminatory prices (or uniform delivered prices) is exactly offset by the smaller demand from nearby consumers who pay higher discriminatory prices (or uniform delivered prices).

Although the welfare effects for the three pricing policies cannot be differentiated distinctively in terms of prices and outputs, they can be ranked with respect to profits. Profit to each firm under the three pricing policies can be derived by substituting the price equations (7.5) and (7.7) in the profit equations (7.4) to obtain

$$\Pi_f^R = \frac{DR}{2b}\left\{(a-c)^2-(a-c)tR+\frac{t^2R^2}{4}\right\}-F \tag{7.12a}$$

$$\Pi_u^R = \frac{DR}{2b}\left\{(a-c)^2-(a-c)tR+\frac{t^2R^2}{4}\right\}-F \tag{7.12b}$$

$$\Pi_d^R = \frac{DR}{2b}\left\{(a-c)^2-(a-c)tR+\frac{t^2R^2}{3}\right\}-F \tag{7.12c}$$

Profit under discriminatory pricing is greater than under f.o.b. mill pricing, which in turn equals that of uniform delivered pricing.

The various pricing policies can also be ranked with respect to consumer surplus. Consumer surplus for each consumer at market point r is given by the shaded area in Figure 7.2; it is the area between the demand curve and the delivered price $p(r)$ to consumers at market point r.

Given the assumption of linear demand, consumer surplus for each consumer at market point r is given by

$$CS(r) = \frac{1}{2}(a-p(r))q(r) = \frac{1}{2b}(a-p(r))^2 \tag{7.13}$$

and total consumer surplus in market area R is

$$CS^R = 2D\int_0^R CS(r)\,dr = \frac{D}{b}\int_0^R (a-p(r))^2\,dr \tag{7.14}$$

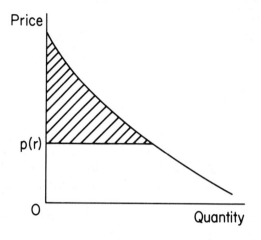

Figure 7.2. Consumer surplus.

Substituting the price equations (6.10) and simplifying gives

$$CS_f^R = \frac{DR}{b}\left(\left(\frac{a}{2}-\frac{c}{2}\right)^2 - \left(\frac{a}{2}-\frac{c}{2}\right)\frac{tR}{2} + \frac{7t^2R^2}{48}\right) \qquad (7.15a)$$

$$CS_u^R = \frac{DR}{b}\left(\left(\frac{a}{2}-\frac{c}{2}\right)^2 - \left(\frac{a}{2}-\frac{c}{2}\right)\frac{tR}{2} + \frac{t^2R^2}{16}\right) \qquad (7.15b)$$

$$CS_d^R = \frac{DR}{b}\left(\left(\frac{a}{2}-\frac{c}{2}\right)^2 - \left(\frac{a}{2}-\frac{c}{2}\right)\frac{tR}{2} + \frac{t^2R^2}{12}\right) \qquad (7.15c)$$

Comparison of equations (7.15) establishes that in a constrained market area, consumer surplus is greatest under f.o.b. mill pricing and least under uniform pricing:

$$CS_f^R > CS_d^R > CS_u^R \qquad (7.15d)$$

What is the intuition behind equation (7.15d)? Figure 7.1 shows that the delivered price to consumers within distance $R/2$ of the firm is lowest under f.o.b. mill pricing and highest under uniform pricing, whereas for consumers at greater distances this relationship is reversed. Thus, consumer surplus is greatest for proximate consumers under f.o.b. pricing and least under uniform pricing, with this relationship again reversed for more distant consumers. It should also be clear, however, from Figure 7.2 that the additional consumer surplus generated for proximate consumers by the relatively low f.o.b. prices charged to them is sufficient to offset the lower consumer surplus that stems from the relatively high prices charged to more distant consumers.

Table 7.1. *Profit, output, and welfare comparisons for f.o.b., uniform, and discriminatory pricing*

Delivered prices	$p_f(r) < p_d(r) < p_u(r)$ for $r < R/2$
	$p_f(r) > p_d(r) > p_u(r)$ for $r > R/2$
Output	$Q_f^R = Q_d^R = Q_u^R$
Profit	$\Pi_d^R > \Pi_f^R = \Pi_u^R$
Consumer surplus	$CS_f^R > CS_d^R > CS_u^R$
Total surplus	$TS_f^R > TS_d^R > TS_u^R$

Finally, we can compare total surplus, defined (Holahan 1975) as the sum of profit plus consumer surplus. From equations (7.12) and (7.15),

$$TS_f^R = \frac{DR}{4b}\left(3(a-c)^2 - 3(a-c)tR + \frac{13t^2R^2}{12}\right) - F \tag{7.16a}$$

$$TS_u^R = \frac{DR}{4b}\left(3(a-c)^2 - 3(a-c)tR + \frac{3t^2R^2}{4}\right) - F \tag{7.16b}$$

$$TS_d^R = \frac{DR}{4b}\left(3(a-c)^2 - 3(a-c)tR + t^2R^2\right) - F \tag{7.16c}$$

Given a constrained market area, total surplus is greatest under f.o.b. mill pricing and least under uniform pricing:

$$TS_f^R > TS_d^R > TS_u^R \tag{7.16d}$$

The greater profit under the optimal discriminatory pricing policy does not offset the greater consumer surplus generated by f.o.b. mill pricing.

The results of the foregoing comparisons are summarized for convenience in Table 7.1. For other elements of this comparison (e.g., with respect to average prices and transport-cost expenditures) the interested reader is referred to Beckmann (1976). These results, particularly with respect to consumer surplus and total surplus, may mislead readers into thinking that statutes such as the Robinson-Patman act in the United States, which favor f.o.b. pricing, have economic validity. On the contrary, however, it should be emphasized that though f.o.b. pricing might be supported by the theory of pure competition, it is not at all clear that the same conclusion applies in a world of imperfect competition. First, it should be noted that the foregoing welfare results, which appear to support f.o.b. pricing, *apply to fixed market spaces only*. It will emerge in later discussion that these welfare results do *not* apply over the entire space economy.

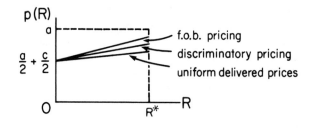

Figure 7.3. Delivered prices for various market boundaries under alternative price policies.

Second, it has already been noted that there are important distributional consequences of the various pricing policies. The additional total surplus generated by f.o.b. pricing arises because of the consumer surplus enjoyed by consumers proximate to the producer. It is dangerous enough to justify policy conclusions by using welfare concepts such as consumer surplus. To justify these conclusions on the basis of the aggregation of consumer surplus in a situation in which some consumers benefit and others lose might well be described as foolhardy!

7.1.3   *The short-run competitive equilibrium price*

A related question arises at this juncture: Which of the three price policies would a firm adopt if there were no institutional constraints? To resolve this question, evaluation of the market boundary prices under the three alternative price policies is in order. Of course, the market boundary price under uniform delivered pricing is identical to the firm's prices at its other market points; thus, given the fixed market area R, (7.8b) is the competitor's market boundary price under uniform delivered pricing. To obtain the market boundary prices under mill pricing and discriminatory pricing, substitute R for r in (7.8a) and (7.8c). This provides

$$p_f(R) = \frac{a}{2} + \frac{c}{2} + \frac{3tR}{4} \tag{7.17a}$$

$$p_u(R) = \frac{a}{2} + \frac{c}{2} + \frac{tR}{4} \tag{7.17b}$$

$$p_d(R) = \frac{a}{2} + \frac{c}{2} + \frac{tR}{2} \tag{7.17c}$$

These boundary-price equations are illustrated in Figure 7.3. They show that *for any given market area*, the market boundary price under mill pricing is higher than under discriminatory pricing, which in turn is higher than that under a uniform-delivered-price policy.

Thus, if price discrimination is allowed, a firm will be able to undercut at the market boundary a competitor who adopts an f.o.b. mill-price policy. This will force the competitor to adopt price discrimination in order to match the price cuts. The mill-price equilibrium breaks down in the short-run equilibrium with a fixed market area.

Can a discriminatory price equilibrium sustain? Will the competitors continue to undercut each other until a uniform-delivered-price equilibrium is reached? As noted earlier, for a given market area the discriminatory price policy leads to the highest profits. Thus, it is likely that a discriminatory-price equilibrium will prove to be an equilibrium-price policy. However, it should be recognized that a uniform-delivered-price equilibrium cannot be ruled out when extreme price competition exists, because the uniform delivered price provides the lowest price at the firms' common market boundary. Section 7.2, therefore, will present a formal analysis of some of the long-run properties of systems of uniform delivered prices.

7.1.4   Long-run competitive equilibrium: individual firm and total output

The comparison of f.o.b. mill, uniform, and optimal discriminatory pricing presented earlier has been essentially short-run in nature, in that it is based on the assumption of a fixed market area. In the longer run, competitive entry can be expected to take place if existing firms are making surplus profits (or exit to occur if losses are being incurred). We assume in the following discussion that competitive entry simply reduces a firm's market area, but does not affect in any fundamental way the underlying pricing model. Later chapters will investigate in more detail the possible price reactions of a firm subject to the threat of competitive entry in the spatial economy.

Under free entry, long-run equilibrium is attained when the market area for each firm is such that profit for each firm is driven to zero (because the cost function is assumed to include an allowance for normal profits). The profit equations under the three pricing systems are given by equations (7.12). The nature of long-run equilibrium in this model can be investigated, therefore, simply by setting equations (7.12) to zero, solving for market radii R, and substituting these values of R into the pricing equations (7.8).

It is clear from equations (7.12) that the zero-profit long-run equilibrium market area under a particular pricing policy is determined by consumer density, by the parameters of the individual demand function, and by production costs. In particular, if demand conditions and marginal production costs are constant, the equilibrium market radius is determined by the ratio F/D of fixed costs to consumer density. This argument can be put another way: Given demand conditions and marginal production costs, equations (7.12) determine for each pricing policy a unique value for the ratio F/D that will give zero (i.e., just normal) profits.

Designate these ratios of fixed costs to consumer densities by γ, θ, and ρ, respectively, for f.o.b. mill, uniform, and discriminatory pricing. Then γ, θ, and ρ are given by the equations [5]

$$\gamma = \frac{R}{2b}\left((a-c)^2 - (a-c)tR + \frac{t^2R^2}{4}\right) \tag{7.18a}$$

$$\theta = \frac{R}{2b}\left((a-c)^2 - (a-c)tR + \frac{t^2R^2}{4}\right) \tag{7.18b}$$

$$\rho = \frac{R}{2b}\left((a-c)^2 - (a-c)tR + \frac{t^2R^2}{3}\right) \tag{7.18c}$$

Equations (7.18) are difficult to solve explicitly, but they can be graphed as the curves γ, θ, and ρ in Figure 7.4. Note that because a spatial competitor never sells beyond the monopolist's market radius $2(a-c)/3t$ under mill and uniform delivered pricing (see Mathematical Appendix I), the relevant range for comparison among the alternative pricing policies must be limited to a market radius smaller than that. Substituting $R = 2(a-c)/3t$ into (7.18a) yields

$$\gamma = \frac{4(a-c)^3}{27bt} \tag{7.19}$$

Thus, in terms of the ratio of fixed costs to consumer density, the relevant range for comparison among the alternative pricing policies is $0 \le F/D \le 4(a-c)^3/27bt$. An arbitrary value for this ratio within this range is shown in Figure 7.4. Long-run zero-profit equilibrium market radii R_f^*, R_u^*, and R_d^* occur at the intersections of the curves γ, θ, and ρ, respectively, with the F/D line.[6]

It can be seen from Figure 7.4 that over all the relevant ranges [i.e., $0 \le R \le 2(a-c)/3t$ or $0 \le F/D \le 4(a-c)^3/27bt$], the long-run zero-profit equilibrium is such that each firm's market area is larger under mill pricing than under discriminatory pricing. Moreover, the equilibrium market areas under uniform delivered pricing and mill pricing are identical. It follows that under free entry, discriminatory pricing will provide more firms (each with a smaller market area) than f.o.b. pricing or uniform pricing:

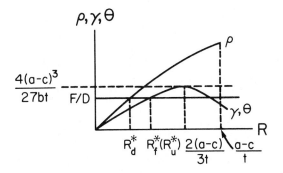

Figure 7.4. Zero-profit equilibrium market radii.

$$R_f^* = R_u^* > R_d^* \tag{7.20}$$

It was noted earlier that outputs for a *given* market area are identical under the alternative pricing policies. As a result, in the long-run zero-profit equilibrium, each single competitor's output is larger under mill pricing than under discriminatory pricing. The equilibrium outputs under uniform delivered pricing and mill pricing are identical:

$$Q_f^* = Q_u^* > Q_d^* \tag{7.21}$$

Equation (7.21) does not allow comparison of *total* outputs under the various pricing policies. Equation (7.29) indicates, however, that more firms can enter the entire market space under discriminatory pricing than under f.o.b. mill (or uniform) pricing. Because for any given space, such as AB in Figure 7.5(a), $Q_f = Q_u^* = Q_D^*$, and because in the zero-profit long-run equilibrium the discriminatory firms must be conceived to be located at sites such as 0 in Figure 7.5(b), the total output under discriminatory pricing exceeds that for f.o.b. mill (and uniform) pricing.[7]

7.2 Long-run equilibria in uniform-delivered-pricing models

It was noted in Section 7.1 that the competitive process may well lead to a system of uniform delivered prices. This section, therefore, examines some of the long-run properties of the uniform-delivered-pricing system. The analysis is based on Gronberg and Meyer (1981a). It is also worth recalling a nonspatial application of this analysis suggested in Chapter 3, in which it was shown that uniform pricing can be applied to the analysis of bundled products. Market separation or overlap of bundled products

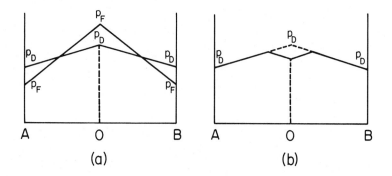

Figure 7.5. Delivered-price schedules under alternative price policies and plant locations.

can then be treated as a function of the degree of heterogeneity of the goods.

Firms are assumed to set a uniform delivered price p and thus will sell to a desired market area $R = (p-c)/t$. This constraint on the market boundary is derived from the condition that at the market boundary the delivered price must be no greater than the marginal costs of production and transport costs. That is,

$$p = c + tR \qquad (7.22)$$

where p is the uniform delivered price, c is constant marginal production cost, t is the transport rate, and R is the market area.

The profit-maximizing uniform-delivered-price equation for a fixed market area R is given by equation (7.8b),

$$p = \frac{a}{2} + \frac{c}{2} + \frac{tR}{4} \qquad (7.23)$$

and is illustrated by the line LL in Figure 7.6. Equations (7.22) and (7.23) provide, respectively, the lower and upper bounds on the uniform price that can be expected to apply in a market of radius R. The former price equation is derived from the condition that gross profits from selling to consumers distance R from the firm are zero, and the latter price equation is that which would be adopted by a uniform-pricing monopolist in a market of radius R.

The largest market radius under uniform delivered pricing is, as was noted earlier, $2(a-c)/3t$, and the corresponding uniform delivered price for this (monopolistic) market radius is $(2a+c)/3$. At this price and market radius combination, the monopolistic firm's delivered price equals its marginal cost of production and transportation; thus, the price equations (7.22) and (7.23) intersect at this price/market-radius combination – the point m in Figure 7.6.

7.2.1 *Uniform delivered prices under alternative competitive assumptions*

Three conditions define the free-entry competitive equilibria of the Gronberg and Meyer uniform-pricing model. First, firms are assumed to have fixed, equally spaced locations. Second, all firms are making only normal profits given their other behavioral assumptions. Equilibrium for all firms in the market area is then characterized by equilibrium for the "representative firm."

In order to simplify the analysis, and without any loss of generality, attention is confined to the case of two firms charging a uniform price p and serving only the consumers located on the line market between them. Assume that the two firms are distance $\bar{R}$ apart and will split the total market between them, each serving customers in the market area $\bar{R}/2$. Then the two firms either will be isolated monopolists or will compete for consumers, depending on how great is the distance $\bar{R}$. If each firm's desired market area $R = (p-c)/t$ is smaller than (or equal to) the given market area $\bar{R}/2$, the firms' desired market areas will not overlap, and each firm will be able to act (and price) as a monopolist. If, on the other hand, each firm's desired market area is greater than $\bar{R}/2$ [i.e., $R = (p-c)/t > \bar{R}/2$], the two firms' desired market areas will overlap, and spatial competition will arise.

The analysis in Chapters 2 through 4 indicates that in the case of nondiscriminatory pricing, a firm's pricing policy is determined in large part by its conjectural variations. The same conditions can be expected to hold under uniform pricing, because, as was noted in equation (7.5b), the profit-maximizing uniform price is affected by the firm's market radius.

If the firms in the industry act under the Hotelling-Smithies (H-S) assumption in which each firm assumes that the other firm will not react to its price reduction, each firm will cut its price. Under such circumstances, equilibrium can occur only when each firm cuts its delivered price to the point that their desired market areas no longer overlap. That is, the uniform price must fall until $(p-c)/t = \bar{R}/2$. Accordingly, the price line $p = c + tR$ in Figure 7.6 is the firm's relevant uniform-delivered-price line under the H-S assumption.[8]

Now consider the case in which the firms operate under the Löschian assumption. It was noted in the discussion of f.o.b. pricing that this type of conjectural variation is more likely to occur when there are few firms

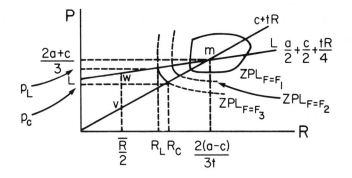

Figure 7.6. Long-run competitive equilibria in the uniform-delivered-pricing models.

in the industry, all producing relatively homogeneous goods. Each firm's manager will then assume his market area to be fixed at $\bar{R}/2$. In such a case, neither will have incentive to cut prices. Each firm will price as a local monopolist within its own market area $\bar{R}/2$. It follows that the Löschian firm's profit-maximizing uniform delivered price in market area $\bar{R}/2$ is given by substituting $\bar{R}/2$ in equation (7.23). This latter pricing equation is depicted by the line LL in Figure 7.6.[9]

7.2.2   Long-run equilibrium uniform prices and market areas

In Gronberg and Meyer's model, firms continue to enter until profits for all firms equal zero. To obtain the firm's zero-profit equation, set the profit equation (7.4b) to zero (where now $p = m_u$) to give

$$\Pi(R, p): \frac{2D}{b}(a-p)\left(pR - cR - \frac{1}{2}tR^2\right) - F = 0 \qquad (7.24)$$

Following Capozza and Van Order (1978), equation (7.24) can be used for each level of fixed costs to define a zero-profit locus (ZPL) in the (R, p) plane (the plane defined by the uniform delivered price and the desired market area R). Three ZPLs are illustrated in Figure 7.6, where we assume $F_3 < F_2 < F_1$.[10]

The long-run zero-profit equilibrium price and market area for a spatial competitor under the Löschian assumption occur at the intersection of the line $p = a/2 + c/2 + tR/4$ and the appropriate ZPL. For example, if fixed costs are F_3, the equilibrium price and market area are the combination (R_L, p_L). On the other hand, the long-run zero-profit equilibrium price and market area under the H-S assumption are represented by the intersection of $p = c + tR$ and the appropriate ZPL. For example, if fixed costs are F_3, the point (R_c, p_c) denotes the firm's price and market area in the zero-profit equilibrium under the H-S assumption.

Comparing the point (R_L, p_L) with the point (R_c, p_c) indicates that the equilibrium uniform delivered price is higher and the market area smaller under Löschian competition than under the H-S assumption. More generally, the qualitative impact on price and market area of different conjectural variations is the same for uniform delivered pricing as for f.o.b. mill pricing.

7.2.3 Comparative statics of the uniform-delivered-pricing model

Because both price equations (7.22) and (7.23) are upward-sloping in the (R, p) plane, the uniform-delivered-price policy does not exhibit any of the more perverse results noted by Capozza and Van Order and others.[11] To appreciate this point, consider a change in fixed costs. Because the profit equation (7.24) is increasing in both p and R, an increase in fixed costs requires a larger market area for any given level of p if zero profits are to be maintained. An increase in fixed costs therefore leads to a shrinking of the ZPL curve from, for example, ZPL for $F = F_3$ to ZPL for $F = F_2$ and to a higher price under both competitive assumptions; see Figure 7.6.

7.3 Conclusions

Given the underlying assumption of linear demand, several main conclusions emerge from this chapter:

1. A firm's total outputs are identical under the three pricing modes within a constrained market area. Moreover, no distinct welfare comparisons can be made in terms of prices.
2. Given the constrained market area, each firm's total profits are greater under discriminatory pricing than under mill pricing or uniform delivered pricing. Total profits are identical under mill pricing and uniform delivered pricing.
3. Consumer surplus and total surplus (the sum of consumer surplus and producer profit) are greatest under mill pricing and least under uniform pricing.
4. In long-run zero-profit equilibrium, the individual firm's market radii and outputs will be identical under f.o.b. mill and uniform pricing and will be greater than under discriminatory pricing. Total output will be greatest under discriminatory pricing, and

the market area will be served by a larger number of smaller firms than under f.o.b. mill or uniform pricing.

5. If a competitor is free of institutional constraints, it will adopt discriminatory pricing given that the firm's area is constrained at a fixed value, but extreme price competition may force the firm to adopt a uniform-delivered-price policy.

6. In the long-run zero-profit equilibrium, uniform delivered price is higher and the market areas smaller under Löschian (restricted entry, homogeneous good) competition than under H-S (unrestricted entry, heterogeneous good) competition.

7. The "perverse" comparative-statics effects found in the f.o.b. mill-price policy by Capozza and Van Order do not arise under the uniform-delivered-price models (even under the linear-demand assumption).

Mathematical appendix I

The spatial monopolist: If the firm is a spatial monopolist, its market area is not fixed, but the price equation will be as in equations (7.8). The spatial monopolist's market area under f.o.b. mill pricing extends to the market point at which demand for the product falls to zero. Hence, from equations (7.1) and (7.2),

$$q(r) = a/b - (m + tr)/b \qquad (A7.1)$$

Setting this to zero gives

$$R_f = (a - m)/t \qquad (A7.2)$$

where R_f is the spatial monopolist's market boundary under f.o.b. pricing. Substituting from (7.5a) gives

$$R_f = \left(a - \frac{a}{2} - \frac{c}{2} + \frac{tR_f}{4} \right) \Big/ t \qquad (A7.3)$$

and solving for R_f gives

$$R_f = \frac{2(a - c)}{3t} \qquad (A7.4)$$

With uniform pricing, the market area extends to the market point at which the delivered price equals the sum of marginal costs of production and transport costs. That is, at the market extremity R_u,

$$m_u = c + tR_u \qquad (A7.5)$$

Substituting from (7.5b) and solving for R_u gives

$$R_u = \frac{2(a-c)}{3t} \tag{A7.6}$$

Note that a spatial monopolist's market boundaries in the case of linear demand are identical for mill pricing and uniform delivered pricing. A spatial monopolist's market area under the general form of discriminatory pricing extends to the market point at which delivered price equals marginal cost of production and transportation. Hence, from (7.2c),

$$m(R_d) + tR_d = c + tR_d \tag{A7.7}$$

Substituting (7.7) and solving for R_d gives

$$R_d = \frac{a-c}{t} \tag{A7.8}$$

Comparison with (A7.4) and (A7.6) indicates that $R_d > R_f = R_u$. The relative delivered prices for the spatial monopolist can be obtained simply by substituting $2(a-c)/3t$ for R in equations (7.8a) and (7.8b) to give

$$p_f(r) = \frac{a}{3} + \frac{2c}{3} + tr \tag{A7.9}$$

$$p_u(r) = \frac{2a}{3} + \frac{c}{3} \tag{A7.10}$$

It follows from (A7.9), (A7.10), and (7.8c) that

$$p_f(r) \gtreqqless p_d(r) \gtreqqless p_u(r) \quad \text{according as} \quad r \gtreqqless \frac{a-c}{3t} \tag{A7.11}$$

Thus, a spatial monopolist's delivered-price schedules under the alternative price policies can be depicted as in Figure 7A.1. To obtain a spatial monopolist's output, substitute $R_f = 2(a-c)/3t$, $R_u = 2(a-c)/3t$, and $R_d = (a-c)/t$ into equations (7.11) to yield

$$Q_f = \frac{2D(a-c)}{3bt}\left(a - c - \frac{a-c}{3}\right) = \frac{4D(a-c)^2}{9bt} \tag{A7.12}$$

$$Q_u = \frac{2D(a-c)}{3bt}\left(a - c - \frac{a-c}{3}\right) = \frac{4D(a-c)^2}{9bt} \tag{A7.13}$$

$$Q_d = \frac{D(a-c)}{bt}\left(a - c - \frac{(a-c)}{2}\right) = \frac{D(a-c)^2}{2bt} \tag{A7.14}$$

Thus, for the spatial monopolist,

$$Q_d > Q_f (= Q_u) \tag{A7.15}$$

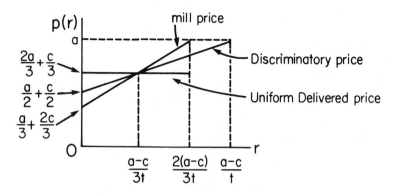

Figure 7A.1. The monopolist's delivered prices.

Detailed comparisons of monopoly outputs in the case of discriminatory pricing and mill pricing have been provided by Greenhut and Ohta (1972, 1975b), Holahan (1975), and Greenhut (1977). For comparisons between mill pricing and uniform delivered pricing, see Beckmann and Ingene (1976).

Mathematical appendix II

Optimal f.o.b. and uniform prices: Differentiation of (7.4a) and (7.4b) gives

$$\frac{\partial \Pi_f}{\partial m_f} = \frac{2D}{b}\left(aR - 2m_f R + cR - \frac{1}{2}tR^2\right) = 0$$

$$\frac{\partial \Pi_u}{\partial m_u} = \frac{2D}{b}\left(aR - 2m_u R + cR + \frac{1}{2}tR^2\right) = 0$$

Equations (7.5) follow.

Optimal discriminatory price: Differentiation of (7.6) gives

$$\frac{\partial \Pi_d(m, r)}{\partial m(r)} = \frac{D}{b}(a + c - 2m(r) - tr) = 0$$

Equation (7.7) follows.

Total output: Substituting from equations (7.8) gives

$$Q_f^R = \frac{2D}{b}\int_0^R \left(\frac{a}{2} - \frac{c}{2} + \frac{tR}{4} - tr\right) dr$$

$$= \frac{2DR}{b}\left(\frac{a}{2} - \frac{c}{2} + \frac{tR}{4} - \frac{tR}{2}\right) = \frac{DR}{b}\left(a - c - \frac{tR}{2}\right)$$

$$Q_u^R = \frac{2D}{b} \int_0^R \left(\frac{a}{2} - \frac{c}{2} - \frac{tR}{4} \right) dr = \frac{DR}{b} \left(a - c - \frac{tR}{2} \right)$$

$$Q_d^R = \frac{2D}{b} \int_0^R \left(\frac{a}{2} - \frac{c}{2} - \frac{tr}{2} \right) dr = \frac{DR}{b} \left(a - c - \frac{tR}{2} \right)$$

Profit: From equations (7.5), (7.7), and (7.4), profit is

$$\Pi_f^R = \frac{2D}{b} \left(\frac{a}{2} - \frac{c}{2} - \frac{tR}{4} \right) \left(\frac{a}{2} - \frac{c}{2} - \frac{tR}{4} \right) R - F$$

$$= \frac{DR}{2b} \left((a-c)^2 - (a-c)tR + \frac{t^2R^2}{4} \right) - F$$

$$\Pi_u^R = \frac{2D}{b} \left(\frac{a}{2} - \frac{c}{2} - \frac{tR}{4} \right) \left(\frac{a}{2} - \frac{c}{2} - \frac{tR}{4} \right) R - F$$

$$= \frac{DR}{2b} \left((a-c)^2 - (a-c)tR + \frac{t^2R^2}{4} \right) - F$$

$$\Pi_d^R = \frac{2D}{b} \int_0^R \left(\frac{a}{2} - \frac{c}{2} - \frac{tr}{2} \right) \left(\frac{a}{2} - \frac{c}{2} - \frac{tr}{2} \right) dr - F$$

$$= \frac{2D}{b} \int_0^R \left(\frac{a}{2} - \frac{c}{2} - \frac{tr}{2} \right)^2 dr - F$$

$$= \frac{2D}{b} \left(\frac{2}{3t} \left(\left(\frac{a}{2} - \frac{c}{2} \right)^3 - \left(\frac{a}{2} - \frac{c}{2} - \frac{tR}{2} \right)^3 \right) \right) - F$$

$$= \frac{4D}{3bt} \left(3 \left(\frac{a}{2} - \frac{c}{2} \right)^2 \frac{tR}{2} - 3 \left(\frac{a}{2} - \frac{c}{2} \right) \frac{t^2R^2}{4} + \frac{t^3R^3}{8} \right) - F$$

$$= \frac{DR}{2b} \left((a-c)^2 - (a-c)tR + \frac{t^2R^2}{3} \right) - F$$

Consumer surplus: From equations (7.8) and (7.14), consumer surplus is

$$\text{CS}_f^R = \frac{D}{b} \int_0^R \left(\frac{a}{2} - \frac{c}{2} + \frac{tR}{4} - tr \right)^2 dr$$

$$= \frac{DR}{3bt} \left\{ \left(\frac{a}{2} - \frac{c}{2} + \frac{tR}{4} \right)^3 - \left(\frac{a}{2} - \frac{c}{2} - \frac{3tR}{4} \right)^3 \right\}$$

Expand and simplify to give (7.15a):

$$\text{CS}_u^R = \frac{D}{b} \int_0^R \left(\frac{a}{2} - \frac{c}{2} - \frac{tR}{4} \right)^2 dr$$

$$= \frac{DR}{b} \left(\frac{a}{2} - \frac{c}{2} - \frac{tR}{4} \right)^2$$

Expand to give (7.15b):

$$CS_d^R = \frac{D}{b} \int_0^R \left(\frac{a}{2} - \frac{c}{2} - \frac{tr}{2} \right)^2 dr$$

$$= \frac{2DR}{3bt} \left\{ \left(\frac{a}{2} - \frac{c}{2} \right)^3 - \left(\frac{a}{2} - \frac{c}{2} - \frac{tR}{2} \right)^3 \right\}$$

Expand and simplify to give (7.15c).

Graphs of γ, θ, and ρ: To graph (7.18a) or (7.18b), differentiate with respect to R, and set the derivative to zero:

$$\frac{d\gamma}{dR} = \frac{(a-c)^2}{2b} - \frac{(a-c)}{b}tR + \frac{3t^2R^2}{8b} = 0$$

$$\Rightarrow \left(\frac{(a-c)}{2} - \frac{tR}{4} \right) \left((a-c) - \frac{3tR}{2} \right) = 0$$

Thus, γ has a turning point at $R = 2(a-c)/3t$ or $R = 2(a-c)/t$. But a spatial competitor's market radius under f.o.b. mill or uniform pricing is less than $2(a-c)/3t$ [see equations (A7.4) and (A7.6)]; thus, the root $2(a-c)/t$ is irrelevant. Further differentiation gives

$$\frac{d^2\gamma}{dR^2} = -\frac{(a-c)t}{b} + \frac{3t^2R}{4b}$$

Thus,

$$\frac{d^2\gamma}{dR^2} \le 0 \quad \text{if} \quad 0 \le R \le \frac{4(a-c)}{3t}$$

Hence, the curves γ and θ are as illustrated (roughly inverse-U-shaped) in the relevant region. Similarly, to graph (7.18c), differentiate with respect to R, and set the derivative to zero to obtain

$$\frac{d\rho}{dR} = \frac{(a-c)^2}{2b} - \frac{(a-c)}{b}tR + \frac{t^2R^2}{2b} = 0 \Rightarrow ((a-c) - tR)^2 = 0 \qquad \text{(A7.16)}$$

Thus, the curve ρ has a turning point at $R = (a-c)/t$. Further,

$$\frac{d^2\rho}{dR^2} = -\frac{(a-c)}{b}t + \frac{t^2R}{b}$$

Hence,

$$\frac{d^2\rho}{dR^2} < 0 \quad \text{for} \quad 0 \le R \le (a-c)/t$$

Thus, the curve ρ is concave over the region $0 \le R \le (a-c)/t$. It follows, therefore, from (A7.8) and (A7.16) that ρ is everywhere increasing, because $d\rho/dR \ge 0$ for all R in the relevant region.

CHAPTER 8

Discriminatory pricing and market overlap

The analysis in Chapters 6 and 7 was based on some relatively restrictive assumptions regarding the nature of competition between firms in an imperfectly competitive economy. It is now time to consider alternative assumptions with respect to the competitive environment of the firm.

The departure point in this chapter involves explicit recognition of the fact that many markets are characterized by partial or complete market overlap. Local monopolists of the type considered in Chapters 6 and 7 exist and are important. However, casual inspection of any department store or a walk along any High Street also indicates that in many industries firms invade and sell in each other's markets. Recognition of such mutual invasion should carry strong implications for the nature of pricing and, in particular, for the degree of price discrimination.

8.1 Market overlap and pricing with homogeneous goods

Greenhut and Greenhut (1975), hereafter referred to as G-G, considered the effects of competition on delivered-price schedules in a long-run market equilibrium in which two or more competing firms sell a homogeneous product to the same market locations. The assumptions on which their model is based are just those specified in Chapter 6, with two exceptions:

> *Assumption 7A:* Firms may share locations, and there may be complete or partial overlap of their market areas.
> *Assumption 8:* There is Cournot-type competition: Each firm believes its rivals' supply to be fixed at any given buying point.

The market is assumed to be a line market of length L, as in Figure 8.1. Suppose there are n firms in this market, with n_1 firms at location 0 and n_2 firms at location R. Further assume, for the moment, that all n firms supply output to each selling location r. Let the supply of firm j to market location r be $q_j(r)$ $(j = 1, ..., n)$. Total supply to market location r is then

$$q(r) = \sum_{j=1}^{n} q_j(r) \tag{8.1}$$

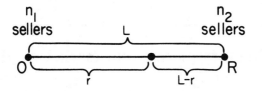

Figure 8.1. The line market.

and price at market location r (see Assumption 5 in Chapter 6) is

$$p(r) = g(q(r)) : g' < 0 \tag{8.2}$$

8.1.1   *The basic pricing equation*

Because it is assumed that all firms face constant marginal-production costs, aggregate profit for any particular firm is maximized if the firm maximizes profit at each and every market location r. Profit for firm i from sale to each consumer at market location r (gross of fixed costs) is[1]

$$\Pi_i(r) = (p(r) - c - tr_i) q_i(r) \tag{8.3}$$

where r_i is the distance of firm i from selling location r.

The profit-maximizing equilibrium-price equation for each and every firm selling to market location r is (see Mathematical Appendix)

$$p(r) \left(1 - \frac{1}{\epsilon(r)n} \right) = c + \bar{T}(r) \tag{8.4}$$

where $\epsilon(r)$ is the elasticity of demand function $g[q(r)]$ at market location r with respect to delivered price $p(r)$, defined to be

$$\epsilon(r) = -\frac{p(r)}{q(r)} \frac{dq(r)}{dp(r)} = -\frac{g}{q(r)g'} \tag{8.5}$$

and $\bar{T}(r)$ is average transport costs of all firms selling to market location r:

$$\bar{T}(r) = \sum_{i=1}^{n} t_i r_i / n \tag{8.6}$$

It is significant that at every market point r, each firm equates marginal revenue to the composite marginal cost and *average* transport cost.

Equation (8.4) applies for *any* inverse demand function $g[q(r)]$, and it is possible to analyze the implications of this fundamental pricing equation maintaining such a general demand specification. Analysis is considerably eased, however, and little generality lost, by using the inverse demand function[2] of Greenhut, Greenhut, and Kelly (1977) (GGK) introduced in Chapter 4:

$$p(r) = \alpha - \frac{\beta}{x} q(r)^x \quad (\alpha, \beta > 0; \ 0 < x < \infty) \tag{8.7}$$

The elasticity of this demand function with respect to delivered price was shown in Chapter 6 to be

$$\epsilon(r) = \frac{p(r)}{x(\alpha - p(r))} \tag{8.8}$$

Substituting (8.8) into (8.4) establishes the profit-maximizing price for a firm facing G-G competitive conditions:

$$p(r) = \frac{1}{n+x}(x\alpha + nc) + \frac{n}{n+x}\bar{T}(r) \tag{8.9}$$

8.1.2　The price effects of local competition

Analysis is confined at this stage to consideration of delivered price at a particular market location r, given that this market point is supplied by n competitive firms. Equation (8.9) then indicates that delivered price is affected by the *average transport costs* $\bar{T}(r)$ to market point r of the n supplying firms. From equation (8.6) it can be seen that average transport costs of the n suppliers will be determined by the locations of these suppliers. It follows that delivered price to any market point r will be determined by the locations of the firms supplying that market point.

Three interesting cases regarding the effects of competition and locational choices on a firm's delivered prices can be considered in the context of the G-G model: (1) effects of local competition on price, (2) effects of distant competition on prices with completely overlapping markets (i.e., all firms from alternative locations compete at each market point), and (3) effects of distant competition on prices with partially overlapping markets (i.e., firms from alternative locations compete over only portions of the total market space). The first of these cases is examined in this subsection, and the remaining two cases in the following subsections.

In the case in which all firms share the same production center, assume that they are located at 0. Then $n_2 = 0$, and $n = n_1$. Hence, the average transport cost to a particular market point, $\bar{T}(r) = (\sum_{i=1}^{n} tr_i)/n$, equals the transport costs to that point, $\bar{T}(r) = tr$. It follows from (8.9) that a firm's delivered-price equation at each market point r becomes

$$p(r) = \frac{1}{n+x}(x\alpha + nc) + \frac{n}{n+x}tr \tag{8.10}$$

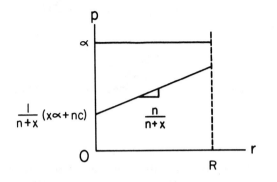

Figure 8.2. DPS for competing firms when all are located at the same production center.

This price equation is illustrated in Figure 8.2 as a delivered-price schedule for given demand conditions and number of firms in the production center.

The delivered-price schedule can be examined in the light of the discussion of spatial price discrimination by reorganizing terms. The effective mill price charged to consumers at distance r from the firm's location (delivered price net of transport costs) is

$$m(r) = p(r) - tr = \frac{1}{n+x}(x\alpha + nc) - \frac{x}{n+x}tr \qquad (8.11)$$

Clearly, because the second term is negative (recall that it is assumed that $x > 0$), there is price discrimination in favor of more distant consumers in that they are being charged a lower net mill price than are proximate consumers.

The degree of price discrimination is given by the slope of the delivered-price schedule, which can be denoted S:

$$S = \frac{n}{n+x}t < t \quad \text{for } x > 0 \qquad (8.12)$$

The effect of competition on prices at an existing production center can readily be obtained by differentiating (8.10), (8.11), and (8.12) with respect to n. Thus,

$$\frac{dp(r)}{dn} = \frac{dm(r)}{dn} = \frac{-x(\alpha - c - tr)}{(n+x)^2} < 0$$

$$(0 < x \le \infty \text{ and } \alpha > c + tr) \qquad (8.13)$$

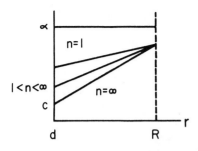

Figure 8.3. Effects of an increase in local competition, assuming $x > 0$.

and

$$\frac{dS}{dn} = \frac{x}{(n+x)^2} t > 0 \quad (0 < x < \infty) \tag{8.14}$$

Note that because α represents the price intercept of the demand function [see equation (8.7)], that is, the highest price consumers are willing to pay, α must necessarily be greater than $c + tr$ for some values of r if firms are to exist over the market space. In addition, no firm will wish to sell to distant markets for which $\alpha < c + tr$. Equation (8.13) therefore carries a negative sign.

Equations (8.13) and (8.14) indicate that an increase in local competition results in decreases in both the mill price and delivered price and in the degree of price discimination. Indeed, (8.13) and (8.14) indicate that as the number of firms approaches infinity, the mill price approaches marginal cost, c, and the slope approaches unity (f.o.b. pricing) regardless of the shape of the underlying basic demand. In such a case, the firm's delivered-price schedule (DPS) becomes $c + tr$, and here the classical result of nondiscriminatory perfect competition obtains, with each firm pricing at marginal cost. Figure 8.3 depicts the effect on delivered prices of an increase in local competition.

8.1.3   *Distant competition with completely overlapped markets*

Now consider the effect of distant competition on the DPS of the firms located at market point 0. Assume that the rival firms are located at R in Figure 8.1, with n_1 firms located at 0 and n_2 firms at R $(n_1, n_2 \neq 0)$. Further assume that firms at both locations can compete for each and every point in the market space. That is, using the G-G terminology, the firms' market areas are completely overlapped, and competition is therefore

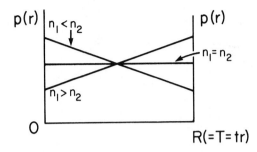

Figure 8.4. DPS when competition is completely overlapped between firms at both locations.

homogeneous throughout the market space. In such a case, the total number of firms supplying each market point is $n = n_1 + n_2$. With distance between the two locations of L, as in Figure 8.1, the average transport cost at each market point r will be

$$\bar{T}(r) = \frac{1}{n}(n_1 tr + n_2 t(L-r)) \tag{8.15}$$

Substituting (8.15) into (8.9) provides the delivered price,

$$p(r) = \frac{1}{n+x}(x\alpha + nc) + \frac{n_2 tL}{n+x} + \frac{n_1 - n_2}{n+x} tr \tag{8.16}$$

the mill price,

$$m(r) = \left(\frac{1}{n+x}(x\alpha + nc) + \frac{n_2 tL}{n+x}\right) - \frac{2n_2 + x}{n+x} tr \tag{8.17}$$

and the slope of the DPS,

$$S = \frac{n_1 - n_2}{n+x} t \tag{8.18}$$

Equation (8.17) indicates once again that there is price discrimination [compare this equation with (8.11)]. The nature and degree of price discrimination are somewhat different, however, in this case. Equation (8.18) indicates that for a given total number of firms n, the slope of the DPS depends on the relative magnitudes of n_1 and n_2.

The interrelationships among the number of firms, their competitive locations, and the resulting delivered-price schedules are illustrated in Figure 8.4. If $n_1 > n_2$, the slope of the DPS for firms at 0 is positive. When $n_1 = n_2$, the DPS becomes horizontal, and uniform pricing between the

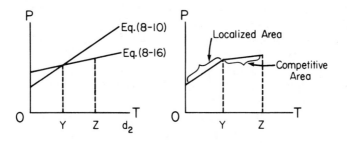

Figure 8.5. Combined DPS of a firm located at 0.

two production centers prevails. Finally, if there is more competition at the distant locations, that is, $n_1 < n_2$, the DPS for the firms at 0 becomes negatively sloped. Converse results apply for firms at R, because these firms charge prices identical with those charged by firms located at 0.

This result reflects the importance of average transport costs for the firm's DPS in the G-G model. If $n_1 > n_2$, average transport costs increase with distance from 0, because more firms are incurring larger transport costs. If $n_1 = n_2$, the average transport costs remain the same as distance from the firms at 0 increases.

What about the effects of increased competition? It can be shown (see Mathematical Appendix) that as the total number of firms is increased, delivered price at any selling location tends toward marginal-production costs plus *average* transport costs to that location: a form of marginal-cost pricing. In particular, if $n_1 = n_2 = \frac{1}{2}n$, delivered price tends to $c + \frac{1}{2}tL$: uniform pricing at "average" marginal cost.

8.1.4 *Distant competition with partially overlapped markets*

An important analytical by-product of the G-G analysis occurs in the situation in which competition is not homogeneous throughout the market space. Consider in this regard the simplified case in which firms at distant location R do not compete at market points proximate to the firms at 0. For simplicity, further assume that competition is homogeneous throughout the overlapped competitive area. Under this simple arrangement, the delivered-price schedules of the firms are combinations of (8.10) and (8.16); at the market points proximate to location 0, (8.10) is the relevant DPS (with $n = n_1$), whereas for the overlapped competitive area, (8.16) is applicable (with n now $n_1 + n_2$). This is illustrated in Figure 8.5, in which $0Y$ represents the localized area, and YZ the overlapped competitive area. Note that Figure 8.5 assumes that $n_1 > n_2$. The portion of the DPS between Y and Z is therefore shown to be positively sloped.

It must be noted that the delivered-price schedule depicted here reflects an important assumption mentioned earlier. Because marginal-production costs have been assumed constant, a firm determines its discriminatory delivered price at each market point by maximizing its profits at that point. As a result, the DPS in the localized area will be unaffected by distant competition.[3] It should also be noted that the number of firms at each market point plays a central role in these results. Significantly, the analysis indicates that a firm's DPS is linear only if it faces homogeneous competitive forces over the entire market space.

8.1.5   *Some suggested applications*

The analysis in this section can be used to interpret pricing behavior in particular spatial and nonspatial markets. Empirical results from such tests applied to pricing in the United States, West Germany, and Japan will be discussed in detail in Chapter 14, but it may be valuable at this stage to give the reader some intuitive feeling for the implications of the analysis.

Essentially, the G-G results indicate that the pricing behavior of competitive firms is significantly affected by the "locations" firms occupy in the markets in which they are competing. This can be seen in purely spatial terms. Thus, if competitive firms are highly concentrated, prices in distant markets can be expected to be relatively high. If, however, competitors are more widely spread, then each firm, in trying to serve a particular market, will have to take into account the strength of competition from local producers.

This story can be used to explain the export pricing policies of, for example, computer and office-equipment firms such as IBM, Honeywell, and Burroughs. So long as there was little domestic competition in Europe, the prices in European markets were relatively high. As domestic competition emerged, perhaps as a result of technology transfer, but also in response to market growth, price discounting became necessary if U.S. firms were to maintain their market shares.

The final step, in which U.S. firms began to produce in the European markets, can then be explained in this way. First, price discounting reduces the profitability of exporting vis-à-vis local production. The switch to local production is therefore the result of a simple economic calculation. Alternatively (or, indeed, in addition), local production in Europe can be seen as an oligopolistic defense (Knickerbocker 1973) by, say, IBM to the threat that its U.S. competitors will switch from exporting to local production.[4]

There are also implications to be drawn for basing-point pricing systems. If the majority of producers are located at one production center, say location 0 in Figure 8.1, price will increase with distance from 0, or fall with distance from R, even for producers located at R. This may explain some of the basing-point pricing systems (such as "Pittsburgh plus") that have been founded on a *single* basing point – the dominant production center.

On the other hand, when competitors are more widely spread, a heterogeneous pattern of prices is likely to arise, as illustrated in Figure 8.5, with each firm aligning on its competitors' delivered prices. Such a pattern is clear in the distribution of motor-car prices in the various national markets within Europe. It may also underlie institutionalized price alignment such as that arising from sales under a *multiple*-basing-point pricing system.

A simple nonspatial application also suggests itself. Assume, as in Chapter 5, that the "space" over which consumers are spread is a preference or characteristics space. If all the competing firms produce a single, identical product, then consumers whose preferences are for that product will enjoy high levels of utility, while competing firms will be under little pressure to discount the price charged to consumers whose preferences are for an unavailable product with slightly different characteristics. In contrast, consider a situation in which one group of firms produces product variant A and another group produces product variant B. If producers of A are to hope to sell this product to consumers whose preferences favor variant B, a price discount will have to be offered – equivalent in spatial terms to spatial price discrimination through freight absorption.

Quite clearly, this analysis can be extended to the situation of multiproduct firms. At some point, producers of product variant A may well decide to switch from price discounting to actual production of *both* variants A and B – note the parallel here with the switch from exporting to multinational production.

8.2 Optimal pricing policies: differentiated products[5]

One limitation of the G-G model is the assumption that the product is homogeneous. As a consequence, all producers charge identical prices at each selling point. If the market is the linear market of Figure 8.1, the slope of the delivered-price schedule (DPS) is determined by the numbers of sellers at the two production points. Thus, if $n_1 > n_2$ (see Figure 8.4), firms located at 0 pass on some proportion of freight costs to more distant consumers, but firms located at R are forced to absorb more than 100 percent of transport costs.

Such an outcome may characterize certain markets, but it is unlikely to be *standard*. It is, in large part, a consequence of the assumed homogeneity of the product. Consider, therefore, a model identical to the G-G model in all but one respect. The one departure from G-G is to assume that the products are differentiated. Because the market is oligopolistic, it follows that the demand for product i is affected by the price of i and by the prices of all related (rival) products. If there are two rival producers, individual demand for product 1, for example, is given by

$$q_1(r) = q_1(p_1(r), p_2(r)) \quad (0 \le r \le L) \tag{8.19}$$

where $p_i(r)$ is the price of product i at location r $(i = 1, 2)$. It is assumed that commodities 1 and 2 are substitutes. Hence,

$$\frac{\partial q_1(r)}{\partial p_1(r)} < 0; \quad \frac{\partial q_1(r)}{\partial p_2(r)} > 0 \quad (0 \le r \le L) \tag{8.20}$$

It should be noted that this type of product differentiation is distinct from, but additional to, product differentiation based on commodity characteristics. We can conceive of product variety in terms of objective characteristics embodied in each product and thus define the "location" of the product and the "location" of each consumer. In addition, we can conceive of more subjective characteristics such as brand name, packaging, and so forth. It is these subjective factors that will allow a particular producer to supply consumers with products that do not necessarily offer the ideal combination of objective characteristics, even if this ideal combination is available from another producer.

Given the assumption that marginal costs are constant, aggregate profit for each producer is maximized by maximizing profit at each selling location. Profit for producer 1 (assumed to have his plant located at 0) from sales to each consumer at location r (gross of fixed costs) is

$$\Pi_1(r) = (p_1(r) - c_1 - tr)q_1(p_1(r), p_2(r)) \quad (0 \le r \le L) \tag{8.21}$$

In maximizing this profit function with respect to price $p_1(r)$, some assumption is required regarding the conjectural variation $\partial p_2(r)/\partial p_1(r)$ held by producer 1 concerning the way in which producer 2 will react to a (marginal) change in the price of product 1. For the moment, the Hotelling-Smithies conjectural variation is assumed:

$$\frac{\partial p_2(r)}{\partial p_1(r)} = 0 \quad (0 \le r \le L) \tag{8.22}$$

Then, maximizing (8.21) with respect to $p_1(r)$ gives the fundamental pricing equation for producer 1 [see equation (8.4)]:[6]

$$p_1(r)\left\{1 - \frac{1}{\epsilon_1(p_1(r), p_2(r))}\right\} = c_1 + tr \tag{8.23}$$

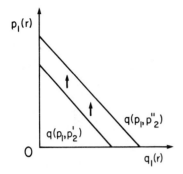

Figure 8.6. Effect on $q_1(r)$ of an increase in $p_2(r)$: $p_2'' > p_2'$.

where $\epsilon_1[p_1(r), p_2(r)]$ is own-price elasticity of demand for product 1 at location r.

The fundamental pricing equation can be solved to establish the DPS for producer 1. The precise shape of this DPS will depend, of course, on the nature of the individual demand functions (8.19) and, in particular, on how the own-price elasticity of demand is affected by changes in own-prices and cross-prices. What this implies is that the degree of spatial price discrimination adopted by producer 1 will depend, at least in part, on the DPS of producer 2.

It is possible to be more specific about the price interdependence of the two producers. Assume that (a) producer 2 charges a uniform price $\bar{p}_2$ at all locations, (b) producer 1 is located at 0 in Figure 8.1, and (c) own-price elasticity of demand $\epsilon_1[p_1(r), p_2(r)]$ is a monotonic decreasing[7] function of price $p_2(r)$: An increase in the price of product 2 reduces own-price elasticity of demand for product 1. This will occur, for example, if an increase in price of product 2 induces a vertical shift in the demand function for product 1, as in Figure 8.6.

These assumptions, particularly assumption (a), allow solution of equation (8.23) for $p_1(r)$. Assume that the resulting DPS is as in the dotted curve in Figure 8.7(a). What has happened is that assumption (a) has reduced the problem to a standard monopoly case, because $q_1(r)$ is now a function solely of $p_1(r)$. Thus, for example, if $q_1(r)$ were linear in p_1 and p_2, the discussion in previous chapters would indicate that the DPS $p_1(r)$, given $p_2(r) = \bar{p}_2$, would have a slope of $t/2$, giving rise to 50 percent freight absorption.

Of more interest is what happens when assumption (a) is relaxed. Consider first the case in which $p_2(r) = p_2'(r)$ in Figure 8.7(b), and in particular

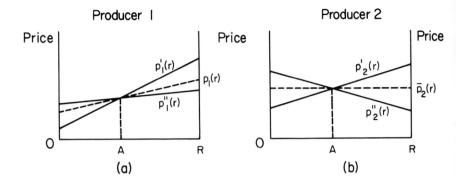

Figure 8.7. Pricing with differentiated commodities.

consider the effect this new DPS for product 2 has on the own-price elasticity of demand for product 1. At selling point A, $p_2'(r) = \bar{p}_2$. Hence, own-price elasticity of demand and price $p_1(r)$ are unchanged at selling point A under the two sets of delivered prices $\bar{p}_2$ and $p_2'(r)$. To the left of A, however, $p_2'(r) < \bar{p}_2$; hence, from assumption (c),

$$\epsilon_1(p_1(r), p_2'(r)) > \epsilon_1(p_1(r), \bar{p}_2) \quad (0 \leq r < A) \tag{8.24}$$

For consumers to the left of A, the change in the DPS of producer 2 from $\bar{p}_2$ to $p_2'(r)$ increases the own-price elasticity of demand for producer 1 and, from the fundamental pricing equation (8.23), leads to a reduction in the price $p_1(r)$. Similarly, for consumers to the right of A, $p_2'(r) > \bar{p}_2$, and price $p_1(r)$ will be increased. In summary, the DPS for producer 1, given DPS $p_2'(r)$ for producer 2, will look like $p_1'(r)$ in Figure 8.7(a) and thus will involve less price discrimination than in the case in which a uniform price is charged for product 2.

By an identical argument, if the DPS for product 2 is $p_2(r) = p_2''(r)$ in Figure 8.7(b), the DPS for product 1 will be as $p_1''(r)$ in Figure 8.7(a). It will therefore involve more price discrimination than the uniform-pricing case.

This analysis can be used to illustrate the effects of location choice on the pricing policies of competitive firms. The DPS $p_2'(r)$ is "more likely" than $p_2''(r)$ if producer 2 is located at 0 rather than R, and vice versa. Thus, as in the G-G analysis, less price discrimination is likely if the two producers adopt coincident locations than if they are located at opposite ends of the market. What is also the case, however, is that the price schedules of the two producers *need not be identical* [e.g., producer 1 may have DPS $p_1'(r)$, and producer 2 DPS $p_2'(r)$, because the products are differentiated].

The discussion of Figure 8.7 is suggestive, but it can be made more specific if particular forms are given to the demand functions (8.19). Assume that individual demand functions are linear:

$$q_1(r) = \alpha_1 - \beta_{11} p_1(r) + \beta_{12} p_2(r) \tag{8.25}$$

$$q_2(r) = \alpha_2 + \beta_{21} p_1(r) - \beta_{22} p_2(r) \tag{8.26}$$

where $\alpha_i, \beta_{ij} > 0$ for $i, j = 1, 2$, and assume zero marginal-production costs: $c_i = 0$ $(i = 1, 2)$.

If both firms are located at 0, the optimal DPS for each firm is[8]

$$p_1(r) = (1/\Delta)[(2\beta_{22}\alpha_1 + \beta_{12}\alpha_2) + (2\beta_{11}\beta_{22} + \beta_{12}\beta_{22})tr]$$
$$p_2(r) = (1/\Delta)[(2\beta_{11}\alpha_2 + \beta_{21}\alpha_1) + (2\beta_{11}\beta_{22} + \beta_{21}\beta_{11})tr] \tag{8.27}$$

where $\Delta = 4\beta_{11}\beta_{22} - \beta_{12}\beta_{21}$. For price to be nonnegative, it is necessary that $\Delta > 0$. This condition will be satisfied so long as the product of the own-price elasticities of demand exceeds a (small) fraction of the product of the cross-price elasticities of demand – a not particularly restrictive condition.

Equations (8.27) give the slopes of the DPS for the two producers:

$$S_1 = \frac{2\beta_{11}\beta_{22} + \beta_{12}\beta_{22}}{4\beta_{11}\beta_{22} - \beta_{12}\beta_{21}} \geq \frac{1}{2}$$
$$S_2 = \frac{2\beta_{11}\beta_{22} + \beta_{21}\beta_{11}}{4\beta_{11}\beta_{22} - \beta_{12}\beta_{21}} \geq \frac{1}{2} \tag{8.28}$$

and the degree of spatial price discrimination is $1 - S_i$ $(i = 1, 2)$. Thus, the two producers adopt less discriminatory prices than would a spatial monopolist (in which case $S_i = \frac{1}{2}$).

Several further points emerge from equations (8.27); see Norman (1983a) for a fuller discussion. First, producer 1 will adopt a more discriminatory DPS than will producer 2 if product 1 is perceived to be differentiated more from product 2 than is 2 from 1. [The idea that product i is more differentiated from product j than is j from i should be intuitively clear if the products are thought of as fulfilling particular functions rather than merely providing utility to the consumer: the Lancaster (1966) "characteristics" approach to consumption discussed in Chapter 5.]

Second, the degree of spatial price discrimination is determined by the parameters of the demand function. In particular, an increase in the cross-price elasticity of product 1 with respect to product 2 (an increase in β_{12}) will result in a reduction in price discrimination for product 1. Similarly, a reduction in own-price elasticity of demand for product 1 (a reduction in β_{11}) will reduce price discrimination for that product. These results follow because an increase in β_{12} signifies an increase in the competitiveness of product 1 with respect to product 2: An increase in β_{12} will, from

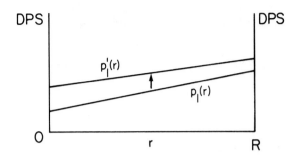

Figure 8.8. Effect on $p_1(r)$ of an increase in β_{12}.

equation (8.25), lead to a general rightward shift in the demand curve for product 1. Thus, with coincident locations, an increase in the competitiveness of one product with respect to other products will give rise to a general increase in prices over distance and a reduction in price discrimination.

When the producers adopt noncoincident locations, some sharp contrasts emerge. Assume in this case that producer 1 is located at 0, and producer 2 at R. Then the slopes of the DPS are

$$S_1 = \frac{2\beta_{11}\beta_{22} - \beta_{12}\beta_{22}}{4\beta_{11}\beta_{22} - \beta_{12}\beta_{21}}$$

$$S_2 = \frac{2\beta_{11}\beta_{22} - \beta_{21}\beta_{11}}{4\beta_{11}\beta_{22} - \beta_{22}\beta_{21}}$$

(8.29)

As is to be expected from the original G-G analysis, noncoincident location leads to greater degrees of price discrimination [compare (8.29) and (8.28)] than would characterize pricing under coincident location. In further contrast to the coincident-location case, an increase in the cross-price elasticity of demand for product 1 with respect to product 2 will result in an *increase* in the degree of price discrimination in the noncoincident-location case, as illustrated in Figure 8.8.

8.3   Collusive oligopoly and nonzero conjectural variation

The pricing policies (8.27) do not maximize the joint profits of the duopolists (Koutsoyiannis 1975, p. 227). Consider, therefore, the case in which the duopolists collude to maximize total (joint) profits. With coincident location, the effects of collusion on the DPS are as in Figure 8.9. A reduction in competitive pressures through collusion allows each producer to adopt a more discriminatory pricing policy.

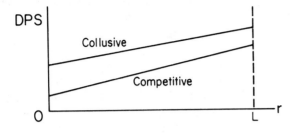

Figure 8.9. Effects of collusion on DPS – coincident location.

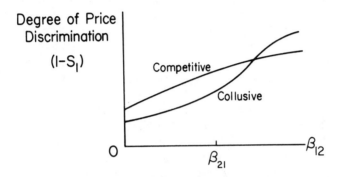

Figure 8.10. Effects of collusion on price discrimination – noncoincident location.

Matters are not quite as straightforward in the noncoincident-location case. The effects of collusion on price discrimination in this case depend crucially on the cross-price effects β_{ij}. This is illustrated in Figure 8.10. If $\beta_{12} < \hat{\beta}_{12}$, collusion reduces the degree of price discrimination, whereas if $\beta_{12} > \hat{\beta}_{12}$ ($> \beta_{21}$), collusion increases price discrimination. What can be said is that collusion between noncoincidentally located duopolists is more likely to increase price discrimination on a particular product the more "competitive" that product is, that is, the greater the extent to which consumers perceive it as being a substitute for other products in the market.

Similar conclusions emerge when nonzero conjectural variations are introduced such that the duopolists recognize their interdependence but do not explicitly collude. An increase in conjectural variations can be expected to lead to an increase in price discrimination in the coincident-location case. When the producers are located separately, there is an ambiguous price effect. In this latter case, a decrease in price discrimination for product 1 is likely to be accompanied by an increase in discrimination for product 2; the overall effect on the "average" degree of discrimination cannot be stated without specific knowledge of the conjectural variation.

8.4   Conclusions

The analysis in this chapter lends strong support to the contention that the existence of price discrimination in particular markets is not a priori evidence of lack of competitive pressures. But neither can a simple connection be drawn between the degree of competition and the degree of price discrimination. Price discrimination between consumers in separated markets (e.g., by means of freight absorption) may indeed reflect and be the result of intense competitive pressures in particular markets, but this is more likely if the competitors in such markets are not themselves concentrated. On the other hand, discrimination may be the consequence of explicit collusive agreements between coincidentally located producers or of attempts by such producers to anticipate the (lead–follow) actions of their competitors.

Certainly, the simple (spaceless) foundations on which current policies with respect to price discrimination, dumping, and so forth, are based need to be reexamined. It would appear, however, that such reexamination must be based on empirical analysis that takes full account of the interconnections between producers, the extent to which they produce differentiated or substitute commodities, and the locational choices they have made.

Mathematical appendix

The fundamental pricing equation: Differentiate (8.2) with respect to $q_i(r)$ to give

$$\frac{dp(r)}{dq_i(r)} = \frac{dg}{dq(r)} \sum_{j=1}^{n} \frac{dq_j(r)}{dq_i(r)} \tag{A8.1}$$

But, from Assumption 8,

$$\frac{dq_j(r)}{dq_i(r)} = 0 \quad (i, j = 1, \ldots, n; \ i \neq j) \tag{A8.2}$$

and, of course,

$$\frac{dq_i(r)}{dq_i(r)} = 1 \tag{A8.3}$$

Substituting in (A8.1) gives

$$\frac{dp(r)}{dq_i(r)} = \frac{dg}{dq(r)} = \frac{dp(r)}{dq(r)} \tag{A8.4}$$

Differentiate the profit equation (8.3) with respect to $q_i(r)$ and substitute (A8.2) and (A8.3) to give the fundamental pricing equation for firm i:

$$p(r) + q_i(r) \frac{dp(r)}{dq_i(r)} = c + tr_i \tag{A8.5}$$

Summing (A8.5) over the number of firms n yields

$$np(r) + \sum_{i=1}^{n} q_i(r) \frac{dp(r)}{dq_i(r)} = nc + \sum_{i=1}^{n} tr_i \tag{A8.6}$$

and dividing by n gives

$$p(r) + \left(\sum_{i=1}^{n} q_i(r) \frac{dp(r)}{dq_i(r)} \right) \bigg/ n = c + \bar{T}(r) \tag{A8.7}$$

where $\bar{T}(r)$ is the average transport cost for all firms selling to market location r. That is,

$$\bar{T}(r) = \left(\sum_{i=1}^{n} tr_i \right) \bigg/ n \tag{A8.8}$$

Substitute (A8.4) in (A8.7) to give

$$p(r) + \left(\sum_{i=1}^{n} q_i(r) \frac{dp(r)}{dq(r)} \right) \bigg/ n = c + \bar{T}(r) \tag{A8.9}$$

Hence, because $dp(r)/dq(r)$ is constant for all i,

$$p(r) + \frac{dp(r)}{dq(r)} \left(\sum_{i=1}^{n} q_i(r) \right) \bigg/ n = c + \bar{T}(r) \tag{A8.10}$$

Finally, substituting from equation (8.1) gives

$$p(r) + \frac{q(r)}{n} \frac{dp(r)}{dq(r)} = c + \bar{T}(r) \tag{A8.11}$$

Equation (8.4) follows from the definition (8.5) of elasticity of demand.

Delivered price as $n \to \infty$ with distant competition: Assume that n_1 and n_2 are kept in proportion, with $n_2 = \gamma n_1$ ($\gamma > 0$). Then $n = (1 + \gamma)n_1$, and delivered price is, from (8.16),

$$p(r) = \frac{1}{n+x}(x\alpha + nc) + \frac{\gamma n t L}{(1+\gamma)(n+x)} + \frac{(1-\gamma)ntr}{(1+\gamma)(n+x)} \tag{A8.12}$$

As $n \to \infty$, $p(r)$ tends to

$$p(r) = c + (tr + \gamma t(L-r))/(1+\gamma)$$

which is just marginal production cost plus average transport cost.

Pricing with differentiated products

Coincident location: Profit from sales to consumers at distance r from 0 is

$$\Pi_1(r) = (p_1(r) - tr)(\alpha_1 - \beta_{11} p_1(r) + \beta_{12} p_2(r)) \qquad \text{(A8.13)}$$

$$\Pi_2(r) = (p_2(r) - tr)(\alpha_2 + \beta_{21} p_1(r) - \beta_{22} p_2(r)) \qquad \text{(A8.14)}$$

Differentiate (A8.13) with respect to $p_1(r)$ and (A8.14) with respect to $p_2(r)$ to give

$$\alpha_1 - 2\beta_{11} p_1(r) + \beta_{12} p_2(r) + \beta_{11} tr = 0 \qquad \text{(A8.15)}$$

$$\alpha_2 + \beta_{21} p_1(r) - 2\beta_{22} p_2(r) + \beta_{22} tr = 0 \qquad \text{(A8.16)}$$

Reorganize:

$$\begin{bmatrix} 2\beta_{11} & -\beta_{12} \\ -\beta_{21} & 2\beta_{22} \end{bmatrix} \begin{bmatrix} p_1(r) \\ p_2(r) \end{bmatrix} = \begin{bmatrix} \alpha_1 + \beta_{11} tr \\ \alpha_2 + \beta_{22} tr \end{bmatrix} \qquad \text{(A8.17)}$$

Multiply each side by the inverse of the left-hand-side (LHS) matrix:

$$\begin{bmatrix} p_1(r) \\ p_2(r) \end{bmatrix} = \frac{1}{\Delta} \begin{bmatrix} 2\beta_{22} & \beta_{12} \\ \beta_{21} & 2\beta_{11} \end{bmatrix} \begin{bmatrix} \alpha_1 + \beta_{11} tr \\ \alpha_2 + \beta_{22} tr \end{bmatrix} \qquad \text{(A8.18)}$$

where $\Delta = 4\beta_{11}\beta_{22} - \beta_{12}\beta_{21}$. Expand to give (8.27).

Noncoincident location: Profit equations are now

$$\Pi_1(r) = (p_1(r) - tr)(\alpha_1 - \beta_{11} p_1(r) + \beta_{12} p_2(r)) \qquad \text{(A8.19)}$$

$$\Pi_2(r) = (p_2(r) - t(L - r))(\alpha_2 + \beta_{21} p_1(r) - \beta_{22} p_2(r)) \qquad \text{(A8.20)}$$

giving the profit-maximizing equations

$$\alpha_1 - 2\beta_{11} p_1(r) + \beta_{12} p_2(r) + \beta_{11} tr = 0 \qquad \text{(A8.21)}$$

$$\alpha_2 + \beta_{21} p_1(r) - 2\beta_{22} p_2(r) + \beta_{22} t(L - r) = 0 \qquad \text{(A8.22)}$$

Reorganization gives

$$\begin{bmatrix} 2\beta_{11} & -\beta_{12} \\ -\beta_{21} & 2\beta_{22} \end{bmatrix} \begin{bmatrix} p_1(r) \\ p_2(r) \end{bmatrix} = \begin{bmatrix} \alpha_1 + \beta_{11} tr \\ \alpha_2 + \beta_{22} tL - \beta_{22} tr \end{bmatrix}$$

Multiplication by the LHS matrix inverse leads to (8.29).

CHAPTER 9

Intraindustry trade: a spatial approach

The analysis in previous chapters, particularly Chapter 8, can be used to interpret some recent developments in international trade. Traditional theories of international trade, summarized in the Heckscher-Ohlin-Samuelson (HOS) model,[1] predict that countries will specialize according to their relatively abundant factors. Thus, trade will take place in *different* commodities.

More recent analysis of international trade data indicates, however, that there is extensive and growing international trade – termed *intraindustry trade* – in identical or nearly identical commodities:[2] Countries both export and import shoes, cement, machine tools, motor cars, and so forth. The extent of intraindustry trade in any industry i can be measured using the Grubel-Lloyd index:

$$B_i = \frac{(X_i + M_i) - |X_i - M_i|}{(X_i + M_i)} 100 \tag{9.1}$$

where X_i equals exports of industry i and M_i equals imports of industry i.

When exports exactly equal imports, the index B_i equals 100. When there are exports but no imports, or vice versa, the index equals 0. If exports equal one-half of imports, or vice versa, the index equals 66.67. In general, the higher the index, the greater the amount of intraindustry trade.

Grubel and Lloyd (1975) measured intraindustry trade in a wide range of industries defined at the three-digit level in the Standard Industrial Trade Classification (SITC) and for ten OECD countries.[3] Table 9.1 gives the unweighted averages of the intraindustry trade indices for these countries in a range of industries, based on 1967 trade data. As can be seen, substantial proportions of trade flows are intraindustry trade flows. There is, therefore, a need for an explanation of these flows complementary to explanations based on the HOS theory.

It has occasionally been suggested that intraindustry trade is merely a consequence of aggregation. If we could get a sufficiently accurate definition of an industry, no intraindustry trade would be found. This argument has, however, been rejected. Even if trade flows are measured at the five-digit or seven-digit level in the SITC, substantial intraindustry trade

Table 9.1. *Ranking of industries by percentage of intraindustry trade*

Rank	SITC class	Description	Percentage
1	5	Chemicals	66
2	7	Machinery and transport equipment	59
3	9	Commodities and transactions not elsewhere specified	55
4	8	Miscellaneous manufactured articles	52
5	6	Manufactured goods classified by material	49
6	1	Beverages and tobacco	40
7	4	Animal and vegetable oils and fats	37
8	10	Food and live animals	30
9	2	Crude materials, inedible, except fuels	30
10	3	Mineral fuels, lubricants, and related materials	30

flows remain. At the same time, it must be accepted that the causes of intraindustry trade lack a strong theoretical underpinning. The growing body of empirical work has underlying it little more than a suggestive set of theoretical ideas.

Because international trade takes place, by definition, between spatially separated markets, it would appear that spatial analysis should be able to shed some light on why intraindustry trade might be expected not only to exist but also to be of increasing importance. It should also be possible to develop some empirically testable propositions with respect to the kinds of industries and countries that can be expected to exhibit high levels of intraindustry trade.

9.1   Intraindustry trade in homogeneous commodities

One obvious situation in which intraindustry trade will occur arises when home and foreign firms in a particular industry produce differentiated goods. This case will be considered in the next section. For the moment, attention is confined to cases in which the firms in the industry produce homogeneous goods. Can intraindustry trade still be expected in such circumstances?

Consider first a case in which each firm is a local monopolist: There is no market overlap. Then each firm, by appropriate choice of location and pricing, will be able to supply a well-defined market area. Two such firms are illustrated in Figure 9.1, where $A + C$ is the market area for firm 1, located at L_1, and $B + D$ is the market area for firm 2, located at L_2. These two firms are assumed to be producing a homogeneous product

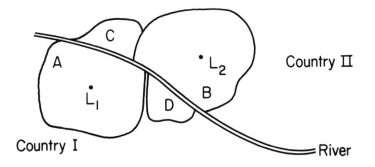

Figure 9.1. Border trade.

(e.g., cement). Now assume that the two firms are located in different countries, with the national boundary following the line of the river in Figure 9.1. Because firm 1 supplies consumers in C in country II, and firm 2 supplies consumers in D in country I, there is simultaneous import and export – intraindustry trade – in this homogeneous-product industry.

Such intraindustry trade – termed *border trade* – is more likely in industries characterized by relatively strong economies of scale, but, perhaps, with relatively high transport costs, and between countries with common international borders. It follows that one limitation of relying on border trade as the sole explanation of intraindustry trade is the limitation that the trading countries be contiguous – have a common border. More fundamentally, such an explanation assumes that each supplier exercises sole control of particular markets: There is no market overlap. It is quite clear, however, that a substantial proportion of intraindustry trade takes place in industries in which there is extensive market overlap. We can all, as consumers, cite cases in which retailers are simultaneously offering identical or nearly identical commodities produced by both domestic and foreign firms.

What is needed is a rather more general theory of intraindustry trade in identical commodities. Such a theory is available in the form of the G-G model discussed in Chapter 8. An essential feature of this model is that there is complete market overlap and thus *two-way (intraindustry) trade* in what are effectively identical commodities. It should be possible, therefore, to treat this model explicitly as an international-trade model and thus make some statements regarding the conditions under which intraindustry trade can be expected to take place.[4]

Assume that our international-trade "world" consists of two countries, 1 and 2, each of which can be represented as a point market (i.e., with zero internal costs of distribution). Firms in these two countries produce a homogeneous product under cost conditions that exhibit economies of scale and are identical for the firms in any one country. Production costs are assumed to be

$$C_i = F_i + c_i q_i \quad (i = 1, 2) \tag{9.2}$$

where, as usual, F_i is fixed cost, c_i is marginal cost, q_i is individual firm output in country i $(i = 1, 2)$. There are assumed to be n_1 producers in country 1 and n_2 producers in country 2.

In order to keep the analysis tractable, aggregate demand in each country is assumed to be linear,[5] with the inverse demand function

$$p_i = a_i - b_i Q_i \quad (i = 1, 2) \tag{9.3}$$

Transfer costs (including any specific tariffs) between country i and country j are T_{ij} per unit exported. It may well be the case that $T_{12} \neq T_{21}$ (e.g., if the two countries apply different tariff policies).

All prices and costs are assumed to be measured in a common monetary unit, which may be, for example, a European Unit of Account or Special Drawing Right.

It follows immediately from Chapter 8 that the fundamental pricing equation in country i is

$$p_i\left(1 - \frac{1}{n\epsilon_i}\right) = \bar{c} + T_i \quad (i = 1, 2) \tag{9.4}$$

where

$$n = n_1 + n_2 \tag{9.5}$$

$$\epsilon_i = p_i / (a_i - p_i) \tag{9.6}$$

$$\bar{c} = (n_1 c_1 + n_2 c_2)/n \tag{9.7}$$

$$T_i = n_j T_{ji}/n \quad (j \neq i) \tag{9.8}$$

In other words,

$$p_i^* = \frac{1}{1+n}\{a_i + n\bar{c}\} + \frac{n}{1+n}T_i \quad (i = 1, 2) \tag{9.9}$$

So long as $p_i^* > c_j + T_{ji}$ (i.e., so long as price in country i is greater than the marginal cost of production and transfer from country j), there can be two-way trade in the homogeneous commodity.

It is of some interest to investigate the extent of such intraindustry trade. In order to do so, it is necessary to identify the market shares of the two sets of producers.

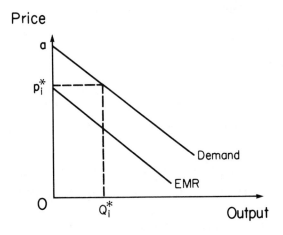

Figure 9.2. The equilibrium marginal-revenue function.

Each firm maximizes profit on its total sales by equating marginal revenue to marginal cost on sales in each market. Because each firm supplies only part of the output in any one market, its marginal-revenue curve is not the simple marginal-revenue curve that would result from the inverse demand function (9.3). This can be seen very simply by noting that an attempt by any single firm to price above p_i^* in country i will result in zero sales.

Greenhut and Greenhut (1975, appendix) resolve this problem by constructing the *equilibrium marginal-revenue curve* for country i:

$$\text{EMR}_i = p_i^* + q_i^h \frac{dp_i}{dQ_i} \quad (i = 1, 2) \tag{9.10}$$

where p_i^* is given by (9.9), q_i^h is individual-firm output supplied to country i, and Q_i is aggregate supply to consumers in country i.

From the inverse demand function, $dp_i/dQ_i = -b_i$, and

$$\text{EMR}_i = p_i^* - b_i q_i^h \quad (i = 1, 2) \tag{9.11}$$

The EMR function is illustrated in Figure 9.2. It has intercept at the price ruling in country i and slope equal to that of the aggregate demand function (Greenhut and Greenhut 1975, p. 418).

Each firm maximizes profit by setting EMR equal to its marginal cost.

Firms in country i supplying consumers in country i: For these firms,

$$\text{MC}_i = c_i \quad (i = 1, 2) \tag{9.12}$$

and profit maximization requires

$$\text{EMR}_i = c_i \quad (i = 1, 2) \tag{9.13}$$

Substitution from (9.9) and (9.11) gives

$$\frac{1}{1+n}\{a_i + n\bar{c}\} + \frac{n}{1+n}T_i - b_i q_i^i = c_i \quad (i = 1, 2) \tag{9.14}$$

where q_i^i is output of each firm located in country i supplied to consumers in country i. Further substitution from (9.7) and (9.8) and simple manipulation give

$$q_i^i = \frac{1}{b_i(1+n)}\{a_i - c_i(1+n_j) + n_j(c_j + T_{ji})\} \quad (i = 1, 2) \tag{9.15}$$

Total output of firms located in country i supplied to consumers in i is

$$Q_i^i = n_i q_i^i \tag{9.16}$$

Firms in country j supplying consumers in country i: For these firms, profit maximization requires

$$\text{EMR}_i = c_j + T_{ji} \quad (i = 1, 2; \ j \neq i) \tag{9.17}$$

and manipulation similar to that earlier gives

$$q_i^j = \frac{1}{b_i(1+n)}\{a_i + n_i c_i - (1+n_i)(c_j + T_{ji})\} \quad (i = 1, 2) \tag{9.18}$$

where q_i^j is output of each firm located in country j supplied to consumers in country i.

Total output of firms located in country j supplied to consumers in country i (exports from j to i) is, as in (9.16),

$$Q_i^j = n_j q_i^j \tag{9.19}$$

[The reader may care to check that $p_i^* = a_i - b_i(Q_i^i + Q_i^j)$.]

The total values of exports from country i to country j (X_{ij}) and of imports to country i from country j (M_{ij}) are, from (9.9), (9.18), and (9.19),

$$X_{ij} = p_j^* Q_j^i$$

$$= \frac{n_i}{b_j(1+n)^2}\{a_j + n_j c_j - (1+n_j)(c_i + T_{ij})\}\{a_j + n_j c_j + n_i(c_i + T_{ij})\} \tag{9.20}$$

$$M_{ij} = p_i^* Q_i^j$$

$$= \frac{n_j}{b_i(1+n)^2} \{a_i + n_i c_i - (1+n_i)(c_j + T_{ji})\}\{a_i + n_i c_i + n_j(c_j + T_{ji})\}$$

$$(9.21)$$

Consider first the case in which the two countries are identical in both consumption and production conditions and in which $T_{ji} = T_{ij}$. Then $X_{ij} = M_{ij}$, and trade is identically overlapped. In terms of the Grubel-Lloyd index of equation (9.1), the index of intraindustry trade is 100. More generally, the intraindustry trade index will be greater the more closely the two countries resemble each other in trade and production conditions. The theory developed earlier, therefore, lends support to the hypothesis, first advanced and given empirical support by Linder (1961), that there will be more intraindustry trade between countries at similar levels of economic development and with cultural similarities.

Even when the two countries are not identical, equations (9.20) and (9.21) indicate that intraindustry trade is likely to occur. It is also a simple matter to investigate the effects on imports and exports of changes in parameter values.

In doing so, recall first that a necessary condition for exports from j to i (imports to i from j) to be feasible (profitable) is that the equilibrium price in country i is sufficient to cover marginal cost of production and transfer from country j: p_i^* increases as T_{ji} is increased, *but only in the proportion* $n_j/(1+n)$. Note that similar comments apply to changes in marginal-production costs, because these are not fully reflected in delivered prices.

There will be lower trade flows between geographically separated countries in commodities that are expensive to transport and between countries with high tariff barriers, conditions that are familiar to trade theorists. *Intraindustry* trade will be less extensive when producers in one country have access to transport facilities that are cheaper or more efficient than those available to producers in other countries, or when there are wide differences in tariff barriers erected by different nations with respect to particular commodities.

There will be more trade in commodities in which value added in production is high (in which the reservation price of consumers is high relative to marginal-production costs). Intraindustry trade is likely to be more extensive between countries with similar cost structures. The effects on prices, exports, and imports of changes in the remaining parameter values are summarized in Table 9.2.[6]

The necessary condition for trade to take place is more likely to be

Table 9.2. *Effects on price, exports, and imports of increases in particular parameter values*

Increase in parameter	p_i^*	Effect on X_{ij}	M_{ij}
a_i	+	0	+
a_j	0	+	0
b_i	0	0	−
b_j	0	−	0
c_i	+	(a)	+
c_j	+	+	(b)
n_i	−	+	−
n_j	−	−	+

(a) <0 if $n_i \leq 1 + n_j$; >0 for n_i "sufficiently large" with respect to n_j.
(b) <0 if $n_j \leq 1 + n_i$; >0 for n_j "sufficiently large" with respect to n_i.

satisfied when the consumers' reservation price (a_i) is high relative to marginal-production costs. Trade is also more likely to take place in oligopolistic industries in which the number of firms (n_i and n_j) is limited. Thus, more intraindustry trade is likely in industries characterized by high concentration ratios and extensive barriers to entry.

An increase in local competitiveness in country i (an increase in n_i) changes the balance between exports and imports. Domestic price will fall, discouraging imports, while the relative attraction of foreign markets is increased, thus encouraging exports.

All of these comments are consistent with empirical investigations of intraindustry trade (Tharakan 1981) and help to give better theoretical support to the analysis of such trade.

9.2   Other considerations

9.2.1   *Product differentiation*

The theory developed earlier assumes a homogeneous product, yet indicates the strong possibility of intraindustry trade. One question that immediately arises is whether or not the introduction of product differentiation will further increase the extent of such trade. It turns out that there are, in fact, good reasons for believing that product differentiation will have an ambiguous effect on intraindustry trade flows.

On the one hand, product differentiation increases the likelihood of trade being feasible (i.e., of the necessary condition for trade being satisfied). The discussion of the Norman model in Chapter 8 indicates that product differentiation gives an exporter more leeway in the price chargeable in foreign markets. It is no longer the case that the exporter must exactly match the foreign price – effectively charging a uniform delivered price. At least part of transport costs can be passed on to consumers in foreign markets, the extent to which this is possible being determined by the degree to which the exporter's good is seen as being "different" from indigenous goods. As a result, exporting will be possible to a more extensive set of markets when products are differentiated than when they are homogeneous.

On the other hand, product differentiation is likely to increase, or encourage producers to engineer differences in tastes between consumers in different countries. The more different are demand patterns, the less intraindustry trade is likely to occur.

These comments are at least suggestive of explanations for the relatively poor performance of product-differentiation variables in empirical investigations of intraindustry trade. It is, of course, difficult to obtain a "good" measure of the degree of product differentiation in any industry, but the theory developed earlier suggests that even if such a measure were available, it could not be expected to have a well-defined effect on intraindustry trade flows.

9.2.2 *Reciprocal dumping and welfare considerations*

The pricing equation (9.9) indicates that prices do not fully reflect either marginal-production costs or transfer costs. It follows quite naturally that there is likely to be reciprocal dumping between the two countries, with firms in both countries charging lower net mill prices on exports than on production for domestic consumption. It must be emphasized, of course, that such dumping is a natural consequence of intense competitive pressures, rather than evidence of the exercise of monopoly power.

One consequence of reciprocal dumping is that the welfare effects of intraindustry trade are not at all clear-cut. There is apparent waste of resources in the cross-hauling of identical commodities. At the same time, pressures from foreign competition may encourage a lower domestic price than would otherwise apply. This lower price is secured, however, by substituting domestic production for what may well be higher-cost foreign production.

The cross-hauling loss is less the lower are transport costs, and the production diversion and cross-hauling costs are higher the higher are transport costs. It is to be expected, therefore, that there is a range of transport costs over which intraindustry trade will lead to a net welfare gain.

9.2.3   *Intraindustry production*

It has been assumed throughout the analysis in this chapter that trade is profitable for the exporting firm. This assumption deserves rather close attention, because there is the distinct possibility that intraindustry *trade* will lead naturally to intraindustry *production* – to the cross-hauling of foreign direct investment. Such a possibility is discussed by Norman and Dunning (1984). The essential point is that oligopolistic competition of the G-G type leads to quite intense pressure on export prices and limits the profitability of exporting. Indeed, as was indicated earlier, this price pressure may become sufficiently severe to make exporting unprofitable to particular markets.

An obvious response in such a case is to replace exporting with foreign production, by establishing subsidiaries in particular overseas markets. Within the oligopolistic structure of the G-G model, it is perfectly possible that producers in different countries will establish subsidiaries in each other's markets, leading to cross-hauling of foreign direct investment.

The conditions under which such intraindustry production can be expected to occur are easily identified. Consider firms in country i exporting to country j. For each exporting firm, profit on exports is given by

$$\Pi_{ij}^e = (p_j^* - c_i - T_{ij})q_j^i \tag{9.22}$$

Assume the simplest case, in which all producers in both countries face identical production costs and in which all consumers are identical. Substitution of (9.9) and (9.18) in (9.22) then gives

$$\Pi_{ij}^e = \frac{1}{b}\left\{\frac{a-c-(1+n_j)T_{ij}}{1+n}\right\}^2 \tag{9.23}$$

Now consider the profit any firm in country i can expect to earn if it produces directly in country j, that is, undertakes foreign direct investment (FDI) in country j. One complication arises in evaluating this profit equation. The "representative" firm in country i has to form some expectation about how it expects other firms in country i will react to its decision to undertake FDI.

Two extreme possibilities can be considered. The representative firm may believe that its decision to undertake FDI will be completely ignored by all other firms located in country i. Alternatively, the firm may believe that its decision to invest abroad will be imitated by its neighbors.

The first possibility might be argued to be less reasonable, but it is consistent with the Cournot-Nash conjecture that characterizes the solution of many oligopoly problems. The second possibility is in some ways more reasonable. Certainly, it is consistent with the proposition advanced, for example, by Knickerbocker (1973) that FDI is often undertaken by a firm as an oligopolistic defense to anticipated or actual FDI by its rivals.

There is little point in trying to resolve this conflict of more/less reasonable conjectures within the confines of this book. In any case, such a resolution is unnecessary given the objectives of our analysis. No matter the relative attractiveness or reasonableness of the two possibilities outlined earlier, they do provide us with two extreme cases for purposes of comparison.

In order to highlight this comparison, assume that the representative firm in country i expects its decision to invest abroad to be imitated by a proportion λ of its neighbors. Then $\lambda = 0$ corresponds to what might be termed Cournot-style beliefs about neighbors' reactions, and $\lambda = 1$ to what might be termed Knickerbocker beliefs.

Profit to the representative firm in country i from FDI in country j is

$$\Pi_{ij}^{f}(\lambda) = (p_j^*(\lambda) - c)q_j^{j}(\lambda) - F \tag{9.24}$$

where $p_j^*(\lambda)$ is equilibrium price in country j, $q_j^{j}(\lambda)$ is quantity sold by each local producer in j when the number of local producers[7] in j is

$$n_j(\lambda) = n_j + 1 + \lambda(n_i - 1) \tag{9.25}$$

and the number of exporters to j is

$$n_i(\lambda) = (1 - \lambda)(n_i - 1) \tag{9.26}$$

It follows (see Mathematical Appendix) that profit to the representative firm in country i from FDI in country j is

$$\Pi_{ij}^{f}(\lambda) = \frac{1}{b}\left\{\frac{a - c + (1 - \lambda)(n_i - 1)T_{ij}}{1 + n}\right\}^2 - F \tag{9.27}$$

FDI will be more profitable so long as $\Pi_{ij}^{f}(\lambda) > \Pi_{ij}^{e}$. The additional profit generated by FDI is

$$\Delta\Pi_{ij} = \Pi_{ij}^{f}(\lambda) - \Pi_{ij}^{e} \tag{9.28}$$

Substitution from equations (9.22) and (9.27) and simple differentiation give Table 9.3 – the impact of particular parameter changes on the relative profitability of FDI vis-à-vis exporting. FDI is likely to be more profitable relative to exporting

1.   the greater is the consumers' reservation price (a) relative to marginal production costs (c),

Table 9.3. *Effects of parameter changes on relative profitability of FDI*

Increase in parameter	Effect on relative profitability $(\Delta\Pi_{ij})$ of FDI
Demand a	+
Demand b	−
Cost c	−
Cost T_{ij}	+
Cost F	−
Reaction λ	−

2. the less is the slope (b) of the demand function,
3. the higher are transfer costs (transport costs and tariff barriers) between country i and country j,
4. the smaller are the fixed costs (F) of operating additional production facilities, and
5. the smaller is the proportion of neighboring firms the representative firm believes will imitate the decision to invest in production overseas.

These conclusions are all in accord with basic intuition on motives for FDI and with empirical investigations of FDI. There are, of course, many further reasons why firms can be expected to invest overseas rather than export, many of which will be considered in subsequent chapters of this book. Nevertheless, even the very simple model presented in this chapter has proved capable of shedding light on motives for intraindustry trade and on reasons why such trade might be replaced by intraindustry FDI.

9.3   Conclusions

The primary aim of this chapter has been to show that theories of spatial pricing have direct relevance for theories of international trade and, in particular, for theories of intraindustry trade.[8]

Simultaneous import and export of identical or nearly identical commodities is a natural consequence of spatial price theories based on market overlap and oligopolistic reaction. The conditions under which such trade is likely are then consistent with many of the available empirical investigations of such trade.

Mathematical appendix

Profit from FDI in country j: Price in country j is, from equation (9.9),

$$p_j^*(\lambda) = \frac{1}{1+n}[a+n_j(\lambda)c+n_i(\lambda)(c+T_{ij})] \tag{A9.1}$$

Substituting from equations (9.25) and (9.26) and simplifying then gives

$$p_j^*-c = \frac{1}{1+n}[a-c+(1-\lambda)(n_i-1)T_{ij}] \tag{A9.2}$$

Output supplied to consumers in country j by each producer in country j is, from equation (9.15),

$$q_j^j(\lambda) = \frac{1}{b(1+n)}[a-c(1+n_i(\lambda))+n_i(\lambda)(c+T_{ij})] \tag{A9.3}$$

Substituting from (9.26) and simplifying gives

$$q_j^j(\lambda) = \frac{1}{b(1+n)}[a-c+(1-\lambda)(n_i-1)T_{ij}] \tag{A9.4}$$

Multiplying (A9.2) and (A9.4) gives (9.27).

CHAPTER 10

Optimal pricing with delivered-price or transport constraints

One implication of spatial models that allow for market overlap, as in Chapter 8, is that any individual spatial firm may be constrained in the price it can charge, even to proximate consumers. In Section 10.1 in this chapter, therefore, we shall consider pricing within a competitive environment that imposes a ceiling-price constraint on the firm's pricing policies.

It has also been assumed in the analysis thus far that the means of product differentiation (e.g., transport) is under the control of the supplier. There are many cases, however, in which the producer does not have this control. For example, the consumer may travel to a retail outlet such as a department store, or the retailer may use his own transport services to collect goods from the wholesaler. It will often be the case that transport services are provided by independent carriers. Storage facilities may similarly be controlled by the buyer rather than the seller. In the context of the product-differentiation example of Chapter 6, the consumer may be able to customize products to his own requirements (e.g., by purchasing and fitting his own radio).

All of these cases have one property in common. In the language of spatial economics, the transport rate becomes one of the decision variables: It is endogenous to the pricing problem. The effects on spatial pricing of such an endogenous transport rate will be examined in Section 10.2.

10.1   Pricing policy with a limit-price constraint

10.1.1   *The Greenhut-Ohta model*

An immediate consequence of allowing for market overlap as in the G-G model discussed in Chapter 8 is that the spatial firm no longer has total freedom in the price it can charge, even to proximate consumers. Constraints are imposed by competition from other firms trying to sell to the same consumers.

This leads to an alternative view of spatial competition initially proposed by Greenhut and Ohta (1975b). They formulated a model in which

166

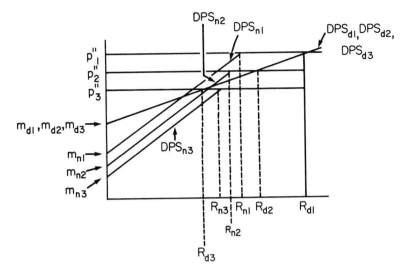

Figure 10.1. Competitive entry and alternative price policies: the Greenhut-Ohta version.

each firm can maintain exclusive control of a particular market (i.e., is a local monopolist) so long as its delivered price does not exceed a given ceiling-price constraint. In other words, they proposed that "the firm visualizes a given maximum delivered price when a distant rival firm competes with it for selected buyers" (Greenhut and Ohta 1975b, p. 129). This maximum price can therefore be seen as the entry-deterring price.

Greenhut and Ohta compared the relative profits and outputs under *discriminatory pricing* with those under *f.o.b. mill pricing*, given this competitive price constraint and subject to the further constraint that the discriminatory pricing policy was that which equated marginal cost and marginal revenue at each selling point – the discriminatory policy discussed in Chapter 6.

Figure 10.1 illustrates their analysis.[1] In the figure, DPS_{d1} and DPS_{n1}, respectively, denote the firm's discriminatory and nondiscriminatory price schedules under the given price constraint p'_1.

As indicated earlier, Greenhut and Ohta assume that the firm maximizes profits at *each* market point under the discriminatory price policy (by equating marginal cost with local marginal revenue). On the other hand, the firm chooses the f.o.b. mill price and its market space to maximize *aggregate* profits in the market by equating marginal cost and aggregate marginal revenue. Under these pricing formulations, as depicted in Figure 10.1, the discriminatory price schedule initially provides a lower average price and larger market space than does nondiscriminatory pricing. Increased competition evidenced as a reduction in the ceiling-price constraint from, say, p_1'' to p_2'', however, shifts the nondiscriminatory DPS down to the point where the lower mill price m_{n2} and smaller market area R_{n2} obtain. On the other hand, because DPS$_{d1}$ is profit-maximizing at each point in the seller's market space, it continues to be the firm's delivered-price schedule under discriminatory pricing, except that the firm now sells over the sharply reduced market area R_{d2}.

Under such a competitive process, if fixed costs are sufficiently low to permit extensive entry, a level of competition will be reached at which the nondiscriminatory price policy will involve still lower mill prices, but eventually a significantly larger market area than that of discriminatory pricing. The price constraint p_3'' in Figure 10.1 illustrates such a level of competitive entry. As a consequence, the firm will switch from the discriminatory pricing policy to the nondiscriminatory policy.

10.1.2   *A factor-input application*

Consider four distinct labor markets: (1) the short run for female workers with varying levels of education, (2) the counterpart for male workers, (3) a market over time with large-scale entry of firms seeking female employees, and (4) correspondingly for males.

In the initial case (1), imagine a demand more convex than a negative-exponential demand for females of high skill and educational background. Such a demand is proposed here because we are referring to a factor market in which cultural or legislated standards now seek reverse discrimination. As practiced recently in the United States, at least with respect to universities, a premium is becoming evident for women with PhDs *plus* well-recognized publications. At the lower end of the spectrum, low-skill females are subject to minimum and low wage levels. Above that level, a sharp drop-off in demand takes place. Thus, it would appear reasonable to suggest that a rather convex demand exists for low-skill, low-wage female workers.

The converse can be expected to hold for males with respect to education. No demand premium applies, for example, to a male PhD. In general, the less convex demand type will apply to this category of worker. At the lower end of the wage/education spectrum, a substantial demand exists above minimum wage levels vis-à-vis female workers, especially because many jobs at this level require the greater physical strength of the male. The plot of wages against education for females thus involves discrimination in favor of high incomes (delivered price) as the education (publication) level rises. For males distributed over the same spectrum, there is more likely to be discrimination in their favor at the low education levels.

Let entry of many firms needing all kinds of workers take place in each market. Let the firms no longer be subject to cultural or legislated standards, but be purely profit-seeking. The lower price constraint in the female wage/education markets will tend to flatten this price schedule, in effect leading to more of an f.o.b. wage/price alignment in place of the discriminatory pattern that favors the high-skill, well-educated female worker. In contrast, entry along the male wage/education spectrum will convert the flat schedule to a steeper one, eventually ending the relative discrimination in favor of low-skill male workers. In time, what will appear as an f.o.b. price schedule will take hold in a form corresponding to *the large-entry spatial price model* that was set forth in Part I of this book.

10.1.3 *An alternative view: the Norman model*

The conclusions of the Greenhut-Ohta model derive in the main from the narrow range of pricing policies from which the competitive firm is allowed to choose. Although situations can be envisaged in which the firm does have such a narrow choice, it will also often be the case that the firm is much freer in its feasible choice of pricing policy. The range of pricing policies open to the competitive firm is considerably extended in the Norman model (1981b). In the Norman model, the firm's pricing policy is constrained solely to be a linear function of distance from the firm or, as will be discussed later in this section, is freely chosen by the firm. (Subsequent chapters will consider nonlinear delivered-price schedules over all or many markets served by the firm.) For the present, delivered price is assumed to be given by

$$p(r) = m + Str \quad (S \geq 0) \tag{10.1}$$

where the firm's decision variables are m, the mill price, and S, the slope of the DPS.

Note that in the Greenhut-Ohta model, S is constrained to either 1 (f.o.b. mill pricing) or $\frac{1}{2}$ (in the case of a linear demand function). Thus, the Greenhut-Ohta solution is a feasible solution to the Norman model.

Norman further simplifies the analysis by normalizing the demand and cost functions as follows:[2]

$$q(r)(=a - bp(r)) = 1 - p(r) \tag{10.2}$$

$$t = 1; \quad c = 0 \tag{10.3}$$

The spatial firm facing a limit-price constraint is then required to solve the following system:

$$\max_{m, S, R} \Pi = 2 \int_0^R D(1 - m - Sr)(m + Sr - r)\, dr - F \qquad (10.4)$$

subject to

$$m + SR \le p' \qquad (10.5)$$

$$m, S, R \ge 0 \qquad (10.6)$$

Three cases should be considered, determined by how "tight" is the price constraint.[3] If the constraint is ineffective, the standard pricing solution of Chapter 6 applies. With the linear demand of equation (10.2), the producer will absorb 50 percent of transport costs – choose $S^* = \frac{1}{2}$.

The more interesting case is that in which the limit-price constraint is binding. Given the normalization of equations (10.2) and (10.3), a distinction has to be drawn between limit price $p' \ge 0.6$ and $p' \le 0.6$. Consider first the case in which $p' \ge 0.6$. Then the solution to (10.4)–(10.6) is

$$m^* = \tfrac{3}{4}(3 - 2p') - \tfrac{1}{4}K \quad (0.6 \le p' \le 1) \qquad (10.7)$$

$$R^* = 2(3 - 2p') - K \quad (0.6 \le p' \le 1) \qquad (10.8)$$

$$S^* = (p' - m^*)/R^* \qquad (10.9)$$

where $K = [(11 - 10p')(3 - p')]^{1/2}$. The optimal pricing strategy and market radius R^* are, as in Greenhut-Ohta, functions of the limit price p'.

These equations are illustrated in Figure 10.2, and the resulting delivered-price equation $[p(r) = m + Sr]$ in Figure 10.3. Consider Figure 10.2, and recall that we confine our attention for the moment to limit prices such that $p' > 0.6$. The lower is the limit price, the higher is the optimal mill price [Figure 10.2(a)], the smaller is the firm's market area [Figure 10.2(b)], and the lesser is the slope of the delivered-price schedule or, equivalently, the more discriminatory are delivered prices [Figure 10.2(c)]. Thus, increased competition leads to an *increase* in the degree of price discrimination. These results are illustrated in Figure 10.3: Compare, for example, delivered prices for $p' = 1.0$ with delivered prices for $p' = 0.8$.

Now consider the case in which $p' < 0.6$. In the absence of the nonnegativity constraint on S [equation (10.6)], the solution (10.7)–(10.9) will be as illustrated by the dotted lines in Figure 10.2. This implies that the slope of the delivered-price schedule is negative, and as shown by the dashed line for $p' = 0.2$ in Figure 10.3, the firm *will never charge less than the limit price*. Because the limit price is a delivered-price *ceiling*, such

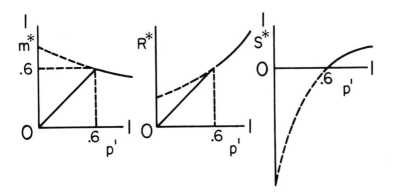

Figure 10.2. Relationships among m^*, R^*, S^*, and p'.

a solution is not permissible and is eliminated by constraining S to be nonnegative.

When this constraint is introduced, it emerges that there is a degree of competition beyond which a firm subject to a limit-price constraint is driven to a uniform pricing strategy. In such competitive situations, the optimal pricing-policy and market-area decisions for the firm are

$$m^* = p' \quad (0 \leq p' \leq 0.6) \tag{10.10}$$

$$R^* = p' \quad (0 \leq p' \leq 0.6) \tag{10.11}$$

$$S^* = 0 \quad (0 \leq p' \leq 0.6) \tag{10.12}$$

as indicated in Figures 10.2 and 10.3.

Equations (10.7)–(10.12) imply that the greater the degree of competition (the lower is the limit price p'), the greater is the degree of price discrimination adopted by the competitive firm, and the more likely it is that the firm will be driven to a uniform pricing policy.

Use of p' as a measure of the degree of competition is legitimate given the normalization assumed by Norman [see equations (10.2) and (10.3)]. In the nonnormalized case, the degree of competition is more properly an amalgam of the limit price, the maximum price consumers are willing to pay, and marginal production costs. Norman then finds

$$p' \leq 0.6a/b + 0.4c \Rightarrow S^* = 0 \tag{10.13}$$

Uniform pricing is more likely the lower is the limit price with respect to the maximum price and/or marginal-production costs. Again, therefore, *increased price discrimination leading to uniform pricing is more likely the greater the degree of competition.*

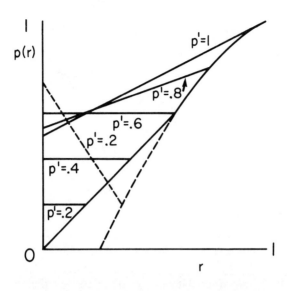

Figure 10.3. Delivered price in Greenhut-Ohta competition.

It can further be shown that the pricing policies (10.7)–(10.9) and (10.10)–(10.12) are more profitable than those discussed by Greenhut and Ohta, a point that should be intuitively clear, because, as noted earlier, Norman's formulation does not preclude the Greenhut-Ohta pricing assumption as a possible solution. In addition, a firm facing Greenhut-Ohta competition will always have the incentive to switch from Greenhut-Ohta pricing to the discriminatory pricing policy (10.7)–(10.12), because by doing so it can undercut the limit price at the Greenhut-Ohta market boundary (R_{n1}, R_{d1}, etc., in Figure 10.1) and thus increase its market area and profit at any level of Greenhut-Ohta competition.

Although the Norman model considerably extends the range of feasible pricing policies in the presence of a limit-price constraint, the interested reader may still feel that this model contains a somewhat arbitrary constraint through the assumed linearity of the DPS embodied in equation (10.1). Such assumed linearity does, in fact, appear to have some justification in observed behavior – as will emerge from the discussion in Chapter 14. Indeed, there is reason for believing that such a pricing policy is easier to administer than the more complex policies that would otherwise emerge. Moreover, empirical analysis of spatial pricing in the United States, West Germany, and Japan (detailed in Chapter 14) indicates that linearity may well appear less discriminatory in the eyes of the regulatory authorities, especially those in the United States.

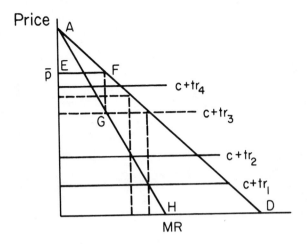

Figure 10.4. The price-constrained model.

Nevertheless, the effects of relaxing the linear restricting equation (10.1) should be considered (Norman 1981c). The profit-maximizing pricing policy then becomes a mixed one. Again, the assumption of constant marginal costs is particularly important to the analysis. With this assumption, aggregate profit is maximized by maximizing profit at each selling point.[4] Solution to the price-constrained model is then as illustrated in Figure 10.4.

Given individual demand AD, marginal revenue is AH. The introduction of a ceiling-price constraint $\bar{p}$ changes the demand curve to EFD, and the marginal-revenue curve to the broken curve $EFGH$. For markets "proximate" to the producer, the ceiling-price constraint is ineffective (e.g., markets r_1 and r_2 in Figure 10.4). The firm adopts the "standard" discriminatory pricing policy discussed in Chapter 6.

For more distant markets, however, the ceiling-price constraint is effective (e.g., market r_4). In such markets, marginal cost cuts marginal revenue in the broken section FG, and price $\bar{p}$ is the profit-maximizing price.

Thus, at those selling points where the limit-price constraint is ineffective, markets within distance r_3, the firm prices as a discriminating monopolist. With a linear demand function, this leads to 50 percent freight absorption. At all other selling points the firm will charge just the limit price and will set its market-area boundary at the point where price equals marginal cost of production and transportation. This is illustrated in Figure 10.5: The DPS is piecewise linear.[5]

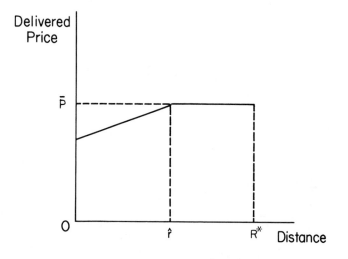

Figure 10.5. Optimal DPS with a limit-price constraint.

The extended Norman solution remains consistent with the general principle that in the absence of institutional constraints, increased competition in an imperfectly competitive economy can be expected to increase the degree of price discrimination. It can be seen from Figures 10.4 and 10.5 that the lower is the limit-price constraint, the greater will be the proportion of selling points in which the firm adopts a uniform delivered price.

10.2   Endogenous transport rates and choice of price policies

The analysis in this and previous chapters indicates that an imperfect competitor will choose to price-discriminate in order to maximize profits if there exist no institutional constraints on pricing behavior. This analysis has been based, however, on the assumption that the transport rate is fixed or exogenously determined across the alternative price policies. If the choice of price policies and the selection of transporters are treated as a simultaneous decision, there is a possibility that firms may adopt the f.o.b. mill-price policy rather than the discriminatory price policy (Gronberg and Meyer 1981b).

We can investigate this possibility using the model specified in previous chapters, with the exception that the transport rate is allowed to vary depending on which individual (firm, consumer, or common carrier) is providing the transport services (Gronberg and Meyer 1981b). For any given transport rate t, profits under f.o.b. mill, uniform, and discriminatory pricing policies are just those identified in Chapter 7. For convenience, these profit equations are repeated here:

$$\Pi_f = \frac{DR}{2b}\left((a-c)^2 - (a-c)tR + \frac{t^2R^2}{4}\right) - F \qquad (10.14a)$$

$$\Pi_u = \frac{DR}{2b}\left((a-c)^2 - (a-c)tR + \frac{t^2R^2}{4}\right) - F \qquad (10.14b)$$

$$\Pi_d = \frac{DR}{2b}\left((a-c)^2 - (a-c)tR + \frac{t^2R^2}{3}\right) - F \qquad (10.14c)$$

Denote the minimum transport rate under f.o.b. mill, uniform, and discriminatory pricing as t_f, t_u, and t_d, respectively. As was noted earlier, the transporting of the product from the firm to the customer must be carried out by one of three parties: the firm itself, the customers themselves, or third-party common carriers, such as trucks or railroads. Hence, three transport rates are available. Denote these respectively as t_1, t_2, and t_3 for firms, the customers, and the third parties. As noted by Gronberg and Meyer (1981b) and Beckmann (1976), if the customer provides the transportation of the product under discriminatory or uniform-delivered-price policies and receives full credit for the transport costs the seller would have paid, distant customers may be able to buy the product at a lower price and resell it to less distant customers. Alternatively, proximate buyers may be able to resell to distant buyers at lower delivered prices than the seller would charge. These arbitrage possibilities preclude the use of t_2 under discriminatory and uniform-delivered-price policies. Assuming the firm chooses the transporter so as to maximize profits, the choice available to the firm under each price policy becomes

$$t_f = \min(t_1, t_2, t_3) \qquad (10.15a)$$

$$t_u = \min(t_1, t_3) \qquad (10.15b)$$

$$t_d = \min(t_1, t_3) \qquad (10.15c)$$

If either the firm or the third-party transporter can deliver the product at a lower rate than the customers themselves (i.e., $t_1 = t_3 < t_2$), then the price policy chosen will not be affected by the existing transport rate. In this case the firm simply chooses the discriminatory price policy so as to maximize profits. If, on the other hand, the customers have a transport advantage[6] (i.e., $t_2 < t_1 \le t_3$ or $t_2 < t_3 \le t_1$), the choice between f.o.b. mill pricing and discriminatory pricing is slightly more complicated. If the seller elects to price-discriminate or to adopt a fully uniform delivered price, his firm is not maximizing profits, because in effect it is utilizing the less efficient transporter, t_1 or t_3. If the firm adopts the mill-price policy to achieve cost minimization in transportation, it also is not profit-maximizing, because the mill-price policy yields less profit for a given market area.

A transport-cost inefficiency range can be derived in which a firm can adopt a discriminatory price policy in combination with utilization of a less efficient transporter while still making more profit than (or at least as much profit as it would) under the mill-price policy. More precisely, a maximum transportation inefficiency value in terms of the ratio t_d/t_f is derived for each given market-area size. For values greater than that ratio, less profit will result under discriminatory policies. For values less than the ratio, the discriminatory price policy can make more profits.

The maximum value of the ratio t_d/t_f can be obtained by first substituting equations (10.15) into (10.14) and then subtracting the total profits for a given market area under mill pricing from those under discriminatory pricing; that is, (10.14c) minus (10.14a) yields

$$\Pi_d - \Pi_f = \frac{DR}{2b}\left(\frac{t_d^2 R^2}{3} - \frac{t_f^2 R^2}{4} - (a-c)t_d R + (a-c)t_f R\right)$$

$$= \frac{DR}{24b}[(4t_d^2 - 3t_f^2)R^2 - 12(a-c)(t_d - t_f)R] \qquad (10.16)$$

The sign of (10.16) depends on the sign of the bracketed term. Clearly, if $t_d = t_f$ (i.e., there is no transport-cost difference between the various carriers), discriminatory pricing is more profitable: $\Pi_d - \Pi_f > 0$. If, however, $t_d > t_f$, the first term of (10.16) is positive, but the second term is negative.[7] There is, therefore, the possibility that (10.16) is negative (i.e., that discriminatory pricing is less profitable than f.o.b. mill pricing).

Equation (10.16) is nonnegative if and only if

$$(4t_d^2 - 3t_f^2)R - 12(a-c)(t_d - t_f) \geq 0 \qquad (10.17)$$

As can be seen, the range of values of the ratio t_d/t_f for which (10.17) is satisfied is dependent on the market radius R. Table 10.1 gives the maximum value of t_d/t_f for various values of R.

The discussion in Mathematical Appendix I to Chapter 7 indicates that a spatial monopolist's market radius $R_f = 2(a-c)/3t_f$ under the f.o.b. mill-pricing policy, and $R_d = (a-c)/t_d$ under the discriminatory pricing policy. Because a spatial competitor can be assumed never to sell to these distances, the relevant market radius for comparison is $R \leq 2(a-c)/3t_f$. Table 10.1 then indicates that if a spatial competitor's market area is fixed at $(a-c)/3t_f$, the transport rate t_d under discriminatory pricing can be as large as $1.036t_f$ (i.e., 3.6% greater than t_f), and the firm will still

Table 10.1. *Maximum* t_d/t_f *for alternative*
values of R

Market area, R	Maximum value of t_d/t_f
$\dfrac{1}{3}\dfrac{(a-c)}{t_f}$	1.036
$\dfrac{2}{3}\dfrac{(a-c)}{t_f}$	1.104
$\dfrac{(a-c)}{t_d}$	1.183

price-discriminate. If the market radius is extended to the maximum relevant radius $R = 2(a-c)/3t_f$, Table 10.1 indicates that the transport rate t_d under discriminatory pricing can be $1.104t_f$ (i.e., 10.4% greater than t_f), and the firm will still price-discriminate. In other words, the greater the competitive firm's market radius, the higher the transport inefficiency that will sustain price discrimination.

Gronberg and Meyer also consider the case in which the firm is a spatial monopolist free to choose its market area. In this case the relevant market areas are those noted earlier: $R_f = 2(a-c)/3t_f$ and $R_d = (a-c)/t_d$. Evaluating the profit expressions at these values of R indicates that the spatial monopolist will choose to price-discriminate so long as $t_d/t_f \leq$ 1.125. That is, in a monopoly market the transport inefficiency could be as large as 12.5 percent and still lead to discriminatory pricing: A spatial monopolist is more likely to price-discriminate than a spatial competitor.

This analysis can be used to say something about the markets in which spatial price discrimination is more likely. It was noted earlier that many household items are purchased on multipurpose shopping trips. In such circumstances the retailer is likely to be a much more inefficient transporter than the consumer, and no price discrimination will be applied.

On the other hand, with bulkier goods such as furniture, refrigerators, freezers, and so forth, the customer is more likely to be at a disadvantage; retailers typically will have their own transportation services or will contract outside carriers for such items and will charge a delivery cost to the customer. Price discrimination is to be expected, in that the delivery cost need not reflect the full cost of delivery.

At the wholesale level, a mixed picture emerges. In many cases the manufacturer provides transportation to the major retail outlets or distribution depots, whereas in others the retailer will collect the goods from the factory. The choice between collection and delivery presumably reflects the relative efficiencies of the two sets of carriers. It is to be expected in this regard that when sellers are small oligopolistic firms, for example, that specialize strictly in one product or a narrow range of products and when their customers are vertically integrated firms that have efficient self-owned carriers, the selling firm will be less likely to price-discriminate than otherwise. Several examples of this type of relationship can be identified. For example, in the United Kingdom, major retail outlets such as Marks & Spencer license to local producers the production of all the goods they sell. M&S provides transportation and centralized warehousing, collecting the goods from the various producers. At the wholesale stage, therefore, the pricing policy is effectively the f.o.b. policy, whereas at the retail stage, M&S does apply some degree of price discrimination across its various department stores.

Heavy manufactured goods and intermediate products (such as steel, cement, or coal) require specialist transport services, and it is to be expected that the manufacturer will best be able to provide these services – it will be better placed to gain economies of scale in transportation, for example, by being able to secure more efficient utilization of specialized transportation equipment. It is of interest in this respect that analysis by Hwang (1979) with respect to coal pricing in the United States and analysis by the Price Commission (1978d) with respect to cement prices in the United Kingdom indicate the application of extensive spatial price discrimination by manufacturers in these industries. The steel industry has long been characterized by a basing-point (Pittsburgh-plus) pricing system, which is one specialized form of discriminatory pricing.

10.3   Conclusions

If competition is such as to impose a maximum-price constraint on the firm (Greenhut-Ohta competition), the effect on pricing policy will depend on the pricing policies available to the firm:

1. If the firm is constrained to choose between f.o.b. mill pricing and the discriminatory pricing policy which is such that marginal revenue equals marginal cost at each selling location, competitive entry ultimately leads to a switching of a firm's price policies from discriminatory pricing to nondiscriminatory pricing when fixed costs are sufficiently low. Under this assumption, discriminatory pricing provides less profit for very small market areas than does f.o.b. mill pricing.

2. If the firm is free to choose either a linear DPS or a completely unconstrained DPS, as proposed by Norman, increased compe-

tition, implying a lower limit price, will lead to an increased degree of price discrimination and, for "strong" competitive forces, to uniform pricing.

If the selection of price policies and choice of transporters are treated as a simultaneous decision, as proposed by Gronberg and Meyer, optimal pricing policy will depend on relative transport costs:

3. The discriminatory price policy may not be the optimal price policy. To utilize the least-cost method of transport or, more generally, of product differentiation, a firm may be forced to adopt a nondiscriminatory policy. This will be more likely the smaller is the competitive radius.

4. A monopolist is more likely to price-discriminate than a competitor if the firm is allowed to choose the mode of transport (i.e., the mode of product differentiation).

International and intranational pricing with a general cost function: an introduction to optimal-control theory

It was noted in previous chapters that if marginal-production costs are constant, the discriminatory pricing policy that maximizes total profit is just that which maximizes profit at each selling location. What happens when this assumption is relaxed?

Consider the simple example illustrated in Figure 11.1, in which marginal-production costs (MC) are assumed to be monotonic increasing. If attention is confined solely to market A [Figure 11.1(a)], profit is maximized in the usual manner with price P_A and quantity Q_A. Now add a second market B [Figure 11.1(b)] in which demand is to be satisfied by shipment from A, with transport cost per unit shipped of t_{AB}.

Because production in market A is already Q_A, the marginal cost of supplying market B with an additional quantity q is

$$MC_B = MC(Q_A + q) + t_{AB} \qquad (11.1)$$

In other words, it is derived by adding transport cost to that portion of the marginal-cost curve in Figure 11.1(a) *to the right of C*. With this marginal-cost curve, the profit-maximizing supply to market B is Q_B at price P_B.

But now consider market A. Total output has been increased to $Q_A + Q_B$; thus, marginal cost in market A has been increased and exceeds marginal revenue in A by the amount CD. If market B is to be supplied, it will be necessary in this example to reduce output in market A from that which would apply in isolation. Put another way, with variable marginal-production costs, the profit-maximizing price/quantity conditions in any one market are no longer independent of price/quantity decisions in other markets.

11.1 Optimal-control theory: an overview

The problem posed earlier has a structure that has much in common with structures to which optimal-control-theory techniques are applied. It is not appropriate in a book of this type to present an extensive discussion of these techniques, far less prove the propositions to which they give

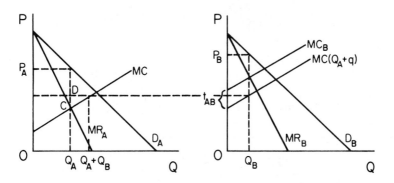

Figure 11.1. Pricing with variable marginal costs.

rise.[1] A brief description of the structure and some of the theory of control problems may, however, prove useful as an introduction to their use in the analysis of pricing in imperfectly competitive markets.

Control problems arise in a number of situations, generally where optimization takes place over time. Thus, for example, we may wish to find the time path of consumption that will maximize the discounted value of utility from future consumption in a situation in which future production and thus income are determined by current saving (forgone consumption).[2] Alternatively, a producer may wish to choose a price policy $p(t)$ over a finite planning horizon $0 \leq t \leq T$ to maximize profit in conditions in which demand at any time t is a function of the current price $p(t)$ and *cumulative* sales $[Q(t)]$ up to time t.[3]

In both cases the decisionmaker has to choose values for a *control variable* – in the pricing example, the price policy or trajectory, $p(t)$ – to maximize an objective function in conditions under which the control variable influences the rate of change of a *state variable* – in the pricing-policy example, cumulative sales $Q(t)$. More generally, the optimal-control problem takes the form[4]

$$\max_{u(t)} \int_0^T f_0(x(t), u(t), t) \, dt \tag{11.2}$$

subject to

$$\left. \begin{array}{l} \dot{x}_i(t) = f_i(x(t), u(t), t) \\ x_i(0) = x_i^0 \end{array} \right\} \quad (i = 1, 2, \ldots, n) \qquad \begin{array}{l} (11.3a) \\ (11.3b) \end{array}$$

Equation (11.2) is the objective function. The control variables are given by the time-dependent vector $u(t) = [u_1(t), u_2(t), \ldots, u_n(t)]$, and the state variables are given by the time-dependent vector $x(t) = [x_1(t), x_2(t), ..., x_n(t)]$. Equations (11.3a) are differential equations that describe the dependence of the state variables on the control variables.

In order to solve the foregoing problem, define a vector of *auxiliary variables* $\lambda(t) = [\lambda_0(t), \lambda_1(t), ..., \lambda_n(t)]$ and the *Hamiltonian function*[5]

$$H[x(t), u(t), t, \lambda(t)] = \sum_{i=0}^{n} \lambda_i(t) f_i(x(t), u(t), t) \qquad (11.4)$$

Necessary conditions for a maximum are then[6]

$$\left. \begin{array}{l} \dot{x}_i = \partial H_i/\partial \lambda_i \\[2mm] \dot{\lambda}_i = -\partial H_i/\partial x_i \end{array} \right\} \quad (i = 0, 1, ..., n) \qquad \begin{array}{l} (11.5) \\[4mm] (11.6) \end{array}$$

$$\partial H/\partial u(t) = 0 \qquad (11.7)$$

In addition, there are *transversality* conditions to be satisfied by the auxiliary variables. These vary depending on the precise structure of the system. In the case specified earlier, the appropriate transversality condition on $\lambda_0(t)$ is

$$\lambda_0(t) = \text{constant} \geq 0 \text{ for all } t \quad (0 \leq t \leq T) \qquad (11.8)$$

while the $\lambda_i(T)$ $(i = 1, 2, ..., n)$ are left unspecified because there are no constraints on the end points of the $x_i(T)$ $(i = 1, 2, ..., n)$.[7]

Finally, a distinction has to be drawn between the cases in which the time horizon is fixed and those in which it is variable. If the time horizon is fixed, the necessary conditions are (11.5)–(11.8). In contrast, if the time horizon is variable, there is an additional degree of freedom (the time horizon) and an extra condition

$$H[x(T), u(T), T, \lambda(T)] = 0 \qquad (11.9)$$

Can any intuitive meaning be given to the conditions for optimization[8] as specified in equations (11.5)–(11.7) and (11.9)? There is, in fact, a very close similarity between these conditions and those that apply in static constrained optimization. Equations (11.5) are just a restatement of the differential equations (11.3a) relating state and control variables, whereas equations (11.7) require that the Hamiltonian be maximized (or minimized) with respect to the control variable. As was noted earlier, there is strong affinity between auxiliary variables and Lagrange multipliers. In nonlinear programming problems to which Lagrangian methods are applied, the Lagrange multiplier on a particular constraint can be interpreted as the marginal valuation of that constraint. In a similar fashion, the auxiliary variable in optimal-control theory is the marginal valuation of the appropriate state variable.

Finally, consider equation (11.9). Given the interpretation of the auxiliary variables, the Hamiltonian can be interpreted as the rate at which the objective function is changing at any time t. When the final time T is open and to be specified as part of the optimization problem, equation (11.9) states that T should be chosen such that the objective function has reached a stationary point at time $t = T$.

11.2 An application: spatial pricing with nonlinear marginal costs

As was noted earlier, optimal-control problems usually relate to time, but the optimal-control theoretical approach can be applied in a wide diversity of situations. In particular, it can be applied in the spatial context of the example discussed at the beginning of this chapter. Consider a situation in which a firm is selling over a market area $[0, R]$, where R may or may not be specified a priori. The objective of the firm is to choose a delivered-price schedule (or trajectory) $p(r)$ to maximize profit, where demand at location r is given by the inverse demand function $q[p(r)]$, transport costs per unit transported to r are $t(r)$, and production cost $C[Q(R)]$ is a function of aggregate output sold in the market area. The production-cost function is assumed not to exhibit constant marginal cost.

In the control theoretical framework, the objective function is total profit, the control variable is the delivered-price schedule $p(r)$, and the state variable is total output $Q(r)$ sold over the market interval $[0, r]$. Total output in this interval is given by

$$Q(r) = \int_0^r q(p(\rho))\, d\rho \qquad (11.10)$$

and the rate of change of total output is given by the differential equation

$$\frac{dQ(r)}{dr} \equiv \dot{Q}(r) = q(p(r)) \qquad (11.11)$$

relating state and control variables. [Recall equations (11.3a), and note that $\dot{f}$ is now defined for any variable f as df/dr.]

The pricing problem is

$$\max \int_0^R q(p(r))\{p(r) - t(r)\}\, dr - C(Q(R)) \qquad (11.11a)$$

subject to

$$\dot{Q}(r) = q(p(r)) \qquad (11.12)$$

Introducing the auxiliary variable $\lambda(r)$, the Hamiltonian is

$$H(Q(r), p(r), r, \lambda(r)] = q(p(r))[p(r) - t(r)] + \lambda(r)q(p(r)) \qquad (11.13)$$

and the necessary conditions for profit maximization, with the appropriate changes of variables, are, from (11.5)–(11.7),

$$\dot{Q}(r) = q(p(r))$$ (11.14a)

$$\dot{\lambda} = -\partial H/\partial Q(r)$$ (11.14b)

H maximized with respect to $p(r) \Rightarrow \partial H/\partial p(r) = 0$ (11.14c)

Consider condition (11.14c). Differentiating (11.13) with respect to price $p(r)$ gives

$$q(p(r)) + q'(p(r))[p(r) - t(r) + \lambda(r)] = 0$$ (11.15)

or, on rearrangement,[9]

$$p(r)\left[1 - \frac{1}{\epsilon(r)}\right] = t(r) - \lambda(r)$$ (11.16)

where $\epsilon(r)$ is price elasticity of demand at market location r and price $p(r)$.

Equation (11.16) closely resembles the fundamental pricing equation discussed in earlier chapters. The left side is marginal revenue derived from additional sales to any market point r, and the right side "looks like" marginal cost, given an appropriate definition of the auxiliary variable $\lambda(r)$.

It is here that the transversality condition is of particular importance. A problem that arises in specifying this condition for our particular problem is that the state variable does not appear in the Hamiltonian (recall that transversality conditions tend to be very problem-specific). Barnett (1975) provides an excellent discussion of the appropriate maximizing condition for a problem of this type. This maximizing condition is

$$\lambda(R) = \left.\frac{\partial(-C(Q(R)))}{\partial Q(r)}\right|_{r=R} = -C'(Q(R))$$ (11.14d)

where $C'[Q(R)] = \partial C(Q)/\partial Q(R)$ = marginal-production cost at output $Q(R)$. Because the Hamiltonian does not contain $Q(r)$ [see equation (11.13)], $\partial H/\partial Q(r) = 0$, and, from condition (11.14b), we have $\dot{\lambda}(r) = 0$ for all r. In other words, $\lambda(r)$ is constant for all r. It follows, therefore, that

$$\lambda(R) = -C'(Q(R)) = \lambda(r) \quad \text{for all } r$$ (11.17)

Substituting into (11.16) gives the optimal-price equation:

$$p(r)\left[1 - \frac{1}{\epsilon(r)}\right] = t(r) + C'(Q(R))$$ (11.18)

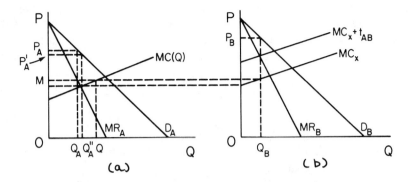

Figure 11.2. Profit maximization with increasing marginal cost.

There is a direct analogy between equation (11.18) and the optimal-pricing equation that applies under a constant-marginal-production cost assumption. It will be recalled that with constant marginal cost, the profit-maximizing price schedule is such that marginal revenue equals marginal cost (of production plus transportation) at each selling location. In the non-constant-cost case discussed in this chapter, the profit-maximizing pricing policy is again that marginal revenue should equal marginal cost of production plus transportation at each selling location, but now the appropriate marginal-production cost is that applicable to *total* output.

This analysis can be applied to the example considered at the beginning of this chapter. The discussion underlying equation (11.18) indicates that the profit-maximizing pricing strategy in that example is to set marginal revenue equal to marginal cost in both markets, where in market B marginal cost includes transport costs, and for both markets marginal-production cost is $MC(Q_A + Q_B)$. In order to illustrate the profit-maximizing price/quantity decision, use is made of a geometric device first suggested by Horst (1973).

Figure 11.2(a) illustrates market conditions in market A, assumed to be the sole producing point, and Figure 11.2(b) shows market conditions in market B. In isolation, output in A will be Q'_A, and price P'_A. Now consider an increase in output to Q. Marginal cost increases to M, and output for market A will be reduced to Q_A. We can also construct what Horst termed a "marginal cost of exporting" schedule, where exports emanate from market A and are sent to market B. At marginal cost M, for example, $Q_A Q = Q_B$ will be exported to market B. Experimenting with different marginal costs allows us to construct the marginal cost of exporting schedule MC_X: At any level of marginal cost, the amount exported to market B is given by the difference between $MC(Q)$ and MR_A in market A. Now add transport costs from A to B to generate the marginal cost (of exporting and transportation) for market B, $MC_X + t_{AB}$. Profit is maximized in market B by equating marginal revenue MR_B with marginal cost $MC_X + t_{AB}$. This gives total output Q in Figure 11.2, with Q_A supplied to market A and $Q_A Q = Q_B$ supplied to market B. Price in A is P_A, and in B is P_B.

Price in market A has risen and quantity fallen from those that applied in isolation. If, in contrast, marginal cost were decreasing, the addition of market B would lead to a reduction in price in market A and an increase in quantity supplied to that market.

One final point is worth noting in closing this section. It has been noted that equation (11.18) is appealingly similar to the profit-maximizing equation that applies with constant marginal costs. It follows from equation (11.18) that the marginal-production-cost function will affect the profit-maximizing mill price (P_A in our example), but the degree of price discrimination[10] is totally determined by the individual demand functions $q(p(r))$. In other words, the degree of price discrimination is independent of the precise form of the marginal-production-cost function.

11.3   Determination of the market boundary

The necessary conditions (11.5)–(11.8) fully define the solution to the optimal-control problem when the boundary point (time or radius) is specified a priori. Condition (11.9) is necessary, however, when the boundary point is to be determined as part of the solution.

Applying this equation to the optimal-pricing example gives

$$H[Q(R^*), p(R^*), R^*, \lambda(R^*)]$$
$$= q(p(R^*))[p(R^*) - t(R^*)] + \lambda(R^*)q(p(R^*)) = 0 \quad (11.19)$$

where R^* is the profit-maximizing market boundary. Substituting from (11.17) gives

$$q(p(R^*))[p(R^*) - t(R^*) - C'(Q(R^*))] = 0 \quad (11.20)$$

Equation (11.20) will be satisfied by a finite value of R^* only if the demand function is such that there is a well-defined maximum price that consumers are willing to pay for the product, that is, only if the demand function has an intersection with the price axis. Assume that this maximum price is $\hat{p}$. Then (11.20) indicates that the profit-maximizing market radius R^* is such that

$$q(p(R^*)) = 0; \quad p(R^*) = \hat{p} \quad (11.21)$$

It should be noted in passing that equation (11.21) implies that price equals marginal cost (of production and transportation) at R^*, because if $q[p(R^*)] = 0$, then $\epsilon(R^*) = \infty$, and from (11.18),

$$p(R^*) = t(R^*) + C'[Q(R^*)]$$

In other words, the bracketed term in equation (11.20) is also satisfied as an equality.

Further, it should be emphasized that the mill price, $p(0)$, is not independent of the market radius, a property that is in sharp contrast to the constant-marginal-cost case. This should be clear from the discussion of Figure 11.2, but it can easily be proved by the interested reader. Merely introduce a third, more distant, market to Figure 11.2. It will then be noted that price in market A (the mill price in our example) will further increase above P_A; it will also be noted, of course, that price in market B will exhibit a similar increase.[11]

11.4 F.o.b. mill and uniform pricing: a brief digression

The reader may be wondering if similar problems arise when the producer is constrained, or decides, to adopt an f.o.b. mill or uniform price. It is, in fact, very easy to show that optimal-control theoretical techniques are not necessary in such situations, even if marginal-production cost is non-constant.

Consider a producer, for example, constrained to an f.o.b. pricing scheme. With mill price m, his total profit over a market of radius R is

$$\Pi_f = \int_0^R \{q(m+t(r))(m+t(r)) - q(m+t(r))t(r)\}\,dr - C(Q(R))$$

$$= m \int_0^R q(m+t(r))\,dr - C(Q(R))$$

$$= mQ(R) - C(Q(R)) \tag{11.22}$$

Hence, the profit-maximizing mill price is obtained by the familiar rule that marginal cost equals marginal revenue, where now marginal revenue relates to the aggregate demand function. In other words, the principles applied in Chapter 2 in determining the optimal f.o.b. mill price carry through directly to the variable-marginal-cost case.[12]

11.5 An illustration: optimal behavior with different tariff rates

It has often been suggested that tariff barriers act in a manner similar to transport costs. The results of this chapter can be used to indicate the extent to which this is true[13] and to investigate the price/quantity effects of different tariff policies within a partial-equilibrium framework.

11.5.1   *Specific tariffs*

Two main types of tariffs can be applied: ad valorem tariffs levied as a percentage of the declared value of the goods imported, and specific tariffs levied as a given sum per unit of the goods imported. This section concentrates on specific tariffs, because, as will be seen later, these act in a very direct way "like" transport costs.

Assume that each selling location r is a different country, that location 0 is the source of a particular commodity,[14] and that the specific tariff applied in r is $\tau(r)$ per unit.

Net receipts from each selling location r are then

$$NR(r) = q(p(r))[p(r) - t(r) - \tau(r)] \tag{11.23}$$

and total profit with a specific tariff is

$$\Pi_S = \int_0^R q(p(r))[p(r) - t(r) - \tau(r)]\, dr - C(Q(R)) \tag{11.24}$$

Comparison with equation (11.11a) indicates that the two objective functions are identical with the transformation

$$T(r) = t(r) + \tau(r) \tag{11.25}$$

In other words, specific tariffs do indeed act identically as transport costs, and the analysis of Section 11.2 carries through directly. Specifically, assume that tastes and income levels are roughly identical across countries such that individual demand functions are identical across countries (an assumption that is more or less reasonable if attention is confined to the Western industrialized countries). Then the proportion of a specific tariff actually charged to consumers in a particular country will be determined by the "shape" of the individual demand functions. For example, if individual demand is linear, then 50 percent of any specific tariff will be charged to consumers.

Now consider the effects on home and foreign markets of a change in tariff rates. To keep the analysis simple, consider, as in Figure 11.2, a two-country model (U.S. and Foreign), where U.S. is assumed to be the exporting country. Assume that production in U.S. is characterized by increasing marginal costs. Further assume that initial transport costs to and specific tariffs in Foreign amount to $T(r)$. Now consider an increase in specific tariffs such that $T(r)$ increases to $T'(r)$. The effects of this change are illustrated in Figure 11.3.

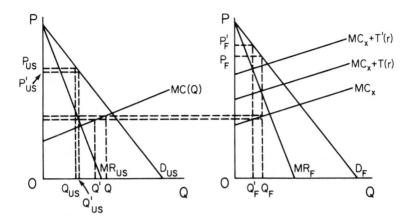

Figure 11.3. Effects of increases in specific tariffs: increasing marginal-production costs.

At the initial tariff level, price/quantity in U.S. and Foreign are respectively (P_{US}, Q_{US}) and (P_F, Q_F), where, as in Figure 11.2, $Q_F = Q - Q_{US}$ and $P_F = P_{US} + \frac{1}{2}T(r)$, because we have assumed linear demand functions. The curve MC_X is just that defined in Figure 11.2: the marginal production cost of exporting from U.S. to Foreign.

When tariffs are increased, price rises and quantity falls in Foreign to (P'_F, Q'_F), as is to be expected, while in U.S. there is an increase in local production and a consequent decrease in price. Total output, however, is reduced.

Now consider the outcome if marginal-production costs are decreasing as in Figure 11.4. An increase in specific tariff again leads to an increase in price and a decrease in quantity for imports to Foreign. For U.S., however, price increases to P'_{US} and quantity falls to Q'_{US} as a consequence of the increased tariff in Foreign, because U.S. producers are now less able to exploit economies of scale in production. In other words, the effects on U.S. of an increase in specific tariff barriers in Foreign are crucially dependent on production conditions in U.S. (It should be clear, but is left to the reader to show, that if marginal-production costs are constant, price/quantity decisions in U.S. are unaffected by changes in tariffs in Foreign.)

11.5.2 *Ad valorem tariffs*

Matters are not quite as straightforward if import markets apply ad valorem tariffs, because these apply to the *declared value* of imports rather

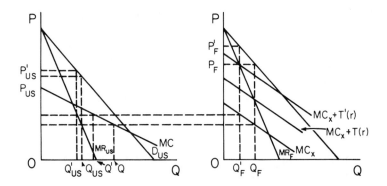

Figure 11.4. Effects of increases in specific tariffs: decreasing marginal-production costs.

than to the quantity imported. In order to analyze the effects of an ad valorem tariff, assume that the declared value of the product exported to location r is $p_d(r)$ and that the ad valorem tariff rate is $\tau(r)$. Then price in location r is

$$p(r) = p_d(r)(1 + \tau(r)) \tag{11.26}$$

and the tax payable by the exporter is

$$\text{tax} = \tau(r)\, p_d(r)\, q(p(r)) = \frac{\tau(r)}{1 + \tau(r)} p(r)\, q(p(r)) \tag{11.27}$$

Net revenue from location r is therefore

$$NR(r) = q(p(r))[p(r) - t(r)] - \frac{\tau(r)}{1 + \tau(r)} p(r)\, q(p(r))$$

$$= q(p(r)) \left[\frac{p(r)}{1 + \tau(r)} - t(r) \right] \tag{11.28}$$

and total profit with an ad valorem tariff is

$$\Pi_A = \int_0^R q(p(r)) \left[\frac{p(r)}{1 + \tau(r)} - t(r) \right] dr - C(Q(R)) \tag{11.29}$$

The ad valorem tariff is not acting identically as transport cost, but there is a strong connection between the two. Given the objective function (11.29), the Hamiltonian for the optimal-control problem is

$$H_A[Q(r), p(r), r, \lambda(r)] = q(p(r)) \left[\frac{p(r)}{1 + \tau(r)} - t(r) \right] + \lambda(r) q(p(r)) \tag{11.30}$$

Applying equations (11.7) and (11.17) gives the necessary condition for the profit-maximizing price

$$\frac{p(r)}{1+\tau(r)}\left[1-\frac{1}{\epsilon(r)}\right]=t(r)+C'(Q(R)) \qquad (11.31)$$

Or, on reorganization,

$$p(r)\left[1-\frac{1}{\epsilon(r)}\right]=(1+\tau(r))(t(r)+C'(Q(r))) \qquad (11.31a)$$

There is a strong similarity between equations (11.31a) and (11.18). The left side of (11.31a) is marginal revenue, and the right side is marginal cost of production and transportation increased by the amount of the ad valorem tariff rate. Profit is maximized by equating marginal revenue with this adjusted marginal cost.

The effect of an ad valorem tax is illustrated in Figure 11.5. Given (11.31a), the effect of an ad valorem is to shift *and rotate* the MC_X+t curve as shown. Not surprisingly, therefore, the ad valorem tariff can be expected to have different quantitative results than a specific tariff. The qualitative consequences of an increase in ad valorem tariffs are, however, as for specific tariffs.

To identify the effects on the declared value of imports of an increase in the ad valorem tariff rate, consider equation (11.31). This can be rewritten, from (11.26), as

$$p_d(r)\left[1-\frac{1}{\epsilon(p(r))}\right]=t(r)+C'(Q(R)) \qquad (11.31b)$$

where elasticity of demand is measured at the *delivered* price. Now assume an increase in the ad valorem tariff rate. If the declared value of imports $p_d(r)$ remains unaltered, the delivered price will increase. Assuming that the individual demand function is well-behaved, in that elasticity is an increasing function of delivered price,[15] the term in brackets on the left side of (11.31b) will increase, necessitating a reduction in the declared value of imports in order to maintain the equality in (11.31b). In other words, not all of an increase in the ad valorem tariff rate will be passed on to consumers as an increase in price. Some will be absorbed by the exporter and be exhibited as a reduction in the declared value of imports.

11.6 The ad valorem tariff and price discrimination

In order to consider the effect of an ad valorem tariff on the degree of price discrimination, we simplify matters by confining attention to the GGK class of demand functions:

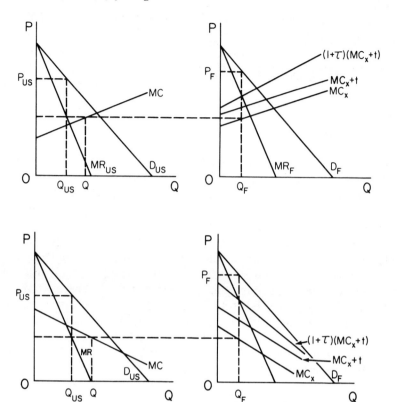

Figure 11.5. Effects of an ad valorem tariff.

$$p = a - \frac{bq^x}{x} \quad (x > -1; \ x \neq 0) \tag{11.32}$$

and assume a constant tariff rate $\tau(r) = \tau \ \forall r$. Elasticity of demand for the GGK class of demand functions is

$$\epsilon = \frac{p}{x(a-p)} \tag{11.33}$$

Substituting into (11.31a) and reorganizing gives

$$p(r) = \frac{ax}{1+x} + \frac{1+\tau}{1+x}(C'(Q(R)) + t(r)) \tag{11.34}$$

The higher the ad valorem tariff, the smaller the degree of price discrimination that will be employed by the producer if $x > 0$, and the more the producer will discriminate against distant markets for $x < 0$: Recall that the degree of price discrimination is given by

$$PD = 1 - \frac{1+\tau}{1+x} = \frac{x-\tau}{1+x} \tag{11.35}$$

A sharp contrast should be drawn between equation (11.34) and the equation that would apply in the absence of any tariff barriers. It is known from Chapter 6 that the optimal delivered-price schedule is defined by

$$p_D(r) = \frac{ax}{1+x} + \frac{1}{1+x}(C'(Q(R)) + t(r)) \quad (x > -1; \ x \neq 0) \tag{11.36}$$

The more convex the demand function (the lower the value of x), the greater is the slope of the delivered-price schedule, and the smaller is the degree of price discrimination.

Now compare equations (11.34) and (11.36). The ad valorem tariff, unlike the specific tariff, acts in large part *as if a change in convexity of demand has taken place*. Thus, if the underlying demand function is only weakly convex ($x > 0$ but $x < \tau$), the ad valorem tariff can act to reverse the direction of price discrimination.

This outcome has a number of important implications. The analysis has been couched mainly in terms of the price effects of tariffs. It applies equally, however, to local sales taxes such as those imposed in the United States or to the value-added taxes that are imposed by the various member states of the European Economic Community. The fundamental pricing equation (11.34) indicates that external evidence of f.o.b. pricing, which is taken by the regulatory authorities to be nondiscriminatory, may well disguise a situation in which there is extensive price discrimination.[16]

In addition, empirical work such as that by Hwang (1979) uses equation (11.36) as a basis for estimating the form of the demand function and, in particular, for estimating the convexity/concavity parameter x. These estimates need to be reevaluated in light of the foregoing discussion. More fundamentally, the analysis lends further support to the assertion by Phlips (1980) and others that adequate empirical analysis of pricing policies requires a richer theoretical background, particularly of discriminatory pricing, than has been available until now.

Why should ad valorem tariffs or taxes raise such issues, particularly because first thoughts would suggest that demand (taste) is a datum and any tax imposed by government is merely an added cost? The answer lies in the fundamental distinction drawn in imperfect competition between the *delivered* price and the *net* price received by the producer. These two sets of prices are related in a well-defined way, determined by cost conditions and the shape of the individual demand functions. Any tax that so impacts marginal cost as to alter its slope then appears as a demand-curve-twisting effect, in the present case a twist toward greater convexity. The ad valorem tax has this effect because its higher rates with higher prices lead to a marginal-cost equality with a much greater marginal revenue, and thus constitute a mapping to (or transform to) the lower elasticity associated with a more convex demand function. Assuming further that a low finite price limit applies in a given country where the demand happens to be relatively convex suggests the possibility that the ad valorem tax will cause the exporter to restrict the firm's market to his own country and to others that do not impose such a tax. The imposition of the tax, combined with (11.34), could yield a delivered price greater than the finite price limit in a country with significantly convex demands.

11.7   Competitive pricing: a brief digression

It has been assumed throughout the analysis that the producer is a monopolist. The pricing equations [particularly (11.34)] are so closely related to the no-tariff spatial pricing equations, however, that the analysis can be extended with little alteration to a competitive environment.

In particular, we can relax the somewhat restrictive assumption that there is no market overlap between competing producers located at different points in the market area and extend the analysis to the case discussed in some detail in Chapter 8.

Given two competitive locations d_2 distance units apart, with m_1 sellers at location 1 and m_2 sellers at location 2, the optimal-pricing equation with demand functions of the form given by equation (11.32) is from Chapter 8:

$$p_D(r) = \frac{ax}{m+x} + \frac{1}{m+x}\{m\bar{c} + m_1 Tr + m_2 T(d_2 - r)\} \qquad (11.37)$$

The analogy with equation (11.34) is direct. It follows that the introduction of a specific tax will appear simply as an increase in transport costs (T). An ad valorem tax, on the other hand, requires that the term $1/(m+x)$ be replaced by the term $(1+\tau)/(m+x)$. In other words, no matter whether we consider a monopolistic or competitive environment, ad valorem tariffs appear in effect as a change in convexity of demand.

11.8   Conclusions

If we relax the assumption that marginal-production costs are constant, then the producer who wishes to adopt a discriminatory pricing scheme will find that he can no longer apply a simple rule that "marginal cost equals marginal revenue in each market." The simple point is that with variable marginal costs, price/quantity decisions in any market r are intimately related to price/quantity decisions in all other markets. Optimal pricing requires a global view rather than a market-by-market approach.

The techniques of optimal-control theory have been developed to cope with just such problems. Although these techniques were initially developed to deal with optimization over time, they can be transferred in a very straightforward fashion to general problems in imperfect competition.

When this is done, the profit-maximizing conditions for an optimal-price policy with variable marginal costs are very appealing. The rule of "marginal cost equals marginal revenue at each location" reemerges, but now the appropriate marginal-production cost is that applying to *total* output over the entire market area. In addition, the degree of price discrimination is determined totally by the individual demand functions; it is independent of the form of the marginal-cost function.

This analysis has a number of potential applications. In particular, it can be applied in partial-equilibrium analysis of the effects on an exporting country of tariffs imposed by importers. Specific tariffs applied to the quantity exported act identically as transport costs. The exporter who is free to do so will therefore absorb tariff costs just as he will absorb freight costs, the proportion of the tariff absorbed being determined by the shape (convexity) of the individual demand functions.

Ad valorem tariffs apply to value exported and do not act totally identically as transport costs. Again, however, the basic spatial-pricing approach can be applied, and the optimal-pricing rule has much in common with that which would apply under specific tariffs. One thing that does emerge is that the degree of price discrimination is affected by the ad valorem tariff rate: Such a tariff is treated partly as an increased demand convexity.

Finally, for both types of tariffs, the effects on price/quantity decisions in the exporting country of an increase in the tariff rate are determined by the shape of the marginal-cost function. If marginal costs are increasing, price will fall and output increase in the exporting country, whereas if marginal costs are decreasing, price will rise and quantity fall.

This analysis demonstrates how underlying conditions that would make the dumping of goods abroad a natural result of consumer or business demands for goods can be converted into a reverse-dumping situation via imposition of an ad valorem tax. For nations obsessed with the goal of protecting home markets (e.g., versus Japanese inroads), imposing an ad valorem tax rather than a specific tax can do the job. Of course, from a "purist" standpoint, a related matter should be determined, namely, whether the comparative or possibly even absolute advantage in prices charged to foreign buyers is due to subsidy or the like in the exporting country or is the natural result of demand conditions and/or, as spatial price theory also emphasizes (Greenhut and Greenhut 1975), greater competition in a more distant market than the local market.

CHAPTER 12

Dynamic market strategy: further application of optimal-control theory

Although control-theory techniques can be applied, as in Chapter 11, to essentially static problems, they were developed principally to allow solution of dynamic systems. In this respect they are of particular relevance to many economic problems. All economic systems are subject to change. Consumers' tastes vary over time; cost conditions alter; a firm may face varying intensities of competition over time.

The traditional method of analyzing changing systems is one that has been used in many chapters of this book: (1) Identify a static equilibrium for a particular system, given known values for exogenous parameters of the system. (2) Change one parameter or a group of the exogenous parameters and identify the new equilibrium. Comparison of the two equilibria will indicate how the system reacts to changes in the various parameters.

This approach, termed *comparative statics*, is valid only if the parameters that are varied are truly exogenous (i.e., determined outside the particular economic system). If they are influenced by decisions made within the system, comparative-statics analysis will not work. In such cases a dynamic approach is necessary, and optimal-control techniques are required.

Many dynamic economic systems can be identified, two particular examples of which will be considered in this chapter. We know from previous chapters that the way in which a firm prices its products in a market is determined at least in part by the intensity of competition it faces in that market. It also seems reasonable to suggest that the prices chosen will themselves affect the intensity of competition. Consider, for example, a firm in an initially monopolistic position. If the firm changes the monopoly price, it will earn supernormal profit. This may attract other firms to the market, increasing total supply, lowering the price, and reducing the monopolist's profit. Would the monopolist not have been better advised to have chosen a lower initial price to control or deter entry by competitors, trading off short-run profits for higher long-run profits?

The second example recognizes explicitly that when the firm is placed in a dynamic framework, managers take account of the firm's ability to store part of its output in any given period. Storage costs will be incurred, of course, and with the aid of optimal-control theory we can investigate the extent to which they are absorbed by the producer. (Note the analogy here with price discrimination through freight absorption.)

12.1   Dynamic market strategy under threat of competitive entry[1]

Chapter 10 analyzed a firm's pricing policy in a situation in which it faced a known, fixed limit price in some or all of its markets. Two important issues were left unresolved by that analysis. First, what determines the limit price? Resolution of this issue will be postponed to a later section, where the appropriate limit price in any given market will be defined. For the time being, let us assume that such a price exists.

The second issue relates to what will happen if the firm does not price at the limit price. In particular, if a firm, which might be termed "the leading firm," prices above the limit price, presumably it will be subject to the threat of competitive entry to some of its markets. In choosing its pricing policy, the leading firm must balance the short-run profits that will accrue if it ignores the limit price against the long-run profits that will accrue if it chooses its prices to maintain a monopoly or near-monopoly market position.

12.1.1   A formal model[2]

In a dynamic context, the firm is interested in more than today's profit levels. Its objective is to maximize the present value of its future net income stream. Norman and Nichols (1982) have analyzed this dynamic problem using a model that employs many of the assumptions of previous chapters. Specifically, all consumers are assumed to be identical, and the leading firm's production costs are assumed to consist of a fixed cost plus a constant marginal cost.[3]

The leading firm is conceived to choose the pricing policy that will maximize the present value of its profits, as given by

$$\Pi = \int_R \int_0^T q(p(t,r),t)(p(t,r)-(c+\tau r))D(r)e^{-\delta t}\,dt\,dr - F \qquad (12.1)$$

where $q[p(t,r),t]$ is demand at price $p(t,r)$ at time t to each consumer at location r, $p(t,r)$ is the price charged at time t to consumers at location r, $D(r)$ is the density of consumers at location r, c is marginal-production costs, assumed to be constant, F is fixed production costs, τ is transport cost per unit product per unit distance, δ is the discount rate, T is the period over which the firm chooses to serve particular markets,[4] R is the market area supplied by the firm. The assumption of constant marginal-production costs enables each local market to be treated separately. The objective of the firm, therefore, reduces to

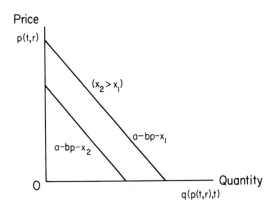

Figure 12.1. Effect on demand of competitors' sales.

$$\max_{p(t,r),T} \Pi(r) = \int_0^T q(p(t,r),t)(p(t,r)-(c+\tau r))D(r)e^{-\delta t}\,dt \qquad (12.2)$$

for each location r.

It is assumed that all consumers are identical. The analysis is further simplified by postulating linear individual demand functions

$$q(p(t,r),t) = a - bp(t,r) - x(t,r) \quad (a,b>0) \qquad (12.3)$$

where $x(t,r)$ is sales by competitors at time t at location r.

All firms are assumed to charge the same price in a particular market. The effect on the leading firm's demand of competitors' sales in market r is then depicted by Figure 12.1. The greater are competitors' sales, the lower is the effective demand allocable to the leading firm.

What causes rivals to enter a particular market? Mansfield (1962) suggested that entry of an "outside" or rival firm to a particular market will occur as a result of the profits the firm expects to make in that market. Following Gaskins (1971), potential entrants perceive the current product price as a proxy for future price and profit. It would then seem reasonable to suggest that the rate of entry of rival firms $[\dot{x}(t,r)]$ into market r is a monotonically nondecreasing function of the current product price in that market. For simplicity, this function is assumed to be linear:

$$\dot{x}(t,r) = k(r)(p(t,r)-\bar{p}(r)); \quad x(0,r)=0, \ \bar{p}(r) \geq c \qquad (12.4)$$

where $k(r)$ is the entry-response coefficient (taken as ≥ 0), $\bar{p}(r)$ is the limit price at r,[5] and $\dot{x}(t,r) = dx(t,r)/dt$.

How the limit price, $\bar{p}(r)$, and entry coefficient, $k(r)$, are determined will be explained in detail later, but a brief economic interpretation of them may be helpful at this point. If the leading firm prices at or below $\bar{p}(r)$ in market r, this will deter the entry of new competitive firms to market r. Indeed, at prices below $\bar{p}(r)$, existing competitive firms will be driven out of the market.[6] The difference between $\bar{p}(r)$ and the leading firm's marginal cost $(c + \tau r)$ in supplying market r can be taken as a measure of the long-run cost advantage enjoyed by the leading firm in market r. As a result, if all potential competitors in that market are indigenous, one possible measure of $\bar{p}(r)$ will be the long-run average costs of production of entrant firms indigenous to r.

The entry coefficient $k(r)$, on the other hand, can be viewed as a diffusion rate of the technology employed by the leading firm. It is smaller the easier it is for the leading firm to maintain the secrecy of its specialized knowledge from potential rivals in r.

This model is a problem in optimal-control theory in which the leading firm chooses a control variable $p(t, r)$ that maximizes (12.2), given (12.3), while being subject to (12.4), where $x(t, r)$ is the state variable. The optimal values of $p(t, r)$ and $x(t, r)$ are written, respectively, as $p^*(t, r)$ and $x^*(t, r)$.

12.1.2   *Analysis*

As is usual in control theory, solution of this dynamic pricing model requires that a number of cases be examined. It turns out that there are four options available to the leading firm in choosing the price to charge to consumers in a market r_i. In other words, the firm's potential markets can be partitioned into four separate sets. These four sets are denoted R_1, R_{2A}, R_{2B}, and R_3 and are illustrated in Figure 12.2: If $0 < r_i \le r_i'$, r_i is in R_1. If $r_i' < r_i \le r_i''$, r_i is in R_{2A}. If $r_i'' < r_i \le r_i'''$, r_i is in R_{2B}. If $r_i''' < r_i \le R$, r_i is in R_3.

Lying at the heart of the rules governing this overall market segmentation is what might be called the "no-entry-threat" monopoly pricing equation. Assume that the leading firm is, in fact, free of any threat of entry. Optimal pricing policy with the linear-demand function (12.3) is then the familiar discriminatory price schedule:

$$p^*(t, r) = a/2b + (c + \tau r)/2 \quad \forall t \tag{12.5}$$

This price schedule is illustrated as the line PP in Figure 12.2.

The first point to note is that the leading firm's potential market area covers all markets for which price $p^*(t, r)$ is greater than marginal cost of production and transportation. The market will extend to distance R in Figure 12.2. Now allow the possibility of competitive entry. Even with such entry threats there are some markets for which the (myopic) mo-

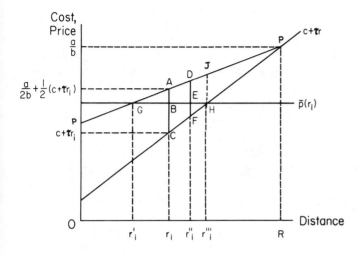

Figure 12.2. Market segmentation.

nopoly price (12.5) is less than the limit price and for which, therefore, price equation (12.5) is optimal. These are the markets R_1 in Figure 12.2, defined by the condition

$$\text{market set } R_1 \equiv \{r : a/2b + (c + \tau r)/2 \le \bar{p}(r)\} \tag{12.6}$$

The limit-price constaint is ineffective for markets in R_1. The long-run cost advantage of the leading firm vis-á-vis potential rivals in R_1 markets is so great that the leading firm can charge the myopic profit-maximizing price without inducing competitive entry.

Now consider markets not in the set R_1. Two possibilities arise, determined by the relationship between the limit price and marginal costs of production and transportation. Consider first those markets in which the limit price exceeds marginal cost of production and transportation: markets in $[r_i', r_i''']$ in Figure 12.2. Denote this set of markets by R_2. The set of markets R_2 is, in fact, the union of the sets R_{2A} and R_{2B}. It is defined by the relationship

$$\text{market set } R_2 \equiv \{r : \bar{p}(r) \ge c + \tau r \text{ and } r \notin R_1\} \tag{12.7}$$

The leading firm is able, by appropriate choice of pricing policy, to ensure its long-run survival as a supplier to all markets in the set R_2. But the leading firm must depart from the myopic profit-maximizing pricing policy (12.5). Failure to do so would result in the leading firm being driven out of markets in R_2, because for these markets, $p^*(t, r) > \bar{p}(r) : p^*(t, r)$ lies in the segment GJ in Figure 12.2.

The leading firm has a further choice to make in choosing prices for markets in R_2. On the one hand, the firm could choose to price exactly at the (entry-deterring) limit price, thus ensuring not only its long-run survival but also its exclusive monopoly position by preempting entry of any potential competitors. Alternatively, the firm could choose to price initially above the limit price, but subsequently allow price to fall to the limit price. In this case, the firm chooses to share its markets with entrants, but to control the number and size of rival firms it allows to enter any given market.

It is to be expected that the choice between these two pricing strategies will be determined by the balance between (1) the short-run profits forgone as a result of any deviation from pricing policy (12.5) (e.g., by pricing at the limit price) and (2) the long-run profits forgone as a result of competitive entry in response to a price greater than the limit price.

In purely technical, mathematical terms, the possibility of a boundary solution to the optimal-control problem must be considered. Norman and Nichols show that the leading firm will indeed adopt such a boundary solution (i.e., *always* price at the limit price), so that

$$p^*(t,r) = \bar{p}(r) \quad \forall t \tag{12.8}$$

in all markets r, which are such that

$$\frac{a/2b + (c + \tau r)/2 - \bar{p}(r)}{\bar{p}(r) - (c + \tau r)} \leq \frac{k(r)}{2b\delta} \tag{12.9}$$

To interpret (12.9), note that for a market r_i the numerator of the left-hand side (LHS) is the difference between the short-run profit-maximizing price and the limit price [see equation (12.5)], and the denominator measures the long-run profit per sales unit that the leading firm will make in r_i on each unit sold at the limit price. Thus, the numerator is a measure of the short-run profits forgone by pricing at the limit price, and the denominator is a measure of the long-run profits secured by limit pricing. The lower is this ratio (the lower are short-run profits relative to long-run profits), the more likely it is that a limit-pricing policy will be applied.

Equation (12.9) can be interpreted geometrically as follows. Consider the market r_i in Figure 12.2. The numerator of the LHS of (12.9) is the distance AB, and the denominator is the distance BC. The LHS of (12.9) is given for market r_i by the ratio AB/BC in Figure 12.2. Now consider the RHS of equation (12.9) for market r_i, which has the value $k(r_i)/2b\delta$. We can identify the distance r for which, *at limit price $\bar{p}(r_i)$ and technology diffusion rate $k(r_i)$*, equation (12.9) is satisfied as an equality. That such a distance exists and is unique for *any* value of the RHS is easy to see from Figure 12.2, because the LHS of (12.9) is zero for $r = r_i'$,

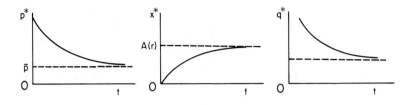

Figure 12.3. Time variation of price, quantity, and competitors' sales: market set R_{2B}.

infinity for $r = r_i'''$, and increases monotonically as r increases from r_i' to r_i'''. Denote this value of r as r_i''. Thus, in Figure 12.2, r_i'' is such that the ratio $DE/EF = k(r_i)/2b\delta$. If r_i lies to the left of r_i'' ($AB/BC < DE/EF$), inequality (12.9) is satisfied for market r_i, and the leading firm will apply the limit-pricing policy (12.8) in r_i. More generally, if all markets have identical limit prices and technology diffusion rates, the leading firm will apply the entry-deterring limit-pricing rule in all markets in the interval $(r_i', r_i'']$ in Figure 12.2. These markets form the set R_{2A} defined by the relation[7]

$$R_{2A} \equiv \left\{ r : \frac{a/2b + (c + \tau r)/2 - \bar{p}(r)}{\bar{p}(r) - (c + \tau r)} \leq \frac{k(r)}{2b\delta} \text{ and } r \notin R_1 \right\} \tag{12.10}$$

The definition of market set R_{2A} confirms the expectation that the leading firm is more likely to adopt a strict limit-pricing strategy the greater are the long-run profits secured by this policy compared with the short-run profits generated by the monopolist's pricing strategy (12.5).

Now consider the case in which (12.10) does not hold. The market set R_{2B} is defined (and characterized) by

$$R_{2B} \equiv \left\{ r : \frac{a/2b + (c + \tau r)/2 - \bar{p}(r)}{\bar{p}(r) - (c + \tau r)} > \frac{k(r)}{2b\delta} \text{ and } \bar{p}(r) > c + \tau r \right\} \tag{12.11}$$

If all markets are characterized by identical limit prices and technology diffusion rates, the market set R_{2B} is defined by the interval (r_i'', r_i''').

The limit-pricing policy (12.8) is feasible in markets in R_{2B} but is rejected by the leading firm. The long-run profits gained by limit pricing in these markets is much smaller than for markets in R_{2A}, whereas the short-run profits forgone are much greater. It is more profitable for the leading firm initially to price above the limit price in markets in R_{2B}, allowing entry and losing its monopoly position. Over time, however, price will be reduced to the limit price. Typical paths for $p^*(t, r)$, $q[p^*(t, r), t]$, and $x^*(t, r)$ are illustrated in Figure 12.3 for a market r in R_{2B}.

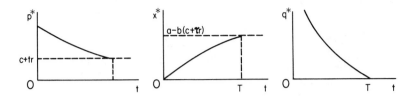

Figure 12.4. Time variation of price, quantity, and competitors' sales: market set R_3.

Equation (12.12) indicates that prices will become more discriminatory over time in markets in R_{2B}, tending in the limit to uniform pricing. For all markets in R_{2B}, the leading firm is willing to sacrifice short-run profits in order to *control* the entry of potential competitors and thus to secure long-run profits. At the same time, however, the long-run profits to be obtained by *total* exclusion of potential rivals are not enough in R_{2B} to offset the short-run profits lost by the limit-pricing policy necessary to effect the exclusion.

The final set of markets is that in which the consumers' reservation price (a/b) is greater than marginal cost of production and transportation $(c + \tau r)$, but in which the limit price is less than marginal cost: markets to the right of r_i''' in Figure 12.2:

$$\text{market set } R_3 \equiv \{r : \bar{p}(r) \le c + \tau r \le a/b\} \qquad (12.12)$$

The leading firm has no long-run cost advantage in such markets. Its only advantage is that of being first in the markets. Sales by the leading firm to markets in R_3 will eventually be driven to zero by competitive entry; all the firm can hope to do is control the speed of such entry to at least some extent by its choice of pricing policy. The nearer its price is to marginal cost in any R_3 market, the longer it can supply that market; the nearer its price is to the no-entry-threat price of (12.5), the more quickly it will be forced out of the market.[8]

Typical time paths for $p^*(t, r), q^*[p^*(t, r), t]$ and $x^*(t, r)$ are illustrated in Figure 12.4 for a market r in R_3. The leading firm chooses the temporal strategy for its pricing policy such that price falls to marginal cost just as the leading firm's sales are driven to zero by competitive entry.

12.1.3 *Determination of market segmentation: some empirical comments*

The four market sets identified earlier are defined by equations (12.6), (12.10), (12.11), and (12.12). Given knowledge of demand, cost, and entry

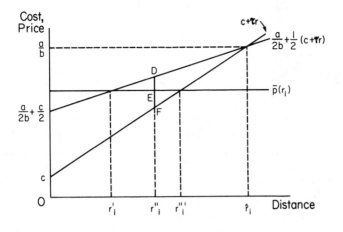

Figure 12.5. Bounds on market sets.

parameters for a particular market r_i, these definitions can be used to identify bounds on a particular market set within which the distance r_i must lie if the market r_i is to be allocated to that set. This is illustrated in Figure 12.5 [note that r_i'' is such that $k(r_i'')/2b\delta = DE/EF$]. Clearly, once the market set in which r_i exists is known, the pricing policy applied by the leading firm in r_i is also known.

Perhaps of greatest interest are the ways in which the parameter values influence whether or not r_i will belong to a market set in which the leading firm can ensure its long-run survival as an exporter: market sets R_1, R_{2A}, and R_{2B}. The bound r_i''' is determined solely by cost conditions and the limit price. *Ceteris paribus*, the lower are costs of production and transport, or the higher is the limit price below which there is no threat of entry, the more likely it is that the firm will be able to survive in the long run as an exporter to r_i.

Exclusive control is exercised over all markets in R_1 and R_{2A}, and for r_i to be in either of these two sets it is necessary that r_i be less than r_i''. The bound r_i'', and hence the probability that r_i will be in R_1 or R_{2A}, is greater (1) the greater the limit price with respect to the maximum price consumers are willing to pay, or with respect to the leading firm's marginal costs of production and transport, (2) the lower the discount rate, and (3) the greater the diffusion rate. Thus, the greater locational advantage of the leading firm over potential competitors in r_i, as measured by the relationship between the limit price and the demand or cost conditions in r_i, the more likely it is that the leading firm will be in position profitably to exclude potential competitors from r_i.

A lower discount rate enhances the value of long-run profits and thus will encourage the leading firm to price to exclude entry over a greater number of its markets.

Similarly, the greater the technology diffusion rate $k(r_i)$, *ceteris paribus,* the more quickly will profits in r_i be eroded by competitive entry. It again follows that it is more likely that the leading firm will then aim for exclusive control of r_i.

Because the way in which the leading firm segments its potential market area is strongly affected by variations in both the limit prices $\bar{p}(r)$ and diffusion rates $k(r)$ over markets in this area, further consideration should be paid to the determination of $\bar{p}(r)$ and $k(r)$ and the factors that cause them to vary between markets.

The limit price $\bar{p}(r)$ has been defined as the minimum price at which potential competitors will be willing to enter the market r. It was noted earlier that $\bar{p}(r)$ can be expected to be related to long-run average costs (LRAC) of production in market r. The precise relationship between $\bar{p}(r)$ and LRAC will be affected, however, by a number of factors.

First, the product in question may have a well-defined image or may rely on a specialist technology. New entrants are faced not only with the problem of competing in price with the leading firm but also with defining a new firm image that can compete with that of the leading firm. If the product relies on a specialist technology, on the other hand, new entrants may have to replicate that technology and comply with patent restrictions, as did Berkey Photo in its competition with Eastman Kodak.

The definition of a new brand image and the replication (and differentiation) of a specialist technology impose high initial setup costs on potential entrants. These become greater the stronger is the existing brand image (e.g., initial advertising expenditures, market research), the more complicated is the technology, and the more is either image or technology the derivative of (or integrated with) other products and technologies, especially those developed by the leading firm.

The appropriate limit price in a particular market is also affected by the quantity sold in that market. If potential competitors are purely local in scope, then for entry to be feasible to market r, price must be sufficiently high to cover LRAC in r. In Figure 12.6, entry into market r_i will be possible for an indigenous firm only if its price exceeds p_i', whereas in market r_j entry will be possible if price exceeds p_j'. The leading firm will be able to control entry into market r_i if marginal costs of production and transport $(c + \tau r_i)$ are less than p_i', but will find it rather difficult to control entry into market r_j. It is perfectly conceivable, therefore, that the leading firm can be a long-run exporter to market r_i, but not to market r_j, even if r_j is the geographically closer market.

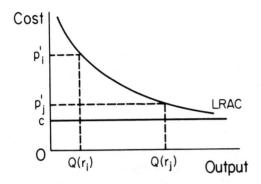

Figure 12.6. Effect of consumer density on limit price.

Now consider the situation in which potential competitors are themselves exporters to several markets. The leading firm will find it more difficult to maintain a long-run market presence as an exporter, because potential competitors will be affected more by marginal costs than by LRAC in deciding whether or not to serve these markets. In addition, this type of competitor is likely to be rather more sophisticated than are purely indigenous competitors and will be better able to overcome the image and technology barriers to entry that were discussed earlier. Control by the leading firm may still be possible, of course, particularly if the leading firm controls certain specialized inputs, whether raw materials, intermediate products, or specialized labor skills, but it is less likely.

Pricing policy by the leading firm will be determined not only by the size of a market but also by the extent to which it is sophisticated and developed. The more developed is a particular market, the more difficult it will be for the leading firm to define and maintain an exclusive brand image or technology. Thus, while the firm may be able to use exports as a long-run supply strategy to less developed markets, it will find it much more difficult to maintain this strategy in developed markets.

A third factor that will determine the appropriate limit price in particular markets is the extent to which the leading firm can influence, or is influenced by, government policy within those markets. Antidumping regulations, for example, will inhibit the extent to which the leading firm can use selective price cutting to limit competition in large but distant markets. The effects of tariff barriers should also be considered. When imposed on the leading firm, tariffs may well move a market from satisfying the conditions for it to be in R_1 or R_{2A}, say, to satisfying the conditions for it to be in R_{2B} or R_3. In either case, local production will be encouraged. Alternatively, if potential competitors are themselves exporters to the market in question, the leading firm may be able to restrict competition by influencing tariff and other trade policies within that market. Clearly, this will be more likely for markets within the same national jurisdiction as the leading firm (e.g., Japanese firms influencing trading conditions confronting firms that attempt to export to Japan). But it is also likely to occur in external markets in which the leading firm "has the ear" of the government.

Consider now the entry coefficient $k(r)$, already interpreted as a measure of the diffusion rate of the technology being exploited by the leading firm. It will be lower in a given market the more able is the leading firm to keep the technology private from its potential competitors in that market. In this sense, $k(r)$ is a measure of appropriability (Magee 1977, 1981); it is a measure of the power the leading firm has to appropriate the returns from investment in new technology and information.

The diffusion rate can be expected to be lower the more complicated the technology. It can also be expected to vary between markets. It will be greater in a particular market the greater is the degree to which potential competition comes from other exporting firms, and the more sophisticated and developed are the individuals and institutions in that market. Finally, the diffusion rate will be affected by judicial arrangements. It will be lower, for example, in markets over which the leading firm can more easily define and enforce its patent restrictions.

It can be seen that there is a commonality in the factors that influence the limit price $\bar{p}(r)$ and the diffusion rate $k(r)$. Markets can be expected to have high limit prices and low diffusion rates, and thus to be in R_1 or R_2, the smaller and less developed they are. Similarly, limit prices can be expected to be low and diffusion rates high in large, developed markets containing sophisticated potential competitors. In the latter markets, whereas the high diffusion rate may induce the leading firm to price to exclude entry and protect its technology (put the market in R_{2A}), the low limit price may well prevent this from being a feasible strategy; it may, in fact, put the market in R_3.

12.1.4 *Alternative supply modes: an application to the multinational enterprise*

The foregoing discussion assumes that the export mode is the sole method of supply considered by the leading firm. This is not a feasible long-run supply mode for markets in R_3 (and, of course, for markets not in R), and for markets in R_2 the export mode is feasible only if the leading firm modifies its pricing strategy so as to control the entry of potential competitors.

Other supply modes are, however, available to the firm. In particular, the firm may consider branch-plant operations, and if its markets are located in different countries, it may consider multinational production through foreign direct investment (FDI).

For FDI to be a feasible supply mode in market r_i, it is necessary that the leading firm be able to exploit a competitive advantage over its potential competitors in r_i (Buckley and Casson 1976; Dunning 1977). Such a competitive advantage will derive from just those factors discussed in Section 12.1.3: possession of a well-defined brand image, specialist technology, or control over specialized resources. Norman and Nichols consider a mixed strategy in which the firm initially exports to r_i and subsequently switches to FDI in r_i. It is to be expected (Buckley and Casson 1981) that exporting might precede FDI, but not vice versa. For any market r_i, the switch from exporting to FDI will be earlier (1) the more distant is r_i from the firm's home base, (2) the lower is the limit price and the higher the diffusion rate in r_i as compared with other markets, and thus (3) the larger and more developed is r_i and (4) the lower the distance and other costs of operating in the initially foreign environment of r_i.

The connections between this analysis and the received theory of the multinational enterprise (Buckley and Casson 1976; Dunning 1977; Vernon 1979) are clear. The analysis explains why FDI by U.S.-based firms could be expected to be directed initially at the developed economies of Western Europe and concentrated on R&D-intensive, consumer-based (rather than intermediate) products. It is in precisely those industries that U.S. firms are considered to have held the strongest competitive advantages. Exploitation of these advantages by exporting may have been feasible, and indeed preferable as an initial strategy. In the longer run, however, the difficulties involved in controlling the diffusion of technology and the loss of export markets, and the profit penalty of pricing policies necessary to exercise such control, might be expected to force U.S. firms to respond by locating production facilities abroad.

The analysis also indicates that as experience in operating abroad is gained, and as other markets grow and develop, FDI can be expected to be channeled to smaller, less developed economies. This extension of FDI is to be expected as competition in particular markets comes increasingly from other, third-country (e.g., Japanese) producers.

12.2   Pricing over time: intertemporal price discrimination

The second application of optimal-control theory to the analysis of pricing policy is taken from the inspired writing on this subject by Phlips (1983). In fact, the remainder of this chapter draws directly on the materials Professor Phlips used to introduce his readers to the subject.

A preliminary note is perhaps in order. Phlips first discussed different industry price patterns in free-enterprise economies, then set forth selected principles of spatial price-discrimination theory. He then converted these principles to the subject of pricing over time, and finally used optimal-control theory to propose how prices over time are affected by a firm's adoption of entry-deterring pricing.

We have, of course, already set forth optimal-control theory in the previous chapter and need not repeat its principles here; similarly, in the previous section of this chapter we discussed an entry-deterrent strategy. Moreover, because we have previously in this book *detailed* the principles of spatial price-discrimination theory, we need give only a selected (limited) review of it. Hence, though the pages that follow are precisely based on Professor Phlips's Chapters 5 and 6, our condensed analysis must (and will) fail to provide the full richness of Professor Phlips's development of this subject.

12.2.1 *Some background on industrial prices*

Phlips recalls for his readers the Oxford Inquiry of the 1930s, which *in substance* concluded that firms price on the basis of normal (average) costs over a (long) set of production periods. An upshot of this practice is that profit maximization is approximated over a long period of time rather than at each point in time. A related effect is that low interest rates are irrelevant to the holding of inventories, comparatively speaking, whereas high interest rates do impact inventory policy and hence prices.

Phlips goes on to note the pervasiveness of rather sticky prices among *storable goods* subject to seasonal price schedules. He illustrates by reference to the Belgian nitrogen fertilizer market, where the basically "sticky" fertilizer prices tend to "rise more when demand is nonexistent than when demand is high."[9] Phlips notes that this reflects the fact that prices are announced twelve months in advance of sale. In partial contrast, he refers to *exhaustible resource goods*, such as those that systematically have been priced upward over time:

> To say that these prices reflect "the laws of supply and demand" is an easy way out and, to my taste, a most unsatisfactory answer, especially since a large part of the oil reserves are controlled by a few producers who are capable of controlling the price of oil. We shall have to find out what kind of economic reasoning is followed by those who actually fix prices.[10]

Phlips next observes that new *durable goods* are typically high-priced when first introduced on the market, with prices then lowered over time (examples provided include television sets, hand calculators, video cassettes, new books). He refers to this as skimming pricing and further

Table 12.1. *Space–time analogies*

Space	Time
Geographical distance	Future date (t)
Point of delivery	Date of delivery
Point of production	Present moment ($t = 0$)
Frontiers of market area	Planning horizon (T)
Transport cost	Storage cost
Delivered price	Future price (Π_t)
Net mill price	Discounted price $[\Pi_t/(1+r)^t]$
Uniform delivered price	Constant future price

illustrates by reference to radios, bicycles, and electronic computers. During his discussion, he derives the conclusion that "after a producer has satisfied" the demands of the wealthy "at the highest possible price – irrespective of the cost of production – ...the producer starts wondering what a normal cost of production could look like and what a normal price could be." [11]

The last set of prices Phlips stresses relates to *nonstorable goods* whose sales values oscillate systematically *or* randomly, as the case may be. Thus, in service industries, variable demands cannot be regularly met by altering the sizes of inventories. In other industries, storage costs may be prohibitive because of bulk or other aspects of the good. He reminds the reader that telephone calls are cheaper at night, that hotels offer special weekend rates, and he refers to the extensive seasonal variations one finds in the utility rates that are charged.

Putting together all of these (different) goods leads Phlips to the problem of administered prices and the question why some of them "change every so often, whereas other prices remain constant for months, if not for years. ... Furthermore, when there is a change in price, the increase (or decrease) is often said to be smaller than with competitive prices. What could be the reason?" [12]

As the reader might anticipate, Phlips's answer (1982, p. 82) is rooted in the conclusion that the concepts and methods of spatial economics can be used to analyze industrial prices over time given the analogy between space and time shown in Table 12.1.

12.2.2 Pricing over time: the basic intertemporal price discrimination

In what follows, we employ Phlips's analysis, departing from him in minor technicalities that do not essentially alter his presentation. Note initially that the basic intertemporal price-discrimination rule requires equality between discounted marginal costs and revenues *throughout the planning period* and that simultaneous determination, over time, of prices, output, and sales (and therefore inventories) is indeed a special case of the theory of the discriminating firm.

Suppose manufacturing processes are completed each week, that output is available for sale that same week, and that managerial decisions are made on Mondays only. Let the planning horizon extend over n weeks, although attention is confined to weeks 1 and 2. Further assume that if production in week 1 is χ_1, and if it exceeds sales q_1 in that week, then χ_2 may fall short of q_2, with part of χ_1 having been retained in inventory s_1 for sale in week 2.

Figure 12.7 (Phlips's Figure 6.4, p. 91) assumes two demand curves in panel (a), the one of smaller magnitude applying to week 1. The cost curves c_1 and c_2 apply respectively to weeks 1 and 2. If the firm were to maximize profits instantaneously each week, production points A and B would determine respective outputs, prices, and sales. Clearly, however, intertemporal price discrimination and inventory investment offer greater profits, as illustrated in panel (b). Specifically, panel (b) is derived by horizontal addition of the demand curves and marginal-revenue curves (to give the curves for aggregate demand and marginal revenue) and by identifying the aggregate marginal-cost curve. Setting $AMR = AMC$ and reading back to panel (a) gives price p_1, sales q_1, and output χ_1 in week 1. Price is higher and sales lower then at point A, while the greater total output χ_1 facilitates stockpiling of inventory. These inventories allow the producer to undertake greater sales in week 2 at the lower price p_2 than production at point B would have allowed; related to this is the reduced output χ_2 that was made possible over the two-week planning period depicted in Figure 12.7.

The intertemporal discrimination rule that underscores Figure 12.7 requires discounted marginal revenues to equal discounted marginal costs. To explain this, recognize that moving production from period 2 to period 1 incurs costs of carrying (the interest cost of) and storing (the storage cost of) inventories. The curve c_2 in panel (a) technically involves a lower cost than the assumed (anticipated) cost of production in week 2, as the inventory cost of $\chi_1 > q_1$ is subtracted from the marginal cost conceived to be applicable to production in week 2. Correspondingly, the anticipated increase in selling price in week 2 that underlies Phlips's example, which in turn provides the producer's incentive to defer sales, requires a discounting for the uncertainty of demand that is part of real-life processes. That is to say, the second week's demand, as drawn in Figure 12.7, is already reduced (discounted) for demand uncertainty as well as discounted for time. (Recognize that any allowance for uncertainty

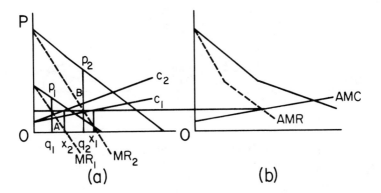

Figure 12.7. Intertemporal discrimination.

must increase with increases in the proposed volume of inventories.) Note finally that not all of the inventory accumulated at the end of week 1 was sold in week 2 (i.e., $|x_1 - q_1| > |x_2 - q_2|$), in accordance with the assumption of a planning horizon extending beyond week 2.

A few final statements are in order. The smoothing-out process of discriminatory pricing (higher in the low demand of week 1 and lower in the high demand of week 2) that would otherwise obtain reflects the price-discrimination pattern that stems from the assumption of linear demands (or, in general, of less convex demands). In its spatial form, the distant buyer is favored; in its temporal form, the second week is favored.

Phlips shows that the resulting intertemporal discrimination rule provides a theoretical underpinning for the practice of normal pricing. To appreciate *this* more readily, let $e^{-rt}\Pi(t)$ $[r = r(0)]$ stand for the present value of price (or net price at the mill). Take demand as $p = \beta - \alpha q$. As with the cost of space where gross demands may be identical but net demands differ, there is here a difference in today's demand and the next period's demand, *ceteris paribus*. (Of course, the analogy differs in the sense that time preference runs in one direction only – the proverbial bird in the hand being preferred to the problematic two in the future.) Again, assume that MC is an increasing function of the rate of production. Putting present price, demand, and cost together, Phlips goes on to assume that the producer aims to maximize the objective function:

$$\int_0^T e^{-rt}(\Pi q - c\chi)\, dt \qquad (12.13)$$

Solution requires appropriate choice of the rate of sales $q(t)$ and rate of production $\chi(t)$, where demand is given by the demand function $\Pi = f(q, t)$, and unit production costs by the function $c = \phi(\chi, t)$. Phlips

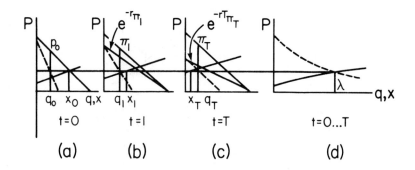

Figure 12.8. Normal-cost pricing.

subjects (12.13) to the constraint that the total quantity sold must equal the total quantity produced over T:

$$\int_0^T (x-q)\, dt = 0 \tag{12.14}$$

Because the difference between output and sales gives the rate of change of inventories, Phlips then rewrites the rate of change of inventories as

$$\int_0^T s'(t)\, dt = 0 \tag{12.15}$$

The solution to this classical variational problem is therefore

$$e^{-rt}\left(\Pi + q\frac{\partial \Pi}{\partial q}\right) = e^{-rt}\left(c + \chi\frac{\partial c}{\partial \chi}\right) = \lambda \tag{12.16}$$

"The rule says that *the discounted marginal revenue from sales* and *the discounted marginal cost of goods produced at all points of time must be equal and constant.*" [13]

The time-discounting process differs somewhat from the space (transport cost) effect on demands, because any discount applied to varying prices converges to a zero discount as the price approaches zero. Hence, the net demand curves drawn in Figure 12.8 differ from those applicable to space (cost) effects.

Further, Phlips ignores the nonnegativity constraint $s(t) \geq 0$ for ($0 \leq t \leq T$) in the equation system (12.13)–(12.16), as in Smithies's (1939) seminal presentation on the subject. Also note that the value of λ is above the MC-MR intersection of period 0 and below that of period T, *a clear reflection of normal pricing.* By further manipulations that are unnecessary for our purposes, Phlips goes on to demonstrate (and justify) the empirical interest-rate and sticky-price effects that were heralded in the Oxford Inquiry. In sum, according to Phlips, intertemporal price-discrimination theory explains normal cost pricing as found empirically in the Oxford Inquiry. As we shall see in Chapter 14, *spatial* price-discrimination theory, in its turn, is also well substantiated by recent empirical studies of pricing over variable distances.

12.3   Conclusions

The main aim of this chapter has been to extend the application of optimal-control-theory techniques to analysis of intertemporal as well as spatial pricing policy.

In the first example considered earlier it was noted that the way in which a firm prices in particular spatial markets and the way in which its pricing policy changes over time depend crucially on the conditions controlling the entry of potential rivals. Pricing policy in any particular market is critically affected by (1) the limit price in the market (the minimum price at which potential competitors are willing to enter the market) and (2) the technology diffusion rate in the market.

Because limit prices and diffusion rates are affected by both product- and market-specific characteristics, it is to be expected that they will vary between markets in a manner that will not be directly distance-related. It follows, therefore, that the factors that determine pricing policy in particular markets will be only partially related to distance between the market and the leading firm's production base. As a result, it is perfectly conceivable that the firm will be a long-run exporter to certain distant markets while being forced to accept partial or total erosion of its exports to other, more proximate markets.

This analysis is of direct relevance to the explanation of economic forces that might lead to a firm changing its mode of market supply. In particular, FDI will be more likely to be preferred to exporting to a market the lower the limit price and the higher the technology diffusion rate in the market.

Our second example is more directly concerned with intertemporal pricing patterns. There is a strong commonality between factors leading to spatial price discrimination and those leading to intertemporal price discrimination, a commonality that is highlighted in a recent analysis by Professor Phlips.

This analysis indicates that the profit-maximizing firm may well choose to discriminate in pricing over time, using inventories to effect such discrimination. Again, the empirical implications of this analysis are highlighted. Support is given to the idea that normal cost pricing may well be a rational response to changing market conditions. In addition, the notion of sticky prices that has previously been an empirical observation without any solid theoretical underpinnings is now shown to be based quite firmly on well-accepted profit-maximizing but time-dependent economic principles.

CHAPTER 13

Heterogeneous prices and heterogeneous goods

One implication of the simpler spatial pricing models is that delivered prices will generally exhibit well-ordered patterns over the space economy. This implication can be challenged on a number of grounds. First, the discussion in Chapter 8 of the Greenhut-Greenhut model indicates that varying competitive pressures might lead to "dip-bump" patterns of delivered prices. Second, the discussion in Chapter 12 of the Norman-Nichols model indicates that heterogeneous spatial prices may well arise as a consequence of heterogeneities in the abilities of potential entrants to enter particular spatial markets. Finally, if there are economic forces that lead to differences in individual (gross) demand functions between spatially separated markets, these forces will generate heterogeneous spatial prices.

In this chapter we examine each of these three challenges to "price homogeneity" by building on or extending some of the models presented in previous chapters. In doing so we confine our attention to showing why *homogeneous* goods might be priced in a *heterogeneous* fashion in the various markets in which they are sold. The assumed homogeneity of goods is quite deliberate. If we can demonstrate heterogeneity in pricing of this type of good, then we should not be surprised to find even more heterogeneity in pricing when we look at heterogeneous goods.

But what do we mean by price heterogeneity? Essentially, what this means is that not only will net prices not reflect the full costs of product differentiation (in the sense discussed in Chapter 6), but also there need be *no definable relationship* between the pattern of full prices charged to consumers and the costs of product differentiation (transport, storage, etc.) involved in supplying them. There may be discontinuities in the pattern of delivered prices, with prices low in some markets and high in others in ways that cannot be explained by simple cost factors.

13.1 Market strategy with variable entry threats

The Greenhut-Greenhut (1975) model discussed in Chapter 8 takes the existence of rival firms as given. This approach can be contrasted with the Greenhut-Ohta (1975c) approach (see Chapter 10), in which a firm in choosing its pricing policy finds this policy constrained by the threat of entry of a competitive firm. To restate: "the firm visualises a given maximum delivered price when a distant rival competes with it for selected buyers" (Greenhut and Ohta 1975, p. 129). The idea of pricing subject to a limit-price constraint also underlies the discussion of the Norman-Nichols model in Chapter 12, Section 12.1. The analysis implies that a firm supplying a number of distinct markets from a concentrated production base, "the leading firm," can be expected to adopt a pricing policy that is sensitive to local circumstances. If competitive forces vary between markets in ways that are not directly distance-related, it is to be expected that the leading firm's delivered prices will vary in ways not directly distance-related.

What is missing from this discussion is an analysis of the economic forces that determine the degrees of competition in particular local markets and cause the degrees of competition to vary between markets. Specifically, rather more detail is necessary with respect to those factors that will determine the appropriate "maximum delivered price" in distinct local markets.

13.1.1 *Some preliminary analysis*

Consider a market at distance r from the leading firm and containing $D(r)$ identical consumers. The only restrictions placed on the individual inverse demand functions, other than that they are identical for all consumers, are the usual ones: first, that they are downward-sloping, and second, that there is some defined maximum price consumers are willing to pay for the product.

The problem facing the leading firm is to choose a price/quantity strategy that will maximize profit in market r subject to the threat of entry of potential competitors to r. Attention is confined for the moment to the case in which a potential competitor in market r supplies only that market; further, there is only one potential competitor in each market. This competitor perceives that the leading firm's price/quantity strategy with respect to its exports to r has left untapped demand in r (demand that would be forthcoming at a lower price) and will enter market r so long as it perceives the possibility of making at least normal profits. In other words, the potential new entrant will enter market r so long as the price at which it can sell its output at least covers long-run average costs (LRAC) of production.

It is assumed that potential entrants produce a product homogeneous with the leading firm's product. Both leading and entrant firms will charge the same price for the product in a particular market once entry has occurred.

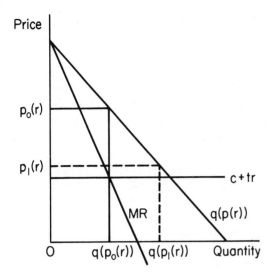

Figure 13.1. Sales of leading firm.

The entry of a new firm in market r will affect both output and price in that market. What is needed is some assumption about the response of the leading firm to the threat, as well as the actuality of entry, and about the way demand will be shared between the firms if entry takes place. The problem here is similar to one we encountered several times in the discussion of pricing given the existence of potential competitors in the market. What is a "reasonable" expectation of the behavioral response by the leading firm?

One of the simplest approaches to adopt, which also has the merit of possessing economic validity, is to follow in the tradition of Bain (1956) and Sylos-Labini (1968) (see also Scherer 1980, p. 244) and assume that the entrant believes that the leading firm will continue to supply and sell the amount it sold prior to competitive entry and will match the price charged by new entrants. In Figure 13.1, if the delivered price to market r is initially $p_0(r)$, and if competitive entry causes the price to fall to $p_1(r)$, the leading firm will continue to sell $D(r)q[p_0(r)]$, and the new entrant will supply demand $D(r)\{q[p_1(r)] - q[p_0(r)]\}$.

Justifications for this type of behavioral reaction by the leading firm (and belief by potential entrants) have been advanced provided entry deterrence is secured thereby (Wenders 1971; Dixit 1979; Scherer 1980). It has, however, been suggested that the leading firm may have to modify its behavior if entry is not deterred, because this strategy may not constitute a credible threat in a once-for-all encounter. It is in this respect that a major advantage is gained from placing the analysis in an explicitly imperfectly competitive context. Within this type of industry, the behavior by the leading firm in one market is likely to be perceived by potential competitors in other markets and thus will affect such competitors' beliefs about the leading firm's future behavior. These potential behavioral interdependencies give rise to all sorts of possibilities that are well beyond the scope of this book to investigate.[1] Suffice to say that "output maintenance" by the leading firm would appear to be a more credible strategy/threat in a spatial model, even if competitive entry does take place in selected markets.

It must be emphasized that the output-maintenance assumption is not equivalent to assuming that the leading firm will pursue myopic profit maximization under the threat of competitive entry. An essential element of the analysis is precisely the choice by the leading firm of its initial price/quantity set, *taking into account the effects this choice will have on potential competitors.*

Denote the leading firm by subscript 0 and potential entrants by subscript 1. Then the model outlined earlier is such that for any initial price/quantity set $[p_0(r), q_0(r)]$ chosen in market r by the leading firm, the potential entrant will choose output $q_1(r)$ to satisfy

$$\max \Pi_1(r) = D(r)\{p(q(r)) - \tilde{c}(r)\} q_1(r) - \bar{F}(r) \tag{13.1}$$

subject to the constraints

$$q(r) = q_0(r) + q_1(r) \tag{13.2}$$

$$\Pi_1(r) \geq 0 \tag{13.3}$$

where $\bar{F}(r)$ is fixed production cost, $\tilde{c}(r)$ is (constant) marginal-production cost for the potential entrant, and $D(r)q_0(r)$ is sales in market r by the leading firm prior to and after entry.

It is perhaps necessary to digress for a moment on equation (13.1). It is assumed that potential entrants face similar cost *structures* as the leading firm: fixed costs and constant marginal costs. But it is not assumed that production costs will be identical across the various firms. Indeed, it is to be expected that

$$\bar{F}(r) \geq F; \quad \tilde{c}(r) \geq c \tag{13.4}$$

That new entrants should face production costs that are no lower than those of the leading firm appears quite reasonable, but the possibility is suggested in equation (13.4) that they may actually suffer production-cost penalties. This possibility is based on the ideas developed in the analysis of multiplant firms and, in particular, multinational firms – see Buckley and Casson (1976), Dunning (1977), and Scherer (1975) and the discussion

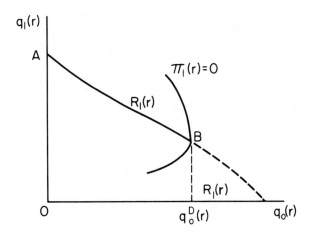

Figure 13.2. Reaction function for firm 1.

in Chapter 12, Section 12.1.3. What is being suggested is that the leading firm may have some advantages over new entrants (defined brand image, trade name, integrated product range, control over specialized resources or technologies, etc.). As a result, new entrants incur additional fixed costs of entry (e.g., in initial advertising or R&D effort). They may also face additional operating costs if the leading firm can control dissemination of knowledge, force new entrants to use inferior or more expensive inputs, or force new entrants into additional, and continuing, advertising or research efforts.

These cost penalties will be greater the more complicated the technology, the more the product is identified with a known set of product characteristics, the more easily the leading firm can keep its specialist knowledge private, and the less sophisticated is either the market r or any potential entrant to r.

Equations (13.1)–(13.3) generate a reaction function for the potential entrant to market r:

$$p'(r)q_1(r) + p(r) - \tilde{c}(r) = 0 \quad \text{if } \Pi_1(r) \geq 0 \tag{13.5a}$$

$$q_1(r) = 0 \quad \text{if } \Pi_1(r) < 0 \tag{13.5b}$$

where $p'(r) = dp(r)/dq(r)$.

This reaction function is illustrated in Figure 13.2; it will be downward-sloping provided that

$$p''(r)q_1(r) + p'(r) < 0 \tag{13.6}$$

We also illustrate the critical isoprofit curve for the entrant: the isoprofit curve for which $\Pi_1(r) = 0$. (The isoprofit curves are just those discussed in any standard microeconomics text.)

It should be noted that the reaction function $R_1(r)$ is discontinuous at B at output $q_0^D(r)$ for the leading firm (Dixit 1979). To the right of B, output by the leading firm is so great as to prevent the potential entrant from breaking even, and so entry is deterred.

Now consider the leading firm. This firm's decision maker is assumed to behave as a Stackelberg market leader (Stackelberg 1952). In other words, in devising his output, he incorporates the potential entrant's reaction function into his own decision-making process. Formally, he chooses $q_0(r)$ to satisfy

$$\max \Pi_0(r) = D(r)\{p[q(r)] - (c + tr)\}q_0(r) \tag{13.7}$$

subject to

$$p(r) \geq (c + tr) \tag{13.8}$$

and subject also to (13.2) and (13.5), with total market area R_0. It is assumed that total profits in this market area at least cover fixed costs F.

Solution for this system for a particular market r is crucially dependent on the reaction function of the potential entrant to r and the isoprofit curves in market r for the leading firm. The reaction function and the leading firm's isoprofit curves are illustrated in Figure 13.3; a superscript M relates to the leading firm's monopoly policy, D to the optimal entry-deterring strategy, and S to the optimal Stackelberg strategy. The lower the isoprofit curve, the higher are profits to the leading firm. As can be seen, various courses of action are possible.

In markets such as s [Figure 13.3(a)], myopic profit maximization by the leading firm generates output $D(s)q_0^M(s)$ and secures long-run exclusive control of the market. For markets such as u [Figure 13.3(b)], output $D(u)q_0^M(u)$ will lead to competitive entry. However, because the discontinuity in R_1 lies to the left of the Stackelberg equilibrium S, entry deterrence is the preferred strategy by the leading firm. Output will be set at $D(u)q_0^D(u)$, and price at $p_0^D(u)$; output by the leading firm is less and price is greater than those that would hold if the Stackelberg equilibrium were feasible.

In markets v [Figure 13.3(c)], the Stackelberg equilibrium is a feasible strategy, but so long as B lies between S and T, entry deterrence is preferred, output being set at $D(v)q_0^D(v)$. Output in such markets by the leading firm will be greater than in the Stackelberg equilibrium, although the Stackelberg equilibrium may involve more output in total.

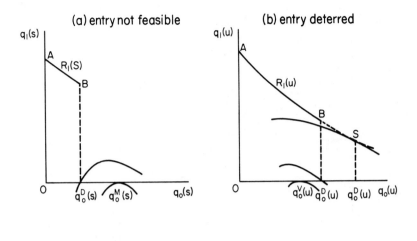

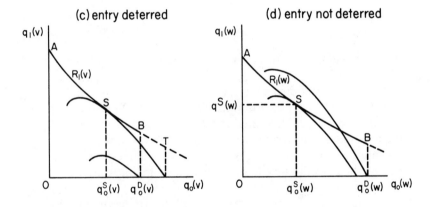

Figure 13.3. Alternative market strategies.

Finally, in markets w [Figure 13.3(d)], whereas entry deterrence might be feasible [if $p_0^D(w) > (c+tw)$ at output $D(w)q_0^D(w)$], the leading firm will find it more profitable to accommodate entry. Output will be set at $D(w)q_0^S(w)$, and the entrant will supply $D(w)q_1^S(w)$.

13.1.2   *Determinants of different strategies*

Merely to present a taxonomy of markets as in Figure 13.3 is not particularly useful unless some economic meaning can be given to the factors

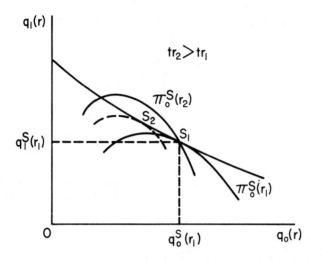

Figure 13.4. Effects of transfer costs on Stackelberg equilibrium.

that will lead to a particular market being in one or another of the four major groups.

The strategy adopted with respect to a market r by the leading firm will be determined by (1) the location of the Stackelberg equilibrium (S), determined in turn by the interaction of the reaction function $R_1(r)$ and the isoprofit curves for the leading firm, and (2) the precise form of the potential entrant's reaction function, both with respect to the location (B) of the discontinuity in this function and with respect to its general position.

Consider initially the factors that will determine the positions of the isoprofit curves for the leading firm. Given the demand conditions in market r, the isoprofit curves will be determined by the marginal costs of production and transportation that are incurred by the leading firm in exporting to r.

For any given marginal and transport costs $(c + tr)$, the slope of the isoprofit curve at the Stackelberg equilibrium is

$$S(\Pi_0^S(r)) = -\frac{\partial \Pi_0^S(r)/\partial q_0(r)}{\partial \Pi_0^S(r)/\partial q_1(r)} = -\frac{p(r) - (c + tr) + p'(r)q_0(r)}{p'(r)q_0(r)} \qquad (13.9)$$

and

$$\frac{\partial S(\Pi_0^S(r))}{\partial (c + tr)} = \frac{1}{p'(r)q_0(r)} < 0 \qquad (13.10)$$

An increase in $(c+tr)$ twists the isoprofit curves for the leading firm, as illustrated in Figure 13.4.

The reaction function, on the other hand, is not affected by $(c+tr)$. It follows, as illustrated in Figure 13.4, that the Stackelberg equilibrium for market r_2, which differs from r_1 only in that it is more distant from the leading firm, lies to the left of that for r_1. The leading firm will therefore find it more difficult to preclude entry from more distant markets and will maintain a smaller share of such markets after entry has occurred. Indeed, it follows from this analysis that the leading firm is more likely to be totally precluded from a market by competitive entry the more distant is that market.

In a more general sense, control will be more difficult, and exclusion of the leading firm more likely, in markets for which there are high transfer costs. These transfer costs might include tariff or other sales taxes, nontariff barriers such as relatively stringent safety or quality standards placed selectively on imported goods, or general costs of product differentiation necessary to design the product for "distant" markets.

A very simple taxonomy of markets is obtained if markets are identical in all respects – market size, production costs facing potential entrants – other than their distances from the leading firm. The leading firm may be able to act as an unconstrained monopolist in very proximate markets, will act to deter entry in slightly more distant markets, will be forced to accept entry and a decline in market share as distance further increases, and will be forced to quit "very distant" markets it would have served as an unconstrained monopolist.

Note the similarity between this discussion and that in Chapter 12 with respect to the Norman-Nichols model. The pattern of delivered price will contain a number of distinct regions, as illustrated in Figure 13.5. In region A, the firm prices as a discriminating monopolist, in region B it charges a uniform price, and in region C it adopts a more general discriminatory pricing policy.

In fact, the analysis gives rise to an even more heterogeneous pricing pattern than implied by Figure 13.5. The leading firm's isoprofit curves are determined in the main by distance-related factors. By contrast, the potential entrant's reaction function in any market r will be determined by factors that need not be distance-related.

From equations (13.1) and (13.5) it can be seen that the fixed costs per consumer, $\bar{F}(r)/D(r)$, incurred by the potential entrant will affect the location of the discontinuity in the reaction function $R_1(r)$, but will not change the overall position of $R_1(r)$. The discontinuity in $R_1(r)$ will lie further to the right, and the leading firm will find it more difficult to deter entry to market r (1) the larger is market r, the greater is $D(r)$, and (2) the lower are fixed costs of production for the potential entrant.

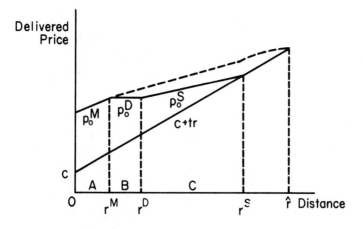

Figure 13.5. Delivered-price schedule for leading firm.

The potential entrant's marginal-production costs, on the other hand, will affect both the location of the discontinuity in $R_1(r)$ and its general position. From equations (13.5) and (13.6) it follows that the greater is $\tilde{c}(r)$, the farther to the left will be the reaction function and the discontinuity in that function.

So long as the general specification of the inverse demand function is maintained, no general conclusions can be derived as to whether greater values of $\tilde{c}(r)$ will increase the likelihood that the leading firm will adopt an entry-deterring strategy as opposed to a Stackelberg strategy. A shift in the reaction function will result in a shift in the Stackelberg equilibrium, and this may increase or decrease the leading firm's market-sharing output level $q_0^S(r)$.

Consider, therefore, the familiar GGK demand function

$$p(r) = a - bq(r)^x \quad (a, b, x > 0)$$

The reaction function $R_1(r)$ for this general form is given by (see Mathematical Appendix)

$$R_1(r): b(q_0(r) + q_1(r))^{x-1}(q_0(r) + q_1(r) + xq_1(r)) - (a - \tilde{c}(r)) = 0 \quad (13.11)$$

It is shown in the Mathematical Appendix that $R_1(r)$ is concave if x is less than one, linear if x equals one, and convex if x is greater than one. More important, at any given value of $q_0(r)$, an increase in $\tilde{c}(r)$ (1) makes the slope of the reaction function more negative if x is less than one, (2) leaves the slope of the reaction function unchanged (at $-\frac{1}{2}$) if x equals one, and (3) makes the slope of the reaction function less negative if x is

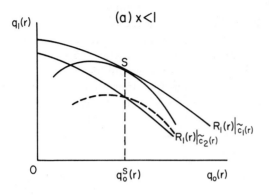

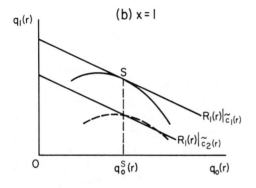

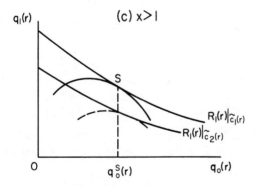

Figure 13.6. Effect of $\tilde{c}(r)$ on Stackelberg equilibrium $[\tilde{c}_1(r) < \tilde{c}_2(r)]$.

less than one. It can also be shown that for any value of $q_0(r)$, the leading firm's isoprofit curves will become flatter as $q_1(r)$ falls.

These properties are illustrated in Figure 13.6. It is clear that the greater is $\tilde{c}(r)$, the farther to the left will be the discontinuity in the entrant's reaction function, and for $x \le 1$, the farther to the right will be the Stackelberg equilibrium. For $x \ge 1$, it can be shown that the increase in the slope of the isoprofit function for any decrease in $q_1(r)$ is greater than the increase in the slope of the reaction function. In this case also, the greater is $\tilde{c}(r)$, the farther to the right will be the Stackelberg equilibrium.

Given, then, that the inverse demand functions are of the specific yet quite general form $p = a - bq^x$ $(a, b, x > 0)$, it can be concluded that all else equal, the entry-deterring strategy is more likely to be preferred by the leading firm the greater are the production costs $\tilde{c}(r)$ incurred by new entrants.

13.1.3   *Some testable implications*

The main implications of this analysis can be summarized as follows:

1. The market taxonomy will be determined in part by distance-related factors. In the absence of differences in production costs or market size, entry deterrence is more likely in markets proximate to the leading firm, and market sharing is more likely to emerge in more distant markets.
2. The market taxonomy will also be determined by factors that are not directly distance-related. Entry deterrence is less likely in large markets, as well as for production processes that impose low fixed costs of production and/or low operating costs on the potential entrant. In other words, the leading firm will find it more difficult to maintain exclusive control of a market

   (a)   the lower are additional cost penalties incurred by new entrants.

   Clearly, control by the leading firm will be easier for complicated technologies, for products that consumers associate with particular characteristics possesed by the leading firm (e.g., a brand name), and for production processes using specialized resources controllable by the leading firm

   (b)   the more sophisticated the market and potential competitors in that market.

   In such cases, new entrants will find it easier to break down the brand image built up by the leading firm and will be more capable of developing competitive technologies.

One further important implication of the analysis is that if the production-cost penalty $[\tilde{c}(r) - c]$ faced by potential entrants varies significantly between locations, perhaps because of differences in local market size, or in the degree of sophistication, or in resource availability between markets, the leading firm may be forced to accept entry, and indeed may find itself excluded from some proximate markets while still being able to supply, and control, other more distant markets.

What this analysis implies is that the leading firm is likely to adopt a heterogeneous market strategy. The choice between unconstrained monopoly, entry deterrence, Stackelberg market sharing, and the possibility of being forced to quit particular markets is determined by technological factors and local market conditions that are only partially distance-related.

It follows that the pattern of delivered prices can be expected to be heterogeneous. There need be no clear relationship between the price charged by the leading firm in a particular market and the transport costs to that market. Rather, prices will be reactive to local competitive conditions. In simple terms, there is more likely to be a connection between price and strength of competition (as measured, perhaps, by the number of firms selling in a particular market) than between price and supply distance.

13.2 Pricing with heterogeneous demand

The alternative source of price heterogeneity that can be considered is in many ways the most obvious: heterogeneity in delivered prices arising from heterogeneity in individual (gross) demand functions. A cautionary note should be struck at this point. It is tempting to explain evidence of heterogeneity in delivered prices as arising solely from differences in demand conditions in different selling locations. The problem with this type of explanation, however, is that without an explanation of *why* demand is heterogeneous, it is no explanation at all. It does not lead to any empirically testable propositions. Rather, it merely provides an ex post rationalization (description) of observed behavior. Our task as economists should be to provide theories that are capable of being tested and that can be used to predict the behavior of economic agents.

Bearing these comments in mind, we now go on to investigate the effects on delivered prices of demand heterogeneity where this heterogeneity in demand arises in two well-defined ways.

13.2.1 *Price discrimination when individual demands are not identical*

It is well known from simple, classical microeconomic theory that the position of the individual (gross) demand function is determined by, among

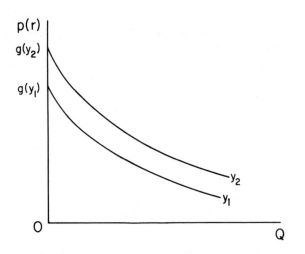

Figure 13.7. Effect of income on demand: $y_2 > y_1$.

other things, consumer incomes. One simple cause of variation in individual consumer demand, therefore, will be variation in individual consumer incomes. Formally, the individual demand function can be written as[2]

$$q = f(p, y) \quad (f_p < 0; \; f_y > 0) \tag{13.12}$$

where y is consumer income, and the good is assumed to be a normal good.

One important result should be noted. If the effect of changing income levels is merely to change the slope of the demand function, but *not* the maximum price consumers are willing to pay, then such a change in income levels will leave price elasticity of demand unchanged at any given price, and thus *will have no effect on the degree of price discrimination*.

Attention is confined, therefore, to cases in which the effect of increased income levels is to shift the demand function vertically, as in Figure 13.7. In order to keep the analysis tractable, while maintaining a reasonably high degree of generality, attention is also confined to the GGK class of demand functions. In other words, it is assumed that each consumer exhibits the inverse demand functions

$$p(r) = \alpha g(y(r)) - \frac{\beta}{x} q(r)^x \quad (\alpha, \beta > 0; \; x > -1; \; x \neq 0) \tag{13.13}$$

where $y(r)$ is consumer income *for each consumer* at location r, and $g[y(r)] > 0$, with $dg/dy > 0$. Note that (for the moment) all consumers at a particular location are assumed to have identical incomes and so have identical demand functions.

Given the usual assumption of constant marginal-production costs, the discussion in Chapter 6 generates the optimal delivered price to consumers at location r:

$$p(r) = \frac{\alpha x g(y(r))}{1+x} + \frac{1}{1+x}(c+tr) \tag{13.14}$$

The slope of this delivered-price schedule $[dp(r)/dr]$ is

$$\frac{dp(r)}{dr} = S = \frac{\alpha x}{1+x}\frac{dg}{dy}\frac{dy(r)}{dr} + \frac{t}{1+x} \tag{13.15}$$

To see what this analysis implies for pricing patterns, assume that the producer is situated in the central business district (CBD) of a large city, that incomes decline as we move from the CBD to the rural fringe, then rise again for consumers located in a neighboring town, as illustrated in Figure 13.8(a). The resulting pattern of delivered prices is illustrated in Figure 13.8(b), where the dotted price line denotes prices that would be charged if all consumers were paid the rural wage, denoted by income level $\bar{y}$.

One natural implication of this analysis is that we would expect to find very different ranges of goods being sold in markets between which there are marked differences in income. Luxury goods, for example, tend to be goods for which demand is particularly sensitive to changes in income: In terms of equation (13.15), dg/dy will be greater for luxury goods than for essentials. We should also expect marginal-production (and, perhaps, transport) costs to be greater for luxury goods – they will contain strong elements of individual styling, quality, complexity, and so forth. It is likely to be the case, therefore, that the price chargeable for luxury goods in peripheral areas will be insufficient to cover the costs of supply: In Figure 13.9, only consumers in the regions $0R_1$ and R_2R_3 will be supplied.

This argument can be taken further by introducing other considerations. The rents payable by retailers for particular locations will be determined in large part by their expected profitability in these locations. Our analysis implies that retailers of higher-quality goods will find particularly strong demand for their goods in high-income areas and thus will be able to outbid retailers of lower-quality goods for retail outlets in the high-income areas.

An example of this in the United States is the location of high-quality stores in the wealthiest, newly developing suburbs [e.g., Sax (Fifth Avenue) in Dallas].

A further corollary of our analysis is that we might expect the range of goods sold in any one store operated by a large-scale retailer to reflect average income levels of those who shop in that general area. In the United Kingdom, for example, it is possible to get a reasonably accurate

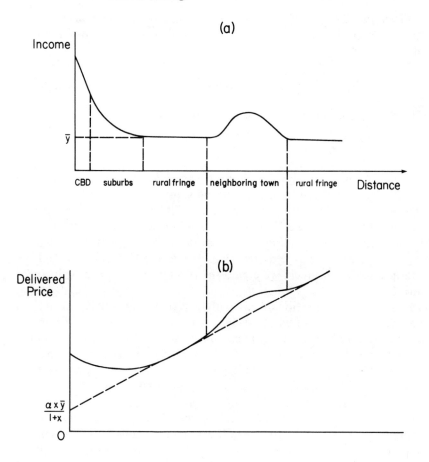

Figure 13.8. Delivered prices with variable consumer incomes.

picture of average income levels and social class in particular towns by looking at the range of goods sold by Marks & Spencer in those towns!

These comments can be extended to pricing policy and commodity bundling. The basic principle of commodity bundling is to extract the surplus of those who appreciate the bundle most and also to extract the surplus of buyers who appreciate only one of the separate products. It is particularly the case that if buyers are wealthy and have strong but disparate commodity preferences, a price-discriminating seller can charge different prices for each good and a low composite price for the bundle, in the process extracting some consumer surplus and earning extra profit. This can be verified using an example given by Phlips, with some minor alterations to the numbers he used (Phlips 1983, p. 179).

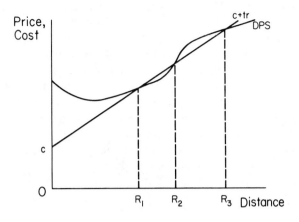

Figure 13.9. Effect of income variation on delivered prices.

Suppose a firm has marginal costs of 20 and 30 in producing goods 1 and 2, respectively, and has four customers, A, B, C, and D, for the goods, each with reservation prices R_1 and R_2 per commodity, as given below, and a reservation price for the bundle (R_B), also as indicated:

A has $R_1 = 10$ and $R_2 = 89$; $R_B = 99$

B has $R_1 = 45$ and $R_2 = 55$; $R_B = 100$

C has $R_1 = 60$ and $R_2 = 40$; $R_B = 100$

D has $R_1 = 89$ and $R_2 = 10$; $R_B = 99$

Three price/production strategies can be considered. Under simple monopoly pricing, profits are maximized and equal 139 when $p_1 = 60$ and $p_2 = 89$. Customer D has a 29 surplus, A and B do not purchase product 1, and B, C, and D are excluded from product 2. On a pure bundling strategy, where only the bundle is offered for sale, profits are maximized by selling the commodity bundle at a price of 99. This generates profits of $99 \times 4 - [(20 + 30) \times 4] = 196$. But a mixed bundling strategy that allows purchase of one or the other single commodity or the commodity bundle generates even higher profits. Assume that the firm sets a price of 89 for commodity 1, 89 for commodity 2, and 100 for the commodity bundle. Then D will buy commodity 1, A will buy commodity 2, and B and C will buy the commodity bundle. Profit climbs to

$$(89 - 20) + (89 - 30) + [(100 - 50) \times 2)] = 228$$

As Phlips observes, this type of pricing extracts maximum consumer surplus when buyer demands are quite different. It accounts for large family Coke bottles, seven-course dinner menus besides à la carte menus, and so on. Shipping goods by an integrated carrier who combines truck pickup and delivery with intermediate shipment by rail or barge will similarly provide advantages to certain firms. Such firms are able to supply more distant markets than those firms who ship all the way by one carrier (truck, rail, or barge). The latter firms are forced to confine their sales to markets other than those that the integrated carrier can open up for the firm. Basically, the mixed bundling strategy (or incremental market segmenting) by sellers is the most profitable sales device. It approaches more closely than other discriminatory systems to what Pigou referred to as first-degree price discrimination. To return to our basic theme, the wealthier are consumers, but the more disparate their individual tastes, the greater will be the alternatives that will profitably be offered them by a discriminating, profit-maximizing seller.

13.2.2 *Price discrimination and income distribution*

An important assumption of the previous section is that all consumers *at a particular location* have identical incomes. Now consider the effects on demand and thus on price discrimination of relaxing that particular assumption. In doing so, attention is again confined to cases in which a change in income level shifts the demand function vertically. By an argument identical with that of the previous section, the degree of price discrimination will be unaffected by changes in income distribution when income merely determines the slope of the individual demand function.

Consider, then, a particular buying location – call it a city – in which buyers are classified into three categories: the rich, the middle class, and the poor. Assume for simplicity that for each category, individual demand is linear. Then, as can be seen from Figure 13.10, aggregate demand in the city will be convex, whereas if all consumers had identical incomes, aggregate demand would be linear.

From analysis in previous chapters, the more convex the demand function at any selling location, the smaller the degree of price discrimination that will be applied on sales to that location. Thus, we would expect, *ceteris paribus*, to find an inverse relationship between income distribution and the degree of price discrimination. More generally, if the distribution of incomes varies *between cities*, between selling locations, this will lead to nonlinear patterns of delivered prices even if individual demand functions are of the GGK class and are identical for all income classes.

13.3   **Concluding remarks**

The main purpose of this chapter has been to identify a number of important factors that are likely to lead to rather more heterogeneous patterns

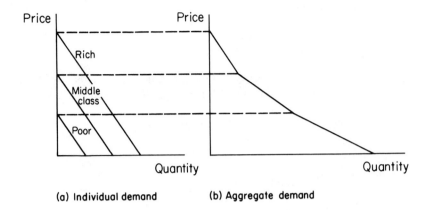

Figure 13.10. Effect of income distribution on aggregate (local) demand.

of delivered prices than would be predicted by the more straightforward analysis of previous chapters. Two major sources of price heterogeneity have been identified:

1. *Variable entry threats.* The ease with which potential entrants can actually enter a particular market will be determined partly by distance-related factors. It is also, however, determined by non-distance-related factors that create greater or lesser barriers to entry: size of local market, technology, brand name, and other quality factors. The more heterogeneous these latter factors are across different markets, the more heterogeneous will be delivered prices to those markets.

2. *Heterogeneous demand.* Heterogeneity in demand can arise, for example, because of variation in income, either between consumers at different buying points or between consumers at a given buying point. In either case, the greater is heterogeneity in demand, the greater will be heterogeneity in delivered prices.

The question that should follow naturally from this and our previous analysis is, *What price patterns are actually used by firms in free-enterprise economies?* It is this question that Chapter 14 addresses.

Mathematical appendix

The reaction function is

$$R_1(r) = p'(r)q_1(r) + p(r) - \tilde{c}(r) = 0 \qquad (A13.1)$$

The demand function is defined as

$$p(r) = a - bq(r)^x \tag{A13.2}$$

Differentiate (A13.2) to obtain

$$p'(r) = -xbq(r)^{x-1} = -xb[q_0(r) + q_1(r)]^{x-1} \tag{A13.3}$$

Substituting (A13.3) into (A13.1) and collecting terms yields (13.11).

We next differentiate (A13.1) with the implicit-function rule to give

$$\frac{\partial q_1(r)}{\partial q_0(r)} = -\frac{\partial R_1(r)/\partial q_0(r)}{\partial R_1(r)/\partial q_1(r)} = S_0/S_1 \tag{A13.4}$$

Further differentiate (A13.4) to obtain

$$\frac{\partial^2 q_1(r)}{\partial q_0(r)^2} = -\frac{S_{00}S_1^2 - 2S_{01}S_0 S_1 + S_{11}S_0^2}{S_1^3} \tag{A13.5}$$

where, from (A13.1), we obtain the following:

$$
\begin{aligned}
S_0 &= \partial R_1(r)/\partial q_0(r) = p''(r)q_1(r) + p'(r) \\
S_1 &= \partial R_1(r)/\partial q_1(r) = p''(r)q_1(r) + 2p'(r) \\
S_{00} &= \partial^2 R_1(r)/\partial q_0(r)^2 = p'''(r)q_1(r) + p''(r) \\
S_{01} &= \partial^2 R_1(r)/\partial q_0(r)\partial q_1(r) = p'''(r)q_1(r) + 2p''(r) \\
S_{11} &= \partial^2 R_1(r)/\partial q_1(r)^2 = p'''(r)q_1(r) + 3p''(r)
\end{aligned}
\tag{A13.6}
$$

We next differentiate (A13.3) to obtain

$$
\begin{aligned}
p''(r) &= -bx(x-1)[q(r)]^{x-2} \\
p'''(r) &= -bx(x-1)(x-2)[q(r)]^{x-3}
\end{aligned}
\tag{A13.7}
$$

Substituting (A13.7) and (A13.3) into (A13.5) and collecting terms gives

$$\frac{\partial^2 q_1(r)}{\partial q_0(r)^2} = \frac{(x-1)p'(r)b^2 x^2 [q(r)]^{2x-4}[xq_1(r) + q(r)]}{(S_1)^3} \tag{A13.8}$$

where $S_1 < 0$. Hence,

$$
\begin{aligned}
\partial^2 q_1(r)/\partial q_0(r)^2 &< 0 && \text{if } x < 1: R_1(r) \text{ is concave} \\
&= 0 && \text{if } x = 1: R_1(r) \text{ is linear} \\
&> 0 && \text{if } x > 1: R_1(r) \text{ is convex}
\end{aligned}
$$

Empirical findings on alternative pricing policies: demand and competitive impacts

One explicit aim of previous chapters has been to show how the system of thought that characterizes the "spatial price theorist" can be applied to a wide diversity of problems in imperfect competition. A secondary but nevertheless important objective has been to outline spatial price theory and to show how this compares with other theories of the firm. In particular, we have been much concerned in the past few chapters in showing that price discrimination will be adopted by monopolistic and competitive firms. That analysis runs the danger of being little more than an interesting intellectual exercise *unless it can be supported by convincing empirical evidence of the use of discriminatory pricing policies.* Such evidence is presented in this chapter.

Before proceeding to more formal econometric analysis, some introductory, suggestive remarks are in order. As Norman (1981, p. 87) states,

[the] use of uniform delivered price systems...is neither new nor particularly exceptional. Any consumer is able to identify a list of products which are sold to all intents and purposes at the same price independent of the point of purchase.

In addition, we are all familiar, as consumers, with cases in which sellers offer free delivery (uniform delivered prices) or charge a delivery cost that bears only a nominal relationship to the actual cost of transportation. Nor is such price discrimination confined to goods bought for final consumption. A major concern of the (now abolished) Price Commission in the United Kingdom was to attack uniform-delivered-price systems applied to a wide range of intermediate products (Price Commission 1978a, 1978b, 1978c).

The policy position adopted by the Price Commission is of more than historical interest, as can be seen from the commission's statements on the (U.K.) prices of aerosol cans. The commission asserted that "[we] have not been persuaded that there is sufficient justification for this method of [uniform] pricing, which leads to cross subsidization between consumers" (Price Commission 1978b, p. 6).

Closer reading of the Price Commission analysis suggests that their thinking was founded on the traditional spaceless theory of perfect competition in which efficiency implies that price should always and everywhere equal marginal cost; viewed geographically, this would appear to

237

imply f.o.b. pricing. By now, the reader should be willing to accept that the perfect-competition paradigm is not applicable to the spatial economy!

Further evidence of the confusion in the Price Commission's thinking is not difficult to find. When investigating the pricing of sugar and syrup products (Price Commission 1978c), they were forced by their previous statements to accept a system of selective consumer discounts, because these eliminated what was otherwise a uniform-delivered-price system!

Many other specific examples of price discrimination can be cited. Thus, the Price Commission (1978d) questioned the U.K. cement pricing policy by which something in excess of 60 percent of delivery costs are absorbed by a major producer. Hwang, in his investigation of coal prices, concluded that "[the] empirical results. . .support the hypothesis that spatial price discrimination characterizes the coal industry. Not only do the monopolists of classical theory discriminate as a general course of action but so do spatial competitors" (Hwang 1979, p. 241).

On a lighter note, Osleeb and Cromley (1978) investigated the location of Coca-Cola plants. They took as given the empirically evident system of uniform delivered prices.

Within the European Economic Community (EEC), concern is being expressed at the extensive price discrimination practiced by the major motor-car manufacturers. Table 14.1 indicates that price differences apply to a wide range of models and manufacturers. One consequence of the type of discrimination involved here is that for many car models, the U.K. consumer gains advantage in purchasing the automobile in Belgium, taking delivery in person, and shipping the car to the United Kingdom, despite the transport costs that this entails. Not surprisingly, the motor-car manufacturers have been trying to prevent such personal importation. This is difficult to accomplish with respect to the majority of European consumers, because such a consumer can claim to be resident in the country of purchase (e.g., Belgium) when ordering the car. Identification of the U.K. consumers is straightforward, however, because they and the Irish are the only ones who demand right-hand drive![1]

In a more general, macroeconomic context there is also increasing acceptance of the idea that prices are unlikely to follow an f.o.b. scheme. Recent attempts to develop a structural model of the United Kingdom's trade in manufactures (Hotson and Gardiner 1983, p. 2) provide econometric support to the proposition that "competitors' prices [are] a key influence on the set of attainable combinations of sales and margins." Put another way, the more competitive are distant (export) markets, the lower (i.e., more discriminatory) will be prices charged by U.K. exporters to those markets.

Table 14.1. *New-car price: comparison net of taxes (in sterling)*

Model	Belgium	Germany	France	Italy	U.K.
BMW 320i	5,716	6,228	6,537	6,681	7,369
Citroen GSA Pallas	3,394	3,642	4,042	4,107	4,444
Fiat Panda 45	1,995	2,293	2,251	2,610	2,484
Ford Escort XR3	4,275	4,824	4,877	5,167	5,440
Mazda 323 GT 1.5	3,325	3,488	3,885	–	4,376
Opel Kadett 1.6 SR	3,729	4,194	4,179	4,415	–
Peugeot 305 GT	3,910	4,188	4,476	4,860	5,130
Renault 5 GT	2,752	2,977	3,016	3,211	3,628
Volkswagen Golf GTi	4,714	5,178	5,193	5,558	6,315

Source: The Times, July 18, 1984; survey conducted by Bureau Europeèn des Unions de Consommateurs (BEUC) on July 2, 1984.

It remains the case, however, that with the exception of the Bank of England analysis, much of the "evidence" presented earlier is somewhat anecdotal. Formal econometric testing of our theories requires a much stronger, sounder data source. We now turn to one such source and test.[2]

14.1 Price findings for sampled firms

Sample surveys were conducted in the United States, West Germany, and Japan intended specifically to identify factors that affect spatial pricing policy. Target study regions were selected in each country to include (1) similar urban/rural proportions, restricted by (2) existing acquaintanceships with professors in or near these urban/rural centers. Survey constraint (2) was imposed after a mailed-questionnaire "pilot-study sample" in the United States had indicated a need for follow-up mailings, telephone calls, and even interviews before a sufficient number of responses from a particular place (e.g., a particular state in the United States) could be expected. After selecting comparable survey areas, firms were picked at random from industrial lists of business establishments in each country, and questionnaires were mailed to them. (The questionnaire is reproduced in the Appendix to this chapter.) The firms that returned questionnaires were compared with nonresponding firms. No distinction in size of firm, industry type, or location was apparent for any country or subregion studied. Among the respondents, all firms that were not subject to significant freight cost (defined to be a 5% *minimum* "freight cost to delivered cost ratio" on sales to at least one distant market point) were

Table 14.2. *Comparison of pricing strategies among different countries*[a]

| Country | Non-discrimina-tory f.o.b. mill pricing | Discriminatory | | | | Total |
		Uniform pricing only	Other discrimina-tory pric-ing only	Mixed pricing	Total dis-criminating	
United States	57(33)	37(21)	28(16)	52(30)	117(67)	174
West Germany	7(21)	11(32)	5(15)	11(32)	27(79)	34
Japan	6(18)	9(27)	3(9)	15(46)	27(82)	33
Overall	70(29)	57(24)	36(15)	78(32)	171(71)	241

[a] The number in each cell indicates how firms in the country (given by the row) use a particular pricing policy (given by the column). The number in parentheses shows the percentage of firms in that country that used the indicated pricing policy. Thus, for example, only 57 firms in the United States priced f.o.b. mill, which number represents 32.7% of all firms sampled in the United States.

dropped from the sample. The findings on pricing strategies are summarized in Table 14.2.

Firms in the United States tend to price discriminatorily.[3] Of 174 sampled firms, less than one-third priced nondiscriminatorily (f.o.b.). The spokesmen for the remaining firms (67%) admitted that they did not add full freight cost to their mill price on all of their distant sales. These firms therefore priced discriminatorily. The tendency to price discriminatorily is even greater in West Germany and Japan, with the percentages of discriminating firms approximately 79 percent and 82 percent, respectively. It is obvious, therefore, that discriminatory pricing not only is possible in countries that have legislated against this practice, such as the United States, but also is the prevalent pricing practice.

To investigate in more detail the possible differences between countries in the tendencies of firms to price discriminatorily, a 3×2 contingency test was applied. The null hypothesis is that there are no intercountry differences in the proportion of discriminatory firms. The χ^2 value rejected this hypothesis at approximately the 10 percent significance level. Intercountry differences may, of course, arise for a number of reasons. Attention will be focused later on the possibility that firms in different countries may not view government restrictions on profit-maximizing pricing in a uniform way.

14.2   The theory and operational model

The delivered prices charged at a set of buying points by competitive firms located at a given production center were derived by Greenhut and Greenhut (1975) (see Chapter 8) as

$$P = \frac{1}{n+x}(xb+n\bar{c}) + \frac{n}{n+x}\bar{T} \tag{14.1}$$

where P denotes the delivered price to a particular market point, n stands for a spatial competition factor (e.g., the number of sellers located together at the production center who supply a particular distant market point), $\bar{c}$ is the average marginal cost of production of the selling firms, and $\bar{T}$ stands for the average distribution (transportation) cost of all firms supplying that market; parameters x and b, in turn, represent demand factors – respectively the demand concavity and price intercept, both assumed positive.

The first term $[1/(n+x)](xb+n\bar{c})$ in (14.1) gives the mill price of the firm at the production center, and $n/(n+x)$ in the second term establishes the slope of the delivered-price schedule (DPS) as transport distances change. Clearly, the greater the number of suppliers (n) at the production center, the lower is the mill price, and the steeper is the slope of the DPS. The spatial price effects of changes in key variables are

$$\frac{\partial P}{\partial n} = \frac{-x[b-(\bar{c}+\bar{T})]}{(n+x)^2} < 0, \qquad \frac{\partial}{\partial n}\frac{\partial P}{\partial \bar{T}} = \frac{x}{(n+x)^2} > 0$$

$$\frac{\partial P}{\partial x} = \frac{n[b-(\bar{c}+\bar{T})]}{(n+x)^2} > 0, \qquad \frac{\partial}{\partial x}\frac{\partial P}{\partial \bar{T}} = \frac{n}{(n+x)^2} < 0$$

$$\frac{\partial P}{\partial b} = \frac{x}{n+x} > 0, \qquad \frac{\partial}{\partial b}\frac{\partial P}{\partial \bar{T}} = 0$$

$$\frac{\partial P}{\partial \bar{c}} = \frac{n}{n+x} > 0, \qquad \frac{\partial}{\partial \bar{c}}\frac{\partial P}{\partial \bar{T}} = 0$$

If a rival production center exists at a distance, so that the n rivals are divisible into two groups, n_1 and n_2, the average distribution costs ($\bar{T}$) of supplying each buying point located between the centers tend to be more nearly equal. Such competition at a distance will also increase the n value and, in turn, generate greater freight absorption at all overlapping buying points, compared with the single-production-center case. Generalization of the model to include sales to buyers located at off-line market points from either production center (or both centers) can also be effected, as can inclusion of other differentially located production centers.

Two of the several principles that were noted in Chapter 8 deserve repetition here:

1. The greater is the concentration of firms at a production center, the lower is the mill price, and the steeper is the discriminatory DPS. In fact, the DPS approaches the f.o.b. price schedule under conditions of extreme localization of industry.
2. Competitive entry at a distance generates lower discriminatory delivered prices at all overlapping market points located between the production centers. A linear DPS may, in fact, give way to curvilinear schedules or kinked linear schedules, and so forth, because of spatial heterogeneities (e.g., in demand and competition).

The operational model stems directly from the foregoing theory, but it requires broader terms than those presented in Chapter 8. Its design relates to the condition that in order to formulate an effective operational model that can explain industrial price policies empirically, the concepts businessmen tend to employ in explaining or evaluating their firms' price policies in different markets must be used. For example, it was evident during the pilot-study phase of this investigation that company officials were reluctant to identify their competitors at specific market points. They would furthermore "fudge" in their identification of where the rival plants were located, asserting simply in their replies that slightly different goods are produced "*around* here or there," warehoused "in this or that *area*," distributed by wholesalers located "near or far," ad infinitum. It was found more practical and consistent to ask for a ranking of competition (i.e., as most intense, least intense, etc.) at a particular buying point rather than to ask for the particular source of the competition.

Even when the origin point of a rival's product was identified – chiefly during personal interviews – it was often the case that no information was given regarding the distribution channels, the exact freight cost, or the mill price (and production cost) existing at that origin point. Fortunately, such specific data are required only in theory. A proxy (intermediate) link that involves simpler (more general) reference terms was acceptable in the survey. Recorded below is the structure of each element of the model.

An implicit form of the space–price theory is given by

$$G = f(n, d, t, o) \tag{14.2}$$

This form indicates that freight absorption (G) is a function of (1) the pattern of competition (n) the firm is subject to throughout its market space, (2) the demand pattern (d) prevailing over its space, (3) the cost of distance (t) on sales, and (4) all other factors (o). It should be stressed that in the empirical studies, no attention was paid to single-factor attributes, such as the number of competitors a firm confronts, the shape of the demand curve (x), or the average marginal costs $(\bar{c})$ and the average transport costs $(\bar{T})$. In fact, it was considered pragmatically necessary to subdivide the parameters into a system of thirteen explanatory variables that would so combine as to approximate the essential components of the theory. The selected regression model is given by

$$G_i^s = \beta_0^s + \beta_1^s \text{HO1}_i^s + \beta_2 \text{HO2}_i^s + \beta_3 \text{TR1}_i^s + \beta_4 \text{TR2}_i^s$$
$$+ \beta_5 \text{TR3}_i^s + \beta_6 T_i^s + \beta_7 L1_i^s + \beta_8 L2_i^s + \beta_9 \text{ND}_i^s$$
$$+ \beta_{10} \text{NI}_i^s + \beta_{11} \text{DD}_i^s + \beta_{12} \text{DI}_i^s + \beta_{13} \text{SFA}_i^s + \epsilon_i^s, \tag{14.3}$$

where superscript s stands for the sth region (e.g., country), and subscript i the ith firm. Other notation needing clarification will be explained briefly later, with all notation and variables explained in the footnotes to Table 14.3. Define G_i^s as

$$G_i^s = 1 - \tfrac{1}{4} \sum_{j=2}^{5} \frac{P_{i,j}^s - P_{i,1}^s}{t_{i,j}^s - t_{i,1}^s} \quad \begin{matrix} (i = 1, 2, \ldots, n \\ j = 2, 3, 4, 5) \end{matrix} \tag{14.4}$$

where this variable stands for the average freight-absorption rate on unit sales by the ith firm in region s.[4] Then $P_{i,1}^s$, $P_{i,j}^s$ and $t_{i,1}^s$, $t_{i,j}^s$ respectively provide the delivered prices and freight costs of the ith firm per unit sale in its 1st and jth markets.

Certain variables in the model lead to lower prices via greater freight absorption, and vice versa. For example: NI in (14.3) is a dummy variable that stands for increasing competition from rivals at more distant market points. When this condition applies, the firm will charge lower prices at such distant points, *ceteris paribus*, in effect absorbing more freight; a positive β_{10} is therefore to be expected. The dummy variable DI in (14.3) stands for greater demands at more distant points. When this condition holds, higher prices obtain, *ceteris paribus*; hence, less freight absorption will apply, and the coefficient β_{12} should be negative.

14.3 Empirical data evaluated

Table 14.3 summarizes the results of the study of spatial pricing practices in the United States, West Germany, and Japan. The overall findings are satisfactory and dovetail closely with our theory. This is especially encouraging, because there are inevitably many factors that could not be included in the operational model but that may well determine the pricing policies of firms in free-enterprise countries.

Table 14.3. *Summary of regression results*[a]

Country	Product types[b]		Types of carriers used[c]			
	HO1	HO2	TR1	TR2	TR3	T
United States	−0.322	−0.017	0.142	0.342	0.342	0.042
	(0.21)	(0.015)	(0.10)	(0.132)	(0.26)	(0.03)
West Germany	−0.173	−0.361	0.334	0.013	−0.113	0.411
	(0.16)	(0.30)	(0.31)	(0.016)	(0.06)*	(0.24)*
Japan	−0.110	−0.137	0.031	−0.058	0.472	0.423
	(0.064)*	(0.088)	(0.036)	(0.085)	(0.44)	(0.32)
Theoretical sign	−	−	n.a.	n.a.	n.a.	+

[a] The regression coefficients and their corresponding standard deviations are recorded under each explanatory variable, with standard deviation provided within parentheses. We use *, **, and *** to denote significance at the 10%, 5%, and 1% levels, respectively.
[b] HO1 (HO2) takes the value 1 if the firm's product is substantially (slightly) different from its competitors, and 0 otherwise.
[c] The TRs stand for using the nation's railway system (1), highways (2), and waterways (3) as the primary transportation mode. If all assume the value 0, the firm uses air carriers as its primary form of transportation. Our theory does not imply whether a negative or positive sign should result. T_i^s takes the value 1 if the firm owns its carrier, and 0 otherwise. Its coefficient should be positive, because firms that own the transportation carrier can be expected to have more leverage in absorbing freight than otherwise.

The data indicate that the locational patterns of competitors and extent of competition, given by variables $L1$, $L2$, ND, and NI, were *in general* the most important factors influencing the sampled firms' spatial pricing policies. Each of these four variables is significantly different from zero *in each sampled country*, highlighting the importance in determining prices (and price policies) over economic space of the "type" of changes in competition that arise as sales distances increase. The spatial demand variables DD and DI were of distinctly secondary importance (Table 14.3).

To elaborate these findings somewhat further, consider the following: Locational patterns $L1$ and $L2$ are consistently significant. This justifies the premise of the theory that the greater is the concentration of firms at a production center, the lower is the mill price, and the steeper is the DPS; the more dispersed is the competition, the flatter is the DPS. Localization of competitors would shift the DPS downward, moving it ever closer to

Competitor location patterns[d]		Competitive impacts[e]		Demand impacts[f]		Distance costs[g]	
L1	L2	ND	NI	DD	DI	SFA	
0.784	0.649	−0.037	1.075	0.735	−0.002	1.734	$R^2 = 0.3297$
(0.37)**	(0.38)*	(0.02)*	(0.51)**	(0.68)	(0.002)	(1.31)	$F = 2.1434*$
0.325	0.142	−0.134	0.654	0.041	−0.012	0.110	$R^2 = 0.2467$
(0.12)***	(0.069)**	(0.078)*	(0.31)**	(0.03)	(0.23)	(0.066)*	$F = 2.1426*$
0.314	0.440	−0.354	0.128	0.034	−0.115	0.326	$R^2 = 0.3142$
(0.18)*	(0.37)*	(0.17)**	(0.075)*	(0.026)	(0.087)	(0.19)*	$F = 2.7834**$
+	+	−	+	+	−	+	

[d] $L1$ ($L2$) takes the value 1 if the firm's competitors are dispersed evenly over the market (located together at a substantial distance), and 0 otherwise.

[e] ND (NI) takes the value 1 if competition decreases (increases) with distance, and 0 otherwise.

[f] DD (DI) takes the value 1 if the underlying [gross] demand for the firm's product is considered to decrease (increase) with distance, and 0 otherwise.

[g] SFA_i^s provides the measure of the firm's *average* spatial friction (i.e., relative importance of freight cost). It is defined by

$$SFA_i^s = \frac{1}{4} \sum_{j=2}^{5} \frac{D_{i,j}^s}{P_i^s} \qquad (j = 2, 3, 4, 5)$$

where $D_{i,j}^s$ and P_i^s are respectively the reported unit freight cost and delivered price to the jth market.

an f.o.b. schedule. In contrast, dispersion of competition will tend to flatten the DPS or, in some cases, cause it to assume a curvilinear form, rising at first before bending down.

Two further observations should be noted. First, the firms in West Germany and Japan were subject to slightly higher freight costs than American firms; this increased the importance of the spatial friction factor (SFA in Table 14.3) in those countries. Second, there is some evidence of a difference in pricing practices across the three countries. An additional test (Chow's test) was run using a slightly different data set to determine if there were in fact any such differences between the pricing practices of the sampled firms of West Germany, Japan, and the United States. For this test, company officials were asked to assign ordinal values to particular spatial demand patterns, besides specifying changes in demand and competition as distances increased. They were also asked to provide

Table 14.4. *Chow's test*[a]

	F statistic from Chow's test	Level of significance	Firms from same universe
U.S. vs. W.G.	9.62	0.5%	No
U.S. vs. Japan	2.819	1.0%	No
W.G. vs. Japan	1.2278	n.s.	Yes

[a] Neither the model underscoring Table 14.3 nor the one that serves as the basis for this table violates the classical linear-regression model. For example, the problem of multicollinearity may appear to be prominent, because if competition increases as distance increases, one might expect respondents to claim that the underlying magnitude of demand will decrease. To evaluate this and other relationships, the incremental contribution of each predetermined variable was calculated and compared with the joint contributions of all variables simultaneously obtained. The differences between the incremental sums and the R^2 for all variables operating simultaneously were checked, and the degree of multicollinearity was found to be very slight.

the number of competitors to which their firms were subject at different market points. (See, for example, items 5d through 5f in the questionnaire.) Table 14.4 shows the results for Chow's test.

The sampled American firms do indeed belong to a different universe than do the firms of West Germany and Japan. Bump–dip changes were prevalent in the delivered prices of firms in West Germany and Japan; in fact, *sharply negative* changes in delivered prices frequently characterized their sales over increasingly costly distances along a given transport line. Thus, a firm located in Karlsruhe, which may have priced in Bonn at a level 110 percent that of its price in Karlsruhe, would quite conceivably price at, say, 90 percent of its Karlsruhe price on sales in Münster. It would do this notwithstanding a greater cost in shipping its product from Karlsruhe to Münster, vis-à-vis Karlsruhe to Bonn. But this type of pricing, though easily explained in theory (Greenhut and Greenhut 1977), was *never found* among the prices of the 174 sampled firms in the United States. Instead, the American firms *always* charged higher prices to more distant buyers, or *at a limit* followed uniform delivered prices over their market space.

Quite conceivably it was the Robinson-Patman act that caused the delivered-price patterns of American firms to differ from those of firms in West Germany and Japan. For example, in one case under the Robinson-Patman statute, the Utah Pie Company was found to have charged a lower (delivered) price in a distant market than the price charged in its

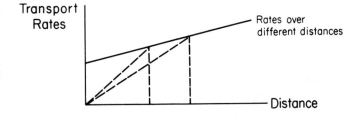

Figure 14.1. A nonlinear transport schedule.

home market. Somewhat analogously, one spokesman interviewed during the Greenhut survey also advised that his company had followed this kind of pricing policy, but on advice of lawyers eliminated the lower (delivered) price at distant market points in favor of a more moderate freight-absorption practice. Notwithstanding intercountry differences in pricing, discriminatory freight absorption nevertheless characterized the pricing schedules of American firms. It is in this particular respect that the pricing policies of the sampled American firms were similar to those of the firms sampled in West Germany and Japan.

14.4 The generality of price discrimination

A customary practice in the United States is transportation of goods by common carrier, where the carrier charges a fixed (load) fee for packing up less than carload (truckload) shipments. By contrast, the shipper (or the consignee at the other end) may undertake the costs of packing the full carload (truckload) lot. In either case, a fixed charge exists that corresponds to the fee one pays to enter amusement parks and the fees charged for telephone or other utility connections. The upshot is that the average price paid by the shipper (or the individual attending the amusement park and purchasing rides, or the householder using the services of the utility company) varies with the distance (the quantities) involved, as in Figure 14.1. A form of price discrimination exists that once helped identify transportation freight rate making (and in turn geographic price discrimination by sellers of goods using common carriers).

This basic form of discrimination not only characterizes freight rate making but more generally is evidenced by the data presented in the previous section of this chapter, as well as in the price practices in the United Kingdom that were mentioned in the introductory section of this chapter. Moreover, the amusement-park and utility-company examples just cited

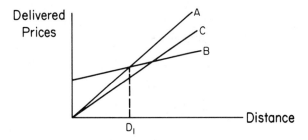

Figure 14.2. Nonlinear and linear price schedules.

suggest the generality of this type of pricing (Phlips 1983). Indeed, it is evident throughout the world in the form of quantity discounts.

These, of course, *could have been* the basis for Figure 14.1. But why, one might ask, do firms price this way? Why do they not tack on the extra load costs by raising the rates per unit distance (or quantity), as given by line A in Figure 14.2? Would a mixed bundle of charges be more profitable, or Pareto-dominant?

Phlips (1983), drawing on Willig (1978), in effect observed that given line A in Figure 14.2, it is always possible to find another line, B, such that customers located beyond D_1 gain more than is lost by those located nearer to the carrier's shipping point. By suitable choice of the carrier's load cost fee (entrance fee, connection fee) and unit distance (quantity) cost, the area between A and B to the right of D_1 can always be made larger than the area between A and B to the left of D_1. The change from the linear to the nonlinear schedule – which lowers the average price for shipments over a greater distance (or for presumably wealthier customers who acquire greater quantities) – can be constructed in such a way as to generate greater consumer surplus than would be gained under, say, line A (where people at shorter distances benefit).

It should be clear that giving customers the option of paying the loading fee (or the entrance, connection, etc., charge) directly, so that they have the right to pay a lower *average* price, enables those shipping beyond (or using services beyond) D_1 to gain an advantage; in turn, others would use the uniform rate of, say, line C.

That the nonlinear schedule Pareto-dominates straight lines through the origin was illustrated by Willig (1978) in a diagram similar to Figure 14.3. Marginal cost is C', and the lower price $(p - t)$ applies for all distances (quantities) beyond D_1. The horizontally shaded area of Figure 14.3 depicts a producer-surplus "loss" due to nonlinear pricing, but this loss is more than offset by the vertically shaded areas gained. The

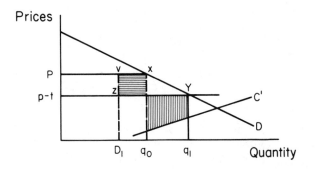

Figure 14.3. Nonlinear price schedules and Pareto optimum.

consumer-surplus gain is given by $VXYZ$. It follows that with a small enough t and a large enough D_1, both the carrier and shipper (the amusement-park owner, the utility company, and their consumers) can be made better off by the two-part price technique. In general, then, familiar types of spatial pricing enable us to identify analogous nonspatial discriminatory pricing policies.

14.5   Conclusions

This chapter began with a series of anecdotes, all of which point to the extensive use of discriminatory pricing policies by both monopolistic and competitive firms. More formal testing of the various facets of pricing under imperfect competition developed in previous chapters demands, however, a much more structured data set, such as that reported by Greenhut (1981). The main results to emerge from econometric analysis of this set can be summarized as follows:

1. The survey data indicate significantly greater use of discriminatory pricing policies, compared with f.o.b. mill pricing, in the countries studied. More specifically, of all sampled firms in the United States, less than one-third priced nondiscriminatorily. The tendency to price-discriminate is even greater in West Germany and Japan.

2. The empirical findings are consistent with the theoretical results derived in the Greenhut-Greenhut (1975) model (e.g., the greater the concentration of firms at a production center, the lower is the mill price, and the steeper is the DPS).

3. The findings also show differences in the pricing practices of firms in different countries. Not only do West German and Japanese

firms discriminate in price more than do American firms, but their discriminatory practices differ significantly from those of the American firms. More specifically, unlike the American firms, which generally absorb only a portion of the freight costs and thus have a positively sloped DPS, negative slopes in the delivered-price schedules of firms in West Germany and Japan were found to be quite common.

Rather significantly, the aftermath of air-fare deregulation in the United States led to intense competition between airlines serving different cities. The upshot in the middle 1980s, for example, has been lower fares on flights by a given carrier from Houston to New York via Dallas than from Dallas to New York (same airline, same plane) and from Los Angeles to New York via Chicago than from Los Angeles to Chicago. In the former case, a Dallas resident would be better off having the travel agent ticket the flight to New York as if departure were from Houston; in the latter case, the Los Angeles resident who wants to go to Chicago will save money by being ticketed from Los Angeles to New York, but deplaning at the stopover in Chicago. These fares, therefore, have negative dips with greater distances.

Appendix

Firm Name _____ Telephone Number _____

Official Supplying Data _____

1. Classify your activity by selecting a standard product or service below. The good manufactured is _____; the service supplied is _____; or the good distributed is _____.

2. Is the item in question (check one):
   a. substantially different, b. slightly different, c. identical to competitors' products.

3. How do you typically transport? a. by highway, b. rail, c. water, or d. air. (check appropriate answer)

4. Do you typically use your own transport facility? a. yes, b. no. (check one)

5. Please describe below a typical shipment of your product (or service) from your facility in _____ to five different buying locations:

	1	2	3	4	5
a. Specify the buyer's location (e.g., Chicago, Ill.)	___	___	___	___	___
b. The delivered price at the buyer's location is	___	___	___	___	___
c. The number of competitors is	___	___	___	___	___
d. How would you rank your competition at these buying points? (1) the greatest your firm faces, (2) the next greatest, (3) etc. (Possibly you will assign the same number to several customer buying points.)	___	___	___	___	___
e. Approximate the percentage of your total sales that your company sells to each of the locations	___	___	___	___	___
f. Using numbers as in 5d, rank the *relative* impact of your firm on the subject market.	___	___	___	___	___
g. The freight cost per unit of shipment to each buying location is	___	___	___	___	___

6. The (general) price of the product considered in question 5 in a sale to a buyer located at your facility (whether or not any sales are made there) "would be" _____.

7. Your competitors are (check one):
   a. located near you, b. spread over the market area, c. located together at a distant point, d. increase with distances, e. decrease at more distant buying points, f. other (please specify) _____.

8. *Assume* you have no competitors supplying the aforementioned 5 buying points. Would the demands for your product generally be (a) greatest among buyers located close to you, (b) greatest among buyers located at substantial distance from you, (c) the same at all locations?

PART III

Pricing, location, and competition

CHAPTER 15

General location and market-area principles

A separation between price theory and location choice has been maintained to this point in the book, with only passing reference made to the fundamental interactions between price and location. It is clear, however, that in many situations price and location choices are mutually interdependent. The remainder of the book will evaluate this interdependence and demonstrate how it contributes to an understanding of the structure and performance of oligopolistic markets.

This chapter provides a survey of some of the more important theories of industrial location, a survey that is, of necessity, brief. The study of how firms locate over an economic space and what kinds of market areas they control actually requires a book of its own; more extensive reviews can be found, for example, in Greenhut (1956, 1970) and Smith (1971).

The present survey is organized along conventional lines, determined in large part by the chronological development of the major theories. We begin in Section 15.1 with a discussion of cost-based theories, then consider locational-interdependence theories in Section 15.2, the market-area school in Section 15.3, and profit-maximization theories in Section 15.4. In each case we point out the major limitations of the available theories, but also indicate how these theories might be and are being applied to contemporary spatial and nonspatial questions.

15.1 Cost theories of location

The central assumption of cost-based theories of location is that in choosing its location(s), the individual firm is required to supply a known, localized demand at parametric prices. It follows, therefore, that the profit-maximizing strategy is the location strategy that minimizes total costs of production and transportation. Of the many early contributions to this particular body of theory, the most significant are undoubtedly those of von Thünen and Weber.[1]

15.1.1 *Von Thünen*

Von Thünen's primary interest was in analysis of the allocation of agricultural land. Given that agricultural produce has to be transported from

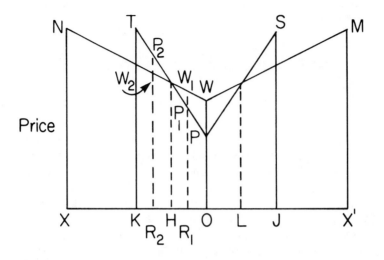

Figure 15.1. Von Thünen rings and transport costs.

the point of production to the point of consumption (a city), how should land be allocated between competing agricultural uses?

The model begins by assuming a uniform homogeneous plain in which the productivities of capital and labor inputs, as well as the cost of producing a given crop, are identical at all locations. The location decision is thus determined by differences in land rents that can be offered by competing producers of the various products. These products are to be transported for consumption to a single city that, for convenience, is assumed to be located at the center of the plain.

The solution to the allocation problem for two products, wheat and potatoes, say, is illustrated in Figure 15.1.[2] Assume that the city is located at 0. Unit production costs for both products are independent of location and are given by $0W$ for wheat the $0P$ for potatoes. Unit transport costs are given by the slopes of WN and PT or WM and PS for wheat and potatoes, respectively. Wheat is assumed to be more costly to produce, but cheaper to transport, than potatoes.

Consider agricultural land at distance $0R_1$ from the city. It can be seen from Figure 15.1 that average costs (of production and transportation) are R_1P_1 for potatoes and R_1W_1 for wheat, with $R_1P_1 < R_1W_1$. In contrast, for agricultural land at distance R_2 from the city, the relative average costs are such that $R_2P_2 > R_2W_2$. Assume that wheat and potatoes sell at identical prices in the city. Then potato producers can outbid wheat producers for land at R_1 whereas wheat producers will outbid potato producers for land at R_2. More generally, all land in the regions $0H$ and $0L$

will go to potato production, and all land in *HX* and *LX'* to wheat production. Taking the analysis further by placing it in a two-dimensional plane market rather than a one-dimensional line market, it can be seen that von Thünen's theory predicts a pattern of land use characterized by a series of concentric rings, each devoted to the type of production that can offer the highest land rent.

Von Thünen, a wealthy landowner, was primarily interested in the allocation of agricultural land, and it might be thought that his ideas would be of little relevance to a modern industrial society. This is not the case, however, in that his framework of thought underscores many developments in urban economics. In fact, there is now a well-developed "demand-oriented" theory of household location within metropolitan areas based on the concept of bid–rent curves (cf. the land rent noted earlier) that predicts a concentric pattern determined by the individual household's willingness and ability to bid for land in the urban area; see, for example, Alonso (1964), Muth (1967), Mills (1972), and Beckmann (1968). In addition, there are "production-oriented" theories that propose a similar concentric pattern of industrial and commercial locations within metropolitan areas; see, for example, Koopmans and Beckmann (1957) and Mills (1972).

15.1.2 *Weber*

Weber's main interest was in industrial-location choice. He was concerned with analyzing the "general factors of location which are applicable to a greater or lesser degree in every industry" (Friedrich 1929, p. 23). The main assumptions of the Weberian model are the following:

1. The firm choosing a location is subject to a fixed-coefficient, constant-returns-to-scale technology.
2. Inputs to production are available in unlimited supply at fixed prices independent of location.
3. These inputs are either ubiquitous (i.e., available everywhere in the market area) or strongly localized at a few known sources. (Note that assumption 2 applies to localized and ubiquitous factors of production.)
4. Demand is concentrated at a number of known points and is fixed at each point.
5. Transport is feasible in any direction, and transport costs for each commodity are directly proportional to weight and distance transported.

The first stage of the analysis is illustrated in Figure 15.2. Assume a technology consuming a_1 and a_2 units, by weight, of two localized inputs

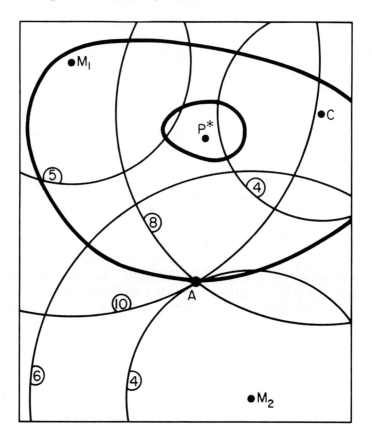

Figure 15.2. Weber's location theory.

to produce one weight unit of output for final demand. The inputs are available at sources M_1 and M_2, respectively, and the consumption site is at C. Transport costs for each commodity are respectively t_1, t_2, and t_c per unit weight per unit distance. Find the least-cost location P^* from which to supply C.

Because all inputs are available at known, constant prices, this is equivalent to finding point P^* that minimizes total transport costs. A geometric solution to this problem is readily developed (Alonso 1964). Construct lines of equal assembly costs around M_1 and M_2 and equal delivery costs around C. These lines, termed *isotims*, are, from assumption 5, circles centered on M_1, M_2, and C. Thus, for example, point A in Figure 15.2 has assembly costs of $10 for input 1 and $4 for input 2. In each case, the input costs are given by the product $a_i d_i$, where d_i is the radius of the isotim

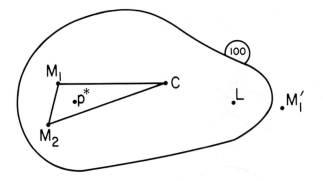

Figure 15.3. Labor orientation.

centered on M_i and passing through A. Delivery costs are \$8 on the final product. Thus, total assembly and delivery costs at A are \$22. Joining points of equal total transport costs generates a series of *isodapanes* – the heavy curves in Figure 15.2. For example, all points on the isodapane through A are associated with total transport costs of \$22. Given assumptions 1 through 5, these isodapanes will radiate from a uniquely best (i.e., least-cost) location P^* somewhere in the *location triangle* $M_1 M_2 C$.

Clearly, the position of P^* is determined by the relative importance of the "transport weights" $t_1 a_1$, $t_2 a_2$, and t_c. Thus, if $t_1 a_1 > t_2 a_2 + t_c$, the least-cost location will be at M_1, but if $t_c > t_1 a_1 + t_2 a_2$, the optimum location will be at C. It is to be expected, for example, that weight-losing production (e.g., steel manufacture) will be located near raw-material sites, or ports if raw materials (e.g., iron ore) are imported, whereas weight-gaining production (e.g., beer production) will be located near consumption sites.

Weber went on to provide two important extensions of his basic analysis. Consider, first, the effect of introducing a source of cheap labor (or some other localized material). Assume that this source is located at L in Figure 15.3 and that use of this labor will reduce unit production costs by \$20. Assume that unit costs of assembly and distribution at P^* are \$80. Now construct the isodapane associated with assembly and distribution costs of \$100 (\$20 + \$80), termed the *critical isodapane*. If L lies inside (outside) this isodapane, then the least-cost location is L (P^*).

Labor orientation of the type implied by Figure 15.3 is more likely when labor costs in production are important relative to other costs. This is particularly the case when a cheap-labor location is also near an alternative source of one or another of the materials used in production (e.g., source M_1' in Figure 15.3). Weber's analysis can easily be used, therefore,

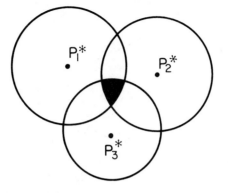

Figure 15.4. Agglomeration of production.

to explain recent trends on the part of major international corporations to locate much of their high-value-added, labor-intensive intermediate production in the Far East and in newly industrializing countries such as Brazil and Venezuela.

The third and final stage of Weber's theory is to modify assumption 1. In doing this, maintain the fixed-coefficient technology, but now assume that there are economies of agglomeration:

An agglomerative factor...is an "advantage" or cheapening of production or marketing which results from the fact that production is carried on to some considerable extent at one place [Weber 1929, p. 126].

Agglomerative factors arise at two stages of production. First, there may be economies from "simple enlargement of plant." Second, there may be advantages from "close local association of several plants" (Weber 1929, pp. 127–8).

Consider a situation in which transport orientation with respect to three demand sites gives the locations P_1^*, P_2^*, and P_3^* in Figure 15.4. Now assume the agglomeration economies are such that if total demand at the three consumption locations is supplied from a single production site, unit production costs will be reduced by \$25. Then if the critical isodapanes – those isodapanes that involve an increase in transport costs of \$25 per unit of production for each P_i^* production site – happen to intersect, agglomeration will reduce total costs. Thus, in Figure 15.4, the least-cost location to supply total demand at the three consumption sites lies in the shaded area (i.e., agglomeration will reduce total production costs).

One of the major limitations of the Weberian and von Thünen analyses lies in the parametric treatment of demand and price. This is justified by some authors on the assumption that the market structure underlying the model is perfectly competitive, but it can also be justified by assuming that the producer is a monopolist with perhaps little control over the final price. In either case, the analysis has limitations, of course, but the latter approach sets the scene for many practical applications of Weber's analysis. Indeed, it can be argued that a major strength of the Weberian model lies in its capacity to be made operational.

Early work in this vein was provided by Hoover (1937, 1948) in classic studies of the shoe and leather industries. Isard (1956) acknowledges the importance of Weberian analysis to his study of the iron and steel industry. The analyses of the optimal locations of hospitals, warehouses, fire stations, and public facilities in general have a strongly Weberian flavor; see Feldman, Lehrer, and Ray (1966), Massam (1975), Greenhut and Mai (1980), and Thisse and Zoller (1983). Similarly, we can point to analyses of the optimum locations for Coca-Cola production (Osleeb and Cromley 1978) and cement production (Norman 1979), as well as allocation of production units of multinational companies (Buckley and Casson 1976), each of which has at its heart a refinement of the Weberian model.

15.2   Locational-interdependence theory

A major limitation of the Weberian model is its treatment of competition. Essentially, each producer is assumed to take the locations of its competitors as given, or is a monopolist. The major contribution of the locational-interdependence theories is to relax this assumption and to consider the spatial implications of noncollusive oligopoly.

The seminal work in this area was that of Hotelling (1929), later extended and summarized by Smithies (1941); see also Lerner and Singer (1937) and Greenhut (1956). Hotelling analyzed the pattern of location for two sellers of a homogeneous product when buyers of that product are evenly distributed over a bounded linear market. Each buyer is assumed to purchase one unit of the product and to bear all transport costs. Thus, the demand side is essentially ignored. Relocation of production is assumed to be instantaneous and costless. A simple illustration will be useful: The best known is the analysis of the location of two ice cream salesmen on a bounded linear beach with each consumer assumed to buy one ice cream cone, purchasing it from the nearest salesman.

The fundamental solution concept underlying Hotelling's approach to the duopoly problem is the assumption that each duopolist holds Cournot conjectures with respect to the rival's reactions to a change in location. For example, assume that the salesmen start at points A and B in Figure 15.5(a). Seller A believes that seller B will not react to a change in

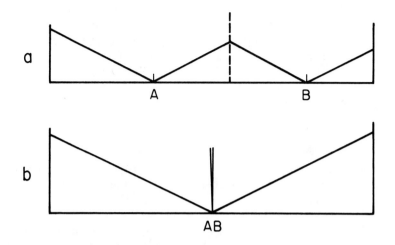

Figure 15.5. Hotelling's model.

seller A's location. It will accordingly benefit A to relocate just to the left of B. But then B will leapfrog over A, and this leapfrogging will continue until the two sellers are located back to back in the center of the market, as in Figure 15.5(b). Note that this solution maximizes the transport costs imposed on the consumers.

Subsequent extensions of Hotelling's analysis have called into question the strength of the agglomerative motives that this model appears to imply. Smithies (1941), among others, shows that with nonzero elasticity of demand, the extent of agglomeration will be severely limited. If the analysis is extended to allow for more than two competitors, then Eaton and Lipsey (1975) and Rothschild (1976) show that sellers will tend to disperse in order to avoid being caught as "pig in the middle." Alternatively, if the sellers are assumed to have some foresight about future sellers' location plans, dispersal of production will again result (Prescott and Visscher 1977).

Nevertheless, the Hotelling model remains an important starting point in the analysis of spatial and nonspatial oligopoly. It has been applied directly, in a manner suggested by Hotelling, in political science; see Downs (1957) and Kramer (1977). In this context, the Hotelling model indicates why first-past-the-post voting systems tend also to be two-party systems, as in the United Kingdom and United States, where each major party fights for the middle ground and squeezes out any third central party. The emergence of the Social Democratic Party (SDP) in the United Kingdom in the late 1970s can be explained by the increasing polarization of the

Labour Party, but the SDP can also be expected to be squeezed out as the Labour Party moves once again to more moderate, although leftist, policies. In contrast, proportional-representation voting systems allow much easier entry. They therefore tend to generate a wider variety of political parties and to lead to coalition governments, with no one party able to obtain a simple majority.

In a strictly economic sense, extensions of the Hotelling model underlie recent advances in spatial oligopoly (as we shall see in subsequent chapters) and are also of considerable use in analysis of nonspatial problems such as that of product differentiation – recall Chapter 5.

15.3   The market-area school

As indicated, it is probably reasonable to place the least-cost location theories within the context of a spatial monopoly and to view locational-interdependence theories in the context of "small-number" spatial oligopoly. The market-area school can then be seen to take the competitive structure one step farther, into a "large-number" spatial oligopoly or into the spatial equivalent of monopolistic competition.

The seminal work and, indeed, the standard work to this day is undoubtedly that of Lösch[3] (1938, 1954). In contrast to Weber, Lösch assumes a homogeneous plain over which consumers are evenly distributed. The demand side is explicitly introduced by attributing to each consumer a downward-sloping demand curve for whichever product is being analyzed. It is assumed that all consumers have identical tastes and incomes and that production costs are identical everywhere on the plain.

The remaining main assumptions indicate the strong intellectual debt Lösch owed to Chamberlin (1933) in the development of his ideas:

1.   The location of an individual (entrepreneur) must be as advantageous as possible (i.e., must be a maximum-profit location).
2.   Locations must be so numerous that the entire space is occupied.
3.   In all activities that are open to everyone, abnormal profits must disappear.
4.   The areas of supply, production, and sales must be as small as possible.
5.   Consumers at the boundaries of economic areas must be indifferent regarding to which of the neighboring locations they belong.

Let us begin the analysis by considering a homogeneous plain containing "nothing but self sufficient farms that are regularly distributed" (Lösch 1954, p. 105). Now let one farmer produce and sell beer, for which individual consumer demand is *dd* in Figure 15.6(a). If the brewery price is

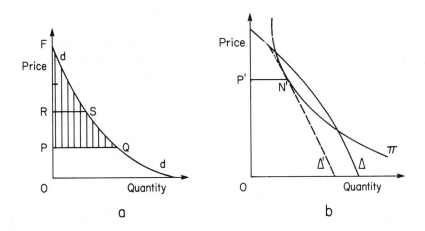

Figure 15.6. Lösch's model – aggregate demand and average cost.

set at $0P$, the individual demand of consumers located at the brewery gates will be PQ. For more distant consumers, transport costs are added. Thus, with transport costs PR, individual demand falls to RS. Finally, at price $0F$, individual demand is zero. Note that the prices $0P$ and $0F$ imply a maximum geographic radius that can be supplied with brewery (mill) price $0P$, the distance being $(0F-0P)/t$, where t is unit transport cost.

Aggregate demand at the brewery price $0P$ is obtained by rotating PQF around PQ as axis, multiplied by consumer density (recall the derivation of aggregate demand in Chapter 2). This exercise can be repeated for different brewery prices to generate the aggregate demand curve Δ in Figure 15.6(b).

The cost side is represented by the planning curve Π. This curve is just the minimum (long-run) average-cost curve; it does not include any element of transport costs, because these are paid by consumers. So long as Δ and Π intersect, brewing is feasible, the brewery price being that which maximizes profit.

The initial stage of the analysis generates a circular market area, as in Figure 15.7(a), and supernormal profits to the brewer. Other producers will enter as a consequence (assumptions 3 and 4). Initially, the brewers will be sufficiently dispersed as to leave each other unaffected [Figure 15.7(c)]. In effect, the aggregate demand curve Δ moves downward, and entry continues until only normal profits remain – with aggregate demand Δ' and brewery price $0P'$ in Figure 15.6(b); also see Figure 15.7(d).

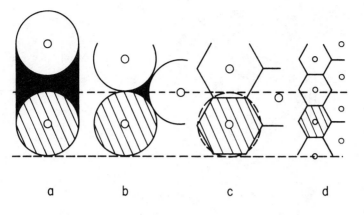

Figure 15.7. Individual long-run market areas in the Löschian model.

The question Lösch addressed was, What will be the shapes of the individual market areas in the long-run, normal-profit equilibrium? An intuitive insight that a system of hexagonal markets will emerge is suggested by Figure 15.7(d). To see more exactly why this should be so, note that circles are optimal, and triangles, squares, and hexagons are the only space-filling regular polygons. Now, the hexagon is nearest to the circle and thus is likely to be optimal.[4] A (technical) formal proof is available (Bollabas and Stern 1972).

The size of the individual hexagons for a particular industry is determined by demand and production conditions – by the factors that determine the position of the aggregate demand function Δ and the average-cost function Π. Hence, different industries can be expected to be characterized by different sizes of hexagons – equivalently, by different plant sizes. For each industry, we can therefore envisage a hexagonal net covering the total market area. The next stage of the analysis (Lösch 1954, pp. 124ff.) is to superimpose these hexagonal nets in an ordered manner – with one common center and a maximum number of intersections of other production centers – in order to minimize overall transport costs. This process generates a hierarchy of production centers, as in Figure 15.8(a): "we suddenly have crowds of economic areas on a plain which we deprived of all spatial inequalities at the outset" (Lösch 1938, p. 75).

The fundamental point Lösch wanted to make was that the process of superimposing the hexagonal nets will give rise to city-rich and city-poor sectors, as in Figure 15.8(b). Nevertheless, Lösch was not really interested in empirical "verification" of his theories.[5] Rather, he asked to what

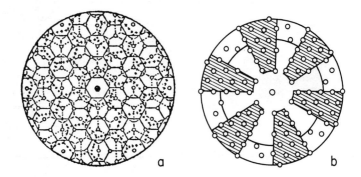

Figure 15.8. Löschian hexagonal nets.

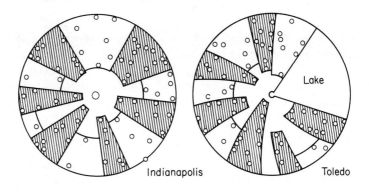

Figure 15.9. Löschian maps.

extent actual location was rational. Thus, in his 1938 article he compared the theoretical distribution of activity with the area within 100 miles of Indianapolis, and in his book he considered the area surrounding Toledo; the resulting "maps" are illustrated in Figure 15.9.

We noted that a major limitation of the Weberian model lies in its very simple treatment of demand. In a sense, the Löschian model, quite deliberately, goes to the other extreme by assuming away all spatial variations in cost conditions. It should be recognized, however, that spatial heterogeneity in factor endowments will tend to strengthen the tendency Lösch identified for a hierarchy of industrial concentrations – *central places* – to emerge (Berry and Garrison 1958).

More fundamentally, although Lösch presented his theory as a "general" theory, it is in fact a partial analysis, because no allowance is made for interaction between industrial sectors. There are no linkages between Löschian "industries"; hence, the Löschian model cannot be applied to intermediate products. With intermediate products there will be spatial variation in production costs, depending on whether or not the intermediate product and the final product are produced at the same location.[6]

Similarly, no allowance is made for the feedback between production concentration and consumer concentration (i.e., for the emergence of cities with intraindustry production-cost advantages and their effects on the distribution of demand). One form of concentration tends to imply the other and would appear to lead to a distortion of the even hexagonal dispersion of productive activity.

Again, of course, it can be argued that introduction of intermediate products and of consumer concentration merely strengthens Lösch's prediction of the emergence of central places. Nevertheless, and perhaps not surprisingly, we are left with a somewhat abstract framework that is quite difficult to apply to analysis and explanation of industrial location.

15.4   Maximum-profit plant location

Our discussion of the Löschian model indicates that a key element of that model – the regular hexagonal net for each industry – might be significantly distorted as soon as spatial variations in costs or demand are considered explicitly. In addition, whereas Lösch predicts a significant degree of interindustrial concentration, his model predicts intraindustrial dispersion. Put another way, cost factors of agglomeration [which implicitly underlie the rotation of the hexagonal nets in Figure 15.8(b)] promote interindustry concentration, whereas demand factors lead to the honeycomb type of intraindustry dispersion.

Even the most casual of empirical investigations indicate that intraindustry concentration characterizes many different types of activity, whether manufacturing, commercial, or retail. What is needed is a true synthesis of cost and demand factors in an explicitly maximum-profit plant-location theory. Such a synthesis was presented by Greenhut (1956, 1970, chap. 12 and 13). It forms the basis for much of the discussion in later chapters of this book. Let it suffice at this point simply to provide a brief statement of that analysis.

Consider a situation in which production costs vary significantly across the landscape. It is nevertheless the case that a producer may be able to operate profitably in a high-cost location. In Figure 15.10,[7] B is assumed to be the lowest-cost location for a particular product, with the producers at B choosing mill price BP and delivered prices PT (and PS). This policy will leave untapped demand at noncentral, high-cost locations. Thus,

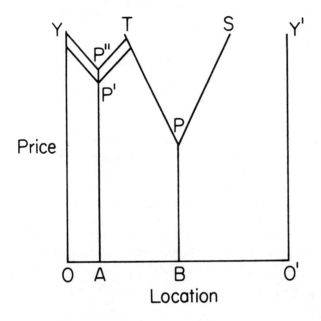

Figure 15.10. Maximum-profit location – Greenhut's model.

it may be possible for a second firm to enter at location *A*. Production costs will be higher than at *B*, but these are covered by the higher price *AP′* chargeable to consumers at this distant location. Indeed, the firm at *A* has some flexibility in the markup over costs that can be applied (e.g., the higher price *AP″* is also feasible).

What then emerges from this analysis is that high-cost locations tend to be inhabited by small-scale firms. One corollary of this, which should not be surprising, is that most industrial structures are characterized by a relatively small number of large firms (and plants) and a relatively large number of small firms (and plants). Distance and transport costs offer some degree of protection even to high-cost producers.

More fundamentally, if the firms competing with firm *B* are to be able to operate at any significant scale, they will be forced to locate very close to *B* and to compete in a very direct way with *B*, as in Figure 15.11(a). In other words, with no difference in cost conditions, it is perfectly reasonable to expect intraindustry dispersion. Once we allow for spatial differences in production costs, however, we should expect to find a greater degree of intraindustry concentration: "The essential difference between the cases of equal and unequal cost is the element of extra doubt" (Greenhut 1956, p. 164). The important point is that although firms *A* and *B* may

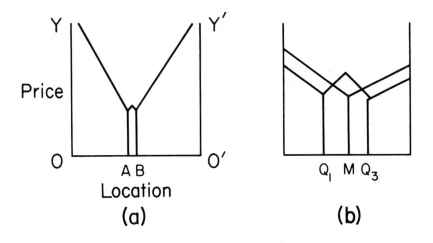

Figure 15.11. Intraindustry production concentration.

gain from dispersion [see Figure 15.11(b)], each may believe it has too much to lose by moving away from the low-cost location – a form of prisoner's dilemma to which we shall return in the next chapter.[8] Producers can quite reasonably be expected to believe that the higher costs of a noncentral location will not be offset by any additional demand gained from lower freight cost. There is, in other words, additional uncertainty caused by the variation in cost conditions that will drive large-scale producers in the industry to adopt relatively concentrated locations, as in Figure 15.11(a).

The agglomerative force is strengthened whenever one recognizes that if the officials in one company can identify the low-cost locations, then officials in other similar companies are likely to identify the same locations. Industrial agglomeration of large firms is therefore to be expected at low-cost, high-demand locations.[9] Location policy is also likely to be characterized by a substantial degree of inertia, as the spatial allocation of resources in a particular industry is likely to change significantly only in response to a major change in technology or in cost conditions.[10]

15.5 Concluding remarks

To summarize, inclusion of demand and cost factors of location leads to potentially significant revisions of prevailing theories of plant location. Some spatial dispersion of activity is still to be expected, either of small-scale activity or in industries (or markets) in which there is little spatial variation in production costs. Where there is significant spatial variation in production costs, however, the additional behavioral uncertainty created thereby tends to favor both interindustry and intraindustry concentrations of activity. It is only in the longer run[11] that we might expect Löschian-style intraindustry dispersion to reemerge. Over time, spatial competitors can reduce the uncertainties with which they are faced. They will gain experience of their rivals and begin to think of more dispersed, branch-plant operations.

CHAPTER 16

Pricing, demand distribution, and location choice

It is clear from even the very brief analysis in Chapter 15 that pricing policy and location choice interact. Moreover, as we noted in Part II, the degree of price discrimination is affected, under certain competitive conditions, by the locations that competing firms select. In this chapter and the remainder of Part III, therefore, we investigate more directly the interactions between price and location. Our hope is that this discussion will give the reader a much deeper understanding of the full range of interdependences between competing producers under imperfect competition.

Specifically, this chapter builds on the brief discussion in Chapter 15 of the maximum-profit theories of location. The most important message to be drawn from those theories is that classical *location theory* has been tied "too restrictively" (Greenhut 1956) to the cost factors of location. The location of industry depends not only on the cost factors of classical location theory but also on demand factors, as evidenced in part by the distribution of customers. In turn, the distribution of demand is affected crucially by the pricing policy chosen by the firm(s). It follows naturally that a connection can be expected to exist between pricing policy and location choice.

16.1 A simple price/location model

One of the major problems in an analysis of imperfect competition is that a slight increase in model complexity can generate an intractable increase in mathematical complexity. This is particularly true of any attempt to investigate the interactions between pricing policy and location choice. As a result, formal analysis in this chapter is confined to location choices under monopoly or duopoly.

This might be felt to be overly restrictive. It will become quite clear, however, that even this simplification leads to very complex analysis. In addition, we believe, and hope to show in the applications of the analysis in Chapter 17, that quite general insights flow from what is, on first sight, a quite restrictive model.

One of the most detailed attempts to investigate the mutual interdependence of price and location is that of Greenhut, Mai, and Norman

271

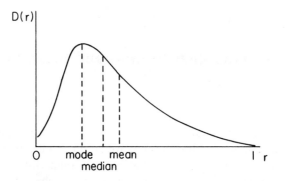

Figure 16.1. Unimodal distribution of consumers in a line market.

(1986) (henceforth referred to as GMN), and this chapter draws heavily on their analysis. The model with which they work is defined by quite familiar assumptions that are, nevertheless, worth repeating here.

1. All firms in the market produce a homogeneous product.
2. Production costs are independent of location and are given by

$$C(Q) = F + cQ \qquad (16.1)$$

   where F is fixed production costs, c is (constant) marginal-production costs, and Q is total output of the firm.
3. The freight rate, or delivery-cost function, to consumers at distance z from the producer is $T(z)$ and is independent of the quantity shipped.
4. All consumers are identical, and each has the demand function

$$Q(z) = f(P(z)) \quad \text{such that} \quad f'(\ ) < 0 \qquad (16.2)$$

   where $Q(z)$ is demand by each consumer at distance z from the producer, and $P(z)$ is delivered price to each consumer at distance z from the producer.
5. Consumers buy only from the producer charging the lowest price, or, where prices are equal, from the more proximate producer.
6. The whole market is served in both monopoly and duopoly market structures.

One departure from what might be described as the "traditional" spatial pricing model is the following assumption:

7. Consumers are distributed over a linear market of unit length, that is, on interval $[0,1]$, with density $D(r) \geq 0$ $(0 \leq r \leq 1)$. The

only restriction to be placed on $D(r)$ is that it is uniform or unimodal, as in Figure 16.1.

16.2 Monopoly location under a heterogeneous distribution of consumers

Assumptions 1–7 allow GMN to draw directly on the analysis by Rydell (1967). Rydell considered a general integral equation of the form

$$\int_0^{\rho^*} g(\rho^* - r) D(r) \, dr = \int_{\rho^*}^1 g(r - \rho^*) D(r) \, dr \tag{16.3}$$

where $g(z) > 0$.

The function $g(z)$ is a weighting function applied to the consumer distribution $D(r)$. This function can take many forms. In particular, in location models it may be interpreted as the marginal cost or marginal net revenue of shipping goods to buyers. The importance of this weighting function lies in the effect of its "shape" on the optimum location choice (ρ^*). Rydell shows that if $g'(z) = 0$ (a constant weighting function), the objective function (e.g., total distance, or profit, or again shipping cost) from which the weighting function is derived will be optimized by ρ^* at the median location of $D(r)$. If $g'(z) < 0$, the increase in, say, the marginal cost of shipping decreases with distance, and hence the weighting function is concave; ρ^* then falls between the median and mode of $D(r)$. If $g'(z) > 0$, the weighting function is convex, and the optimal location ρ^* will fall between the median and mean of $D(r)$.

In applying Rydell's results to price/location interdependence, all that is needed is identification of the appropriate weighting function for each pricing policy. For any pricing policy $P(z)$ and plant location ρ, the monopolist's total profit is

$$\Pi = \int_0^{\rho} f(P(\rho - r))(P(\rho - r) - c - T(\rho - r)) D(r) \, dr$$

$$+ \int_{\rho}^1 f(P(r - \rho))(P(r - \rho) - c - T(r - \rho)) D(r) \, dr - F \tag{16.4}$$

The integral equation (16.3) is just the first-order condition[1] $\partial \Pi / \partial \rho = 0$, which, from (16.4), gives the weighting function $g(z)$:

$$g(z) = f'(P(z)) P'(z)(P(z) - c - T(z)) + f(P(z))(P'(z) - T'(z))$$

$$(z = \rho^* - r, \ r - \rho^*) \tag{16.5}$$

The appropriate weighting functions for the three pricing strategies (f.o.b. pricing, uniform pricing, and the profit-maximizing positively

Table 16.1. *Pricing strategies and weighting functions*

	F.o.b. pricing[a]	Uniform pricing	Profit-maximizing discriminatory policy
Pricing strategy, $P(z)$	$m+T(z)$	p	$P(z)$ satisfies (16.7)
Weighting function, $g(z)$	$-(m-c)f'[p+T(z)]T'(z)$	$f(p)T'(z)$	$f[P(z)]T'(z)$
$g'(z)$	$-(m-c)f''[p+T(z)][T'(z)]^2$ $+f'[p+T(z)]T''(z)$	$f(p)T''(z)$	$f'[P(z)]P'(z)T'(z)$ $+f[P(z)]T''(z)$
Elements determining the sign of $g'(z)$	$f''[P(z)], T''(z)$[b]	$T''(z)$[c]	$T''(z)$[d]

[a] m stands for mill price.
[b] Because $(m-c)$ is constant, $f'[p+T(z)]<0$, $[T'(z)]^2>0$.
[c] Because $f(p)$ is constant.
[d] Because $P'(z)>0$.

sloped discriminatory pricing schedule) are detailed in Table 16.1. The negative sign on the weighting function under f.o.b. pricing is necessary to ensure $g(z)>0$, because $f'[p+T(z)]<0$, and $T'(z)>0$. Some comments are perhaps necessary on the conditions that must be satisfied by the profit-maximizing discriminatory price schedule. The basic model's specification (16.1) and (16.2) is such that revenue (ignoring fixed cost) from sales to consumers distance z from the producer is

$$NR(z) = (P(z)-c-T(z))f(P(z)) \qquad (16.6)$$

In addition, assumption 2 that marginal-production costs are constant is such that the profit-maximizing discriminatory pricing policy is the one that maximizes $NR(z)$ at each selling location z (recalling the analysis in Chapter 6). Differentiating (16.6) with respect to $P(z)$ and setting the derivative to zero establishes the first-order condition

$$(P(z)-c-T(z))f'(P(z))+f(P(z))=0 \qquad (16.7)$$

which can be substituted into (16.6) to give the weighting function in column 3 of Table 16.1.

Some very simple conclusions can be drawn immediately from Table 16.1. The first is that the shape of the transport-cost function plays an important role in location choice no matter the pricing policy. More specifically, optimal location will be affected in a significant manner depending

Table 16.2. *Location choice under f.o.b. pricing*

Delivery-cost function [$T(\ )$]	Demand function [$f(\ )$]		
	Concave ($f'' < 0$)	Linear ($f'' = 0$)	Convex ($f'' > 0$)
Concave ($T'' < 0$)	g' uncertain; ρ uncertain	$g' < 0$; ρ between median and mode	$g' < 0$; ρ between median and mode
Linear ($T'' = 0$)	$g' > 0$; ρ between median and mean	$g' = 0$; $\rho =$ median	$g' < 0$; ρ between median and mode
Convex ($T'' > 0$)	$g' > 0$; ρ between median and mean	$g' > 0$; ρ between median and mean	g' uncertain; ρ uncertain

on whether transport costs are linear [$T''(z) = 0$], concave [$T''(z) < 0$], implying that there are economies to long hauls, or convex [$T''(z) > 0$], implying more expensive transport rates with the length of haul.

In contrast, the effects on location choice of the concavity or otherwise[2] of the demand function vary significantly depending on the choice of pricing policy. At one extreme, optimal location is *independent* of the individual demand function under uniform delivered pricing. To see why this should be so, note that any change in price or in the individual demand functions under a uniform delivered price merely multiplies the individual quantity demanded at every location by a constant. Thus, whereas the *distribution of customers* will affect the choice of location under uniform delivered pricing, *the amount each customer purchases* (which is constant across all buyers) will not.

At the other extreme, f.o.b. pricing gives an important role to the shape of the individual demand function in determination of optimal location, in the sense of whether location is drawn toward the mean or mode of the consumer distribution. Optimal discriminatory pricing leads to an intermediate case. The *precise* choice of location is "affected" by the individual demand function. Whether this location is between median and mode or between median and mean, however, is determined by the concavity/convexity of transport costs, but *not* by the concavity/convexity of individual demand.

Details of the effects on location choice of alternative forms of the demand function and transport-cost function are given in Tables 16.2, 16.3, and 16.4.

The importance of the concavity/convexity of delivery costs is quite clear and consistent across all three pricing policies. Concave delivery costs imply economies of long hauls. Such economies enable the producer

Table 16.3. *Location choice under uniform delivered pricing*

Delivery-cost function [$T(\ )$]	Location
Concave ($T'' < 0$)	$g' < 0$; ρ between median and mode
Linear ($T'' = 0$)	$g' = 0$; $\rho =$ median
Convex ($T'' > 0$)	$g' > 0$; ρ between median and mean

Table 16.4. *Location choice under optimal discriminatory pricing*

Delivery-cost function [$T(\ )$]	Location
Concave ($T'' < 0$)	$g' < 0$; ρ between median and mode
Linear ($T'' = 0$)	$g' < 0$; ρ between median and mode
Convex ($T'' > 0$)	g' uncertain; ρ uncertain

to locate at or near to the modal location (i.e., the major concentration of consumers), while still being able to maintain sales to more distant consumers. Convex delivery costs, on the other hand, penalize long-distance transportation – they may arise, for example, if the goods being transported are perishable or subject to information loss as distance grows. With convex delivery costs, therefore, location is drawn toward the mean, or geographically central, location.

The impact of the shape of the demand function on location choice is, as noted earlier, "significant" only under f.o.b. pricing. That this should be so is not, perhaps, too surprising, because f.o.b. pricing gives rise to the greatest differences in the delivered prices actually charged to consumers in separate markets.

Take, for example, the case in which the demand function is convex and the delivery function is concave, which, as noted earlier, implies economies to long hauls. Then location will be chosen between the median and mode of the consumer distribution and will tend to favor the modal point (i.e., the major concentration of consumers). To see why this is so, note that the ratio of quantity demanded at the mill price (i.e., at the seller's location) to the quantity demanded at a higher price (i.e., at a location distant from the seller) is greater when the demand function is convex

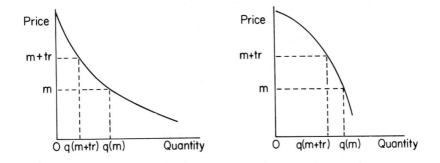

Figure 16.2. Convex demand and concave demand.

than when that function is concave, as illustrated in Figure 16.2. All else being equal, the weighting function derived from a convex demand function will tend to favor the major consumer concentration – the modal location.

This influence is reinforced if the delivery-cost function is concave, because with such a function, freight *rates* fall with distance, and thus delivered prices do not increase particularly rapidly with distance. This means that the producer will more easily be able to maintain sales to buyers skewed at the greatest distances from the plant location. The two effects – demand and transport-cost effects – together generate a composite weighting function that draws the seller to the modal consumer location, in effect strengthening the pull of the major consumer location vis-à-vis more distant, smaller markets.

By the same token, if the demand function is concave and the delivery-cost function is convex, the pull of the major consumer distribution is significantly weakened. Using an argument similar to the one advanced earlier, concave demand functions tend to give more weight to distant consumers (i.e., to reduce the relative importance of the major consumer concentration). At the same time, convex delivery-cost functions cause delivered prices to increase rapidly with distance and thus tend to penalize a location choice that is not geographically central; in other words, location near the mode implies a substantial loss of sales to distant consumers. Location will be drawn, therefore, toward the mean of the consumer distribution – toward the location that is the geographically central location.

Two possible exceptions arise when the demand function and delivery-cost function are either both concave or both convex. In either case, what might be called the demand effect and the delivered-price effect tend to work in opposite directions. For example, concave demand functions decrease the relative importance of the major consumer concentration, but concave delivery-cost functions reduce the penalty of deviating from the geographically central location. The combined effect is uncertain.[3]

The vital contrast in location choice under the three pricing policies is that the pull of the major consumer concentration (the mode) is greatest when the monopolist is able to adopt the pricing policy (16.7) that discriminates in favor of more distant buyers. Systematic absorption of freight costs allows the producer more easily to maintain sales in more distant markets. The pull of the modal location is therefore increased, or, put another way, there is less need for the monopolist to adopt a geographically central location.

It might be felt that this argument should apply with at least equal force to uniform delivered pricing, because this is an even more discriminatory pricing policy than that implied by equation (16.7). Yet it is clear from Tables 16.2 through 16.4 that the locational strategy under uniform delivered pricing is much more akin to that which arises under f.o.b. pricing. The point here is that a producer operating under uniform delivered pricing effectively absorbs all delivery costs. Convex delivery costs then impose a heavy cost penalty on a noncentral location sufficient to reduce the pull of the major consumer concentration: The delivery-cost effect, in other words, dominates the demand effect and encourages location nearer to the geographic center of the market.

It is impossible to be more precise with respect to location choice so long as the very general specification of demand and delivery-cost functions is maintained. GMN considered, therefore, the case in which both demand and delivery-cost functions are linear. With such a demand function, equation (16.7) will lead to 50 percent freight absorption (recall Chapter 6). GMN then showed[4] that there is remarkable symmetry in the monopolist's location choice. The location chosen will always be somewhere between the median and the mode of the customer distribution *no matter the degree of spatial price discrimination.* Further, location choice moves from the median toward the mode as freight absorption increases from zero (f.o.b. pricing) to 50 percent, but moves back to the median as freight absorption increases from 50 percent to 100 percent (uniform delivered pricing).

It further emerges that the monopolist's profit-maximizing conditions are identical under f.o.b. and uniform delivered pricing. As a result, the remarkable equivalence between f.o.b. pricing and uniform pricing that was first noted by Beckmann and Ingene (1976) is much more extensive than those authors perhaps realized. The profit and output equivalence of these two pricing policies, assuming a fixed location choice, extends to the case in which location can be freely chosen.

16.3 Duopoly, pricing policy, and location choice

The discussion in Section 16.2 virtually exhausts all that can or need be said about the single-plant monopolist. What happens to this story when a second firm is introduced? The first point to note is that the firms need not compete merely on price; they can also be expected to compete in location choice. In a more general context, firms can compete on price and also, perhaps even more fiercely, on such factors as product specification.

In order to continue to keep the technical (mathematical) complications within manageable bounds, attention is focused solely on the case in which demand and delivery-cost functions are linear and on a duopolistic market.

As GMN point out, the duopolists can be expected to compete for consumers: The location choice of any one firm will affect the consumers that can be supplied by the second firm (recall the discussion of spatial locational-interdependence theory in Chapter 15). As a result, the duopolists will interact with each other, and some assumption is needed regarding the way in which each duopolist expects its rival to react in the competitive "game." It has been noted by a number of authors that specification of such an assumption meets with severe problems in this price/location formulation. It is worthwhile considering these problems briefly, particularly because they carry implications for the existence and stability of equilibrium in the much more general setting of imperfectly competitive markets.

In order to deal with these problems, it is generally assumed that each duopolist in choosing price and location has zero conjectural variation regarding the effects of its choices on the other firm's price and location, [5] with one significant exception. If one firm's choice of location or price results in undercutting of the other firm's price at the latter's location, it is believed that the latter firm will respond by cutting price to marginal cost.

Arguments in favor of this type of behavioral assumption, termed *modified zero conjectural variation (MZCV)*, and reasons for it being necessary have been advanced by several researchers; see, for example, Eaton (1972), Eaton and Lipsey (1978), and Kohlberg and Novshek (1982). Without it, as Kohlberg and Novshek point out, "no Nash equilibrium in price-location pairs is possible except in the case where the market is so large that all firms are unaffected by their neighbors" (Kohlberg and Novshek 1982, p. 9, fn. 4). Or, as Eaton (1972) indicates, there will be "a hopelessly unstable situation with no determinate solution" (Eaton 1972, p. 269).

Assume, therefore, that behavior is characterized by MZCV in the duopoly case. Further assume that the duopolists adopt identical pricing strategies, competing solely through location choice, and that firm 1 is located to the left of firm 2. Attention is confined to a comparison of f.o.b., uniform, and optimal discriminatory pricing systems and, to keep the mathematical analysis tractable, to the case of linear demand and delivery-cost functions.

The objective of firm i is to choose the location ρ_i $(i = 1, 2)$ that will maximize profit, on the assumption that the location of the other firm is fixed. Even within this apparently simple formulation, however, a technical difficulty arises that, quite fortunately, has an important economic interpretation.

It is quite within the bounds of possibility that the first-order conditions for optimal location choice cannot be satisfied, in which case there will be a corner solution in which $\rho_1 = \rho_2$. This is equivalent in economic terms to the Hotelling case discussed in Chapter 15, in which the duopolists choose coincident locations. Two cases should therefore be considered: first, the case in which the duopolists are *assumed* not to adopt coincident locations, and second, the conditions under which this assumption is invalid and Hotelling-like concentration emerges.

The linearity assumptions are such that the transport rate is assumed to be t per unit weight per unit distance, and the individual demand functions to be

$$Q(z) = a - bP(z) \quad (a, b > 0; \; 0 \leq z \leq 1) \tag{16.8}$$

GMN normalize the model by assuming

$$a = b = t = 1; \quad c = 0 \tag{16.9}$$

It also proves convenient to adopt the approach suggested by Norman (1981a) and respecify the delivered-price function $P(z)$. Thus, each firm is assumed to charge the delivered price

$$P(z) = p(\alpha) + \alpha t z = p(\alpha) + \alpha z \quad (0 \leq \alpha \leq 1) \tag{16.9'}$$

where $p(\alpha)$ is the mill price and α is the proportion of transport costs passed on to consumers by the producer. Note that $\alpha = 1$ is equivalent to f.o.b. pricing, and $\alpha = 0$ to uniform delivered pricing. The degree of spatial price discrimination, or freight absorption, is given by $\beta = 1 - \alpha$.

16.3.1 Competitive location: noncoincident location

Because it is assumed that both producers charge identical prices, it follows, as illustrated in Figure 16.3, that they will share equally the intermediate market [i.e., the market in the interval (ρ_1, ρ_2)]. Firm 1 will supply consumers in the market area $[0, (\rho_1 + \rho_2)/2)$, and firm 2 consumers in the market $((\rho_1 + \rho_2)/2, 1]$. The market boundary $(\rho_1 + \rho_2)/2$ is denoted $\bar{\rho}$.

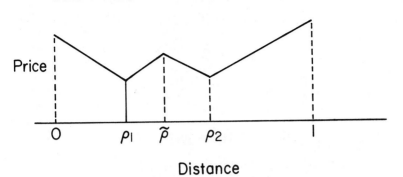

Figure 16.3. Market shares.

Given the linearity and normalizing assumptions (16.8) and (16.9), the profit functions for the two firms are

$$\Pi_1 = \int_0^{\rho_1} (1-p(\alpha)-\alpha(\rho_1-r))(p(\alpha)+\alpha(\rho_1-r)-(\rho_1-r))D(r)\,dr$$

$$(16.10)$$

$$+\int_{\rho_1}^{\tilde{\rho}} (1-p(\alpha)-\alpha(r-\rho_1))(p(\alpha)+\alpha(r-\rho_1)-(r-\rho_1))D(r)\,dr - F$$

$$\Pi_2 = \int_{\tilde{\rho}}^{\rho_2} (1-p(\alpha)-\alpha(\rho_2-r))(p(\alpha)+\alpha(\rho_2-r)-(\rho_2-r))D(r)\,dr$$

$$(16.11)$$

$$+\int_{\rho_2}^{1} (1-p(\alpha)-\alpha(r-\rho_2))(p(\alpha)+\alpha(r-\rho_2)-(r-\rho_2))D(r)\,dr - F$$

In each case, the first term gives profit (gross of fixed costs) from consumers to the left of the plant location, and the second term profit from consumers to the right of the plant location.

Differentiating (16.10) with respect to ρ_1 and (16.11) with respect to ρ_2 (assuming MZCV : $\partial\rho_1/\partial\rho_2 = 0$) generates a pair of first-order conditions that are, in fact, Cournot reaction functions. These reaction functions are (see Mathematical Appendix)

$$(\alpha-1)\left\{\int_0^{\rho_1} (1-p(\alpha)-\alpha(\rho_1-r))D(r)\,dr\right.$$

$$\left. -\int_{\rho_1}^{\tilde{\rho}} (1-p(\alpha)-\alpha(r-\rho_1))D(r)\,dr\right\}$$

$$-\alpha\left\{\int_0^{\rho_1} (p(\alpha)+(\alpha-1)(\rho_1-r))D(r)\,dr\right.$$

$$\left. -\int_{\rho_1}^{\tilde{\rho}} (p(\alpha)+(\alpha-1)(r-\rho_1))D(r)\,dr\right\} +$$

$$+ \tfrac{1}{2}(1 - p(\alpha) - \tfrac{1}{2}\alpha(\rho_2 - \rho_1))(p(\alpha) + \tfrac{1}{2}(\alpha - 1)(\rho_2 - \rho_1))D(\tilde{\rho}) = 0$$

$$(16.12)$$

$$(\alpha - 1)\left\{ \int_{\tilde{\rho}}^{\rho_2} (1 - p(\alpha) - \alpha(\rho_2 - r))D(r)\,dr \right.$$

$$\left. - \int_{\rho_2}^{1} (1 - p(\alpha) - \alpha(r - \rho_2))D(r)\,dr \right\}$$

$$- \alpha\left\{ \int_{\tilde{\rho}}^{\rho_2} (p(\alpha) + (\alpha - 1)(\rho_2 - r))D(r)\,dr \right.$$

$$\left. - \int_{\rho_2}^{1} (p(\alpha) + (\alpha - 1)(\rho_2 - \rho_1))D(r)\,dr \right\}$$

$$- \tfrac{1}{2}(1 - p(\alpha) - \tfrac{1}{2}\alpha(\rho_2 - \rho_1))(p(\alpha) + \tfrac{1}{2}(\alpha - 1)(\rho_2 - \rho_1))D(\tilde{\rho}) = 0$$

$$(16.13)$$

F.o.b. pricing ($\alpha = 1$) *and uniform delivered pricing* ($\alpha = 0$): Setting $\alpha = 1$ and $\alpha = 0$ in (16.12) and (16.13) generates the reaction functions for f.o.b. and uniform pricing, respectively (see Mathematical Appendix). These two sets of reaction functions are identical provided that

$$p(0) + p(1) = 1 \tag{16.14}$$

They are

$$\int_0^{\rho_1} D(r)\,dr - \int_{\rho_1}^{\tilde{\rho}} D(r)\,dr = \tfrac{1}{2}[1 - p(1) - \tfrac{1}{2}(\rho_2 - \rho_1)D(\tilde{\rho})]$$

$$(16.12')$$

$$\int_{\rho_2}^{1} D(r)\,dr - \int_{\tilde{\rho}}^{\rho_2} D(r)\,dr = \tfrac{1}{2}[1 - p(1) - \tfrac{1}{2}(\rho_2 - \rho_1)D(\tilde{\rho})]$$

$$\int_0^{\rho_1} D(r)\,dr - \int_{\rho_1}^{\tilde{\rho}} D(r)\,dr = \tfrac{1}{2}[p(0) - \tfrac{1}{2}(\rho_2 - \rho_1)D(\tilde{\rho})]$$

$$(16.13')$$

$$\int_{\rho_2}^{1} D(r)\,dr - \int_{\tilde{\rho}}^{\rho_2} D(r)\,dr = \tfrac{1}{2}[p(0) - \tfrac{1}{2}(\rho_2 - \rho_1)D(\tilde{\rho})]$$

Equation (16.14) is, in fact, just the fundamental pricing equation shown by Beckmann (1976) and Beckmann and Ingene (1976) to characterize optimal monopolistic f.o.b. and uniform delivered pricing. Given this fundamental pricing equation, it follows that profits, outputs, and market sizes for the duopolists will be identical under the two pricing schemes,[6] yet a further extension of the Beckmann and Ingene results.

The reaction functions for the duopolists are such that they are unlikely to choose the median locations in their respective market areas. Median location arises under f.o.b. pricing only if demand is zero at the joint market boundary, and under uniform delivered pricing only if net

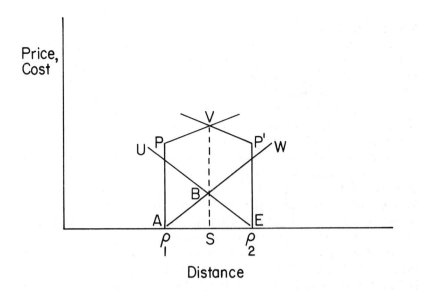

Figure 16.4. Optimal discriminatory pricing – case 1.

revenue (price minus marginal-production plus transportation costs) is negative at the joint market boundary. This should not be particularly surprising; either case implies, in effect, that the duopolists are not inter-acting.

In any other case, the location of firm 1 will be to the right and that of firm 2 to the left of the medians of their respective consumer distri-butions. Now the duopolists are competing for consumers on their joint market boundary. The force of this competition draws the firms together; effectively, they fight for the "middle ground."

Optimal discriminatory pricing policy ($\alpha = \frac{1}{2}$): When the duopolists are given free choice of the degree to which they can price-discriminate, then the assumption of constant marginal-production costs is such that profit is maximized over a given market area by setting marginal cost (MC) equal to marginal revenue (MR) *at each selling point,* and this whether the pro-ducer is a monopolist or duopolist. Assuming that the demand curve is linear, the delivered-price schedule (DPS) is also linear, with slope one-half the transport rate; in this case, $\alpha = \frac{1}{2}$, implying 50 percent freight absorption.

A quite interesting problem arises with this pricing policy, however, in the context of a duopolistic (or oligopolistic) market. It is best illustrated in terms of Figure 16.4. Assuming that the two firms have located at ρ_1

and ρ_2, the DPS on the MR $=$ MC rule is PV for firm 1 and $P'V$ for firm 2. Marginal production and transport costs are respectively ABW and EBU.

The problem that must be resolved is that the pricing policies PV and $P'V$ do not constitute a simple Nash equilibrium. Firm 2 can undercut firm 1 in markets in $\rho_1 S$ and will do so if its manager believes that firm 1 will not react. Similarly, firm 1 may try to undercut firm 2 in $\rho_2 S$ if it does not expect retaliation (acts as a simple Cournot-Nash competitor). Quite clearly, however, the attempted price undercutting will not be successful in that each firm will in fact react to the other's attack.

In order to resolve this problem, two alternative situations need to be considered. Assume first that the locations of the duopolists are sufficiently close that AW cuts EP' as in Figure 16.4. Then the assumption of MZCV can be used to argue that neither firm will attempt the price undercutting noted earlier. Each believes that the other firm will respond by immediately cutting price to marginal cost.

This argument in its literal form is not sufficient, however, to deal with the case illustrated in Figure 16.5. Now the DPS on the MC $=$ MR rule is PUV for firm 1 and $P'WV$ for firm 2. Marginal costs are respectively $ABCW$ and $EDCU$. Firm 1 can attempt price undercutting in the region SR' (because costs CW lie below firm 2's prices WV), and firm 2 can attempt price undercutting in the region RS. Given the locations of the duopolists, the only stable Nash equilibrium with the possibility of aggressive price-undercutting behavior is delivered-price schedule PUC for firm 1 and $P'WC$ for firm 2. This is a type of pricing policy first discussed by Hoover (1937).

GMN show that the price policies PUC and $P'WC$ are the outcomes of a prisoner's dilemma (Luce and Raiffa 1957). Both firms earn more profit with price policies PUV and $P'WV$, but their myopic competitive beliefs lead them into a price war and the less profitable Hooverian pricing policies.

How can this apparently rational, yet obviously misguided, behavior be resolved? There are two reasons for arguing that the predatory Hooverian pricing schedules will not emerge. First, there is the institutional point that this type of pricing is illegal in certain countries (e.g., the United States) and violates antidumping regulations between countries (price schedule PUC, for example, implies dumping in markets in RS). In terms of the prisoner's dilemma, such institutional forces eliminate the possibility of price undercutting and thus constrain the duopolists to simple discriminatory pricing.

Second, there are appealing theoretical reasons for believing that the prisoner's dilemma will be resolved in this spatial setting. In particular, the basic philosophy of MZCV can be extended to the belief by both duopolists that any attempt at price undercutting by predatory pricing will

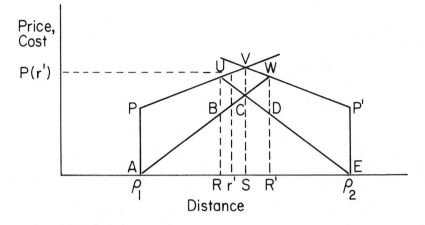

Figure 16.5. Optimal discriminatory pricing – case 2.

be met by the competitor cutting price to marginal cost. As Greenhut and Ohta (1975a) argue,

There is...no compelling economic reason why firms should compete with each other to such an extent that these competitive Hooverian price schedules appear ...derived as they are from excessive competition stemming from erroneous expectation that a rival's price schedule is unaffected by the price schedule established by a competitive firm. [Greenhut and Ohta 1975a, p. 126]

As a consequence, only the discriminatory price schedules *PUV* and *P'WV* will be chosen.

It might be thought that this kind of reasoning implies that the duopolists confine themselves to a limited form of price competition. Although that is indeed the case, it should be noted that the firms continue to compete on location choice (subject, of course, to MZCV). There is, therefore, an analogy to be drawn between the competitive behavior assumed to characterize spatial markets and that which characterizes oligopolistic competition based on product differentiation or advertising rather than on competitive price cutting and recurring price wars. As will be seen later, just as competing oligopolists produce more and closer product variants than they would if they colluded, so the spatial duopolists locate nearer to each other than they would if they colluded.

The outcome of this admittedly lengthy discussion is that the duopolists can be expected to adopt the pricing policies implied by *PUV* and *P'WV* in Figure 16.5 (i.e., the optimal discriminatory pricing policy that would be chosen by setting MC = MR at each selling location). It follows from the discussion in previous chapters that with normalized linear-demand and delivery-cost functions this gives

$$\alpha = \tfrac{1}{2}; \quad p(\alpha) = \tfrac{1}{2} \tag{16.15}$$

Substituting these values in equations (16.12) and (16.13) gives the reaction functions:

$$\int_0^{\rho_1} D(r)\,dr - \int_{\rho_1}^{\bar{\rho}} D(r)\,dr$$

$$= \rho_1 \int_0^{\bar{\rho}} D(r)\,dr - \int_0^{\bar{\rho}} rD(r)\,dr + \tfrac{1}{4}(1 - \tfrac{1}{2}(\rho_2 - \rho_1))^2 D(\bar{\rho}) \tag{16.16}$$

$$\int_{\rho_2}^{1} D(r)\,dr - \int_{\bar{\rho}}^{\rho_2} D(r)\,dr$$

$$= \int_{\bar{\rho}}^{1} rD(r)\,dr - \rho_2 \int_{\bar{\rho}}^{1} D(r)\,dr + \tfrac{1}{4}(1 - \tfrac{1}{2}(\rho_2 - \rho_1))^2 D(\bar{\rho}) \tag{16.17}$$

The right-hand sides of both reaction functions can be expected to be nonnegative. In common with f.o.b. pricing and uniform delivered pricing, competition will draw the duopolists toward each other. Optimal location for each firm deviates farther from the median of the consumer distribution within its market area than it would if the firms were to adopt the monopolist's location in the same market areas.

16.3.2 *Competitive location: coincident location*

It was noted in the introduction to Section 16.3 that an essential assumption underlying the analysis of Section 16.3.1 is that the first-order conditions for location choice can be satisfied as equalities and thus do not give rise to a corner solution (i.e., do not give rise to coincident location). It was also noted that this assumption may well be violated. We now turn to a consideration of those situations in which production concentration will in fact arise.

Because precisely the same arguments apply to both firms, we need only consider the location choice of firm 1.

F.o.b. pricing and uniform delivered pricing: For a corner solution (i.e., a solution in which $\rho_1 = \rho_2 = \bar{\rho}$), it is necessary that the profit equation still be increasing when $\rho_1 = \bar{\rho}$:

$$\left. \frac{\partial \Pi_1}{\partial \rho_1} \right|_{\rho_1 = \bar{\rho}} \geq 0 \tag{16.18}$$

Substitute $\rho_1 = \bar{\rho}$ and $\rho_2 = \bar{\rho}$ in the reaction function. Then (16.18) requires

$$\int_0^{\bar{\rho}} D(r)\,dr \leq \tfrac{1}{2}(1 - p(1))D(\bar{\rho}) \quad \text{(f.o.b. pricing)}$$

$$\int_0^{\bar{\rho}} D(r)\,dr \leq \tfrac{1}{2}p(0)D(\bar{\rho}) \quad \text{(uniform delivered pricing)} \tag{16.19}$$

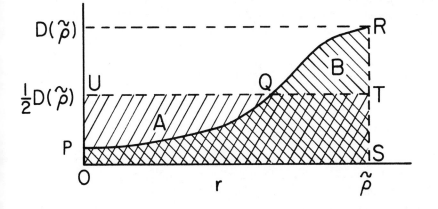

Figure 16.6. Coincident location – f.o.b. pricing.

Providing the fundamental pricing equation (16.14) holds, the consumer distributions that generate coincident location are identical for f.o.b. mill and uniform pricing. In other words, the locational equivalence of f.o.b. pricing and uniform pricing carries through to the coincident-location case.

Consider first the case in which consumers are evenly spread over the market area. Then it is to be expected that both firms will locate in the center of the market (as in the simple Hotelling case). In other words, $\tilde{\rho} = \frac{1}{2}$, and (16.19) cannot be satisfied for any nonzero price. Put another way, *Hotelling-like production concentration cannot occur if consumers are evenly distributed over the market and firms adopt f.o.b. or uniform delivered pricing.*

What does equation (16.19) imply about the types of consumer distributions that will lead to coincident location? For sales to be nonnegative on the left-hand boundary for firm 1 ($r = 0$), it is necessary that

$$(1 - p(1)) > \tilde{\rho} \quad \text{or} \quad p(0) > \tilde{\rho} \tag{16.20}$$

Hence, a sufficient but not necessary condition for (16.19) to hold is

$$\int_0^{\tilde{\rho}} D(r)\, dr \le \tfrac{1}{2} \tilde{\rho} D(\tilde{\rho}) \tag{16.21}$$

This condition is illustrated in Figure 16.6. The left-hand side of (16.21) is given by the area under the curve PQR, and the right-hand side is given by the area of the rectangle $0STU$. Equation (16.21) will be satisfied so long as area A is at least equal to area B. This gives the intuitively appealing result that Hotelling-type production concentration is more likely the more peaked is the consumer distribution around the mode. On the other hand, and again appealingly, if there is some "significant" number of consumers at peripheral locations (locations near to either the left- or right-hand boundary of the market), production concentration will not arise.

Optimal discriminatory pricing: Substituting $\rho_1 = \tilde{\rho}$ and $\rho_2 = \tilde{\rho}$ in equation (16.16) indicates that coincident location requires

$$\int_0^{\tilde{\rho}} (1 - \tilde{\rho} + r) D(r) \leq \tfrac{1}{4} D(\tilde{\rho}) \tag{16.22}$$

There is no simple way of determining if a consumer distribution that gives rise to coincident location under f.o.b. or uniform pricing will also give coincident location under optimal discriminatory pricing. What can be said, however, is that (16.22) is not satisfied by a uniform distribution of consumers. More generally, and in common with f.o.b. and uniform pricing, (16.22) is more likely to be satisfied by strongly peaked consumer distributions, which have "few" consumers at peripheral locations.

16.3.3   *Location choice under alternative market structures: some comments*

Our analysis of the duopolists' location choices has not considered the possibilities that one firm might be better informed than the other or that the two firms might collude. Assume, for example, that one firm (firm 1, say) is sufficiently sophisticated to recognize that its competitor is acting on the MZCV assumption. The sophisticated duopolist will incorporate this knowledge in its reaction function and thus act as a Stackelberg (1952) market leader (recall the analysis in Chapter 13).

In such a case, GMN show that there will be an increase in production concentration, but also a general rightward movement of the production locations; that is, the market leader will take a rather greater share of the market than would be the case under MZCV assumptions.

Alternatively, if the duopolists collude to maximize joint profits, there will be a considerable reduction in the drive to compete for "central" consumers. Quite naturally, therefore, the collusive equilibrium will be more dispersed than the MZCV equilibrium: It is unlikely, for example, that a collusive equilibrium would generate coincident location except under very special restrictions on the distribution of consumers.

16.4   Concluding remarks

Before presenting our main conclusions, a caveat is in order. The discussion in this chapter has been based on several fundamental assumptions that provide results sensitive to changes in the number of firms (i.e., the degree of competition) and hence to changes in the conjectural variations among the firms, changes in the distribution of customers throughout the market, and changes in the nature of the demand and delivery-cost functions. They call to mind the statement by Professor Chamberlin that

Wherever, for any reason, population is unevenly distributed, it is evident that the distribution of stores will conform to it. This is a proposition which is of great importance in the light of the interpretation which must now be given to the phrase, "distribution of population.". . . Variations in the scale of production, in rents, and in profits also take place from unevenness in the distribution of population, not in the sense of the existence of certain areas where it is on the whole more dense, but in the sense that the markets of different sellers fit into each other in highly irregular fashion. [1962, pp. 262–4]

The optimum-location principle set forth by Quinn (1943), Alonso (1964), Rydell (1967, 1971), and Snyder (1971) indicates that the median location is the cost-minimizing location of a monopolist in a one-dimensional market. However, under a heterogeneous distribution of customers, a monopolist's optimum location under alternative pricing policies depends crucially on the shapes of the demand and delivery-cost functions. Few general statements are possible, although it would appear that the monopolist is more likely to be drawn toward the major consumer concentration if freight rates decrease with distance, or if he can adopt the optimal discriminatory pricing policy.

If it is assumed that demand and delivery-cost functions are linear, there is a remarkable equivalence of locational choice under f.o.b. and uniform pricing that carries through to various types of market structures. Criticisms of uniform pricing vis-à-vis f.o.b. pricing must therefore be based mainly on their effects on consumer surplus (Beckmann 1976; Norman 1981a) but are then weakened by the need to make interpersonal welfare comparisons.

In the duopoly market it emerges once more that different pricing strategies lead to different location choices. In addition, the more peaked is the consumer distribution, the more likely it is that we shall find Hotelling-type concentration, no matter the pricing policy.

If the Cournot assumptions are relaxed to allow collusion between the duopolists, production will become more dispersed, whereas if one of the producers acts as a "sophisticated" duopolist, we shall expect some concentration of production.

These results lead us to emphasize that whereas production location is of course affected by cost considerations, general demand conditions are also powerful influences on location choice. The firm's optimal location depends, in general, on the firm's pricing policy, which in turn depends on the shape of the individual demand functions, the form of the delivery-cost functions, the conjectural variations of the managers of firms, the particular distribution of customers, and the degree of competition in the industry. Standard location theory also requires full recognition of the demand (price) factor of location (Greenhut 1956).

Mathematical appendix

Total profit under f.o.b. pricing:

$$\Pi_f = \int_0^\rho (m-c)f(m+T(\rho-r))D(r)\,dr$$

$$+ \int_\rho^1 (m-c)f(m+T(r-\rho))D(r)\,dr - F \tag{A16.1}$$

Differentiate with respect to ρ, and set the derivative to zero to give

$$\int_0^\rho (m-c)f'(m+T(z))T'(z)D(r)\,dr$$

$$= \int_\rho^1 (m-c)f'(m+T(z))T'(z)D(r)\,dr \tag{A16.2}$$

Comparing (A16.2) to (16.3) yields the weighting function

$$g(z) = (m-c)f'(m+T(z))T'(z) \tag{A16.3}$$

Differentiate (A16.3) to give

$$g'(z) = (m-c)f''(m+T(z))(T'(z))^2 + f'(m+T(z))T''(z) \tag{A16.4}$$

Total profit under uniform delivered pricing:

$$\Pi_u = \int_0^\rho (p-T(\rho-r)-c)f(p)D(r)\,dr$$

$$+ \int_\rho^1 (p-T(r-\rho)-c)f(p)D(r)\,dr - F \tag{A16.5}$$

Differentiate (A16.5) and set it to zero to give

$$\int_0^\rho f(p)T'(z)D(r)\,dr = \int_\rho^1 f(p)T'(z)D(r)\,dr \tag{A16.6}$$

Compare (A16.6) to (16.3) to obtain the weighting function

$$g(z) = f(p)T'(z) \tag{A16.7}$$

Further differentiate (A16.7) to obtain

$$g'(z) = f(p)T''(z) \tag{A16.8}$$

Total profit under discriminatory pricing:

$$\Pi_d = \int_0^\rho [(m(\rho-r)-c)f(m(\rho-r)+T(\rho-r))]D(r)\,dr$$

$$+ \int_\rho^1 [(m(r-\rho)-c)f(m(r-\rho)+T(r-\rho))]D(r)\,dr - F \qquad (A16.9)$$

Differentiate (A16.9), substitute (16.7) into the derivative, and set it to zero to give

$$\int_0^\rho f(m(z)+T(z))T'(z)D(r)\,dr$$

$$= \int_\rho^1 f(m(z)+T(z))T'(z)D(r)\,dr \qquad (A16.10)$$

Again compare (A16.10) with (16.3) to give

$$g(z) = f(m+T(z))T'(z) \qquad (A16.11)$$

Differentiate (A16.11) to give

$$g'(z) = f'(p(z))p'(z)T'(z)+f(p(z))T''(z) \qquad (A16.12)$$

Reaction functions (16.12) and (16.13): Differentiate (16.10) with respect to ρ_1 using the Leibniz formula to give

$$(\alpha-1)\int_0^{\rho_1}(1-p(\alpha)-\alpha(\rho_1-r))D(r)\,dr$$

$$-\alpha\int_0^{\rho_1}(p(\alpha)+(\alpha-1)(\rho_1-r))D(r)\,dr+(1-p(\alpha))p(\alpha)D(\rho_1)$$

$$-(\alpha-1)\int_{\rho_1}^{\bar\rho}(1-p(\alpha)-\alpha(r-\rho_1))D(r)\,dr$$

$$+\alpha\int_{\rho_1}^{\bar\rho}(p(\alpha)+(\alpha-1)(r-\rho_1))D(r)\,dr-(1-p(\alpha))p(\alpha)D(\rho_1)$$

$$+\tfrac12(1-p(\alpha)-\tfrac12\alpha(\rho_2-\rho_1))(p(\alpha)+\tfrac12(\alpha-1)(\rho_2-\rho_1))D(\bar\rho)=0$$
$$(A16.13)$$

Simple manipulation gives equation (16.13).

Differentiate (16.11) with respect to ρ_2 using the Leibniz formula to give

$$(\alpha-1)\int_{\bar\rho}^{\rho_2}(1-p(\alpha)-\alpha(\rho_2-r))D(r)\,dr$$

$$-\alpha\int_{\bar\rho}^{\rho_2}(p(\alpha)+(\alpha-1)(\rho_2-r))D(r)\,dr+(1-p(\alpha))p(\alpha)D(\rho_2)-$$

$$-\tfrac{1}{2}(1-p(\alpha)-\tfrac{1}{2}\alpha(\rho_2-\rho_1))(p(\alpha)+\tfrac{1}{2}(\alpha-1)(\rho_2-\rho_1))D(\bar{\rho})$$

$$-(\alpha-1)\int_{\rho_2}^{1}(1-p(\alpha)-\alpha(r-\rho_2))D(r)\,dr$$

$$+\alpha\int_{\rho_2}^{1}(p(\alpha)+(\alpha-1)(\rho_2-\rho_1))D(r)\,dr-(1-p(\alpha))p(\alpha)D(\rho_2)=0$$

$$(A16.14)$$

Simple manipulation gives equation (16.13)

Reaction functions under f.o.b. and uniform pricing: Substitute $\alpha=1$ in equation (A16.13) and (A16.14) to give the reaction functions under f.o.b. pricing:

$$-\int_{0}^{\rho_1}p(1)D(r)\,dr+\int_{\rho_1}^{\bar{\rho}}p(1)D(r)\,dr$$

$$+\tfrac{1}{2}(1-p(1)-\tfrac{1}{2}(\rho_2-\rho_1))p(1)D(\bar{\rho})=0$$

$$-\int_{\bar{\rho}}^{\rho_2}p(1)D(r)\,dr+\int_{\rho_2}^{1}p(1)D(r)\,dr$$

$$-\tfrac{1}{2}(1-p(1)-\tfrac{1}{2}(\rho_2-\rho_1))p(1)D(\bar{\rho})=0$$

Cancel $p(1)$ and reorganize to give equations (16.12′).

Substitute $\alpha=0$ in equations (A16.13) and (A16.14) to give the reaction functions under uniform delivered pricing:

$$-\int_{0}^{\rho_1}(1-p(0))D(r)\,dr+\int_{\rho_1}^{\bar{\rho}}(1-p(0))D(r)\,dr$$

$$+\tfrac{1}{2}(1-p(0))(p(0)-\tfrac{1}{2}(\rho_2-\rho_1))D(\bar{\rho})=0$$

$$-\int_{\bar{\rho}}^{\rho_2}(1-p(0))D(r)\,dr+\int_{\rho_2}^{1}(1-p(0))D(r)\,dr$$

$$-\tfrac{1}{2}(1-p(0))(p(0)-\tfrac{1}{2}(\rho_2-\rho_1))D(\bar{\rho})=0$$

Cancel $[1-p(0)]$ and reorganize to give equations (16.13′).

CHAPTER 17

Optimal location in nonspatial markets: a spatial approach

The analysis in the previous chapter can be applied to a wide variety of spatial and nonspatial problems. It can, for example, be applied directly to the analysis of product differentiation and the optimal "locations" of competing product variants. Indeed, this application is so direct that we shall merely sketch out its basic principles in Section 17.1. The reader can then return to Chapter 16 and change the spatial "labels" to product-differentiation "labels."

Rather more attention is paid to a second possible application. It will be shown in Section 17.2 that the analysis of optimal location choice has direct relevance to current debates on transportation policy and the development of transportation services.

17.1   Product differentiation: some brief comments

Much of this application is perfectly straightforward, given the analysis in Chapter 5. The line market becomes a characteristics line, consumer location is the consumer's preferred product variant, and producer location is the product variant actually made available by each producer.

The only potential complication relates to the interpretation of f.o.b. mill, uniform delivered, and optimal discriminatory pricing in our differentiated-product world. Here the comments in Section 6.4 of Chapter 6 are directly relevant.

The product-differentiation analogue of f.o.b. pricing presents no problems. Such a pricing system arises naturally out of one of two situations:

1.   The consumer pays a full price consisting of the price charged by the producer (the mill price) plus the loss of utility involved in his having to consume a product that is not his most preferred product – this is just the situation analyzed in Chapter 5.

There is an alternative possibility:

2.   The consumer pays the producer's (mill) price for the basic commodity, then customizes the commodity to his own requirements (e.g., by painting it or adding particular "extras" at his own expense).[1]

293

Table 17.1. *Analogy between transport scheduling and production location*

Space	Scheduling
Production location	Offered departure (shipping) time
Consumer location	Preferred departure (shipping) time
Distance	Time
Mill price	Flight (shipping) cost
Transport cost	Waiting time, storage cost, inconvenience

It is, of course, assumed that the more customizing is necessary to convert the basic product to the consumer's most preferred product – the greater the "distance" between producer and consumer – the more expensive the customizing will be.

It should also be emphasized that customizing is assumed to change the characteristics content of goods, but not their quality. In other words, in Phlips's language, customizing leads to horizontal, but not vertical, differentiation.

What about uniform delivered pricing? In fact, the product-differentiation analogue is now quite simple: The producer offers to customize the product and charges identical prices for all customized products.

Finally, consider optimal discriminatory pricing. Again the producer offers to customize the product, but now he charges a different price for each variety. This is just the case considered in Chapter 6. It follows directly that the price charged by the producer for customizing need not be the actual cost of such customizing. Price discrimination is possible.

Again, of course, account has to be taken of the problems raised by Gronberg and Meyer. In this case it is assumed that the producer does not offer the consumer the option of customizing the product himself. All products leave the factory painted in some way, or all cars are automatically fitted with some kind of radio. In a spatial sense this is equivalent to the producer denying the consumer the option of collecting the product at the factory gates.

The concavity/convexity of transport costs in the previous chapter can now be interpreted as the shape of the "customizing-cost curve," and the concavity/convexity of individual demand is captured if, for example, demand is generated by a Lovell type of utility function [see Chapter 5, equation (5.32)].

On this basis, the analysis in Chapter 16 applies directly to product differentiation in markets in which the distribution of consumers is not uniform. The spatial "labels" can be reinterpreted using the space/product-differentiation analogy of Table 5.1. In particular, it is to be expected that competing product variants will be located more closely together the greater the consensus among consumers regarding the most preferred product. By contrast, collusion among the producers, or multiproduct production by a monopolist, will lead to more differentiation (distance) between the varieties offered to consumers.

The reader is left to reinterpret the remaining conclusions of Chapter 16 in this differentiated-product world.

17.2 Scheduling of transport services

Throughout this book we have been concerned with showing how a spatial approach to imperfect competition can be used to shed light on important microeconomic policy debates, whether or not the questions being debated relate explicitly to spatial markets. Two debates that have been ongoing (we are tempted to say raging) over the past few years relate to transportation regulations – in particular, to freight shipping and airline travel. We show in this section in a rather intuitive way how the analysis of Chapter 16 can contribute to these two debates. The reader should then see quite readily how the ideas can be applied to any area of transportation policy.

Why is it that a spatial model can be transformed into this nonspatial context? The essence of the transformation is summarized in Table 17.1. Just as indivisible production units have to be given well-defined geographic locations, so indivisible transportation units (ships, airplanes) have to be given well-defined departure times. Whereas in geographic markets consumers are located at particular buying points, consumers in the market for transport services have preferred departure times, whether in the day, month, or year. Rather than "distance" in Figure 16.1, there is now "time." Corresponding to the transport costs incurred by consumers not located at the factory gates, there is the waiting time, inconvenience, and storage costs or overtime costs incurred by those whose desired departure time does not coincide with a scheduled freighter or airline departure.

17.2.1 *Freight shipping*

A significant proportion of all international freight shipping carried in freight liners is under the control of what are known as "shipping conferences." The term "conference" relates to a cartel arrangement between shipowners that regulates competition on particular freight routes or between particular types of freight carriers. Shipping conferences can take many forms, their main intention being to fix freight rates and, in many cases, market sharing and scheduling of services on the routes to which they apply. [For a discussion of some of the properties of shipping conferences, see Gilman (1983).]

Shipping conferences are restrictive practices; yet they are allowed to continue in operation by the authorities in both developed and developing countries. Why should this be? A clear statement of the attitude of the U.K. government was given by the Rochdale Committee of Inquiry into Shipping (1970), commissioned by the Board of Trade of the United Kingdom. In looking at the advantages of conferences, the committee pointed out that

[many] shippers...seek scheduled services to minor as well as major ports.... They appreciate having freight rates which in general...do not change frequently. [Rochdale Committee 1970, para. 414]

Liner operators contend that in the absence of conferences,

shippers would suffer in the long run through deterioration of service....[If] an intruder creamed off the most profitable traffic by offering cut prices,...the regular liner operators would no longer be able to provide a reasonably profitable and regular service for other traffic. [Rochdale Committee 1970, para. 416]

Although the committee recognized the potentially inefficient aspects of shipping conferences, they stated that

[it] has long been the policy of the UK Government (and of the Governments of all major European maritime nations) to acquiesce in the freedom of shipping companies to join conferences. This policy has been founded on the belief that conference arrangements are necessary if shippers are to be provided with regular and efficient services at stable prices. [Rochdale Committee 1970, para. 428]

In looking in more detail at conferences as restrictive practices, the committee further contended that

the shipper is concerned with more than stability of freight rates; he also looks for a quality of service which includes the characteristics of reasonably regular and frequent sailings.... It follows that the rationalisation of sailings is the most desirable feature of conferences since it...prevents bunching and gaps in services....

[Liner] operators can best provide a service with rationalzed sailings only within a [closed conference]. [Rochdale Committee 1970, para. 465–6]

They concluded that

[the] closed conference with fully rationalized sailings therefore appears to us most likely to service the best interests of both shippers and shipowners. [Rochdale Committee 1970, para. 469]

Similar comments underlie the current debate on shipping conferences within the European Economic Community (EEC). Industrial and commercial policy in the EEC operates under constraints laid down by the Competition Directorate, whose basic philosophy is rooted in the concept of "free competition." Cartels are prohibited, and any dominant market position can be investigated. Nevertheless, the EEC is in the process of ratifying legislation to allow the continuance of shipping conferences. The reasons have much in common with those already stated. In recent analysis by Böhme (1983, p. 334) it was stated that "the Council of Ministers [of the EEC] has considered the stabilising function of the conference system." They noted "the excessive variations of freight rates that are frequently observed in liner markets under conditions of unregulated competition." As a result, shipping conferences are likely to be made exempt from the competition rules of the EEC so long as

[the] agreement between the conference members...serves the stated objective of offering shippers a reliable service at low and relatively stable rates by rationalising the service. [Böhme 1983, p. 334]

How can this consistent policy stance be explained in terms of a theory of spatial pricing and competitive plant location as developed in Chapter 16? Consider first the question of price stability. It was noted in the discussion of discriminatory pricing that considerable difficulties lie in the way of identifying any stable price/location pair. Where competition is unregulated and spare capacity exists – as appear to characterize many unregulated freight routes – price undercutting at particular times is likely to be no more than a broad trend. The typical situation can be expected to be one of price wars interspersed with periods of price stability.

So far as scheduling is concerned, spatial analysis can again be applied in a direct fashion. Recall that competitive zones tend to draw firms toward the more concentrated market locations (between the median and mode) and to encourage more spatial competition than would a collusive market structure. Translating this to the time dimension of transport scheduling, in the absence of conferences it is probable that there will indeed be the "bunching and gaps in services" referred to by the Rochdale Committee. Only with the collusive agreement (a conference) is there any reasonable guarantee that less popular locations (departure times) will be chosen.

17.2.2 Airline services

A similar line of reasoning can be applied to airline services. Some significant differences should, however, be noted. A major reason for govern-

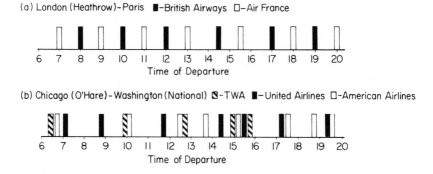

Figure 17.1. Comparison of airline schedules – December 1977.

ments accepting shipping conferences is the belief that shippers desire regular services at stable rates. Given the indivisibilities involved in the provision of international freight services, competition is unlikely to satisfy these desires. It is not clear that those who use airline services have the same requirements, nor that the same indivisibilities apply.[2] Thus, arguments for and against deregulation of airlines must be related to somewhat different considerations.

It is, however, possible to point to one aspect of airline deregulation that accords well with spatial price theory. A major consequence of deregulation has been the move to extensive price discrimination (Meyer et al. 1981). Quite clearly, different travelers (tourists, business travelers, those visiting friends) have different elasticities of demand for travel at particular times. Once regulations on pricing are relaxed, it is to be expected that airlines will make extensive use of special discounts at particular times, on advance purchase, for return fares, and so forth.

In a more general context, there should be some connection between "competition" and airline scheduling. The smaller the number of airlines operating a particular route (perhaps because of regulations on entry), the more likely it is that those operating the route will enter into a tacit or explicit market-sharing agreement. By contrast, with greater numbers of competitors, market sharing is more difficult to sustain, and some bunching of departure times can be expected.

Some (suggestive) evidence of this is given by Figure 17.1, which compares flight scheduling on two routes: between London (Heathrow) and Paris and between Chicago (O'Hare) and Washington (National) during December 1977. In the former case, the route was controlled by the two national airlines (British Airways and Air France). On the latter route,

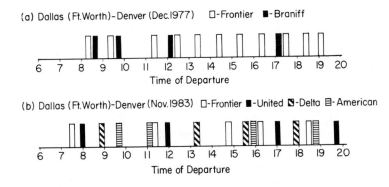

Figure 17.2. Comparison of airline schedules before and after deregulation.

service was provided by TWA, United Airlines, and American Airlines. It was to be expected that the individual carriers would adopt a more collusive attitude on the former route. This is reflected in the much more dispersed and regular pattern of flight departures.

Flight schedules for the Dallas/Ft. Worth–Denver route before and after deregulation are compared in Figure 17.2, which illustrates flights scheduled in December 1977 and November 1983. The competing airlines were, for December 1977, Braniff and Frontier, and for November 1983, Frontier, United, Delta, and American. Although there was some bunching in schedules in 1977 (compare this with London–Paris), it would appear that the post-deregulation schedules exhibit a much less even pattern of departures, with wide gaps and then groups of competing departures – a picture that is, again, consistent with expectations based on the production-location analysis of Chapter 16.

In a simpler but more general context, assume that under regulated (collusive) arrangements, three airlines, say A, B, and C, have scheduled morning departures from Houston to St. Louis at 6:00 a.m., 8:00 a.m., and 10:00 a.m. Further assume that passage on each flight is comparatively high in price and that 8:00 a.m. is the most preferred time. Let the 6:00 a.m. plane be typically two-thirds full, the 8:00 a.m. plane be invariably completely booked, and the 10:00 a.m. plane, like the 6:00 a.m. flight, usually two-thirds full. In arriving at this scheduling, we suppose that airline regulators have acceded to selected consumer interest groups that prefer *very early* and *much later* morning departure times. Of course, the airline awarded the 8:00 a.m. flight can be expected to have a 6:00 a.m. scheduled departure from some other city.

Now deregulate. Assuming the cities have not grown in size, it is to be expected that after deregulation only two airlines will continue servicing Houston–St. Louis in the morning, each of which charges a lower fare than it did under regulation, with one departing within a few minutes of the other, say 7:50 a.m. and 8:05 a.m. What originally was a quartile-median-quartile time dispersion proves not to be the perfect maximizing schedule under competition. Rather, the lower-cost-per-passenger 8:00 a.m. flight of our example justifies localization of the industry and leads to the possibility that some travelers will not be able to find a convenient flight.

It is worth noting that although this example is hypothetical and intuitive, it was inspired in part by an airline executive who has often complained to one of the authors about the effects on scheduling of airline deregulation. His complaints appear to be justified. The maximum-profit theory of location predicts a greater short-run *tendency* to localize as a consequence of the behavioral uncertainty that characterizes competitive markets vis-à-vis what is *in fact* the profit-maximizing (time) location. However, the same location theory indicates that as firms and their industry mature, locational (time) dispersion takes place in response to the greatest (possible) profit signals. It is, in fact, in the long run that locational (product-variant) efficiency obtains. The final three chapters of this book center attention, accordingly, on the long run in the spatial economy.

17.3   Concluding remarks

The analysis presented in this chapter has been kept deliberately intuitive and suggestive. This in no way reduces its power or relevance. It is quite clear that a spatial theory of competitive production-location under different pricing regimes is easily and directly translated into a theory of competing-product differentiation.

The spatial production-location approach is equally directly applicable to the analysis of transport scheduling. It lends support to policy statements with respect to the effects of shipping conferences and is consistent with the apparent consequences of airline deregulation.

It should be further recognized that complaints against regulation of transportation have centered on (1) the static-deadweight loss caused by rates in excess of long-run marginal cost, (2) the so-called dynamic-welfare loss that stems from excess capacity that is related, in turn, to exit regulations that prevent the curtailing or elimination of a service,[3] and (3) the adverse effect of regulation on technical change and productivity (Winston 1985). Estimates by Harbeson (1969) and later by Levin (1978) and others (Winston 1985) of the welfare loss that stems from insufficient use of rail services vis-à-vis motor transport carriage have – on the average – approximated $1 billion. The consensus appears to be that rates should be set at marginal cost to eliminate the welfare loss. However, as Chapters 19 and 20 will demonstrate, marginal cost must be measured by space-economy requirements, not by classical economic estimates.

Many of the recent complaints regarding the effects of regulation and excess capacity have centered on airline regulation. Though one result has been the favorable effect of minimizing the "frequency delays and stochastic delays" (i.e., the utility loss referred to in Chapter 5), more stress has been placed on the welfare loss attributable to excess capacity, as in the hypothetical example used in this chapter. The complaints against the Civil Aeronautics Board (CAB) in the United States extend to the Interstate Commerce Commission (ICC); among other critiques, MacAvoy and Glass (1967) and Gellner (1977) have mentioned the delay in introducing trainload services for coal and the stifling of the innovative facets of piggyback operations, the introduction of aluminum hopper cars, and the backlash restrictions in trucking, all of which have discouraged the development of equipment that could carry liquid or dry freight. Central to the literature on the economics of regulation, we suggest, is the need for far-reaching conceptions of differentiated products, location theory, and, as noted previously, a complete measure of long-run marginal costs in oligopolistic industries. Only when armed with spatial concepts will transportation models be capable of comparing equilibrium levels of fares and services in regulated and deregulated environments.[4]

CHAPTER 18

Competition, free entry, and long-run profit

The analysis in Chapter 16 is essentially a short-run analysis, in that it considers a given number of firms locating within a particular market area. We now turn to the analysis of price/location choices in a long-run setting.

One of the standard assumptions used in the derivation of long-run market equilibria in imperfectly competitive markets under free-entry conditions is that firms will continue to enter until profits are driven to zero. It may be recalled, for example, that extensive use was made of the Capozza and Van Order zero-profit locus (ZPL) in the analysis of f.o.b. and uniform delivered pricing. The ZPL is also implicit in the Salop model of product differentiation.

To a large extent, the zero-profit assumption is drawn from Chamberlin's analysis (1933) of monopolistic competition and, by implication, product differentiation. It is also the case, however, that the zero-profit assumption was called into question almost as soon as Chamberlin's analysis appeared. It should not be surprising, therefore, that the growing awareness of the importance and general relevance of imperfect competition has raised the question whether or not long-run imperfectly competitive equilibria are, or should be, assumed to be zero-profit equilibria.

In this chapter we show why it is that "pure" or excess profit might persist in the long run in imperfectly competitive markets, even under free-entry conditions.

It is, of course, the case that whereas the analysis in this chapter is couched in terms of spatial competition, nothing would change if we were to rewrite the analysis as an analysis of product differentiation and long-run profits. The formal models would be identical, as would be the conclusions.

18.1 The existence of long-run profit: some intuitive remarks

Criticisms of Chamberlin's view that in a monopolistically competitive world free entry will drive profits to zero (or, in a microeconomic textbook sense, down to the point at which only normal profit remains) have come from two major sources. On the one hand, Demsetz (1964) emphasizes the problems that arise with product differentiation:

Product differentiation which is used to confront firms with negatively sloped demand curves, and free entry, basically are inconsistent assumptions. The most plausible source of product differentiation is to be found in the laws of trademark, copyright, and patent. The laws clearly are barriers to imitative entry; they may be socially justified by the incentive that they give to new product production or by the reduction in information cost that they help to bring about, benefits which should, of course, be taken account of in judging the overall efficiency of markets in which products are differentiated. Nonetheless, these barriers provide neither more nor less than the prerequisites for simple monopoly. In the presence of such barriers it is difficult to apply or interpret the assumption of free entry. If a firm produces a profitable brand, "entry" need not eliminate profits because there is not free entry into the production of that brand. Product differentiation undermines the logic of using "free entry" to deduce the familiar zero profit Chamberlin equilibrium. As a result, the equilibrium rate of output for a firm to the left of the low point of its average cost curve is no more necessary than for simple monopoly. Entry via a different brand or product variety analytically is no different than entry into the electricity market to compete with natural gas. Such indirect entry need never succeed in reducing profits to zero because the electricity output, or in the case in hand, the output of rival brands, that is required to reduce profits to zero may be so large that "entering" firms, in order to accomplish this, would need to accept losses. The zero-profit equilibrium is not a correct deduction of the monopolistic competition model; it is a hidden assumption, and one that is difficult to reconcile with product differentiation.

A slightly different, but related, argument was advanced much earlier by Kaldor (1935):

Let us now introduce indivisibilities and economies of scale. The movement of new firms into the field will then not continue until the elasticities of demand for the individual producers become infinite, it will be stopped long before that by the increase in costs as the output of producers is reduced. But there is no reason to assume that it will stop precisely at the point where the demand and cost curves are tangential. For, on account of the very reasons of economies of scale, the potential producer cannot hope to enter the field profitably with less than a certain magnitude of output; and that additional output may reduce demand, both to his nearest neighbours and to him, to such an extent that the demand curves will lie below the cost curves and will be involved in losses. The interpolation of a third producer in between any two producers may thus transform profits into losses. The same reason therefore which prevents competition from becoming perfect – i.e. indivisibility – will also prevent the complete elimination of "profits." It will secure a monopolistic advantage to anybody who is first in the field and merely by virtue of priority. The ultimate reason for this is that it is not the original resources themselves, but the various uses to which they are put that are indivisible – you can divide "free capital," but you cannot invest less than a certain amount of it in a machine – and consequently the investment of resources cannot be so finely distributed as to equalize the level of marginal productivities.

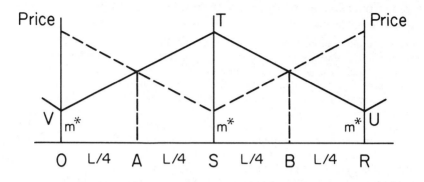

Figure 18.1. Locational equilibrium.

The arguments advanced by Demsetz and Kaldor have a common strand that can be highlighted by means of a simple geometric example. Figure 18.1 illustrates one segment of a spatial or differentiated-product market. Two firms are assumed to exist in this market segment: firm 1 located at 0 and firm 2 at R, with the distance $0R$ being L. Consumers are identical and evenly spread over the market; f.o.b. pricing is assumed, and it is also assumed that both firms charge the same mill price m^*. Delivered prices to consumers in the market segment $0R$ are given by VT and UT.

Now consider firm 3, contemplating entry somewhere between firms 1 and 2. Under not particularly restrictive conditions (discussed in Section 18.2) firm 3 is best advised to locate at the midpoint of $0R$ – at S. The mill price for firm 3 will be at least m^*. As a result, firm 3 will capture a market AB that is no larger than $L/2$, whereas the existing firms supply markets of size L (because firm 1, for example, sells to consumers both to the right and to the left of 0).

It follows that the effective aggregate demand curve facing firm 3 will lie everywhere below and to the left of that facing either firm 1 or firm 2. This is illustrated in Figure 18.2, in which dd_3 is the aggregate demand curve facing firm 3, whereas DD is the aggregate demand curve for firm 1 (and firm 2). It is perfectly conceivable, as shown in this diagram, for DD to lie above long-run average costs (LRAC) over some region, whereas dd_3 lies everywhere below LRAC. Firms 1 and 2 will make pure profit so long as mill price m^* is chosen somewhere between m_1 and m_2. For example, at mill price m_1^*, pure profit to firm 1 (and firm 2) is given by the shaded area $ABCD$. But firm 3 cannot enter the market: Because the demand curve dd_3 lies below LRAC, there is no price that firm 3 can choose that will allow it to break even.

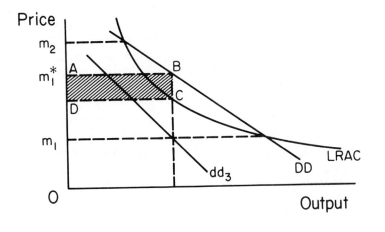

Figure 18.2. Positive-profit equilibrium.

This analysis is, of course, very intuitive. It is consistent with the remarks of Kaldor and Demsetz, but it is by no means a formal model. In particular, no account is taken of the interdependences between producers implied by Figure 18.1. For example, even if Figure 18.2 applies and firm 3 does not enter, why is it that competition between firms 1 and 2, and between these firms and firms in other market segments, does not drive price down to the point at which pure profit is zero, for example, to price m_1 in Figure 18.2? What are the essential elements that give rise to the positive profit illustrated in Figure 18.2?

18.2 A formal model: Eaton and Lipsey

The arguments advanced by Kaldor (and by Demsetz for differentiated products) have been formalized by Eaton and Lipsey (1978) using a model that has much in common with those used throughout this book. The most important assumptions are as follows:

1. The market is an unbounded line market over which consumers are evenly spread.
2. Total production costs are identical for all firms and are given by

$$C(Q) = F + cQ \tag{18.1}$$

where F indicates fixed costs, and c is constant marginal cost.

3. Fixed capital is immobile and cannot be resold at its original cost. This implies, first, that there are heavy costs to relocation of existing plant and, second, that there are sunk costs.
4. All producers own only one plant. This avoids the problems that would arise if firms were able to use a multiplant strategy as a barrier to entry.
5. Transport costs are t per unit distance per unit product.
6. All producers employ f.o.b. pricing, and consumers buy from the firm offering the lowest delivered price.
7. The individual demand functions are identical for all consumers:

$$q = f(p_d) \quad (f' < 0) \tag{18.2}$$

where p_d is delivered price.

The reader may question the f.o.b. pricing assumption given the strong connections between pricing policy and location choice. In fact, all of the analysis in this chapter could be reworked either for uniform pricing or for general discriminatory pricing. The quantitative details of the solution would change, but the basic principles would not. No matter the pricing policy, an equilibrium can be shown to exist such that firms in the market earn positive pure profit but such that no "outside" firms can enter the market. Because the sources of this pure profit are independent of the pricing system, it is sufficient to concentrate on f.o.b. pricing.

In common with all models of imperfect competition, some assumptions must be made regarding each firm's beliefs about its rival's reactions to a change in price or location. It was noted in Chapter 16 that this presents problems in a price/location model that are much more troublesome than those that characterize a simple price model (where locations are fixed).

Eaton and Lipsey assume the following:

1. Each firm, in choosing its location, takes the locations of its rivals as given – denoted zero locational conjectural variation (ZLCV).
2. All firms, in choosing price, have the same price conjectural variations (PCV), but these may lie anywhere between the Löschian extreme of price matching (denoted UPCV) and the Hotelling-Smithies (or Bertrand-Nash) extreme of no price change (denoted ZPCV). (The zonal price effect of the Greenhut-Ohta model is not considered.)

This simple specification is not sufficient to prevent instability in price/location markets, because there remains the possibility that a new entrant will attempt to undercut an existing firm. By doing so, the new entrant hopes to drive the existing firms from the market, while making almost as much profit itself as the existing firms.

A lengthy discussion was presented in Chapter 16 to indicate why this kind of behavior on the part of an entrant can be considered to be irrational. The reactions of oligopolistic competitors are particularly difficult to specify. There is, however, one thing of which a new entrant can be certain: No existing firm will stand passively by and see itself driven from the market. The existing firm will react, and because it *does* exist (has sunk costs), it can compete price down to a level that makes entry unprofitable for the potential entrant. Whereas in a formal sense the Eaton-Lipsey model assumes a relatively simple PCV, it has underlying it the modified PCV discussed in Chapter 16. Price undercutting is ruled out by this modified PCV.

The next question to be resolved is what is meant by equilibrium in this price/location model. Eaton and Lipsey show that it is convenient to split the concept of equilibrium into two parts: a *constant-numbers* equilibrium and a *free-entry* equilibrium. In doing so, they distinguish *pure profit,* which is total revenue minus long-run total cost, and *gross profit,* which is total revenue minus variable cost.

A necessary and sufficient condition for a constant-numbers equilibrium to exist is that no firm can find a combination of price and location that offers it a larger anticipated gross profit than that obtained with its present combination of price and location. This constant-numbers equilibrium is purely a short-run condition. It could, for example, be satisfied by prices and locations that generate negative pure profit (or, indeed, negative gross profit) for some or all existing firms. In other words, constant-numbers equilibrium could exist in a situation in which existing firms are covering their (short-run) variable costs but not their (long-run) total costs. If that is the case, then of course some firms will exit the market in the longer run.

This leads to the second equilibrium concept. Free-entry equilibrium gives the long-run counterpart to constant-numbers equilibrium. For free-entry equilibrium it is necessary that (1) all existing firms be in constant-numbers equilibrium, (2) all possible combinations of location and price for a new entrant offer anticipated gross profit less than F (i.e., anticipated negative pure profit), and (3) no existing firm earn actual gross profit of less than F (i.e., all existing firms are at least covering their long-run total costs).

The first condition ensures that no existing firm will want to change its price or location; the second condition ensures that no new firm will want to enter the market; the third condition ensures that no existing firm will

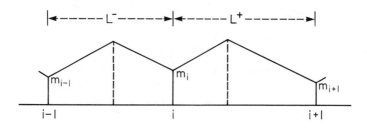

Figure 18.3. Constant-numbers equilibrium.

want to leave the market. In other words, if a free-entry equilibrium can be identified, it will be a stable long-run equilibrium.

The two stages of the Eaton-Lipsey analysis can be outlined very easily. Consider first whether or not positive pure profit can persist in constant-numbers equilibrium. The counterargument would be that even with a fixed number of firms, competition between them will drive price down to the level at which pure profit is zero.

To show that this counterargument will not hold, consider firm i in Figure 18.3. Pure profit for firm i can be written as a function of the mill prices m_i, m_{i-1}, and m_{i+1} and of the distances L^- and L^+, respectively, between firm i and firms $i-1$ and $i+1$:

$$\Pi_i = (m_i - c)Q(m_i, m_{i-1}, m_{i+1}, L^-, L^+) - F \tag{18.3}$$

where Q is the aggregate demand function for firm i.

Maximizing Π_i with respect to m_i gives the general first-order condition

$$\frac{\partial \Pi_i}{\partial m_i} = Q + (m_i - c)\frac{\partial Q}{\partial m_i} + (m_i - c)\left\{ \frac{\partial Q}{\partial m_{i-1}}\frac{\partial m_{i-1}}{\partial m_i} + \frac{\partial Q}{\partial m_{i+1}}\frac{\partial m_{i+1}}{\partial m_i} \right.$$

$$\left. + \frac{\partial Q}{\partial L^-}\frac{\partial L^-}{\partial m_i} + \frac{\partial Q}{\partial L^+}\frac{\partial L^+}{\partial m_i} \right\} \tag{18.4}$$

The terms in brackets are defined by the conjectural variations PCV and LCV. No matter their values, the crucial property of equation (18.4) is that *it is independent of fixed costs F.* It follows that *no matter how the price and location conjectural variations are specified,*[1] *the profit-max-imizing price in constant-numbers equilibrium is independent of fixed costs.*

Eaton and Lipsey go on to show that a constant-numbers equilibrium can be identified that is symmetric in price and location (i.e., such that all firms are evenly spaced and charge the same mill price m^*). This analysis has been extended by Novshek (1980) and allows the following very straightforward argument: For any given optimal mill price m^* that satisfies (18.4), there will be a value for fixed costs, $\hat{F}$, say, that generates a zero value for pure profit. In other words, if m^* is substituted in equation (18.3) for m_{i-1}, m_i, and m_{i+1}, and if $\hat{F}$ is substituted for F, then $\Pi_i = 0$. Therefore, *so long as fixed costs are less than $\hat{F}$, positive pure profit will be earned and will persist in constant-numbers equilibrium.*

The intuition behind this result is very simple. In imperfectly competitive markets we are always dealing with "small-numbers" competition. Each competitor looks to his immediate neighbors in determining price and location. It follows that the relevant solution concept is an oligopolistic one based on specification of the reaction functions of the various competing firms. But it is well known that within any oligopolistic market, profit will generally not be driven to zero through oligopolistic competition. Price competition will exist, but will, in general, result in a positive pure-profit equilibrium.

This first stage of the analysis demonstrates, then, that if firms are in constant-numbers equilibrium, price competition between them will not necessarily drive pure profit to zero. Only an accidental coincidence of m^* and $\hat{F}$ would give zero pure profit.

The second stage of the analysis is to consider whether or not *entry* will drive pure profit to zero.

Assume that the existing firms are in constant-numbers equilibrium, spaced L distance units apart and charging the common price m^*. Now let a new firm enter somewhere between two existing firms. Eaton and Lipsey show (and it should be intuitively clear), that the new entrant will locate midway between the existing firms (recall Figure 18.1).

Now consider the aggregate demand functions for the existing firms, denoted Q^E, and for the new entrant, denoted Q^{NE}. Eaton and Lipsey show, again as intuition should lead us to believe, that Q^{NE} *lies everywhere strictly below* Q^E: Recall the discussion of Figure 18.2, where now $Q^E = DD$ and $Q^{NE} = dd_3$. It is then easy to see that it is possible for Q^{NE} to lie everywhere below long-run average total cost (LRATC), but for Q^E to lie somewhere above LRATC, as in Figure 18.4. Free-entry equilibrium *may* be characterized by zero pure profit, but this can be expected to be no more than an accidental outcome arising from a particular combination of fixed costs, transport costs, and individual demand functions. The much more likely outcome is one in which positive pure profit exists in long-run equilibrium.[2]

That the situation in Figure 18.4 is a free-entry equilibrium is easily seen. Each existing firm is in constant-numbers equilibrium (m^* maximizes pure profit), no new firm wishes to enter (Q^{NE} lies everywhere below

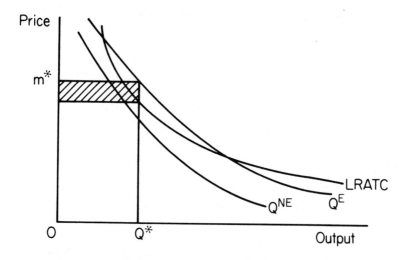

Figure 18.4. Free-entry equilibrium.

LRATC), and no existing firm wishes to exit (pure profit is positive – the shaded area in Figure 18.4).

18.3   Sources of positive pure profit

The Eaton-Lipsey analysis relies, inevitably, on a number of potentially restrictive assumptions. The question that should now be resolved is whether the existence of pure profit in free-entry equilibrium is a general phenomenon or is merely a consequence of the model's assumptions.

Eaton and Lipsey themselves consider the effects of relaxing some of the more restrictive assumptions. They show that their results are robust to quite general specification of the demand functions. Further, they indicate that more general specification of the cost function leaves the analysis unaltered. The critical element in their proof in this connection is that aggregate demand Q^E lies everywhere above Q^{NE}. No matter the shape of LRATC, there will exist an equilibrium in which Q^E lies somewhere above LRATC (thus giving positive pure profit), while Q^{NE} lies everywhere below LRATC (thus ensuring no entry).

In contrast, consider the assumption of zero locational conjectural variation (ZLCV). Under what conditions is this likely to arise? It implies that relocation is costly, perhaps because there are location-specific fixed costs or there are costs of moving fixed capital. This is perfectly reasonable in a spatial world in a wide variety of cases: Moving a factory or an office is expensive both in terms of liquidating existing buildings and infrastructure and in terms of moving machinery and key skilled staff. There are, however, situations in which relocation is relatively costless. For example, in the Hotelling model discussed in Chapter 15, relocation by the ice cream salesman merely implies driving the ice cream van to a new location on the beach.

What happens if ZLCV is not appropriate? Eaton and Lipsey show that if a proportion λ of fixed cost is "location-specific," then ZLCV is appropriate for $\lambda > \frac{1}{2}$, in which case a positive pure-profit equilibrium can be identified. But if $\lambda < \frac{1}{4}$, then ZLCV is not appropriate. Existing firms will choose to relocate if a new firm enters, and *zero profit will characterize the final equilibrium*. This analysis is extended and refined by Capozza and Van Order (1980). If capital is mobile (λ is "low") and the market is large relative to the indivisible unit of capital, then ZLCV is not appropriate, and zero-profit equilibrium will result.

What does this mean in terms of product differentiation? Again, it implies that a distinction must be drawn between markets in which product relocation is straightforward and inexpensive and those in which product relocation is difficult and expensive. If product differentiation is merely a function of packaging or color, then relocation of a product will be relatively straightforward, and pure profit can be expected to be competed away. A simple example here is in the market for pocket calculators, in which the technology is relatively standard; almost all that changes is the external appearance, and this can be altered simply and quickly.

In contrast, if product differentiation requires extensive advertising, or the development of a definably "different" good,[3] or is associated with a brand name, then relocation by existing firms will prove difficult and costly, and fixed costs of entry will be high. Positive pure profit is likely to persist in the long run. Obvious examples here are breakfast cereals (existing firms will incur heavy advertising expenditures in any attempt to relocate a product by giving it a new image), medical drugs (patent protection prevents imitation, and the need to satisfy stringent safety checks makes relocation expensive, because it will generally involve development of a new drug), and microcomputers (now that IBM has entered the market, any new entrant faces a much more difficult task).

Next, it should be recognized that the persistence of positive pure profit is a consequence of the assumed motives of potential entrants. A new firm is presumed to attempt to enter the market only if its *expected* pure profit is nonnegative. This can be contrasted with what will happen if the new firm bases its behavior on the profits of *existing* firms. In the latter case, so long as existing firms are making any level of pure profit, entry will be attempted even though the new firm will incur losses after entry.

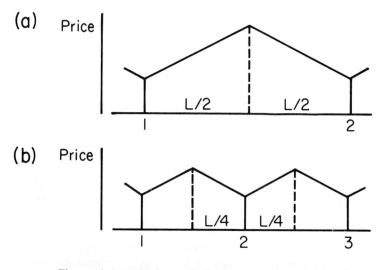

Figure 18.5. Multiple equilibria: case 1.

This appears to be a very myopic way of behaving, and it conflicts with recent analyses of rationality in oligopoly markets (Ulph 1983). If such behavior characterizes a market, then that market will be unstable in any situation in which positive pure profit exists. Some such markets may be identifiable. Our view, however, is that this is not a particularly important theoretical or empirical case. Entry is much more likely to be based on projected profits of the entrant rather than existing profits of the incumbents: What firm would seriously attempt, for example, to compete with IBM based purely on the fact that IBM is earning pure profits?

The final assumption that might be questioned is the assumption that all firms face identical costs. This is a question with which we shall be much concerned in the next chapter. Suffice it to say at this point that if firms of varying sizes and efficiency levels are allowed in the spatial economy, the zero-profit condition can be obtained even with capital immobility. In fact, there is nothing in empirical realities or classical purely competitive theory that requires uniformity of size and efficiency. By the concept of natural rents for differential skills and capacities, firms of varying sizes can be brought to the same average cost level as, let us say, the representative firm.

This (brief) discussion generates an appealingly intuitive conclusion. Positive pure profit is likely to persist in industries in which entry costs are "high" relative to market size (advertising, indivisible investment in machinery, technology, product testing, etc.), where relocation is costly, and where the range of sizes of viable firms is "small." The lower are entry

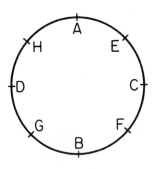

Figure 18.6. Multiple equilibria: case 2.

and relocation costs, the less indivisible are these costs, and the wider the range of viable firm sizes, the lower will be positive pure profit.

18.4   Multiple equilibria: some comments

One of the features of the Eaton-Lipsey analysis is that many possible equilibria can result in a particular market. Two reasons can be advanced as to why this might be the case. First, given the basic behavioral assumptions of the Eaton-Lipsey model, the "shape" of the final equilibrium in a particular market will be quite strongly determined by the history of that market. Consider Figure 18.5, which illustrates two possible equilibria for a particular market. Assume that, given demand functions and conjectural variations, new firms must capture a market of radius at least $L/2$ to break even. Then entry is "just" deterred by the equilibrium illustrated in Figure 18.5(a) and is much more strongly deterred by the equilibrium illustrated in Figure 18.5(b). In this example, existing firms can command market radii of anything between $L/2$ and L while maintaining a free-entry equilibrium.

There is a further reason why multiple equilibria might be expected. It has been assumed throughout the analysis that only one new firm enters at any one time. Consider, however, the market illustrated in Figure 18.6 – assumed to be the perimeter of a circle. Assume that firm 1 enters at point A. Then firm 2 will enter at B. A third firm considering entry will enter at point C or D. But if one firm enters (at C, say), why should it not be the case, as suggested by Grace (1970) and illustrated by Eaton (1976), that two firms will enter, one each at C and D? This implies that entry will follow the sequence $1, 2, 4, 8, \ldots$ As Eaton (1976) demonstrates, this dynamic entry process produces a final equilibrium different from that obtained with only single-firm entry at any given time.

This should be neither surprising nor disturbing. In many ways these results confirm casual empirical investigation. It demonstrates once more that the space economy is capable of sustaining a much richer variety of market equilibria than is implied by simple, spaceless microeconomic theory.

18.5   An example

It is of some interest to investigate what will be the likely extent of excess pure profit, and how this is affected by market conditions. The mathematical implications of the Eaton-Lipsey model are such that this investigation can proceed only on the basis of a numerical example. One such example is presented in their 1978 paper, based on the individual demand function

$$q = e^{-pd} \tag{18.5}$$

They then show that, given ZLCV and UPCV,[4] the rate of return consistent with free-entry equilibrium can be as much as twice the normal rate of return on capital. The rate of return will be higher, *ceteris paribus,* the lower are the fixed costs of entry: With high fixed costs of entry, the market will be capable of sustaining very few firms, each of which will find it difficult to break even.

Rather than repeat the Eaton-Lipsey analysis, we can consider the extent of positive pure profit in the case in which individual demand is of the GGK form,

$$p = a - bq^x \quad (a, b, x > 0)[5] \tag{18.6}$$

and production costs are given by (18.1).

In order to simplify the analysis, the model is normalized by assuming

$$a = b = 1; \quad c = 0 \tag{18.7}$$

Given ZLCV and a symmetric, constant-numbers equilibrium of existing firms, a new entrant will enter midway between two existing firms. The price the new entrant will charge is then dependent on (1) the market area it expects to capture and, related to this, (2) the expected reactions of the existing firms: the entrant's PCV with respect to existing firms.

The constant-numbers equilibrium is determined, in turn, by (1) the minimum market area a new firm must capture in order to consider entering and (2) each existing firm's PCV with respect to other existing firms.

Even in the simplest, linear case, no explicit solution to this example can be obtained.[6] Solution is based, therefore, on a computer simulation with the following parameter values:[7] (1) fixed costs, 0.005–0.030; (2) demand exponents, 0.50–2.50.

As Eaton and Lipsey indicate, fixed costs of F arise from a capital expenditure of F/i, where i is the normal rate of return on capital. Thus, the return on capital associated with a pure profit of Π^E is

$$r = i(\Pi^E + F)/F = i(1 + \Pi^E/F) \qquad (18.8)$$

The ratio $(1 + \Pi^E/F)$ is denoted by M, and Figures 18.7(i) and (ii) illustrate the values of M that result under (i) Hotelling-Smithies (ZPCV) and (ii) Löschian (UPCV) price conjectural variations, respectively.

These figures confirm that the rate of pure profit is determined by the following:

1.   The precise specification of the demand function: The more concave the demand function (the greater is x), the greater is the rate of return.
2.   The price conjectural variation: The rate of return is higher under UPCV than under ZPCV. More generally, the greater the extent of price matching that is expected to occur, the greater the rate of return.
3.   Fixed costs: The higher the level of fixed costs (more correctly, the higher are fixed costs relative to consumer density), the lower the rate of return.

Note also that the rates of return generated by this model lie within the range found by Eaton and Lipsey (1978) using the demand function (18.5). In fact, we find a generally narrower range for M. With ZPCV, the "typical" value of M would appear to be in the range 1.6–1.7 (so long as demand is not strongly convex), whereas with UPCV it would appear to be in the range 1.7–1.9.[8]

18.6   Conclusions

The central conclusion to be drawn from the Eaton-Lipsey analysis is that positive pure profit can exist in spatial equilibrium and will not be competed away either by price competition among existing firms or by the threat of entry of new firms.

This positive pure profit derives in the main from the immobility of capital. If capital investment can be freely moved, then it is to be expected that long-run equilibrium will be characterized by something approaching zero pure profit. Capital indivisibility also plays a role, mainly in ensuring that long-run costs will exhibit some range of increasing returns: decreasing average costs.[9]

Price competition will not proceed to the point at which pure profit disappears, precisely because of the spatial analogy. Each firm has "few" competitors. Thus, oligopolistic behavior characterizes price setting and

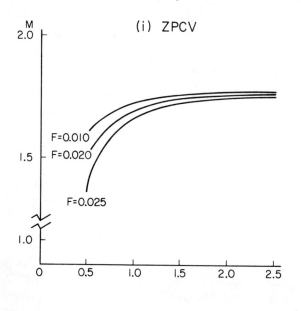

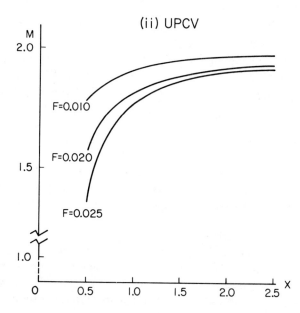

Figure 18.7. Rate of return.

is unlikely to proceed to the point at which price is driven down to the level of average cost.

The threat of entry is modified also because of the spatial context of the model. A crucial property of spatial (imperfectly competitive) markets is that new firms entering such markets need not expect to achieve the same level of sales as existing firms. Rather, new firms can, in general, be expected to sell less than incumbents. As a consequence, an equilibrium will exist (and, in fact, is to be expected) in which incumbents' demand lies above average cost, whereas the new firms' demand lies below average cost. Pure profit exists and will not be competed away.

This does not mean, however, that all of our previous analysis must be reworked to take account of the existence of positive pure profit. Whenever the zero-profit condition has been used, it is a relatively simple matter to rework the analysis using the Eaton-Lipsey "zero profit for an entrant" condition. Thus, for example, instead of using the Capozza-Van Order zero-profit locus, this locus could be redefined to relate to zero profits for potential entrants. The precise *quantitative* results will change, of course, but this is of little consequence. The *qualitative* conclusions remain unaltered.

Perhaps more fundamentally, the final assumption that is necessary for the existence of positive pure profit is that each industry be populated by firms with identical cost structures (this relates to capital indivisibility to an extent). If this assumption is relaxed, then even with immobile capital, positive pure profit might disappear.

For this latter result to hold, we have to introduce further considerations mainly relating to behavioral uncertainty. The Eaton-Lipsey analysis, in common with all of the models examined to this point, presumes certainty on the part of competing firms. But it would appear reasonable to claim that immobile and indivisible capital will imply risk and uncertainty. It is on this point that the next chapter focuses.

Mathematical appendix

1. Assume f.o.b. pricing, with price to consumers at distance r from the firm given by

$$p(r) = m + tr = m + r$$

(because t is assumed normalized to unity). Then profit to a firm selling in a market of radius R, facing individual inverse demand of the form $p = 1 - q^x$ $(x > 0)$, and with consumer density D, is

$$\Pi(x, R) = 2D \int_0^R m(1 - m - r)^{1/x} \, dr - F =$$

$$= 2Dm\frac{x}{1+x}[(1-m)^{1/x+1} - (1-m-R)^{1/x+1}] - F \qquad \text{(A18.1)}$$

2. The profit-maximizing price is given by the first-order condition

$$\frac{\partial \Pi(x, R)}{\partial m} = 0$$

which, from (A18.1), is

$$2D\frac{x}{1+x}[(1-m)^{1/x+1} - (1-m-R)^{1/x+1}]$$

$$-2Dm[(1-m)^{1/x} - (1-m-R)^{1/x}]$$

$$+2Dm(1-m-R)^{1/x}\frac{\partial R}{\partial m} = 0 \qquad \text{(A18.2)}$$

3. Equation (A18.2) holds both for existing firms (which will be subscripted e) and for new entrants (subscripted n), giving the two equations

$$2D\frac{x}{1+x}[(1-m_e)^{1/x+1} - (1-m_e-R_e)^{1/x+1}]$$

$$-2Dm_e\left[(1-m_e)^{1/x} - \left(1 - \frac{\partial R_e}{\partial m_e}\right)(1-m_e-R_e)^{1/x}\right] = 0 \qquad \text{(A18.3)}$$

$$2D\frac{x}{1+x}[(1-m_n)^{1/x+1} - (1-m_n-R_n)^{1/x+1}]$$

$$-2Dm_n\left[(1-m_n)^{1/x} - \left(1 - \frac{\partial R_n}{\partial m_n}\right)(1-m_n-R_n)^{1/x}\right] = 0 \qquad \text{(A18.4)}$$

4. The entry condition is that no new entrant can earn positive profit:

$$2D\frac{x}{1+x}m_n[(1-m_n)^{1/x+1} - (1-m_n-R_n)^{1/x+1}] - F = 0 \qquad \text{(A18.5)}$$

5. Finally, the price charged by the entrant will equal the price charged by a neighboring existing firm at the market boundary between them:

$$m_e + R_e = m_n + (R_n - R_e)$$

or

$$m_e + R_e - m_n - 2R_n = 0 \qquad \text{(A18.6)}$$

6. We now have four equations (A18.3)–(A18.6) in four unknowns, m_e, R_e, m_n, R_n. These are solved assuming, under ZLCV, that $\partial R/\partial m = -\frac{1}{2}$ (from Capozza and Van Order), and, under UPCV, that $\partial R/\partial m = 0$.

CHAPTER 19

An efficient long-run allocative equilibrium

19.1   Introduction

It was noted in our discussion of Lösch's theory, and the work of Eaton and Lipsey, that spatial economics has been tied to Chamberlin's *Theory of Monopolistic Competition* (1933). One of Chamberlin's principal objectives was to examine the nature of equilibrium in markets in which products are differentiated, whether by characteristics or by some spatial attributes. A central element of his equilibrium concept is the tangency between a downward-sloping average-revenue (demand) curve and the long-run average-cost (LRAC) curve. This implies that each firm in monopolistically competitive equilibrium[1] will be producing on the downward-sloping part of the LRAC curve. In other words, each firm will have some excess capacity in equilibrium – will not be operating its production facilities at the lowest possible cost.

Chamberlin's conclusion that excess capacity characterizes equilibrium in imperfectly competitive markets has been the subject of much debate. In the most important of the early critiques, Professors Harrod (1934) and Kaldor (1935, 1938) forced Chamberlin himself to rethink the entire issue of "large-group equilibrium" and excess capacity (Robinson 1971), although Kaldor's views were subsequently criticized (Paul 1954) as well as defended (Edwards 1955).

Harrod (1952) reiterated his own position that a competitor can be expected to produce an output corresponding to the low point on its LRAC curve, given (1) the uncertainty of future competition (i.e., a firm would not sacrifice markets available to it for the sake of "transitory" profits) (Harrod 1952, p. 147), (2) a dynamic inconsistency between pricing and investment policies such that an entrepreneur, when faced with competition, would always be "out of sync" with the scale of plant originally built to maximize profits (Harrod 1952, pp. 148–9), and (3) the existence of "potential competition" that tends to lead competing firms to the low point on the LRAC curve (Harrod 1952, pp. 155–6). Harrod did recognize the *possibility* of excess capacity due to demand deficiency, as Edwards (1955, p. 115) suggests, but he discounted it as a main feature of the imperfectly competitive model. Edwards concluded (1955, p. 116) that the existence of "unexploited economies of scale," coupled with efficient and enterprising entrepreneurship, explained the instability of the Chamberlinian tangency equilibrium in the long run.

The theorem of excess capacity and inefficient production was challenged a few years later in a series of papers by Demsetz (1959, 1967, 1968), who derived a least-cost equilibrium possibility under monopolistic competition. Demsetz's argument engendered a new round of debate on the issue. First, Archibald (1962, 1967) attacked Demsetz's theory by arguing that excess capacity must apply to monopolistic competition, although Demsetz (1967) did not accept his critique. Barzel (1970) and then Schmalensee (1972) critically evaluated Demsetz's theory. Demsetz apparently conceded to "Barzel's methodological criticism and to Schmalensee's mathematics," although he argued that monopolistic competition as set forth by Chamberlin fails to add anything of substance to the classical competition and monopoly models because of its internal and external inconsistencies. Ohta (1977) supported Demsetz on the basis of analysis that has something in common with the arguments to be presented in this chapter.

More recently, Baumol (1982) has argued that imperfect competitors in the form of oligopolists operating under conditions of free entry and exit will be efficient[2] producers. Rather uniquely, he freed his analysis of oligopoly markets from "its previous dependence on the conjectural variations of incumbents" (Baumol 1982, p. 2).

There are many points of agreement between the conclusions of Demsetz and Baumol and those to be presented in this chapter, but there are also quite considerable differences in the analysis that supports these conclusions. In particular, we shall concentrate on the concept of oligopolistic behavioral uncertainty mentioned in Chapter 18.

19.2   Decisionmakers of the spatial firms and their objectives

Two kinds of decisionmakers can be distinguished in our model of the firm: (1) the entrepreneur(s) managing the sole proprietorship or partnership unit and (2) the owner(s) of the corporate firm. Because the distinction between owners and entrepreneurs is, however, somewhat unnecessary for our purposes, they are treated as a single decisionmaking unit of the firm: the owner-entrepreneur.

19.2.1 *Maximizing profits subject to two constraints*

The owner-entrepreneur is generally assumed to be concerned with maximizing profits, but he does so subject to two constraints:

1. a predetermined level of optimal input I_0 reflecting (planned) technological efficiency and
2. a particular (lost-opportunity) rate of return r_0 for the risk involved in investing the amount of equity capital that will provide the efficient input quantity I_0.

Before discussing these two constraints, it should be noted that each constitutes a necessary but not sufficient condition for owner-entrepreneur satisfaction with his business activity. Taken together, they constitute the necessary and sufficient conditions for such satisfaction as well as the stable-equilibrium state.

The concept of a predetermined level of optimal input I_0 reflects the condition that every owner-entrepreneur, and every potential owner-entrepreneur, possesses some amount of talent and energy and ability to utilize investment sums that can be expended optimally in the production of goods or services. The ability to work and to produce goods varies, of course, from person to person.[3] As a result, entrepreneurial ability/enterprise will vary from firm to firm and will give rise to a heterogeneous size distribution of firms, even among firms in the same industry.

19.2.2 *A residual return*

Associated with the concept of an optimal amount of expenditure by the human factor of production is the required optimal rate of return conforming to the talent the individual applies in a particular venture: the manager's compensation, which should be treated as an imputed cost. But in addition to this is a required optimal rate of return for the uncertainty undertaken by the owner or owners as a result of their equity investment in the firm, where the term "uncertainty" is used for simplicity to include the concepts of behavioral uncertainty and spatial indivisibilities (e.g., machines come in certain sizes, the landscape is heterogeneously endowed, and so on). Note here the connection to the technological indivisibilities and spatial immobility discussed in Chapter 18.

It should be noted in passing that uncertainties such as those of war and peace, which impact demand curves, or inventory policies, or the programming of the firm's input/output levels over time, are not relevant to our interests. Our objectives simply require the idea that uncertainty is a business hazard for which owner-entrepreneurs require compensation. The rate of return on equity investment thus includes, in effect, a *residual* (i.e., earnings over and above what might be termed functional returns). This extra return must conform in the long run to the degree of uncertainty applicable to the activity in question. The degree of uncertainty, in turn, is viewed intuitively (and subjectively) by the owners of the individual firms in the given industry. As with Knight (1971), uncertainty relates to all calculated subjective probabilities.

The important distinction is the distinction between the return to the owner-entrepreneur for his *functional* inputs and the return to the owner-entrepreneur for his *nonfunctional* inputs.

The functional inputs of the owner-entrepreneur relate to the inputs he provides in order to maintain an effective production line and produce a marketable product. The nonfunctional inputs of the owner-entrepreneur, in contrast, relate to the definition of the owner-entrepreneur as the risk-taker or, equivalently, as the provider of equity capital. This concept of the owner-entrepreneur and the firm applies to any kind of firm, small or large, the latter whether structured along the U lines of organization or the M lines of organization (Williamson 1981). The firm may be a local enterprise, a regional enterprise, or a national, multinational, or conglomerate firm.

The returns to the owner-entrepreneur's functional inputs are treated identically as the returns to other factors of production. In classical theory, returns on the proprietor's land, labor, and capital stock are added as lost-opportunity costs to the explicit costs of the hired factors of production. These imputed costs – now including the corporate manager's labor – relate to *functional performances* on the part of the relevant factors of production. Whether or not the firm is viable, large or small, is determined by whether or not the director(s) can combine his (their) own inputs efficiently with the hired factors of production. *Conformability* of all factors in work-load capacity and efficiency is necessary for viability of competitive firms in the long run. Taken in combination with the law of variable proportions, *factor conformability* yields the classical lowest-cost U-shaped average-cost curve. This average-cost curve is the sum of an explicit-payments average-cost curve, whose costs involve the hired factors of production, and an imputed-payments average-cost curve, whose costs include owner/manager opportunity costs.

Relating this directly to the returns an owner-entrepreneur will expect to earn, we argue in effect that directing a privately owned business, as well as managing a corporation, yields a functional return classifiable as a cost (or rent), which is why the wages of management are treated later as imputed costs.[4] Any additional uncertainty in receiving these wages increases their level, but this additional return is not of the same (residual) order as the return required to cover the impacts on equity investment of oligopolistic behavioral uncertainty.

The latter return is the return to the owner-entrepreneur's nonfunctional inputs. Behavioral uncertainty underlies all oligopolistic activity. Decisionmakers in a world of oligopolies act in anticipation of the effects their actions will have on others. An action/reaction uncertainty exists that increases the likelihood of losses and bankruptcies. It is reasonable to argue, therefore, that the imputed returns for investing in uncertain conditions should be distinguished from the returns for functional inputs.

It is integral to imperfect competition that some competitive oligopolistic industries will be characterized by hypercompetitive pricing, whereas other oligopolistic industries will engage in milder forms of competitive pricing. Certainly, the more volatile are the profits on unit sales, the greater will be the long-run returns required by investors. Thus, Greenhut (1966) proposed that a monotonicity of returns underscores the spatial (oligopoly) economy, with investors applying their own subjective probabilities to the alternative states of uncertainty that exist across industries. This monotonicity of returns is marked by greater net payoffs over time for recognizably more uncertain investments. But how are the *differentials for uncertainty* (distinct from those for owner-manager skill, or land, or capital stock) imputed for firms in imperfectly competitive industries?

Chamberlin (1956) appears to have ascribed rents to the average-cost curve of the pure competitor (p. 23) but not to the monopolist (p. 13). He argues with respect to profit rents for monopolistic competitors (which presumably would also include oligopolistic competitors) that the average-cost curve "includes the minimum profit necessary to secure the entrepreneur's services" (p. 77). This statement would appear to imply ascription of a scarcity profit (rent) to the average cost of any competitor. Thus, if behavioral uncertainty characterizes an oligopoly economy, a scarcity rent will apply to it.

The important characteristic distinguishing imputed costs for land, labor, and capital stock from the imputed cost for oligopolistic uncertainty on the owner's investment is that the income required for uncertainty on an investment is a residual return. It seems reasonable, therefore, to impute this return as a fixed cost independent of output levels, not as a variable cost that applies to functional inputs. In particular, it is proposed that the return for uncertainty exists essentially in the mind's eye of the investors in a given industry; it is not measurable by the firm's engineers or accountants.

What this implies is that profit in the mind's eye of owner-entrepreneurs must be large enough to include the (nonfunctional) payment for the uncertainty or lost-opportunity cost on the investment required by the planned optimal input I_0. Equally, because the return for uncertainty exists only in the mind's eye of the investor, it cannot be readily included in the marginal-revenue (MR) marginal-cost (MC) profit-maximizing calculus. In other words, the payment required by the owner-entrepreneur that is associated with uncertainty is not identified precisely by non-owner-managers in their bookkeeping process. Whatever residue remains over explicit and imputed costs is fundamentally the bookeeping extra or surplus conventionally referred to as economic profits. Owner-entrepreneurs view this surplus *relative* to what they could have earned elsewhere. It is accordingly evaluated with respect to their own concept of what their investment is worth.[5]

It is the case, of course, that *any* level of investment equating MR with MC is profit-maximizing and optimal in the classical view of monopoly. Correspondingly, the Demsetz-Archibald-Barzel-Schmalensee statements on imperfect competition relate to *any* investment level at which the marginal equality happens to obtain. The theory of imperfect competition to be presented in this chapter, however, is based on the behavioral objectives enumerated earlier. As a consequence, the maximizing activities of the owner-entrepreneur, together with market forces, will *mirror* the classical theory of perfect competition. We shall demonstrate the existence of a specially positioned marginal equality that can provide a long-run stable-equilibrium state.

19.3   The short run: some comments

As an introduction to the nature of long-run equilibrium, it may be useful to review briefly some of the properties of the short-run state.

The world we live in is characterized by spatial heterogeneities (water barriers, mountains, deserts, international boundaries). Not only do f.o.b. sellers price their goods by zones over distance, but also their carriers (public or private) price by zones. Moreover, products and personalities are differentiated in fact, fancy, and even simply by date of origin in a market. It is to be expected that when new firms enter the market, whether at a distant site or next door to an existing firm, an inexorable urge exists to collude or (even more often) to extend the firm's custom.

Sooner or later, *competitive* presences, especially at nearby sites, induce decisionmakers to forestall the impact of the new entrant by lowering the prices of their goods. In the classical view of Chapters 2–7, the representative firm lowers its price and extends its market (its farthest zone) in a manner determined by the prices of its distant rival. Over time, tendencies to reduce prices prevail, and we can envisage something like a "now me, then you" type of price reduction among the *competitive* firms of a spatial economy. This form of behavior can be expected to hold even if a Sweezy-type kinked demand curve or conscious parallelism of action exists from time to time in retaining (fixing) price (and even pushing price up). In the absence of binding collusive agreements, f.o.b. prices tend to fall over time.

It is clear that the same basic result holds under conditions of price discrimination. The essential difference under price discrimination is that lowering of prices as industries mature will be marked by specific price changes rather than a lowering of the entire price schedule. Competitive entry thus implies lower prices, not in the perfectly flexible form described in the theory of perfect competition, but in the erratic yet inexorable form generated by the oligopoly of the few.

No matter what form behavioral interactions take in the short run, whether Löschian, Hotelling-Smithies (Bertrand-Nash), or some unclassified highly erratic patterns, competitive pressures will ultimately involve a leftward shift of the average-revenue (demand) curve from the classical firm's perspective. This shift in demand carries with it a reduction in the maximum price the firm can charge for its product.

19.4 Imputation of rents: ascribing lost-opportunity costs

What happens in the imperfectly competitive economy in the long run? It is by resolving the issue of the required minimum amount of economic profit to reflect behavioral uncertainty that we can demonstrate the existence of a stable tangency solution for the oligopoly market. This solution will be shown to require use of the lowest-cost input combination of the firm's productive factors.

As a preliminary to deriving this result, it is necessary to distinguish in greater detail what is meant by "costs." Three types of long-run average-cost curves can be defined:

1. Explicit average costs, denoted AC_e. These are long-run average costs including only explicit payments to factors of production.
2. Classical average costs, denoted AC_c. These are explicit average costs plus all classical imputations for differentials in skill, land fertility, and so forth. In other words, AC_c is AC_e plus rents to functional inputs.
3. Average costs including uncertainty, denoted AC_u. These are classical average costs plus the imputed costs for behavioral uncertainty. Thus, AC_u is AC_c plus payments for the nonfunctional inputs of the owner-entrepreneur.

Both rents to functional inputs and the imputed costs for behavioral uncertainty can be conceived of as either fixed or variable costs. Our view of opportunity costs leads us to prefer to ascribe differential rents for managerial skills (i.e., to ascribe these rents as variable costs).[6] In contrast, a fixed cost is ascribed for behavioral uncertainty.[7]

There remains the question of just what should be the fixed cost of behavioral uncertainty. This can be resolved if an industry is defined as one

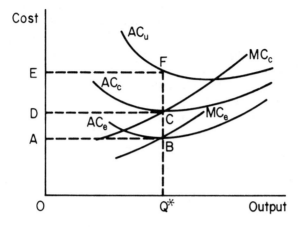

Figure 19.1. Imputed costs.

in which homogeneous goods are produced and in which each firm is subject to an identifiable common uncertainty: The concept of "common uncertainty" corresponds to the concept of "adjusted risk classes" in the finance literature.

The ascription for uncertainty, therefore, is obtained by multiplying the appropriate uncertainty rate for a particular industry by some investment (classical) total cost. For the moment, and without verification, assume that this total cost is the total cost incurred when the firm is producing at the minimum point on its AC_c curve. The relationships between the three average-cost curves and their associated marginal-cost curves are then illustrated in Figure 19.1.

Because the return for behavioral uncertainty is imputed as a fixed cost, MC_u and MC_c are identical (and denoted MC_c). The fixed cost for behavioral uncertainty is given by the area $CDEF$, and the imputed rents for functional performance are given, at output Q^*, by the area $ABCD$. The rate of return for behavioral uncertainty is obtained by measuring the ratio of area $CDEF$ to area $0Q^*CD$.

The fixed cost of behavioral uncertainty is obtained by applying the uncertainty rate of return for the industry to total cost *at the lowest-cost production point* on the firm's classical average-cost curve AC_c. This cost (investment) total is the logical starting point for evaluating returns *both in the selected activity and in the (best) lost opportunity,* because optimal factor use obtains only at the (classical) least-cost input-output point. Note also that this relationship derives from the definition of a competi-

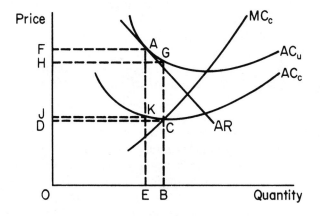

Figure 19.2. Unstable equilibrium.

tive factor that can be technologically efficient only when its relative (energy) cost expenditure is least, or, equivalently, when its relative return is maximized.

That the owner-entrepreneur will select the least-cost point on the firm's classical LRAC curve in his investment decision also has intuitive appeal. Note, for example, that if lost opportunities form a continuum, any use of the rate of return currently prevailing in the best alternative in establishing the rate of return required in the chosen activity must immediately and always yield zero profits or losses. The meaning of lost opportunities, accordingly, requires reference to the long-run competitive rate of return (not present return) in the factor's best alternative use.

Indeed, the investment of the optimal cost position on the classical LRAC curve of the firm reflects more than just the requirement that opportunity costs be based on the absolutely lowest acceptable (long-run) returns. It extends to the principle that *in the long run,* owner-entrepreneurs require assurance that *given the worst expected* condition (i.e., the situation in which competition has pressed the firm's price over time to the lowest likely set of net returns), the firm will still be competitive with respect to the other (viable) members of the industry. In other words, the lowest point on the classical AC_c curve must be a viable, competitive position.

These remarks can be used to illustrate some of the "mechanics" of the long-run model. Let the point A in Figure 19.2 represent a characteristic Chamberlinian tangency point. Total revenue equals total cost (including *all* imputed costs), and their derivatives, MR and MC, will also be equal. Profits appear to be zero, and market stability seemingly holds. When the classical cost curve AC_c is considered, however, it emerges that A is an unstable equilibrium.[8]

To see why this is so, consider the following argument. For any well-defined average-cost curve such as AC_c, total cost (or total investment) rises with greater output; average cost may fall or rise with output, but total cost always increases. Total investment is therefore greater at the lowest average-cost output point than at any smaller output, and less at that output point than for any greater output. However, the fixed-cost ascription for uncertainty was predicated on the optimal-size classical investment (i.e., $0BCD$ in Figure 19.2). The return for uncertainty at point A, or at any other point along AC_c, thus includes the same (given) *total* return for uncertainty as that related to the investment $0BCD$.

It follows that point A offers a *higher percentage rate of return* for the uncertainty on investment than that which was projected. The total return for uncertainty at point A is $JKAF$, which is equal to the total return at point G ($DCGH$), because uncertainty is imputed as a fixed cost. Total classical cost at output $0E$ is $0EKJ$, and at output $0B$ is $0BCD$. Because total cost increases with output, $0BCD > 0EKJ$. The rate of return for uncertainty at point A, the ratio $JKAF/0EKJ$, is then greater than the rate of return at point G, given by the ratio $DCGH/0BCD$.

The additional return at A is effectively a windfall related to a total investment (and use of capital) that is less than that planned by the entrepreneur. So long as such windfalls accrue, there will be pressures to increase output and investment – to move to a point such as G – by all firms in the industry, and a threat of entry by potential producers.[9]

A brief summary of this analysis may be of value. The theory sketched out earlier conceives of normal profit per unit of output as having been lost on all unproduced output that applies whenever the $AR - AC$ tangency leaves the firm with excess capacity. If owner-entrepreneurs wish to utilize their talents (and equity capital) fully, they will be dissatisfied with excess capacity and will decide that they can earn even higher profits for their talents (and capital) by fully utilizing them elsewhere. In fact (although not yet formally established), owner-entrepreneurs can be in an equilibrium position if and only if they operate their plants at full capacity (defined as the minimum-cost point of the classical AC_c curve).

Because the real business world is populated by imperfect competitors who are subject to the unpredictable behavioral reactions of rivals, a return for behavioral uncertainty is required. A hierarchy of premiums results among the activities in the economy. This hierarchy follows the principle that the greater the uncertainty in a particular activity, the greater the required returns, *ceteris paribus*. Owner-entrepreneurs must recover in the long run the uncertainty premium on their investments, in addition to all other costs.

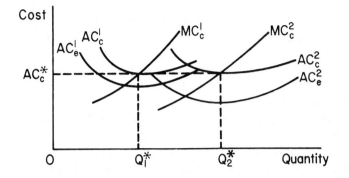

Figure 19.3. Imputation of Marshallian rents.

Because the capacities of men, and hence of firms, vary, the final equilibrium will consist of different-size firms that, as will be shown later, will be adjusted optimally to the varying talents and energies of their owner-entrepreneurs. And in each firm the entrepreneur will be seen to earn the differential rent related to his extra efficiency or greater capacity. In turn, the viable firm will be found to cover the premium required by the size of the planned investment and uncertainty that characterize the firm in its selected activity.

19.5   A stable tangency point

Assume, for simplicity of presentation, that the representative "industry" consists of two firms of different sizes, each utilizing a common technology and producing a homogeneous product. Take the Marshallian view of costs, including all classical imputations. Then the classical theory of the long run indicates that the minimum average costs of all firms in the industry will be at the same level *after all Marshallian (classical) rents are imputed.* The full imputation process is illustrated in Figure 19.3. It has much in common with the analyses of Robinson (1934, chap. 9) and Machlup (1952, pp. 285–97). The only point of difference is that rents have been imputed for functional inputs as differential rents rather than as fixed rents.

A commonality of viewpoints based on the same minimum average-cost level (AC_c^*) thus exists in the long run. In addition, the allocation of demands across the different-size firms can be expected to conform to the relative (minimum classical average-cost) outputs of the surviving firms. The consequence of this allocation is a stable long-run equilibrium for homogeneous-product oligopolists.

Long run equilibrium requires three conditions:

1. There is a common approach to lost opportunities. This means that the fixed cost for oligopolistic uncertainty, when expressed as a return on output, is conceived of identically for all surviving firms in an industry, being based on the minimum-cost point of the Marshallian (rents included) AC_c curve.
2. Identical prices prevail in a given product market.
3. A monotonically increasing order of returns relates to greater uncertainty throughout the hierarchy of industries.

Fulfillment of these conditions generates AR (demand) schedules allocable by sizes of firms. Nonfulfillment involves contradictions and denial of any logical microeconomic structure. To support this thesis, we first derive the equilibrium solution for homogeneous-product oligopolists and then demonstrate that failure to fulfill the three specified conditions will violate the basic structure of neoclassical microeconomics.

It must be stressed that different-size firms can exist in this model, both in the short run and in the long run. As a result, if any excess profit exists above the return to all factors (including the compensation for uncertainty), the excess must be temporary. This may appear to conflict with the analyses of Eaton and Lipsey and of Capozza and Van Order (Chapter 18). We shall return to this point later. Suffice to say at this stage that no such conflict exists. The introduction of the returns for behavioral uncertainty and the relaxation of the assumption that all firms are of identical sizes will be seen to lie at the heart of what might at first sight have appeared to be conflicting results.

Consider initially the total (classical) costs of the two firms illustrated in Figure 19.4 at their respective optimal-cost (AC_c) outputs. These costs can be defined as $Q_1^* f(Q_1^*)$ for firm 1 and $Q_2^* g(Q_2^*)$ for firm 2, with $Q_1^* < Q_2^*$. The Q^* values provide the output levels for firms 1 and 2 at their points of minimum (and equal) average costs of production $f(Q_1^*)$ and $g(Q_2^*)$. Ascribe fixed costs for oligopolistic uncertainty of FC_1 for firm 1 and $(Q_2^*/Q_1^*)FC_1$ for firm 2. In other words, ascribe the fixed costs for behavioral uncertainty in the ratio of the output levels Q_1^* and Q_2^*. This particular ascription will be justified later.

It follows that total (with uncertainty) costs are

$$TC_u^1 = Q_1 f(Q_1) + FC_1$$
$$TC_u^2 = Q_2 g(Q_2) + (Q_2^*/Q_1^*)FC_1 \quad \text{where } f(Q_1^*) = g(Q_2^*) \tag{19.1}$$

and average costs are

$$AC_u^1 = f(Q_1) + h(Q_1) \quad \text{where } h(Q_1) = FC_1/Q_1$$
$$AC_u^2 = g(Q_2) + (Q_2^*/Q_1^*)FC_1/Q_2 \tag{19.2}$$

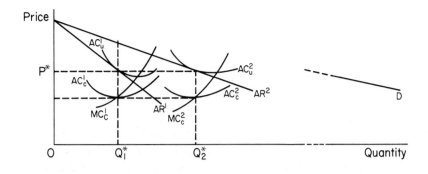

Figure 19.4. Oligopolistic equilibrium.

It can be seen from Figure 19.4 that $f'(Q_1^*) = g'(Q_2^*) = 0$. As a result, the slopes of the average-cost curves (19.2) at the output levels Q_1^* and Q_2^* are respectively

$$\left.\frac{d(AC_u^1)}{dQ_1}\right|_{Q_1=Q_1^*} = f'(Q_1^*) - \frac{FC_1}{(Q_1^*)^2} = \frac{-FC_1}{(Q_1^*)^2}$$

$$\left.\frac{d(AC_u^2)}{dQ_2}\right|_{Q_2=Q_2^*} = g'(Q_2^*) - \frac{(Q_2^*/Q_1^*)FC_1}{(Q_2^*)^2} = \frac{-FC_1}{Q_1^*Q_2^*} \qquad (19.3)$$

Clearly,

$$\frac{FC_1}{(Q_1^*)^2} > \frac{(Q_2^*/Q_1^*)FC_1}{(Q_2^*)^2} \qquad (19.4)$$

so that the (negative) slope of AC_u^1 at Q_1^* is greater than that of AC_u^2 at Q_2^*. Further, the ratio of the slopes of the two average-cost curves at outputs Q_1^* and Q_2^* is given by Q_2^*/Q_1^*.

Even though multiple decisionmaking differences may prevail in the short-run equilibrium (Greenhut 1966, 1974, chap. 2) an intraindustry commonality in decisionmaking can be conceived in the long run as managers of firms in mature industries know and accept their industry's characteristics. As a consequence, the allocated (long-run) demand curves AR_2 and AR_1 of Figure 19.4, which are based on the total market-demand curve D, are in the proportion Q_2^*/Q_1^*. The slopes of these demand curves at outputs Q_1^* and Q_2^* are also in the ratio Q_2^*/Q_1^*, thereby yielding a single equilibrium price with all Marshallian costs covered.

Might another imputation for uncertainty also yield a stable equilibrium? It is easy to show that such an imputation is not consistent with the three equilibrium conditions specified earlier. Redefine equation (19.1) as

$$TC_u^x = Q_x f(Q_x) + FC_x$$

$$TC_u^y = Q_y g(Q_y) + (FC_x) a Q_y; \quad a Q_y = b \neq Q_2^* / Q_1^* \quad (0 < a < \infty)$$

(19.5)

Then average costs are

$$AC_u^x = f(Q_x) + (FC_x / Q_x)$$

$$AC_u^y = g(Q_y) + b(FC_x / Q_y)$$

(19.6)

Quite clearly, any resulting tangencies will involve different prices and elasticities across the two firms, hence violating the commonality of prices required of a homogeneous-product duopoly/oligopoly market and the virtual commonality required for heterogeneous goods, where only differentiated demands should elicit differences in demands and elasticities.

What will happen if Q_y and Q_x are in the same proportion as Q_2^* / Q_1^*, with $(Q_y, Q_x) \gtrless (Q_2^*, Q_1^*)$? In such an event, the resulting tangencies are not *necessarily* at identical prices, because neither $f(Q_x) = g(Q_y)$ nor $FC_x / Q_x = (a Q_y) FC_x / Q_y$ holds, even if $f(Q_1^*) = g(Q_2^*)$. But even in the special case in which identical prices and elasticities *happen to obtain* at outputs Q_y, Q_x, what would appear as another Chamberlinian tangency equilibrium would not in fact be a stable tangency. It would not be stable because the system in question would involve different imputational processes among the different industries of the economy and would also imply the existence of a nonmonotonicity in returns for different degrees of behavioral uncertainty.

The equilibrium identified in Figure 19.4 is based on a proportionate allocation of the aggregate demand function. In fact, the entire allocated AR curve is a decreased image of the industry demand curve. The equilibrium price that ultimately obtains is determined by the number of competing firms (2, 3, ...) necessary to eliminate returns in excess of lost-opportunity costs. The final demand allocation is in strict proportion to the optimal cost outputs of the two firms. But why have the AR_1 and AR_2 curves of Figure 19.4? Why should we not consider a *parallel* leftward shift of the aggregate demand function in defining the long-run effects of competitive entry? The answers to these questions lie in the logical contradictions implicit in the concept of AR curves being shifted parallel leftward for the member firms of a *mature* competitive industry. On sales to any given market, viable homogeneous-product competitors must view the same reservation price for the good rather than the contrasting reservation prices implied by parallel-shifted curves. Equally fundamental is the condition that elasticity differs at any given identical price on parallel AR curves. As a result, tangency to the AC_u curves at the required "same" price would involve different elasticities. Indeed, the price elasticity of the smaller firm would be greater than that of the larger firm at the given price, and hence its MC would be greater than that of the larger firm.[10]

It can be concluded that the imputation process described earlier satisfies the requirements of stability, greater returns for greater uncertainty, and identical prices per market for homogeneous goods relevant to the world of free enterprise. Anything else entails rejection of tendencies toward stability in our economic world and severely undermines our speculation of a microeconomic order, and probably of a macroeconomic order as well.

In consequence, a logical ordering of economic returns and a common approach to lost opportunities are proposed such that the conformability argument previously cited applies. Simply put, each cost component for which an imputation is required, including that for the behavioral uncertainty characteristic of oligopolistic markets, must be predicated on a comparable, identical basis. It is then shown that an equilibrium exists in which different-size firms of different efficiencies survive in the long run and regularly produce at the lowest-cost point on their own classical average-cost curves.

19.6   Special spatial features: the Eaton-Lipsey and Capozza-Van Order theses

When markets are viewed in a spatial framework, one can readily expect small firms to enter at different points of an existing market space and to survive alongside much larger dominant firms. Of perhaps more importance, we can be reasonably happy as a consequence of the free-entry/exit assumption that existing firms will be unable to indulge permanently in strategic behavior to control potential competitors. So we conceive of small and large firms dotting the economic landscape, some localized, some at distances, all in time becoming price-competitive (if not originally so), some industries characterized by discriminatory pricing, some by f.o.b. pricing. For the latter group, what long-run conjectural variation might we propose in the economy?

Is it not likely *over time* (as Greenhut has often stressed) that successful practices breed successful practices? For example, successful plumbers act as do other successful plumbers, successful bankers act as do other successful bankers, successful professors act as do other successful professors. As an industry matures, as we conceptually approach the long run, each firm in an industry, no matter how basically identical are their products, develops a trade-name identification. Its market space *in effect* appears fixed and predetermined, with only minor alterations, and these in economic short-run periods between the long-run comparatively static points in time. In other words, with entry taking place at a distance *and* at, or very near, the representative firm's site, the maximum price possible is lowered sufficiently to produce the long-run tangencies of Figure 19.4.[11]

But what about the analysis of Chapter 18 and the claims of authors such as Eaton and Lipsey and Capozza and Van Order that the spatial economy is marked by positive (excess) profits in the long run? As has been noted, this would appear to be in direct conflict with the view expressed in this chapter that if excess profits exist, then sooner or later the right number of firms and locational distribution will emerge such that these profits will disappear; in this respect, even two firms would appear to suffice.

There is, in fact, no conflict between the two sets of ideas. Inherent to the Eaton-Lipsey model are the assumptions of immobile capital and a single, most efficient size of firm in a particular industry. It has already been noted that Eaton and Lipsey themselves recognized the effects of allowing some mobility of capital: Excess profit is reduced and will disappear if capital is "sufficiently" mobile. It should not be surprising, therefore, that when different-size firms are allowed to populate an industry (implicitly reducing the indivisibility of capital) and when a return for behavioral uncertainty is imputed (based in part on industry characteristics such as capital indivisibility and immobility), excess profit again disappears.

19.7   Conclusions

A conclusion containing some caveats is needed. It has been argued in this chapter that a competitive free-entry/exit (space) oligopoly economy will be efficient in the classical welfare-economics sense,[12] and we shall propose in the next chapter that it is also efficient in terms of location. This is, of course, not to say that we get the very best results in our world, distinct from, say, second-best results. The fact of the matter is that only some individuals and firms will be "best." However, even historical mistakes (e.g., developing an industry in the "wrong" city) are, in a fundamental sense, offset in time by newly developed infrastructures.

This, to repeat, does not mean that a free-enterprise economy produces *perfect* results: The very condition of bankruptcies indicates the second-best nature of any system involving men. Rather, the ideas proposed in this chapter simply imply that short-run errors in investment and location decisions tend to be eliminated in time, with the final distributional equilibrium proving to be economically efficient.

Appendix A

There are many facets to the theory in Chapter 19 that warrant further specification for interested readers. Initially, note that in our basic presentation we described the entrepreneurial function as consisting of two sides: services and investment. The service facet does *not* include promotional services. They are conceived of as a sunk cost to the business, not entrepreneurial at all. Our focus on oligopolies further suggests that emphasis in this appendix on large corporations is desirable; the fact that such emphasis carries the advantage of also including small single proprietorships in our thought framework suffices to justify the following analysis of entrepreneurship in a large corporate firm.

The entrepreneurial function

Under the aforementioned conceptual basis, entrepreneurial services in our framework are the managerial services that typically are paid for in the form of salaries and bonuses. Notwithstanding the explicit payments, our theory assumes only an implicit cost for all top-echelon manager services reflective of lost-opportunity costs. In effect, the salaries and bonuses paid to the firm's managers are conceived over time to dovetail with the implicit costs charged to the firm, in which costs we include the differential rent payments for the greater skills of a firm's managers than those of managers of other firms.

Our conception of the firm further requires that the investment funds of stockholders approach – in the long run – the capacities (capabilities) of the firm's managers. This condition means that though the stockholders and managers in the real world of corporate-form organizations may be two different sets of people, our representative firm is based on a conformability between the optimal cost investment and managerial capacities. This conception is counterpart to the single-proprietorship firm that is made up of an entrepreneur whose investment funds match his physical (mental) abilities (capacity). The same consequence also applies as the lowest-explicit-cost production point plus all differential rents (e.g., for skill) enable the firm to be competitive. Then, given sufficient "stick-to-itiveness" in overcoming short-run disappointments, the firm survives in the long run. It further follows that our counterpart view for the large firm requires varying short-run sizes as managers and investors (including the amount of equity investments) change over time, stabilizing ultimately for the surviving firms at a certain size; that size, in turn, is based essentially on the type of people attracted to the firm as its managers. Across industry lines and within each industry, we therefore have a full set of different-size firms, each characterized by managers who conform to the underlying technology (state of the art) that generates the most efficient production possible for that firm.

Our view of the firm and industry can be depicted quite simply. Conceive of an industry in which the costs and outputs of all *potentially viable firms* appear flat-lined. Of course, there exist outputs and costs beyond

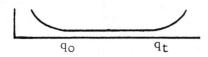

Figure 19A.1. Cost curve.

the efficient range (i.e., firms that are too small and too large), because only the flat-line section in Figure 19A.1 offers a chance for survival in the long run. As in Chapter 19, *which firms survive* depends on short-run events. In other words, we can have many firms of size q_0 or a few firms of size q_t, or a set of in-between sizes. Firms smaller or larger than q_0 or q_t, respectively, will disappear over time. Our theory thus specifies that long-run survivors in the industry are efficient, but not necessarily managed by the most capable men, who may, of course, be in other industries; all that is required is that the viable firms look like the representative firm described and depicted in Chapter 19, whose AC, including differential rents, places it somewhere between (and including) the q_0 and q_t sizes.

It should also be noted that the industrial divisibility conceived of under our theory (i.e., optimum-cost firm sizes anywhere between q_0 and q_t in the sketch) involves some number of firms, determined in part by short-run luck and ultimately by long-run demand. The alternative sizes of individual firms further explain the differences between our theory and those of Eaton and Lipsey or Capozza and Van Order. Profits in our theory are squeezed to the (normal) level commensurate with the behavioral uncertainty underscoring divisible investments (within the q_0–q_t range) in the industry.

Imputing the cost of behavioral uncertainty as a variable not fixed cost

Let us define

$$r = Rs = RAC_0 q_0 \qquad (A19.1)$$

where, here, R stands for the lost-opportunity rate of return (i.e., r_0 in the basic Chapter 19 presentation), and s is the optimal cost investment on AC_c; hence, $r = RAC_0 q_0$. Next, conceive of a variable cost imputation, in fact two alternative forms of it, as either

$$r' = Rs' = RAC_a q_a \qquad (A19.2)$$

where subscript a relates to the actual output, or

$$r' = Rs' = RAC_0 q_a \qquad (A19.3)$$

Refer to (A19.2) as the ψ variable cost adjustment and (A19.3) as the ϕ variable cost adjustment. Next define

$$C = f_1(Q) \qquad\qquad\qquad\qquad \text{(A19.2a)}$$

where $f_1(Q)$ is a cubic function that generates a monotonically increasing cost as total output Q increases. Then,

$$C^* = f_1(Q) + u \qquad\qquad\qquad\qquad \text{(A19.2b)}$$

where $u = u(Q) = f_2(Q)$, and where $f_2(Q) = \psi f_1(Q)$. Thus,

$$C^* = f_1(Q) + \psi f_1(Q)$$

so that

$$MC^* = \frac{dC^*}{dQ} = f_{1Q} + f_{2Q} = (1 + \psi)f_{1Q} \qquad\qquad \text{(A19.2c)}$$

and

$$AC^* + \frac{C^*}{Q} = \frac{f_1(Q)}{Q} + \frac{f_2(Q)}{Q} = \frac{(1+\psi)f_1(Q)}{Q} \qquad \text{(A19.2d)}$$

Alternatively, from (A19.3) we have

$$C = f(Q) \qquad\qquad\qquad\qquad \text{(A19.3a)}$$

Then,

$$C^* = f(Q) + u \qquad\qquad\qquad\qquad \text{(A19.3b)}$$

where $u = u(Q)$ now equals ϕQ. Therefore, $C^* = f(Q) + \phi Q$, so that

$$MC^* = \frac{dC^*}{dQ} = fQ + \phi \qquad\qquad\qquad \text{(A19.3c)}$$

and

$$AC^* = \frac{C^*}{Q} = \frac{f(Q)}{Q} + \frac{\phi Q}{Q} = \frac{f(Q)}{Q} + \phi \qquad \text{(A19.3d)}$$

It is manifest that the (A19.2) conception of r' entails

$$r' = \psi f_1(Q) = \psi AC_a q_a \qquad\qquad\qquad \text{(A19.2')}$$

Therefore,

$$\psi = R \qquad\qquad\qquad\qquad \text{(A19.2'')}$$

(rate of return on some actual dollar investment). The (A19.3) conception of r' in turn establishes

$$r' = \phi Q = RAC_0 q_a \qquad\qquad\qquad \text{(A19.3')}$$

which means

$$\phi = RAC_0 \qquad\qquad\qquad\qquad\qquad\text{(A19.3'')}$$

(the dollar requirement due to the percentage R on the AC_0 amount). Of course, $AC_a > AC_0$ for all $a \neq 0$.

Note that the tangency to the fixed-cost (r) adjusted curve induces entry at points short of the technological optimal cost output; this result occurs because of the windfall profits that exist over such points. Now we find, via our variable-cost (r') conception, a disparity between MR and MC for all AR tangencies to the r' adjusted AC curve due to equating MR with MC*. Note that this disparity applies when uncertainty is imputed by the entrepreneur-investor as a variable input in perfect conformance to technology (the ψ adjustment) or when it is imputed per unit of output (the ϕ adjustment). In each case, new entry into the market by erstwhile accountants, engineers, and economists is encouraged by the apparent failure of the entrepreneur to produce where MR equals the MC that appears on the firm's books.

We favor the fixed-cost r approach. But more important, the final results of the variable-cost r' approach match the fixed-cost approach. To see this, recognize that imputing a cost for the behavioral uncertainty that underlies investments in oligopoly markets can be effected only by the investor. No accountant, engineer, economist, or any other individual knows another person's lost-opportunity costs, including the way the person conceives of investment returns. It is only in the mind's eye of the individual investor that an adjustment to marginal cost exists, and this adjustment obtains if and only if we want to imagine the investor changing the firm's income requirement in conformance to the actual investment. Thus, if we let MC change as inputs or outputs change, we have lost the basic property of the firm, namely, that all individuals require a return for their services and investments based on their conceptions of their lost opportunities. In turn, we have lost the idea that when selecting a given activity, the individual has in mind a total work and investment performance [symbolized by s in (A19.1)] and a lost-opportunity rate of return [symbolized by R in (A19.1)]. The product r of Rs, in other words, is our target. It is the belief that one will gain r returns, which justifies selecting a given employment or, as is of sole interest here, a given investment.

It follows from the foregoing that if we conceive of variable-cost adjustments for uncertainty based on inputs and technology (the ψ adjustment) or based directly on output quantities (the ϕ adjustment), an artificial adjustment is also needed for marginal revenues. This adjustment is also strictly in the mind's eye of the entrepreneur, who, simply put, aspires to the return r, not r'. So we define the several adjustments required under variable imputations in the particular activity as

$$\psi' = \frac{r}{q_a} = \frac{RAC_0 q_0}{q_a} = (RAC_0) \quad (RAC_0 > 1) \tag{A19.4}$$

for all tangencies where $q_0 > q_a$. And we define proxy-related ψ^* for the ψ involved in (A19.2) as

$$\psi^* = \frac{r'}{q_a} = \frac{RAC_a q_a}{q_a} = RAC_a \tag{A19.5}$$

And for (A19.3) we then have

$$\phi^* = \frac{r'}{q_a} = \frac{RAC_0 q_a}{q_a} = RAC_0 = \phi \tag{A19.6}$$

Note that the numerator in the third term of (A19.4) is greater than in (A19.5). Thus, $\psi' > \psi^* > \phi^*$. So, besides the hired expert's disequilibrium view of MR > MC at any tangency to an r' adjusted curve, the entrepreneur is also in disequilibrium as he conceives of an adjusted MR greater than MC. Moreover, for all output points beyond the technological optimal cost point where AR may equal the r' adjusted value, we have

$$\psi' = (RAC_0) \quad (RAC_0 < 1)$$

$$\psi^* = RAC_a$$

$$\phi^* = RAC_0$$

Hence, $\psi' < \phi^* < \psi^*$. Of course, where $q_a = q_0$ in the third terms of (A19.4), (A19.5), and (A19.6), $\psi' = \psi^* = \phi^*$. The long-run equilibrium marked by the Chapter 19 tangency of AR to the r adjusted curve at the optimal technological cost output is therefore directly counterpart to what variable cost imputations would generate.

To sum up our findings: Tangency of AR to the r adjusted curve at what would be a typical Chamberlin excess-capacity point involves profits and potential entry. Tangency to the lower adjusted average-cost curves, the ψ and ϕ adjusted AC curves, involves disequilibrium, because (in his mind's eye) the entrepreneur has not fulfilled his objective $r = Rs$; moreover, the hired experts of the firm are favorably inclined to quit the firm and enter the market with their own enterprise, because, by their books, the entrepreneur is producing at an MR > MC point. It further follows that any tangency to some AC adjusted curve falling (by some process) between the r adjusted and the r' adjusted curves of (A19.2) and (A19.3), and which is short of the technological optimal cost point, still makes the entrepreneur appear not to be maximizing. Moreover, though the entrepreneur himself may be approaching the return r for a smaller investment than the s investment he had intended, we can expect either entry by others and/or the entrepreneur's desire to expand by investing more.

Simply put, either the industry is profitable or it is not yielding enough to the firm's entrepreneur-managers and to the stockholders on the equity investments that the firm has accumulated with the objectives of conforming to its management's capacities.

Final statement

One might ask, What are the effects of different proportions of funded debt to equity investment on our theory? Our answer to this question can be quite terse. We define an industry narrowly as involving (1) a product that is a member of an identifiable group of products, (2) identical risk-uncertainty structures among firms, and (3) financial structures that are also identical among all member firms (i.e., identical funded debt/equity ratios based on that which *over time* has appeared to be the successful financial balance). This definition applies strictly to our long-run conception, which in turn only signifies the position toward which the industry moves before a new exogenous shock sets it off on another new long-run trend. More broadly, we can view as members of the (almost) same industry all firms (1) whose products are among those of an identifiable group of products, (2) provided that among its producing firms, identical (or sufficiently similar) underlying uncertainty structures prevail. Pursuant to this designation, financial contrivances are then considered to alter the levels of uncertainty and required return on the equity investment in the particular firm. But, most important, the monotonicity of yields per dollar investment based on uncertainty levels remains the basic requisite.

Appendix B: Recent approaches to excess capacity in imperfectly competitive markets

From Chamberlin to Demsetz

One of Chamberlin's best-known theorems (1956) was that excess capacity prevails in the long-run equilibrium of monopolistically competitive markets. This theorem was challenged in a series of papers by Demsetz (1959, 1964, 1968), who conceived of the quantity of product and selling costs varying simultaneously. Specifically, Demsetz claimed that an optimal sales-promotion effort applies to each and every saleable quantity of the firm's output. He further asserted that sales-promotion efforts could be expected to conform to classical rules of diminishing returns. From this vantage point, he conceptualized a uniquely different bell-shaped type of average-revenue (AR) curve, the curvature of which relates to the sales-promotion efforts of the firm.

Demsetz (1959) referred to his AR curve as the MAR curve (M for *mutatis mutandis*). The greater-quantity/higher-price section of the bell-shaped curve reflects the portion of selling costs subject to increasing returns to scale. Manifestly, the rise in profit-maximizing prices applicable to (some) greater quantities of the good can be compared to the lower prices applicable to the smaller quantities of the good for which no sales-promotion effort is warranted. The downward portion of the MAR that extends over still greater quantities of the good relates, in turn, to the decreasing-returns-to-scale effect. This portion of MAR involves the classical combination of greater quantities/lower prices.

Demsetz observed that average total cost (equal to average production cost plus average selling cost) could be at its minimum in the zero-profit equilibrium state of monopolistic competition. This possibility follows from the condition that profits of monopolistically competitive firms will induce entry, and with enough entry the bell-shaped MAR curve could become tangent to the U-shaped average total-cost (ATC) curve. This tangency, of course, could take place at diverse points on the ATC curve, including its lowest-cost point, which particular possibility is sufficient condition to rule out excess capacity as an intrinsic, inviolate property of monopolistic competition.

Demsetz's theory was first attacked by Archibald (1962, 1967) on grounds that quality variation alone would reveal the existence of excess capacity.[13] His critique was not accepted by Demsetz (1967).[14] Barzel (1970) then attacked Demsetz's theory on the basis that the slope of the properly measured quality-adjusted price locus must be negative, and hence excess capacity must exist.[15] Still later, Schmalensee (1972) objected to Demsetz's theory with the aid of a simple algebraic model. His model included advertising and product-improvement possibilities. Via an *assumed* negative partial derivative of price to quantity, he, too, was led to the classical conclusion that excess capacity exists in the long run.[16]

Demsetz (1972) continued to defend his approach, notwithstanding the methodological critiques of Archibald and Barzel and Schmalensee's postulational disclaimers. At the same time, he continued to contend in Chicago-school fashion that because of both the internal and external inconsistencies of the model, monopolistic competition fails to add anything of substance to the classical competitive and monopoly models.

Our own view of imperfectly competitive markets rules out the MAR curve (which, as the other writers noted earlier had suggested, is an irrelevant dynamically formulated AR curve); instead, we prefer viewing the traditional static AR curve. But, unlike Archibald, Barzel, and Schmalensee, we conclude that excess capacity can *never exist* in the imperfectly competitive long-run equilibrium. The requirement of a single price for a homogeneous good sold by more than one firm in competition with another (others) generates tangency to the average-cost curve (i.e., the one that includes the return for uncertainty) at a point directly above the minimum-cost point on the average-technological-cost curve.

From Chamberlin to Baumol and associates

Baumol, Panzar, and Willig (1982) produced a theory of imperfectly competitive markets that in some ways rejected a high-cost Chamberlinian solution and yet did not fully reject a high-cost, no-further-entry equilibrium for a monopolistically competitive market. Fundamentally, they appeared to subscribe to the view (Chapter 2) that competitive entry, even just potential entry, would cause prices to approach the minimum-cost level. Under certain conditions, however, they noted that an intersection of the AR curve with the AC curve could take place in a Chamberlinian world at a point involving costs higher than minimum average costs (Chapter 11).

Specifically, Baumol, Panzar, and Willig (henceforth BPW) assumed frictionless entry and exit. They further proposed that certain costs of an existing (incumbent) firm were sunk, and hence irrelevant to that firm's pricing policy. For potential entrants, however, *all* production costs counted and would thus be price-determining. It followed that in the absence of fixed costs for the incumbent firm (because all such costs would be sunk), there could be no production scale economies. Thus, average costs of production were nondecreasing over all quantities. Given that condition, along with frictionless (no-fixed-cost) entry, the incumbent firm would then be forced to price at its lowest possible cost; otherwise, an entrant would produce that quantity or a smaller one and sell at the same or lower price. The related assumption of identical-size firms (as in Eaton-Lipsey) appeared to support the idea of pricing at the minimum AC level (Chapter 2).

Schwartz and Reynolds (1983) recognized that the full significance of the frictionless-exit assumption of BPW necessitated the conclusion that the incumbent firm could immediately adopt the monopoly price and wrench existing profits before entry of the prospective competitor. Of course, the incumbent firm could subsequently exit the market on entry of the new firm; in the process, it would have earned a profit instead of pricing at the lowest possible cost in order to restrain entry. Weitzman (1983) was even more implacable. Besides treating the BPW assumptions as absurd, he contended that contestable-market theory is misleading, because, by necessity, the existence of sunk costs, and hence nondecreasing AC for the incumbent firm, must always lead to intensely competitive entry possibilities. The BPW model was simply too unrealistic and produced a desired solution via the assumptions set that would generate that result. Still more recently, Shephard (1984) argues that contestability (or ultrafree entry) rests on unrealistic assumptions and that the conclusions of the model are contrary to reality. He asserts that "little has been added to the pre-existing entry and exit analysis" (p. 585).

It is relevant for us to propose that a cleaner theory of contestable markets, in our opinion, requires truly frictionless entry along with different-size firms. The frictionless-entry assumption signifies no fixed costs for either the incumbent or the entrant and in fact no need to specify costs as sunk. Greater output, of course, implies nondecreasing average costs with scale. Then it follows that a friction-proofed entrant could indeed produce (and always so) a smaller quantity than an incumbent firm at the same or lower price. The incumbent firm is therefore also led to pricing at its minimum AC level. Note, finally, we would also reject the BPW requirement of frictionless exit, for, given that condition, the incumbent would price monopolistically and would exit on entry by another. What remains with our modification or without it (as in BPW) is a rather non-classical view of imperfectly competitive markets. Unlike the simple inclusion of a residual sum required for uncertainty, as in Chapter 19, the theory of contestable markets discards the concepts and also rejects the relevance of the classical model of the firm. We believe the classical model provides vistas that are needed in microeconomic theory.

CHAPTER 20

Long-run locational equilibrium

The analysis in Chapter 19 was concerned in the main with *price* efficiency. There remains the question, however, of *locational* efficiency in spatial and differentiated-product markets. It is quite clear from the analysis in Section I of this book, for example, that the Löschian firm's delivered price exceeds its marginal-production cost, where marginal-production costs includes transport costs. A number of authors have claimed that this leads to inefficient allocation of resources in the Löschian spatial economy. Long-run equilibrium is characterized by an inefficient number of firms, each operating on an inefficiently small scale.

Stern (1972) questioned this argument. He indicated that whether or not the Löschian market area is optimal depends to a large degree on the level of fixed costs and the elasticity of individual demand. It would appear, therefore, that it is almost impossible to derive other than ambiguous conclusions regarding the question of locational efficiency.

Fortunately, this ambiguity has been resolved in subsequent analyses by Greenhut and Hwang (1979) and Benson (1981a, 1984), and it is to the analyses of these authors that we now turn.

20.1 The Löschian hexagonal network and spatial economic discontinuities[1]

Recall from Chapter 15 that the Löschian hexagonal network for a particular industry was derived on the assumption of a homogeneous plain – a plain over which all consumers and resources are evenly spread. An immediate question that arises is whether or not such a set of equal-size hexagons (identical firm sizes) applies when the market area is heterogeneous.

It is one thing to establish a uniform hexagonal arrangement for an industry producing in a homogeneous space. It is another thing to claim that it exists in the long run in a real, heterogeneous world regardless of the price policies competitive firms pursue. Indeed, how can homogeneous hexagons prevail for an industry dispersed over an economy that ranges over mountainous regions to plains to desertlike regions, and where heterogeneous cost conditions exist?

344

Using the basic analytical tools presented in Chapter 19, Greenhut and Hwang (1979) have shown that the hexagonal pattern proposed by Lösch does, in fact, underscore the economic landscape in much the same way as the perfectly competitive economy can be used to explain basic economic relationships.

20.2 The markup for uncertainty

It was shown in Chapter 19 that for any given homogeneous-product industry there will be an efficient intraindustry price m for all viable producers in the industry in the long run. Because long-run equilibrium has been assumed to be characterized by zero profits, it follows that this mill price equals long-run average costs inclusive of uncertainty: denoted AC_u. Further, the price m is greater than minimum classical average costs (AC_c) by the rate of return required for the degree of uncertainty applicable to the particular industry. Denote this return by R. Greenhut and Hwang show that these pricing equations will generate identical-size intraindustry hexagons even if member firms in an industry have different optimal output capacities and are distributed over a heterogeneously endowed space.

To reiterate, the basic theorem that generates this outcome is totally described by three conditions:

$$m > AC_c^*; \qquad m - AC_c^* = R; \qquad m = AC_u \qquad (20.1)$$

In applying this theorem to the problem of market-area determination, let both the equilibrium mill price m and the AC_u curve be raised by the average freight cost per unit of sales made by each seller. In effect, it is being assumed, for reasons of simplicity, that the firm is operating an f.o.b. pricing system. It charges the representative buyer its mill price plus freight cost (i.e., a delivered price p, with the freight cost being paid by the buyer to the carrier). (It should be noted in passing, however, that the analysis applies equally to a price-discriminating industry.)

This approach has the same effect as leaving m and AC_u unaffected by freight cost on the final product (a property that characterizes f.o.b. pricing systems). In other words, the statement $m = AC_u$ is equivalent to the statement that m plus the average freight cost per unit sold equals AC_u plus the average freight cost per unit sold.

Firms in a given industry may be of different sizes and capacities, and thus different profit-maximizing outputs. Nevertheless, the long-run requirement is that mill price m plus average freight costs must be the same across these firms. This is equivalent to the requirement that average freight cost per unit sold must be the same for all intraindustry firms. It follows that the large-size firm must be selling over a market space characterized by a greaer density of buyers, *ceteris paribus*. The firm simply sells a larger, but fixed, proportion of its output at each distance in its market space than does the small firm in the same-size space.

Many other examples can be envisaged that satisfy these long-run conditions. The small firm may be located at a peripheral market point, the surrounding trading area of which is characterized by a lower density of buyers. Or the smaller firm may be viewed as having located next door to the larger firm, where it simply sells a smaller share of its total output to each buying point within the same market space.

Consider what would arise if the specified long-run conditions did not hold (e.g., if consumer densities were not proportional at each distance in the two market spaces, or, alternatively, if sales distributions by small and large firms were not proportional at each market point within the given market space). In such cases there would be differences in intra-industry mill prices and returns. Profits or losses would be made, and the theorem used as a starting point would be violated. The basic equilibrium requirement is the same mill price m plus average freight cost per unit sold.

To embellish on this argument, assume that there are two firms in *adjacent market spaces,* each of which is managed by men of identical capacities. But though the firms will otherwise be identical in size, *ceteris paribus,* suppose further that the distribution of customers is economically superior in one space compared with the other. The greater consumer density close to the site of the more advantaged seller implies a lower average freight cost for that seller compared with his competitor on the same quantity of sales. This condition again implies greater profits for the more advantaged seller (i.e., $m > AC_u$), thus violating the long-run norm. So entry by a smaller firm at a proximate site can be expected whenever a superior distribution of buyers exists in one space compared with another. Such entry requires an increase in the market space of the original seller before sales (capacity operations) of the assumed firms are again the same. One might propose more completely an entry-relocation-exit type of process throughout the system over time. In other words, the entry-exit process that underscores the theory of perfect competition can be expected to apply in basically the same way in bringing about the long-run spatial oligopoly equilibrium.

What about cost differences across regions? In particular, may not labor costs, raw-materials costs, and land costs differ, and, accordingly, would not market sizes differ so that other polygons emerge, as in the Eaton-Lipsey (1976) computer simulations? Greenhut and Hwang argue simply this: If the explicit average-cost curve is lower in, say, market space

1 than in market space 2, rents will emerge in time, as noted in Chapter 19. These rents lead to the $m = AC_u$ relations. The firm in a low-cost area may appropriate as a monopoly rent the extra product produced by its more highly skilled labor or by its better resources. In the long run, however, labor mobility and competitive bidding for resources will apply to the competitive spatial economy. Only the more highly skilled and higher-quality factors will receive the differential rent advantage they possess. Costs throughout the economy thus tend toward the same level in the long run.

It further follows that a heterogeneous landscape, which, at first blush, would appear to require heterogeneous-size hexagons for a particular industry, must be marked in the long run by identical-size hexagons. This surprising result also applies because (as noted earlier) greater population density (shorter hauls for a given volume of sales) will provide different (enhanced) profits. The locationally advantaged firm will therefore encounter greater local competition. A change in its market area can be expected over time.

Different cost levels may also stem from different freight rates, and different freight rates may occur as a result of natural (terrain) advantage or because of institutional forces. In the former (natural) case, rents arise (as with better land fertility or location). In the institutional case, irregular-shaped markets *will emerge*. This is, however, neither surprising nor contradictory to the theory. The same outcome will result from any artificial interference with the natural rent-cost basis required in order for the theorem to hold ($m > AC_c^*$ by the same R) for all firms in a given industry.

The foregoing analysis might be countered on pragmatic grounds by asserting that firms clearly do not ship over hexagonal market spaces. *Of course they do not!* Greenhut and Hwang recognize that the theory applies to the long run only. It indicates the tendencies and trends that underlie the space economy. Even when products are heterogeneous and market spaces overlap, the trace of identical-size hexagons can be imagined if consumers throughout the landscape happen to conceive of the alternative products as actually being identical. *For these consumers,* the hexagonal spaces will be identical, whereas for those who view the products differently, the overlapping of markets applies. In a similar manner, only irregular polygons will emerge when markets are formed at a single point or a few special points in space.

To sum up this theory, the average-cost levels (including all rents) and the mill prices of the product in a particular industry must be identical in a long-run stable equilibrium in that industry. In addition, the average freight costs on sales of the product must be the same for all intraindustry firms. An identical intraindustry hexagonal market shape thus exists except in specially selected cases, such as where only a single demand point or a sharply limited number of demand points dot the landscape. In general, when demand is distributed over space, Lösch's intraindustry hexagonal network applies in the long run for the competitive free-entry/free-exit spatial oligopoly economy.

20.3 Allocative efficiency in the spatial economy

There remains the question of allocative efficiency in imperfect competition. It was noted in the introductory comments to this chapter that a number of authors have suggested that Löschian competition, in particular, leads to allocative inefficiency. Price exceeds site-specific marginal-production costs, leading to a market containing too many inefficient, small firms. This inefficiency argument has been challenged by Benson (1981a, 1984), who claims that "[the] zero profit Löschian equilibrium yields the optimal number of optimally sized market areas" (1981a, p. 1080). In outlining Benson's analysis, we consider a very simple model. Assume that the market is the circumference of a circle and is of finite length T. Consumers are evenly distributed over that market at density D per unit distance. All consumers are identical, with individual demand for a single homogeneous product

$$q = f(p) = a - bp \quad (a, b > 0) \tag{20.2}$$

(i.e., linear demand, where p is delivered price).

Production costs for this commodity are assumed identical throughout the market and are given by the equation

$$C(S) = F + cS \tag{20.3}$$

where F indicates fixed costs, c indicates marginal costs, and S is individual-plant output (sales). Finally, all firms are assumed to adopt an f.o.b. pricing policy. Delivered price to consumers at distance r from a particular supplier is

$$p = m + tr \tag{20.4}$$

where m is mill price, and t is transport costs.[2]

It might be felt in the light of the analysis in Chapters 2–4 that the linearity assumptions will generate little more than a special case. In purely quantitative terms this is true, but in qualitative terms it is not. Benson's analysis is based on totally general cost functions for demand and production. The analysis that follows *illustrates* his general propositions by using a specific example that is mathematically more tractable.

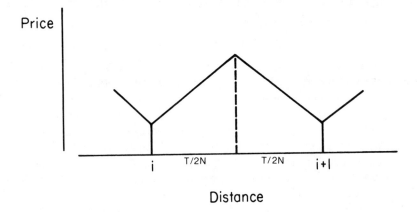

Figure 20.1. Multiplant monopoly.

20.3.1 *The multiplant monopolist*

Consider the case in which the market is served by a multiplant monopolist. Because such a monopolist is assumed to aim to maximize aggregate profit in the market, it is reasonable to expect that the total market area will be served. Further, the assumed uniform distribution of consumers and homogeneous cost conditions imply that each plant will adopt the same mill price and serve the same market area. If there are N plants in the market, each plant will have a market area T/N and market radius $T/2N$, as in Figure 20.1.[3]

Aggregate demand (sales) for any one plant is (recall Chapter 2)

$$S = 2D \int_0^{\hat{R}} f(m+tr)\, dr \quad (\hat{R} = T/2N) \tag{20.5}$$

Substituting from equation (20.2) gives

$$S = D[(a-bm)T/N - btT^2/4N^2] \tag{20.5'}$$

Aggregate demand for the monopolist is therefore

$$Q = NS = D[(a-bm)T - btT^2/4N] \tag{20.6}$$

The demand-increasing effect: Consider first the effect on aggregate demand of adding additional plants. To do so, we adopt a "trick" commonly used in this kind of analysis and treat the integer variable N as if it were a continuous variable. So long as N is "sufficiently large," this trick is a perfectly acceptable approximation. As a result, the effect of an additional plant on aggregate demand is

$$\partial Q/\partial N = S + N\partial S/\partial N = Dbt^2/4N^2 > 0 \tag{20.7}$$

Additional plants reduce the average distance of each consumer from the nearest supplier; or, in a differentiated-product setting, additional product variants allow consumers, on average, to purchase a commodity that accords more closely with their preferred variety. As might be expected, therefore, additional plants increase aggregate demand. But it is also clear from equation (20.7) that the increase in aggregate demand diminishes with additional plants. In the limit with $N = \infty$, one firm serves each market point. Transport costs are no longer relevant, and market demand is maximized.

This increase in market demand is not costless. There is a reduction in transport costs as N is increased, but plants cannot be established at zero cost. A need arises to strike a balance between the two sets of costs.

Profit maximization: Aggregate profit for the multiplant monopolist is

$$\Pi(m, N) = (m - c)Q - NF = N(m - c)S - NF \tag{20.8}$$

where the decision variables for the firm are the mill price and the number of plants.

Consider first the optimal mill price. The relevant first-order condition is just the fundamental pricing equation derived in Chapter 2 under Löschian competitive conditions:

$$m(1 - 1/e_{Sm}) = c \tag{20.9}$$

where e_{Sm} is the elasticity of individual plant demand with respect to mill price. Marginal revenue [the left-hand side of (20.9)] equals (site-specific) marginal-production cost (the right-hand side).

Making the appropriate substitutions from equation (20.5′) gives the mill price:

$$m^* = a/2b + c/2 - tT/8N \tag{20.10}$$

Now consider the optimal number of plants. Because N is treated as a continuous variable, the first-order condition is

$$\partial \Pi/\partial N = (m - c)S + N(m - c)\partial S/\partial N - F = 0 \tag{20.11}$$

which gives the general condition[4]

$$m = \frac{F + cS + cN\partial S/\partial N}{\partial Q/\partial N} \tag{20.12}$$

Equation (20.12) has an appealing interpretation. The numerator of the right-hand side consists of (1) the cost of the new plant $(F + cS)$ plus (2) the marginal cost of the change in individual-plant demand resulting from the increased total capacity. The denominator is the increase in aggregate demand resulting from the increased capacity.

In other words, the numerator is simply the full marginal cost to the industry (or to society) of adding an additional plant. This is multiplied by $1/(\partial Q/\partial N)$: the increment to the number of plants required to produce a unit change in output. Thus, the right-hand side of (20.12) represents the marginal cost of obtaining one more unit of output by adjusting the number of plants.

This marginal cost has been defined in a different context by DeVany (1976) as long-run marginal cost (LMC). In a spatial world, the right-hand side of (20.12) can be reinterpreted as spatial LMC (SLMC). The optimum (profit-maximizing) number of plants requires that price should equal SLMC.

Equation (20.12) can also be interpreted by substitution from equation (20.7):

$$m = c + \frac{F}{\partial Q/\partial N} \qquad (20.13)$$

Price equals site-specific marginal-production cost plus the individual plant's share of a charge for the use of capital to establish additional locations, thus covering the opportunity cost of capital for establishing the last location.

There is nothing in the solution to the system given by (20.13) that requires $m =$ long-run AC. Clearly, a monopolist's surplus may exist. A sort of second-best (or even third-best) type of result exists. Of course, if the monopoly price were the efficient price, the monopolist would also have the efficient number of plants, because the marginal benefit of an additional unit of output (price) would be equal to the marginal cost of obtaining that unit by means of another location. This marginal cost, of course, includes both the marginal-production cost and the opportunity cost of capital used to establish the plant.

20.3.2 *Competition*

Will the efficient price for spatial competitors (Chapter 19) also be equated to LMC, thus implying locational efficiency? One fact can be stated immediately. The demand-increasing effect noted earlier for the multi-plant monopolist also holds within a competitive market. Benefits accrue to consumers and to society as a result of the increase in the number of (spatially separated) competing firms. Such an increase in demand also imposes costs, of course, in the provision of additional productive units (spatial firms). Efficiency in resource allocation requires that the marginal value of the product should equal its full marginal cost.

Consumers' marginal valuation of the product is measured by the mill price they are willing to pay. In order to identify marginal cost, we must first specify the cost function of the individual spatial firm. Maintaining the simplifying linearity assumptions, total production cost for each competitor is

$$C = F + cS + R(N) \qquad (20.14)$$

It will be noted that (20.14) differs from (20.3) by the addition of an uncertainty premium $R(N)$ – recall the discussion in Chapter 19. It is to be expected that the return for behavioral uncertainty will increase *up to a point* with the number of firms in the market: $\partial R/\partial N > 0$ over a relevant domain. Intuitively, a monopolist ($N = 1$) with a given time horizon faces little or no oligopolistic uncertainty. As N increases, oligopolistic rivalry becomes more intense up to some level of entry. Clearly, as firms get closer and closer, they compete for fewer customers and a smaller pool of potential profits. This causes incorrect conjectures to become increasingly costly relative to potential returns. Thus, with competitive oligopolistic entry (i.e., with increased N), a greater premium for uncertainty is required regardless of the underlying character (i.e., basic level) of uncertainty in the industry.

Total industry production cost is NC. The full marginal cost to the industry (and to society) of increasing the number of firms in the market is just the spatial equivalent of DeVany's LMC: the SLMC noted earlier. Recalling equation (20.12), SLMC is defined as

$$\text{SLMC} = \frac{F + cS + cN\partial S/\partial N + R + N\partial R/\partial N}{\partial Q/\partial N} \qquad (20.15)$$

SLMC, to repeat, is the full marginal cost of output when output is changed by changing the number of plants in the market. Locational efficiency requires that price should equal SLMC.

20.3.3   Competitive equilibrium

Assume free entry and that production sites are independently owned. Then N represents the number of independent single-plant firms. Because N is no longer controlled by a single entrepreneur, the costs of establishing additional locations do not enter into any one firm's profit-maximizing decisions. Each entrepreneur considers only his own site-specific marginal cost, his share of the market, and his expectations of rival responses to his pricing policy as he sets his profit-maximizing price.

All of this does not mean that the costs of multiple locations do not exist. The multiplant monopolist was able to account for these costs directly in his profit-maximizing decisions. Independent firms do not, even though the opportunity cost of capital must still be borne by society. Nevertheless, it can be shown that locational efficiency holds in this (spatially) competitive world.

In deriving the competitive equilibrium, assume that all firms in the market are located symmetrically and adopt identical mill prices (Novshek 1980). Assume further that each firm currently in the market has a supply area of radius U'. Then total sales are, from (20.5),

$$S(m, U') = 2D \int_0^{U'} f(m + tr) \, DR$$

$$= 2D((a - bm)U' - bt(U')^2/2) \tag{20.16}$$

With N firms in the market, $U' = T/2N$. In other words, U' (and thus S) is a function of the number of firms.

Each competitor's profit equation is

$$\Pi = (m - c)S - F - R(N) \tag{20.17}$$

Independent rival firms maximize profits over their own supply areas rather than over the entire market T. T is exogenously fixed, but U' is variable with competition and depends on the mill price charged by any one firm relative to the mill prices of its nearest competitors.

The profit-maximizing mill price is, from (20.17), again given by the fundamental pricing equation:

$$m(1 - 1/e_{Sm}^c) = c \tag{20.18}$$

It must be emphasized, however, that the elasticity e_{Sm}^c of equation (20.18) need not be identical with that of the monopolist.

In the competitive framework, a change in mill price gives rise to a demand effect and a competition effect (recall Chapter 2), the latter arising from the expected increase in market area consequent upon a reduction in mill price. Using the notation of Chapter 2,

$$e_{Sm}^c = -(\partial S/\partial M + v_i \, \partial S/\partial U')m/S \tag{20.19}$$

where v_i is a conjectural variation.

It will be recalled that

1. Löschian competition implies $v_i = 0$.
2. Hotelling-Smithies competition implies $v_i = -\frac{1}{2}t$.
3. Greenhut-Ohta competition implies $v_i = -1/t$.

The appropriate mill prices with linear individual demand are then just as in Part I of this book.

The second condition to be satisfied by the competitive equilibrium is that individual-firm profit, and thus industry profit, is driven to zero by competitive entry:[5]

$$N\Pi = N(m-c)S - NF - NR(N) = 0 \tag{20.20}$$

Equations (20.18) and (20.20) define the competitive system and give two equilibrium conditions in the two unknowns: competitive mill price m and the number of firms N. However, the equilibrium condition (20.20) does not provide any direct information about marginal conditions or, in particular, about the locational efficiency of the final equilibrium.

The locational efficiency of the long-run equilibrium is derived from an additional constraint on the long-run equilibrium that recognizes that three cases exist: $\partial LRAC/\partial N \gtreqless 0$. For example, if the "less than" sign applies, prospective entrepreneurs anticipate profit opportunities even though profits of current firms may be zero. It follows that (20.20) does not assure a long-run equilibrium. The long-run equilibrium requires

$$\partial LRAC/\partial N = 0 \tag{20.21}$$

$$AR = \overline{LRAC} \tag{20.22}$$

where $\overline{LRAC} = [cS + F + R(N)]/S$.

Next note that (20.22) implies

$$cS = mS - F - R(N) \tag{20.23}$$

Hence,

$$LRAC = (mS - F - R(N))/S \tag{20.24}$$

Evaluation of the derivative in (20.21) based on (20.24) gives

$$\frac{\partial LRAC}{\partial N} = \frac{(m\partial S/\partial N - \partial R/\partial N)S - (mS - F - R(N))\partial S/\partial N}{S^2} = 0 \tag{20.25}$$

which can be rewritten

$$\frac{\partial LRAC}{\partial N} = \frac{F + R(N)}{S}\frac{\partial S}{\partial N} \tag{20.26}$$

or, substituting (20.23) in (20.25),

$$\partial R/\partial N - m\partial S/\partial N = -c\partial S/\partial N \tag{20.27}$$

Thus, in the long run, the increased cost of an additional firm [the left-hand side of (20.27)] must actually equal the marginal-cost reduction of the new firm [the right-hand side of (20.27)].

To see that (20.26) implies $m = $ SLMC, rewrite (20.22) as

$$m = c + (F + R(N))/S \tag{20.28}$$

Then multiplying and dividing (20.28) by $\partial Q/\partial N = S + N(\partial S/\partial N)$ gives

$$m = \frac{c\left(S + N\frac{\partial S}{\partial N}\right) + \left(S + N\frac{\partial S}{\partial N}\right)\left(\frac{F + R(N)}{S}\right)}{\partial Q/\partial N} \tag{20.29}$$

and because $[(F + R(N))/S](\partial S/\partial N)$ is $\partial R/\partial N$, we obtain

$$m = (cS + cN\partial S/\partial N + F + R(N) + N\partial R/\partial N)/(\partial Q/\partial N) \tag{20.30}$$

It follows that the locational-efficiency condition of m equal to SLMC holds if, as in Chapter 19, the spatially competitive market moves to a long-run equilibrium. The long-run mill-price equation implies social marginal cost equal to social marginal benefit, with the entry-exit process generating the marginal adjustments that produce the zero-profit equilibrium. At the same time, the difference between mill price and firm-specific marginal-producion cost is

$$m - c = (F + R + N\partial R/\partial N)/(\partial Q/\partial N) \tag{20.31}$$

Note from (20.20) that $\Pi = (m - c)S - F - R(N) = 0$ in the long-run equilibrium. Thus, equation (20.31) has the appealing interpretation that the difference between mill price and firm-specific marginal-production cost reflects the firm's share of the social cost of establishing additional locations. The greater that cost, the greater the potential losses involved, and the greater the behavioral uncertainty, *ceteris paribus*. The argument that spatial competition leads to locational inefficiency is in error. Benson contends that those who advance this argument have specified the wrong maximand. He states: "[There] are more costs to consider than just firm specific production costs and more benefits than those derived directly from these costs" (Benson 1981a, p. 1081).

To summarize Benson's theory of the spatially competitive equilibrium to this point in our development of it, note initially that in his view the cost of uncertainty, as derived in Chaper 19, is just one of *two* extra long-run costs imposed on the firm by *economic space*. The other cost, we find from (20.31), is the fraction of added-capacity costs that consumers pay to a seller in exchange for the reduced waiting time, delivery time, and/or service time that derive from the last added (equilibrium-level) capacity. To be sure, because the mill price goes up by only a small amount, consumers view unchanged "full" price to be the consequence of the last increment to capacity in the industry. Meanwhile, the manager of the representative firm recognizes that the new entrant has blocked his firm off spatially from part of the market. This blockage has the effect of raising *opportunity costs* in the industry, particularly as seen by "outside" entrepreneurs who are evaluating alternative investments. Though it is the case that at some substantial levels of entry the $N\partial R/\partial N$ factor will turn negative, the more crowded is the industry, the fewer are the entrepreneurial opportunities for achievement; hence, the personal costs of management are greater in crowded industries. Benson's long-run view of the spatial economy thus captures the consumers' added-demand perspective along with the entrepreneurs' full-cost view of opportunities in the final equilibrium. The difference between m and c includes the equilibrium-level changes in the costs of uncertainty and capacity.

20.4 Impact of conjectural variations on long-run equilibrium

In a sense, Benson's equilibrium arises *independent of the firm's conjectural variations,* because the only requirement is that intraindustry entrepreneurs adopt the same conjectural variations. However, this is not to say that conjectural variations do not impact the final equilibrium. Rather, the fact is that the number of firms in the equilibrium of an industry does depend directly on the conjectural variations in that industry. Given different conjectural variations, different equilibria can be expected to obtain (Benson 1981a).

One might expect, therefore, that *nonunique* long-run equilibria would characterize the spatial economy. However, it is only the uncertainty level in the equilibrium that is determined by the oligopolistic behavior pattern in the industry. This condition is reflected in the mill price and number of firms and thus, to some extent, F in the final equilibrium [equation (20.20)]. In other words, every oligopolistic industry is subject to *its own* level of behavioral uncertainty, as the relevant range of uncertainty that characterizes the industry in the long run reflects the decisionmaking processes that were successful in that industry (Greenhut 1966). It further follows that the very decision processes that lead to certain business practices also lead to the level of behavioral uncertainty that underlies a given industry. To complete the paradigm, this level stems in part from the competitive conjectural variations that the typical viable decisionmaker (and firm) has adopted.

Quite possibly, certain industries in any free-enterprise economy are characterized by Löschian competition, some by H-S competition, and so forth. No comparison *between* them is relevant; in fact, each industry is subject to this or that level of behavioral uncertainty. Benson concludes that whatever the industry case be, the stable-equilibrium value depicted in Chapter 19 results. More specifically, he proposes that for industries in which the decisionmakers typically ignore their rivals (i.e., as in H-S competition), not only will the mill prices be lower than in industries operating under Löschian competition – given otherwise identical demand and cost conditions – but because behavioral uncertainty is typically less in industries marked by less aggressive forms of price competition, the return to behavioral uncertainty can be expected to be low. By contrast, returns for behavioral uncertainty can be expected to be greatest in industries characterized by Löschian competition.

To sum up Benson's thesis, the greater the cost of a new location, the greater the level of behavioral uncertainty. The more aggressive the form of conjectural variation, the greater the level of behavioral uncertainty. Investments in industries involving the greatest degrees of behavioral uncertainty (not necessarily those with the highest new-entrant cost of capital nor most aggressive form of price reaction) require the greatest residual return. All relevant forces involved in the spatial equilibrium of the individual firm combine to determine uncertainty and the number of firms in the industry's long-run equilibrium.

20.5 Conclusion

In classical microeconomics we include nonuser depreciation in the fixed costs of the firm, not in its marginal costs. Short-run decisions involve marginal costs only. In the long run, the number of firms and (if you will) the number of plants per firm require price equal to average cost. In the world of oligopoly, where AC includes uncertainty, and is denoted $\overline{AC}$ perhaps, we must have price equal to $\overline{AC}$. As a consequence of entry and exit, the allocated average revenue covers the nonuser cost depreciation of the oligopolist in the long run.

Now, DeVany incorporated the capacity of a firm (i.e., the number of its plants) directly into his analytical framework. He did this rather than maintain the classical position that requires a downward-shifted AR curve when $P > AC$ and an upward-shifted AR curve when $P < AC$. DeVany attained the long-run view directly without need for imagining shifting AR curves with entry or exit by means of the requirement that $\partial \Pi / \partial N = 0$, where N is the number of plants operated by the firm.

Benson, in effect, converted (1) DeVany's single-firm, yet somewhat classical, result, where AR = LMC, and also (2) our oligopolistic transform of the classical result, where $P = \overline{AC}$, into a world in which, *in effect,* not only does the single firm achieve DeVany's AR = LMC position but also the whole industry's capacity is included in the calculus of the single oligopolistic firm. This is done by means of the conjectural variation. In other words, by including behavioral uncertainty, DeVany's price-taking competitive firm converts to the spatial oligopolistic world where diverse conjectural (price) variations apply. It follows that the spatial long-run equilibrium takes hold the same way as it would if each (viable) spatial oligopolist had directly taken into the firm's profit-maximizing calculus the costs and benefits of new locations (and changed capacity). Moreover, by including the DeVany perspective, it appears that the number of firms is an optimum, given $\Pi = 0$, and, using the spatial oligopoly theory of Chapter 19, that each firm is efficient.

It is tempting to conclude that if people were robots, with perfect foresight and knowledge, so that no cost of behavioral uncertainty would apply, the perfectly competitive (nonspatial) classical model would describe the free-enterprise economies of the world. The facts of life are otherwise. The theory of spatial oligopoly nevertheless predicts efficient conformance on the part of competitive firms to the real forces characterizing their particular industry.

CHAPTER 21

Epilogue – Regulatory controls:
a spatial economics view of governmental
constraints on free enterprise

An underlying theme throughout this book has been a questioning of the interference of legislators with the free-enterprise economy. In particular, we have suggested that the antimerger and price policies of the United States, as evidenced by the Celler Antimerger Act and the Robinson-Patman Act, are based on spaceless economic theory but are applied to spatial economic behavior. We also stressed the excess-capacity welfare losses attributed to regulative interference in the transportation industry, particularly by the Interstate Commerce Commission and the Civil Aeronautics Board. These restrictive interferences were shown to be directly subject to the analysis of spatial microeconomics. In contrast, consumer-product protection controls and worker safety requirements stand prominent among governmental interferences designed to improve living standards and health, with respect to which spatial microeconomics can offer, at best, only a broad change in perspective.

What we mean by this can best be explained in this concluding chapter by centering our attention on government bureaus in general and the U.S. Federal Trade Commission in particular. We use these reference points because the former can easily be revealed to be inefficient vis-à-vis the private-enterprise firm, and the latter can easily be shown not to have recognized that the real free-enterprise world (spatial-economy world) is one marked by oligopolistic industries that, in themselves, can be efficient rather than naturally tending to the inefficient, excess-capacity state proposed by classical economic theory.

First of all we shall evaluate the governmental bureau itself, then the Federal Trade Commission. Next we shall return to the government bureau using the perspective on the bureau that was set forth by Stigler (1971), Posner (1976), and Bork (1978), and finally we shall briefly consider municipal regulation of cable television and the Federal Communications Commission's control of the spectrum in the United States.

21.1 Government enterprises: the government agency or bureau

The annual cost of all government in the United States runs over the trillion-dollar level: almost $5,000 per person. But probably the government cost that most Americans would like to minimize is that in the nation's capital. In particular, interference from the federal bureaucracy touches the lives of everyone, directly and indirectly, the latter through federal government impacts on state bureaucracies. Most likely the Internal Revenue Service (IRS) stands foremost on the list of agencies the public resents, with the Food and Drug Administration (FDA) also prominent on the list of agencies people wish could be managed more effectively; in a dream world, the former would be eliminated outright, and the latter altered considerably.

Why do we have a vast, growing bureaucracy when virtually everyone laughs at bureaus, wishes they did not exist, regards them as boondoggling, wasteful enterprises, fears their personnel during necessary exchanges, and criticizes them harshly in private conversation? As Herbert Spencer reportedly noted (Roche 1983, p. 17), one can, on any given day, read two stories in the newspapers about the failures of government programs – and three stories requesting *new* government programs to do even more for us! To be sure, all too often people trace economic and social shortcomings to the behavior impact of bureaucracy. Yet in the same instance they seek higher ethical-moral standards; so their legislative representatives create bureaus to rectify perceived malfeasances *and* misfeasances. Beyond this, our courts have unwittingly expanded the powers and controls of the federal bureaucracy on the pretense (belief?) that the creating statutes intended even greater *totalitarian* interference in the lives of Americans than, one suspects, legislators really intended. Note that our words are deliberately chosen, for we are convinced that most observers will agree that bureaucracy interferes with otherwise free people via the rigid rules that are established. On top of this, courtroom expansion of bureaucratic power amounts to legislative enactment far beyond what the public would have initially accepted, hence far beyond what the legislature actually dared establish.

We have proposed two premises here quite strongly, and they require substantiation: (1) Bureaucracies are totalitarian, and basically undesirable, organization forms that must be minimized in terms of impact, powers, and size. (2) The courts, at least in the United States, are unnecessarily effecting the opposite. We shall support these propositions under a twofold format, initially by explaining why bureaucracies are and must be characterized as we have described them, and then demonstrating the courts' complicity in the problem growth of bureaucracies, doing this by references to the Federal Trade Commission Act of 1914 (and juristic extensions therefrom).

21.2   The essential ingredients of bureaucracy: its totalitarian base and inefficiency

Consider the American business enterprise, long scorned publicly by many in the world, yet privately admired by most observers. The never-ending search for maximizing profits provides it with purpose and motivation. In the competitive marketplace, an enterprise must serve others and fulfill their needs if that enterprise is to succeed and reach its goal. The upshot (regardless of individual motivation, including love for fellow men, decency, if you will, etc.) is people serving other people; as Roche (1983, p. 79) puts it, social cooperation. In contrast a governmental bureau does not offer *quid pro quo*. It need not please anyone.

The consequence is that the competitive business firm obtains profits over the years if and only if it fulfills the wants and expectations of consumers as a matter of practice. It deals in a world of uncoerced exchange. A bureau, on the other hand, is typically, if not invariably, the product of a deal between politicians and some vested interest: labor, consumer advocates, business firms seeking protection against other business firms. As such, the bureau tends naturally to be licentious, even corrupt. All it sells is protection for some and control over others, a protection that the unprotected envy and *in time* obtain from later legislatures. This protection and the privileges gained continue to be sought by all who remain outside the inner group. Pressure mounts for politicians to extend the bureaucracy. So, in one form or another, the country becomes dominated more and more by the bureaus (and their bureaucrats). What protection is gained against some erstwhile rival competitor is reduced many times over as a result of the proliferation of protection and privilege. The bureaus multiply and control more and more people, and previously "free values" become circumscribed (witness the IRS, its growth, the increasing complexities of its forms, the increasing paperwork, the legalized shelters and exceptions, *ad infinitum*).

In free-market exchanges, an item of lower value in the want system of one party is provided to another that values it more. A continuing distribution, exchange, desire for things and willingness to expend effort to increase personal gratifications and fundamental pleasures lead participants into actions benefiting others; these actions and exchanges do *not* impose loss on nontransactors. But a natural consequence of the actions of the bureau is to benefit the privileged set at the expense of others. The government bureau is naturally a one-way "exchange" in which only one party typically benefits, and another is controlled. The incentives and privileges of outsiders are reduced.

It is the case that in many ways the circumscribing impact of the bureau approximates in effect that of strict dominance: a one-way transfer opposite to the free voluntary exchange between two parties in the market. Let us see an example of how and why American courts have exacerbated "a problem" that Congress had attempted to resolve by creating a bureau (or commission). Using the perspective of spatial microeconomics and imperfect competition, we shall suggest that it would have been preferable for the courts to have sought to find other ways to handle the problem in question.

21.3   The incipient Sherman and Clayton Act violations: judicial legislation

The fact of judicial legislation was first expressed in the *Standard Oil* case by the dissenting Justice Harlan.[1] A more pronounced form of it than simply an interpretation of a clause in a statute that enacting legislators later denied having intended[2] appeared subsequently with the passage of the Federal Trade Commission Act of 1914.[3] Section 5 of that statute made illegal unfair "methods" of competition *which have antitrust effects,* where inclusion of the word "methods" was designed to support litigation extending beyond the practices of the common law that had for centuries censured business practices considered to be unfair competition – such as passing off goods of one company as those of another. Thus, Senator Reed of Missouri, in response to an earlier (proposed) bill, had stated:

It is my opinion that if we employ the term "unfair competition" as it is employed in this bill, without adding anything to it, the courts will adopt as the meaning of Congress that meaning which has been affixed to the term by all of the law dictionaries and by a great many legal authorities. [51 *Congressional Record* 12936]

It is generally accepted that the term "unfair [methods of] competition" was designed to encompass the forms of competition considered illegal at common law as well as the new forms of questionable rivalry that had been emerging with the development of more advanced technology and commercial activity. Most significantly, the body of methods was to be evaluated in part by a new bureau, a commission, the Federal Trade Commission.[4] This commission was designed to serve not only as an administrative bureau (executive) but also as a judiciary bureau; as we shall see, in time it became a legislative bureaucracy as well. For the purposes of this chapter, let us *accept* the Supreme Court's premise that

The Congress intentionally left development of the term "unfair" to the Commission rather than attempting to define "the many and unfair practices which prevail in commerce. . . ."[5]

It is the full *scope* of Section 5 of the Federal Trade Commission Act, as *now* allowed by the Supreme Court, that is to be questioned herein. But first, some further background is in order.

21.3.1 *Sherman and Clayton Act violations*

Section 5 was held to encompass all Sherman Act violations in the *FTC* v. *Cement Institute* case.[6] This holding signified that Federal Trade Commission (FTC) jurisdiction reaches whatever action violates the Sherman Act; in other words, conduct illegal under the Sherman Act also violates Section 5 of the FTC Act:

on the whole the Act's legislative history shows a strong congressional purpose not only to continue enforcement of the Sherman Act by the Department of Justice and the federal district courts but also to supplement that enforcement through the administrative process of the new Trade Commission.[7]

Activity detrimental to competition was condemned by each statute. And the same holds for Clayton Act violations (or, for that matter, Robinson-Patman and other antitrust statutes). In fact, the FTC is authorized to enforce the Clayton Act directly (i.e., bring a suit under the Clayton Act distinct from the FTC Act, if preferred). This having been said, we are therefore in position to bring our concern (critique) to the fore, accepting as we do all of the foregoing, but later questioning the courts' extensions to incipient (oligopolistic) violations of any antitrust law.

21.3.2 *Commission control includes incipient violation of any antitrust law*

The Supreme Court held in the *Fashion Originators* case[8] that it was an object ". . . of the Federal Trade Commission Act to reach not merely in their fruition but also in their incipiency." This extension, reflecting oft-expressed desires to check "monopoly in the embryo,"[9] presumes that large size is per se bad. But clearly a spatial-oligopoly industry is not the monopoly firm of economic theory. Allowing a set of FTC commissioners (five in number) plus their bureaucracy the power to object to business practices that per se may not provide courses of action by the competitors or the public, but that are objectionable on the spurious, undefined grounds of potentially generating a market in which only *one firm* exists, is tantamount to unrestricted power. Among the most troublesome questions of Sherman Act enforcement has been that centering on behavior referred to as conscious parallelism of action (Löschian competition!). The *incipiency* action makes virtually every oligopoly illegal; hence, all industry in the United States, including the service fields, and retailing, can easily be considered as lawbreakers. Consider the following instance.

In *Triangle Conduit and Cable Co.* v. *FTC,*[10] the manufacturers of electrical conduits were found to have utilized a basing-point scheme in order to stabilize price competition among themselves. The Seventh Circuit Court held this to be a conspiracy, a "present" violation of the Sherman Act. And we agree fully with this and would condemn it accordingly.[11] What we object to here is the obiter dictum of the court (which, as we shall subsequently see, has become the present law) that *unilateral adoption of basing-point systems by individual firms could also be prohibited* as long as those firms were aware that other firms were adopting similar practices and that pricing systems of this kind, *even if unilateral at the start,* represented the first steps toward a conspiracy.

The Clayton Act carries extension similar to that of the Sherman Act. This holds notwithstanding the argument that the wording of the Sherman Act refers to present conspiracies, whereas the Clayton Act deals *futuristically* with conduct whose effect *may* be to lessen competition substantially or tend to create a monopoly. Manifestly, it would appear to follow that an "incipiency" application to the Clayton Act is clear-cut, certainly in contrast to the Sherman Act.

This issue was faced squarely in the *Brown Shoe* case. It was held there that the FTC could arrest trade restraints

in their incipiency without proof that they amount to an outright violation of section 3 of the Clayton Act or other provisions of the antitrust laws.[12]

The cases that followed, chiefly under the Sherman Act and Clayton Act, provide some evidence of a few guidelines. Thus, the incipiency rule clearly applies where a per se offense exists (e.g., price fixing under the Sherman Act or conspiring to receive illegal discounts under the Robinson-Patman extension of the Clayton Act). Simply put, an incipiency price-fixing conspiracy would be bad, as in the *Grand Union* case,[13] because *soliciting* discriminatory advantages is tantamount to granting them, and granting them would surely be illegal. But the extension may have gone so far as not even to require allegation of harm to competition, besides not fully understanding the economic meaning of discrimination. Thus, in *E. B. Muller and Co.* v. *FTC,*[14] the court held:

The purpose of the Federal Trade Commission Act is to prevent potential injury by stopping unfair methods of competition in their incipiency.

Note further from the *Brown Shoe* case, where potentially little vertical foreclosure was involved (Brown Shoe's sales were about $110 million of $1.8 billion total), that the Section 5 incipiency test reached conduct that carried very little chance or even a reasonable possibility that it would eventually lessen competition substantially. It is apparently the extended Court-approved law for the FTC that neither actual nor present harm need be shown and that only some basis for predicted harm will suffice.

A related extension, which we shall not detail, is the condemnation of competitive actions that violate the spirit of the antitrust laws. But what are the goals of the antitrust laws: to stave off asset concentration, prevent undue growth of a company, prevent monopoly, eliminate concentration of social-economic-political power, create a just society, protect small enterprises?

Could each of these (essentially Sherman) goals be part of the FTC Act, including a just society of keeping Ma and Pa in business? Certainly if the latter two goals could be said to be in the *spirit of the Sherman Act,* then Section 5 of the FTC Act is all-encompassing. Fortunately, an action based on the spirit of a law (e.g., the Sherman Act) should be kept close to the original legislative intent. Any action under Section 5 that challenges, say, a merger would contradict the spirit of the Clayton Act unless it also involved substantial lessening of competition. To this extent, the FTC would be restrained. But in this regard, consider the conscious-parallelism-of-action cases.

21.3.3 *Virtually unlimited control of the bureaucracy*

People trained in antitrust law can be expected to condemn as anticompetitive any collusive-like action, even though no conspiracy can be shown. Of course, the theory of incipient conspiracy would appear to apply to situations in which firms exhibit interdependent behavior, albeit not explicitly colluding. But all of oligopoly involves taking account of rivals' actions.[15] The theory of spatial pricing and the action-reaction practices of *competitive* firms have focused on Löschian behavior (which in the antitrust context would amount to conscious parallelism of action) or Hotelling-Smithies behavior, or alternatively G-O behavior, the spatial economy's reflection of pure competition with the extreme requirement noted by Capozza and Van Order of the pricing-by-zone requirement noted in Chapter 2.

A principal case along these lines under Section 5 was the *FTC v. Beech-Nut Packing Co.* litigation,[16] as supported by the *FTC v. Cement Institute* case.[17] The elaborate resale-price-maintenance system of the defendant was condemned in the district court, reversed on the appellate level, and finally struck down by the Supreme Court. This system had been imposed by the manufacturer on its jobbers and dealers. The Court held that the spirit of the Sherman Act damned parallel actions in restraint of trade, even in the absence of agreement.

To appreciate fully how the courts have extended FTC powers, *possibly* beyond those contemplated by legislators and certainly beyond those that a general public that typically ridicules bureaucrats and their practices would contemplate, let us return to the *Brown Shoe* case. Note here that exclusive dealing was proscribed by the Clayton Act (a substantive provision), whereas the Court condemned exclusive dealing in the *Brown Shoe* case only if the practice would have substantially lessened competition. But recall further that the Court nevertheless struck down the practice of Brown Shoe *on the premise of an incipient violation.* It went even further than that by adding as an alternative basis for its decision that *the practice violated the spirit of the Clayton Act.* It allowed this in terms that presumed that the FTC is free to extend substantive Clayton Act provisions via Section 5 to the "spirit" of the Clayton Act. And it confirmed the presumption alluded to here in recent cases. [18]

21.3.4 *Extensions: pro and con*

The extended role for the FTC was also approved in *FTC* v. *Gratz* [19] and *FTC* v. *R. F. Keppel and Bro., Inc.,* [20] as well as in many later cases. In the words of Mr. Averitt,

the Commission seems to be empowered to determine and enforce recognized standards of fair competitive behavior, whether these have been declared by statute or have emerged as the generally accepted norms of the community. [Averitt 1980, p. 274]

Beyond all this, the decision in *FTC* v. *Sperry-Hutchinson Co.* [21] allows the FTC to pursue "public values" that are not contained in the letter or spirit of the antitrust laws. Small wonder that John Roche is concerned over the takeover of the country by bureaucrats when the nation's Supreme Court endows a bureau with the authority to *serve as the expert* in advising courts what the public considers to be ethical and unethical. To be sure, the FTC will (probably) have to demonstrate significant adverse effects on competition (the proper minimum level, on which even economists who are supposedly expert in the subject cannot agree), and then if and only if they "are not outweighed by other consumer benefits or by *bona fide* business justification" (Averitt 1980, p. 275). The scope of the FTC's power is therefore virtually unlimited. In Mr. Averitt's view,

The Commission is empowered to decide a case based on principles of conduct that have not yet won universal acceptance in the business community. [Averitt 1980, p. 279]

Most significantly, Averitt's study of the legislative background to the enactment of the FTC Act convinces him that Congress *intended* broad FTC scope, and hence the courts are properly interpreting the intention of

Congress (Averitt 1980, pp. 279–81). And this is no surprise, because the U.S. Congress is the designer of layers upon layers of bureaucracy, as if that were the answer to all problems. American Congresses have failed to understand that matters of this kind can best be left to market actions.[22] By offering private parties triple, sextuple, and even higher damages in the event of unfair methods of competition that tend to lessen competition substantially, they would have left it strictly to the courts to determine what are unfair methods of competition.

Other problems with the statute relate to the words "may substantially lessen competition." If one asks a legislator what this means, the answer one can expect is "a significant decrease in the number of competitors." Quite conceivably, bureaucrats, lawyers, judges, and even many economists would think the same way. But is competition between two teams of ten men each who are engaged in a tug-of-war more intense than the competition between two prizefighters? Manifestly, the "let Charles fight harder" practice is more readily accepted by any tug-of-war combatant than if there were no Charles around in one's fight with the champ.

Is it not equally clear, especially from our analysis of potential entry, that the number of competitors is also a ridiculous basis for determining the existence or nonexistence of competition? Presumably the purpose of the antitrust law is to maximize the well-being of consumers by preventing a firm's control over its market. Maintaining the potential for effective entry and/or the existence of distant-location competition with transitive spillover effects will suffice to assure consumers they will not be "fleeced." This signifies that the main purpose of the law should simply be to maintain proper *ethics,* and this is not a matter for a bureau to determine or even to be considered expert on. By means of a lawsuit of one firm against another, or a suit for a consumers group (via the Wheeler-Lea Act), or suit by the Department of Justice to protect businesses or consumers, sufficient force can be exerted that courts will serve as the ultimate arbiter of what the nation considers to be proper or improper business behavior. It is small solace to recognize that the expertise and authority of the FTC is considered to be circumscribed to the extent that "social or political considerations alone cannot carry the entire weight of the argument" (Averitt 1980) and that instead the economic effects of the competitive method in question must be evaluated – small solace particularly because apparently some lessening in number of competitors along with social or political (annoying) considerations are said to be relevant (Averitt 1980, p. 283). It is most interesting that Averitt's interpretation of the FTC's power, based on the *Sperry-Hutchinson* case,[23] is that the Supreme Court considers the FTC to be "empowered to frame public competition policy on its own initiative" (Averitt 1980, p. 298). That judicial review by the courts provides a safeguard is far from satisfactory, because consent decrees, in effect, will make the bureau not only the executive and (substantially) the judicial authority but also the legislative authority in one fell swoop; in turn, it then is the determiner of public policy as well as of business standards and morality.

In conclusion, early questions concerning legislative delegation of powers were, in the words of Averitt (1980), "eroded by the courts during the New Deal." Apparently agreeing with this result, Averitt goes on to say that

The doctrine is now largely defunct. The increasing complexity of modern government has made delegation a practical necessity, while the safeguards of modern administrative procedure have simultaneously made it less threatening. The Supreme Court now regularly upholds legislation embodying such vague standards as "just and reasonable," "public interest," or "public convenience, interest or necessity." [Averitt 1980, p. 283]

21.3.5   *Historical reversal?*

Some retrenchment in the direction of not requiring an economic basis for antitrust actions took place under William Baxter's leadership of the Antitrust Division of the Department of Justice. Adopting the view that economic power is more effectively checked by competition and the threat of entry of new rivals, the division's thoughts and practices were changed significantly. Indeed, antitrust itself was treated as a form of regulation that, as such, should be minimized. Even control of dealer pricing (resale-price maintenance) was no longer to be necessarily considered as an antitrust violation, because competition among manufacturers (suppliers) would protect consumers. If, as Ernest Gellhorn (1984) suggests, Baxter leaned heavily toward the use of economic analysis as the sole determinant of antitrust enforcement, it may be the case that, in time, the awesome powers of the FTC will be restricted not only by whomever happens to head the FTC (e.g., James Miller, along the lines of William Baxter) but also by changed legislative and judicial approaches to the antitrust problem and the federal bureaucracy. The focus of spatial economics is, of course, central to the subject of antitrust laws, competition, bureaucracies, and the public welfare. The FTC, the ICC, the DOJ, and the FAA (and, in the past, the powerful CAB) engage in activities that involve the costs of distance and/or time.

21.4   Clearing up the antitrust paradox[24]

Bork observes that

to study antitrust at length, to wonder at the manifold errors of economics and logic displayed, to see that the errors move the law in one direction, is to begin to suspect that a process much deeper than mere mistaken reasoning is at work. It seems as though the intellectual terrain is regarded as important not in and for itself but as a field of action upon which the political order moves against the private order. . . . I will not attempt here an explanation of that process. [Bork 1978, p. 423]

We propose a "deeper process" and the consequence that antitrust policy is really not paradoxical at all. Indeed, when a "special-interest" view of antitrust is adopted, the several observations that troubled Bork are easily understood. Certainly, his dichotomy of the welfare of groups versus the general welfare is no longer a paradox. Rewards according to political status rather than merit and reductions in liberty (attenuation of property rights) are all apparent, as is the government's concern with producer well-being rather than with competition.

The special-interest-group model (Stigler 1971) predicts that most political choices will be made by the antitrust enforcers and legitimized by the courts rather than by Congress. The very nature of the governmental rights transfer for the benefit of active interest groups creates incentives for more and more interest-group formation, and therefore greater demands for transfers (Benson 1981b). If one does not understand oligopoly action–reaction economics, the interest group can appear to warrant support.

It is also likely that legislators seeking reelection will respond to increasing pressure by delegating more and more rule-making powers to commissions and bureaus. The FTC, for example, was given authority to enforce sixteen new statutes during the 1970s, and in the process, they developed more than forty new rules and sixty new programs to regulate business (Clarkson and Murio 1982). Naturally, the agencies' powers and budgets grew in the process: The FTC's budget was $3\frac{1}{3}$ times larger in 1980 than it had been in 1970, for instance. A couple of implications of this process are worth noting. First, as agency power expands, the ability of Congress effectively to monitor agencies diminishes; so opportunities for inefficiency and overenforcement increase. Second, the commissioners and bureaucrats themselves become more powerful political-interest groups as their resources and political clientele are expanded; so the interests of those in government become relatively more important, as compared with the interests of those being governed.

21.5 Economic efficiency as a possible goal

Is there much hope for reforming the antitrust process in the United States and elsewhere in the free-enterprise world? Can one expect it ever to be used actually to support competition? Can the goal of economic efficiency be pursued, rather than providing rents to special interests through restrictions on market competition?

The Nader report on the FTC (Cox, Fellmeth, and Schultz 1969) concluded that the problems with the FTC were entirely attributable to the people employed there; it went on to suggest wholesale changes in staffing. But are enforcers (judges, legislators, and members of special-interest groups, for that matter) irresponsible, inefficient, or "bad" or "immoral" people? Of course they are not! It is the political process itself that sets in motion forces that induce people to act as they do. The antitrust process cannot be reformed by replacing people. A fundamental institutional change that would alter the incentives of commissioners, agency managers, and legislators would be necessary for radical adjustments to be observed. Behavior is more a function of the institutions and incentives (property rights) that are brought about by the development of such institutions, rather than a function of the individuals involved.

Bork suggests that if the actors in the antitrust process (particularly the judges) simply understood basic microeconomic theory they would do a better job. He argues that "[the reason] for the inadequate performance of the legal institutions that shape antitrust is a complex topic. No single institution is wholly responsible, but perhaps it can be said that the factor common to the performance of all of them was, and is, the absence of a rudimentary understanding of market economics" (Bork 1978, p. 409). This view accepts economic efficiency as the goal of antitrust. When it is recognized that this is not the case, then economists will be put to the test. As Clarkson and Murio (1982, p. 148) note,

fundamental inconsistencies regarding economic analysis surface frequently in the FTC programs. . . . In general, the agency takes three approaches to economic analysis. Sometimes. . .the FTC concurs with the most accepted view of economists. In other cases, the commission enthusiastically and arbitrarily chooses one side in a raging debate among economists. . . . In still other cases, FTC decisions run counter to mainstream economic analysis. . . . In this last group of cases, the agency not only deemphasizes economists' data but also often relies on ad hoc impressions of industry participants or observers.

Posner (1976) and Bork (1978), among others, suggest the need for major legislative changes, including repeal of most of the antitrust statutes that have been heavily employed in the interest-group process (e.g., Robinson-Patman, Clayton, and Sherman, Section 2). But Congress is not going to make such changes unless a very strong political constituency arises to demand them. And even if such changes were made, the interest-group process would continue. After all, whatever the antitrust laws effect, they are subject to interpretation by the antitrust enforcers and the courts. The nature of the interpretations and the level of enforcement are subject to the same political forces that operate under the current statutes. Retention of Sherman, Section 1, is unlikely to change this, because as Neale (1970) pointed out, there is nothing in the Sherman Act that can ensure that it will be used to promote economic efficiency, and "the courts have consistently refused to take economic consequences as the criterion of antitrust right and wrong."

The conclusions reached here are quite pessimistic. They imply that economists' continual complaints about the inefficiency-enhancing results of antitrust policy are going to fall on deaf ears. And that is probably true if the complaints are directed only at legislators, antitrust enforcers, judges, and other economists. On the other hand, if economists can convince a substantial number of the people who are losers in the antitrust process (e.g., consumers) that they would be better off with policies that protect competition rather than competitors, perhaps a political constituency that will demand efficiency can arise. The free-rider problems that are intrinsic to large-group actions where per capita gains are relatively small do not bode well for such a result. However, Stigler (1971) and, unfortunately, the most visible so-called consumer advocates who denounce regulators and antitrust enforcers inevitably advocate more reform plus even more government control as the solution. This was indeed the Nader study group's conclusion.

Unfortunately, the fact of the matter is that in a representative democracy dominated by interest-group politics, more government is not likely to solve the problems that the governing process itself creates. The essence of spatial economics is predicated on competitive entry and pricing. Promoting this is the role it accepts for the governments of free people. Though our analysis in prior chapters indicated that regulatory controls could provide better time and location dispersion, the excess capacity and price-welfare loss appear to override fully any short-run scheduling advantages. Most fundamentally, the long run was seen to generate dispersals that conform to demands and consumer distributions. Consumer-product controls, unregulated medical fees, input prices of labor based on sex and education, normal cost mark-up pricing, airline and rail regulations, public-utility pricing policies, along with all forms of antitrust actions extending from merger policies to so-called geographic price discrimination, to tying and bundling contracts, to parallelism-of-action practices, to antidumping and international trade regulations, including tariff policies and multinational enterprises, all appear in new light in the context of spatial microeconomics. Hopefully, the obvious relevance of the subject will, in time, be so forceful as to offset the special-interest group appeals by farmers, small and large businesses that seek protection from competitors, workers, insurance companies, and so forth. A viable free-enterprise spatial economy cannot hand out dole after dole and remain efficient.

21.6 Cable television and Federal Communications Commission regulations

The final subject we shall cover in this chapter is so broad as to require the detailed analysis that one can provide only in an academic paper or, at a minimum, a full chapter in a book. Our objective, however, is *not* to resolve an issue definitively here; rather, it is to suggest the special insights one can gain from applying spatial microeconomics to the subject of government bureaus and regulations. We shall, in this context, conclude this chapter by considering very briefly the regulation of cable television in the United States and the broader regulation of the communications networks in the country by the Federal Communications Commission (FCC).

21.6.1 *Municipal regulation of cable television*

American politicians, with judicial approval, have contended that laying cable lines involves the use of public streets and hence comes under the public right-of-way. The fact that sales of newspapers require use of public streets has not been accepted as analogous to the way a cable firm operates. Hence, some form of permission is needed. (Apparently distribution of newspapers does not disrupt the public domain, litter the streets, or inconvenience the citizenry significantly and therefore does not warrant municipal regulation.)

Local authorities, therefore, franchise one or only a few cable operators, depending on the size of the city. Under the typical agreements between a cable operator and a local government, the firm is regarded as a natural monopoly; the upshot in the United States is that no two or more companies compete for the same subscriber. In practice, "the municipality and cable company form a partnership, with the city preventing other cable firms from entering the market" (Lee 1984). The unwillingness to franchise others raises the city's power to "demand pork-barrel prices" (Lee 1984).

Now consider the product-differentiation spectrum. The consumers of cable television are distributed along a line (or over a circle), and the franchisee is situated at some point along the line (or in the center of the circle). The δ_{ij} loss can be so great that some consumers will not have sufficient effective want for the cable.[25] Moreover, it is well known[26] that regulation of rates has had little effect on monopoly prices, as most rate-increase requests have been granted; indeed, the fact that competitive (unregulated-market) rates are only slightly higher than in regulated markets, which would appear in spaceless economic theory to be a plus for regulation, appears as a minus in the full-cost, product-differentiation (spatial) context of our Chapter 5.

21.6.2 The Federal Communications Commission

A corresponding regulatory impact that appears in special light in the perspective of spatial economics is that involving the FCC. As with the FTC under James Miller, the FCC under Mark Fowler is following along the lines of the Reagan administration by pursuing deregulation as a goal. Nevertheless, the "airwaves" are regarded as public property, and broad frequencies only have been assigned. Spatial microeconomics proposes use of the price system for allocating airwave lengths. If localizations should occur, the consumer-distribution and product-performance requirements would have warranted it; otherwise, the firms and spectrum would be uneconomic. Manifestly, if X and Z are transmitting without interference, and Y comes along, pays the price required, but mistakenly ends up interfering with X and Z, diverse remedies could be applied. Legal damages would be one; other alternatives could include required coordination between, say, X and Y so that Z is not interfered with (Mueller 1982), or remedies and policies along the lines suggested by Coase (1959) or Hayek (1973) could apply.

Spatial microeconomics centers on the need for free entry rather than allowing established communications firms the use of the FCC's control of frequencies as a shield from competition. That government regulations are often obsolete as technology (in communications) changes rapidly is manifest. The fact that the spectrum is not a natural resource but depends on the transmitters and receivers that are produced suggests that the locations of firms and of products should be based on market realities rather than outdated regulations.[27] There being no spectrum, but only transmitters and receivers, it would seem that consumers and the economy would benefit by allowing the space economy the freedom to have the *oligopolists compete* for the prizes of the marketplace.

Notes

Chapter 1

1 This property holds whether or not the demand curve is linear.

2 Subscript L denotes a line market.

3 We shall consider in a later chapter the form that individual demand functions would have to take for optimal discriminatory mill prices to be equal – and so lead to f.o.b. pricing. Essentially, the demand functions have to be convex in a well-defined manner.

4 Again, these arguments will be presented more formally in discussion in later chapters.

5 This example is presented more formally in Chapter 3.

Chapter 2

1 The original analysis by Greenhut et al. (1975) assumed a homogeneous plane. Mathematical analysis is eased considerably and no generality is lost if a line market is assumed. All that changes is the precise equation for the best f.o.b. price.

2 From the Leibniz formula, a function of the form

$$G(v) = \int_{a(v)}^{b(v)} f(t, v) \, dt$$

can be differentiated as follows:

$$G'(v) = \int_{a(v)}^{b(v)} f_v(t, v) \, dt + f(b(v), v) b'(v) - f(a(v), v) a'(v)$$

3 Because $p(r) = m + tr$,

$$\frac{df}{dm} = \frac{df}{dp} \frac{dp}{dm} = \frac{df}{dp} = f'$$

4 It is shown in the Mathematical Appendix that this function meets the curvature condition $f'' = (f')^2 / f$.

5 This is easily recognized given that $p(r) = m + tr$:

$$\frac{d(-f'/f)}{dr} = \frac{d(-f'/f)}{dp} \frac{dp}{dr} = \frac{td(-f'/f)}{dp}$$

(because $dp/dr = t$ and $t > 0$).

374

6   The proof is obvious and is left to the reader. Simply apply Lemma 1 to (2.20).
7   These relations were derived by Capozza and Van Order (1978). The analysis
follows their interpretation of G-O competition, in which the rival firm raises its
mill price, so that the assumption of a fixed limit price at the market boundary applies. Capozza and Van Order recognized that this is a somewhat forced interpretation of G-O competition.

Chapter 3

1   The work of Eaton and Lipsey to be discussed in later chapters of this book
explicitly considers the persistence of long-run supernormal profits in spatial markets.
2   More formally, the Löschian pricing equation is

$$m_L(1 - 1/e_L(R, m_L)) - c = 0$$

and from equation (2.22a) this gives

$$m_L \left[1 + \frac{\int_0^R f(m_L + tr)\, dr}{m_L \int_0^R f'(m + tr)\, dr} \right] - c = 0$$

$$\rightarrow (m_L - c) \int_0^R f'(m_L + tr)\, dr + \int_0^R f(m_L + tr)\, dr = 0$$

3   To see this latter condition, assume that the ZPL passes through point E in
Figure 3.1, i.e., passes to the left of ABC. Then, because $\partial\Pi(R, m)/\partial R > 0$, profit
at F is positive. But F lies on ABC and is not the profit-maximizing price for market radius R_t^*; hence, profit is negative at F. Thus, there is a contradiction, and
the ZPL must lie to the right of ABC.
4   Derivation of the precise shape of the pricing equations in Figure 3.2 is complex. Rather than disrupt the discussion, the derivation is presented in the Mathematical Appendix to this chapter.
5   The reader may wish to produce the same diagram for individual demand
more convex than a negative exponential.
6   We wish to thank Charles Smithson and the editors of *Economic Journal* for
permission to use selected materials contained in our paper with Professor Smithson (Greenhut et al. 1985).
7   A highly simplified alternative that is more closely allied with the formulation
used in spatial economics is to consider the firm's "distance time."
8   The reader might find it interesting to note the similarity of this result to the
proposition made by Satterthwaite with respect to the impact of entry on the elasticity of the demand curve facing the service provider. See, for example, Pauly
and Satterthwaite (1981, p. 489).
9   All that is required is direct application of Theorem 3 in Chapter 2.
10   In a recent paper, Newhouse et al. (1982) examined an allied issue: the physician's location decision. It is interesting to note that in this context, they found
demand creation to be flawed both theoretically and empirically. Instead, they
found that physicians' location behavior conforms to the predictions of standard
location theory.

Chapter 4

1   Discussions of this demand function can be found in Greenhut (1977), Greenhut and Greenhut (1975, 1977), Greenhut and Ohta (1978), and Greenhut and associates (1977), where different Löschian effects of the linear demand curve and other types of demand curves are demonstrated.

2   Demand function (4.1) is not defined for $x = 0$. In the paper in which this functional form is derived, however, Greenhut and Greenhut (1975) show that if $x = 0$, the appropriate demand function is the negative exponential.

3   Total revenue is $pq = \alpha q - \beta q^{x+1}/x$. Thus, marginal revenue is

$$MR = \alpha - \beta(x+1)q^x/x$$

and the slope of the MR curve is

$$d MR/dq = -\beta(x+1)q^{x-1}$$

When $x < -1$, the MR curve is upward-sloping; that is, we have increasing marginal revenue, and no determinate solution is possible.

4   Throughout the remainder of the analysis, a subscript p denotes positive demand exponents ($x \geq 0$), and n denotes negative demand exponents ($x < 0$).

5   The analysis in this and subsequent subsections draws heavily on Benson (1980a). Benson confined his analysis to the Löschian case. It is a simple exercise, as here, to extend his conclusions to encompass H-S competition.

6   Recall Chapter 1, Section 1.3, and see Greenhut and associates (1977) for the following discussion.

7   See Greenhut (1956, chap. 2, sect. 2.3 and 3.5) for an original discussion along the lines recorded here.

8   See Greenhut (1956, sect. 2.2, Tables 2 and 3).

9   But note, for example (Greenhut 1956, sect. 2.2, Tables 2 and 3), that the opposite situation, a significantly large increase in the basic freight rate, causes only a slight increase in freight absorption, a result that contradicts the long-held belief that analysis of the impact of freight rates on price follows the same laws that determine the shifting and incidence of taxes on commodities. The reason that freight rates are not analogous to excise taxes is founded in the variable size of the sales radius as compared with the dimensionless content of the models used to portray the effects of the excise tax.

10   The following comments are discussed more fully in Shieh and Goldberg (1985).

11   We would like to thank C. C. Mai for allowing us to draw fully in this section from "Spatial Competition and Merger Policy" (unpublished mimeograph).

12   Diseconomies of scale do not represent a significant problem under conditions of free entry. If both free entry and freedom to merge were allowed, competitive forces would drive the multiunit firm toward its optimal (least-cost) size.

13   Williamson (1968) has shown, using benefit–cost analysis in a spaceless world, that cost reductions may still translate into deadweight welfare losses as a result of the price increases that result from the merging of firms. This monopolistic price effect tends to outweigh the modest unit-cost saving that may arise. He further proposes that with a market demand elasticity of unity, a unit-cost reduction of less than 0.5% would be sufficient to offset the related allocative inefficiency that would stem from a 5.0% increase in concentration. His analysis assumes that a merger lowers costs and that society is unconcerned about any redistributions of income from consumers to monopolists resulting from a merger.

14 See Shull (1963), Greenhut and Ohta (1972), Greenhut, Greenhut, and Li (1980), and Greenhut (1978, 1981).

Chapter 5

1 We cannot hope to give a full treatment of Lancaster's work here. The interested reader should consult the original.

2 Note that C is not an equilibrium, because it is dominated by prices on CF.

3 The maximum number of brands occurs when the monopoly occurs with demand function DED'' in Figure 5.7(a).

4 See Salop (1979) for derivation of these equations.

5 The reader is left to analyze the effects of increases in the value of product differentiation (c) and in market size (L).

6 A simple change in the utility function (5.32) will generate the demand function of Greenhut et al. (1977) used in Chapter 4.

7 This chapter has, inevitably, merely scratched the surface. Other contributions in this area are from Schmalensee (1978), Dixit and Stiglitz (1977), Hart (1980), and Lancaster (1975).

Chapter 6

1 Note further that storing a commodity "transports" it from one period to the next and so is also a form of product differentiation.

2 This is to be distinguished from the freight absorption discussed with respect to f.o.b. pricing. Under f.o.b. pricing, the firm can be considered to be absorbing some proportion of *total* freight costs, but not to be distinguishing between each individual selling location (buyer).

3 This gives rise to potential for resale between consumers. It is assumed for the moment that such resale possibilities are not available to consumers. This will be discussed in more detail in Chapter 7.

4 Recall footnote 3.

5 If marginal production costs were not constant, marginal production costs at location r_i would be affected by the quantity supplied, and so the price charged to consumers at r_j. In other words, the pricing policy at any one selling location would be intimately connected to the pricing policy at every other location: The firm would have to choose its *complete* price trajectory rather than price at each individual selling point. The control-theory techniques of later chapters are required for such simultaneous solutions.

6 This can be contrasted with the somewhat less obvious (but equivalent) proposition in Greenhut and Ohta (1975c, p. 71) that the slope of the DPS is

$$\frac{dp(r)}{d(tr)} = \frac{e(r)}{\xi(r) - (1 - e(r))}$$

where $e(r)$ is elasticity of demand and

$$\xi(r) = \frac{de(r)}{dp(r)} \frac{p(r)}{e(r)}$$

7 If $f = g^{-1}$, then the inverse-function rule states that

$$f' = 1/g' \quad \text{and} \quad f'' = -g''/(g')^3$$

8 $$\frac{dm(r)}{dr} = \frac{dm(r)}{d(tr)} \frac{d(tr)}{dr} = t \frac{dm(r)}{d(tr)}$$

where $dm(r)/dr$ is the rate of change of mill price with respect to distance.

9 To appreciate this, first rewrite (6.9) as

$$dm(r)/d(tr) = -(f'^2 - ff'')/(2f'^2 - ff'') = \tfrac{1}{2}[(f'^2 - ff'')/(f'^2 - \tfrac{1}{2}ff'')]$$

If $f'' > 0$, the term in brackets is less than 1, whereas if $f'' < 0$, it is greater than 1.

10 Such a marginal-revenue curve would arise, for example, from a cubic inverse demand function of the form $p(r) = 10 - 4q + 2q^2 - q^3/3$.

11 The reader is left to check Proposition 2.

Chapter 7

1 Recall the discussion in Chapter 6.

2 Throughout this section, a subscript f refers to f.o.b. mill pricing, subscript u to uniform pricing, and subscript d to optimal discriminatory pricing.

3 Such a constraint may be the outcome of a competitive process or, as suggested by Beckmann (1976), may be the consequence of collusion or oligopolistic interdependence.

4 Mathematical details of the derivation of these and subsequent equations in this section are provided in Mathematical Appendix II to this chapter. See also Beckmann (1976).

5 As an example of the derivation of these equations, rewrite (7.12a):

$$\frac{DR}{2b}((a-c)^2 - (a-c)tR + t^2R^2/4) - F = 0$$

Hence,

$$\frac{R}{2b}((a-c)^2 - (a-c)tR + t^2R^2/4) = F/D = \gamma$$

6 See Mathematical Appendix II to this chapter for derivation of the graphs of γ, θ, and ρ.

7 It should be noted that in a slightly different context in which entry is viewed as imposing a lower competitive price constraint, Greenhut, Ohta, and Scheidell (1972) demonstrated that in the zero-profit equilibrium, discriminatory pricing invariably generates greater output.

8 Under the G-O assumption, each firm ignores the rival, thus cutting price to $(p-c)/t$. Thus, for present purposes, G-O and H-S are the same. We shall accordingly refer to them together.

9 Gronberg and Meyer use a somewhat different argument to justify the use of the pricing equation (7.23). This pricing policy will emerge if the firms "overtly collude, deciding to split the market between them exactly" (Gronberg and Meyer 1981a, p. 760).

10 By an argument identical with that presented in Chapter 3, the ZPLs have infinite slope at the point of intersection with the Löschian pricing equation LL.

11 See the discussion in Chapter 3.

Chapter 8

1 It should be noted that in the G-G model the marginal-production costs c are allowed to vary between firms, even though each firm's c is assumed to be constant with respect to output. The analysis here assumes a constant c across firms as well as with respect to output. A constant c across firms is reasonable because over time a standardization in production technology can be expected to take place among firms. In addition, this simplification will not distort the results generated by Greenhut and Greenhut (1975), but does make mathematical manipulation easier.

2 The reader may wish to refer to Chapter 4 to review some of the properties of this demand function. Note also that in subsequent analysis, x is constrained to be nonnegative. The reader should check the implications of assuming $-1 < x < 0$.

3 See Chapter 6.

4 The analysis of pricing and sourcing strategies of multinational companies is discussed by Casson and Norman (1983).

5 A more extended discussion of the issues outlined in this section is given in the paper "Spatial Pricing with Differentiated Products" (Norman 1983a). We wish to thank the editors of the *Quarterly Journal of Economics* for permission to quote selected materials from that paper.

6 The reader will appreciate that there is a similar equation for producer 2. For the moment we concentrate on the pricing decisions of producer 1.

7 As usual, own-price elasticity is measured as a positive number.

8 See Mathematical Appendix. Rather than give a full derivation of Norman's results, we content ourselves with a summary of his main conclusions.

Chapter 9

1 See, for example, Södersten (1980) for an exposition of this model.

2 The seminal work is by Grubel and Lloyd (1975). See Tharakan (1981) for a recent survey.

3 Canada, United States, Japan, Belgium-Luxembourg, Netherlands, Germany, France, Italy, United Kingdom, Australia.

4 Brander (1981) develops a model of intraindustry trade in identical commodities that bears a close resemblance to the G-G model.

5 The interested reader may wish to investigate the effects of using a GGK demand function.

6 This table has been constructed by simple differentiation of the price, import, and export equations.

7 If country i has n_i local producers, then the representative firm has $n_i - 1$ neighbors. If a proportion λ of these neighbors imitate the representative firm and invest in local production in country j, this leads to an increase of $1 + \lambda(n_i - 1)$ in the number of local producers in country j and to a reduction of $1 + \lambda(n_i - 1)$ in the number of exporters to j.

8 Nor is this the only application of spatial analysis to trade theory. Modern advances in international trade theory are increasingly concerned with international trade in the presence of economies of scale, or under imperfect, particularly monopolistic, competition. Much of this new body of theory is based on the kind of spatial analogy being presented in this book; see, for example, Kierzkowski (1984).

Chapter 10

1 For a rigorous mathematical derivation, see Greenhut and Ohta (1975b, pp. 124–41). See also Greenhut et al. (1972) for analogous arguments concerning the relation between competitive entry and alternative price policies. It should be noted that the exposition here is illustrated under the linear-demand assumption.

2 The normalization is purely in the interest of mathematical simplicity.

3 See Norman (1981b) for details.

4 If marginal-production costs are not constant, the control-theory techniques of Chapter 11 will be necessary to solve the optimal pricing problem.

5 More formally, for selling points in $(\hat{r}, R^*)$, the firm will charge ϵ below p', where ϵ is arbitrarily small. Such a pricing policy is indistinguishable from that illustrated in Figure 10.5.

6 This may arise, for example, if the customer makes multiple purchases during a shopping trip: The marginal transport cost to the customer of any one item purchased during the shopping trip then approaches zero, and average transport costs exhibit strong economies to shopping agglomeration.

7 Note that, from equation (10.15), t_d can never be smaller than t_f.

Chapter 11

1 The interested reader will find an excellent discussion of optimal-control theory by Takayama (1974, chap. 8). More detailed analysis is provided by Hadley and Kemp (1971) and Kamien and Schwartz (1981). Although optimal-control theory is usually applied to temporal problems, Phlips (1976, 1983) has indicated the many close parallels between space and time. Fratrik (1981) has also applied control-theory techniques to spatial pricing problems.

2 This example is discussed by Takayama (1974, chap. 8).

3 This example is discussed by Kamien and Schwartz (1981, pp. 119ff).

4 See Takayama (1974). Note that $\dot{x}_i(t) = dx_i(t)/dt$.

5   There is strong similarity between auxiliary variables and Lagrange multipliers, and between the Hamiltonian and Lagrangian functions.

6   It is well beyond the scope of this book to give a proof of these necessary conditions! The interested reader is referred to Takayama (1974). A more detailed, but mathematically complex, treatment is given by Hadley and Kemp (1971). Note that equation (11.7) assumes the Hamiltonian to be continuous and differentiable in $u(t)$.

7   The transversality conditions are probably among the most awkward to specify in optimal-control problems, because they are peculiarly "problem-specific." See Kamien and Schwartz (1981, part II, sect. 4) for more extensive discussion.

8

9   From (11.15), $p(r)+q[p(r)]/q'[p(r)]=t(r)-\lambda(r)$; hence,

$$p(r)\left[1+\frac{q(p(r))}{p(r)q'(p(r))}\right]=t(r)-\lambda(r)$$

and, by definition,

$$\epsilon(r)=-\frac{p(r)q'(p(r))}{q(p(r))}$$

10   If the slope of the delivered-price schedule is S, the degree of price discrimination (equivalent to the proportion of freight costs absorbed by the producer) is $PD=1-S$.

11   The reader is left to derive the price effect with decreasing costs.

12   The reader is left to show that the same result applies in the uniform-pricing case.

13   The discussion in this section owes much to the analysis of Horst (1971, 1973).

14   For the reader who finds this assumption difficult to accept, it may prove simpler to envisage a finite number of countries (S, say), where each country s covers the "small" interval $[r_s, r_s+\Delta]$, ($s=1,\ldots,S$), with $q(r)\neq0$ for $r\in[r_s, r_s+\Delta]$ ($s=1,\ldots,S$), and $q(r)=0$ elsewhere.

15   Note from footnote 9 that by convention we measure elasticity as a positive number.

16   Phlips (1983) observes that so-called normal cost pricing (which we would propose would probably strike regulators as desirable competitive pricing) is, at its roots, discriminatory pricing.

Chapter 12

1   The analysis here borrows heavily from Norman and Nichols (1982). The authors are grateful to the editors of the *Journal of Industrial Economics* for permission to quote from that article.

2   This model owes much to the analysis of Gaskins (1971). Note, however, that the Gaskins analysis is spaceless and thus applies to only part of the spatial market defined here.

3   The analysis is difficult enough without introducing the further complications of assuming variable marginal costs!

4 T can be written $T(r)$.

5   For reasons to be discussed later, both $\bar{p}(r)$ and $k(r)$ can be expected to vary from market to market.

6   Norman and Nichols depart from Gaskins in assuming $x(0, r) = 0$, i.e., in assuming that there is no initial competitive fringe.

7   Note that the leading firm will charge a uniform price $\bar{p}$ throughout R_{2A} if the same limit price $\bar{p}$ holds in all markets.

8   Attention is confined at this stage to the case in which the leading firm considers only the export mode for serving markets in R_3. Alternative strategies, e.g., local production in a branch plant, may, of course, be feasible, and will be considered later.

9   Phlips (1983, p. 74).

10   Ibid., p. 73.

11   Ibid., p. 77.

12   Ibid., p. 81.

13   Ibid., p. 93.

Chapter 13

1   Some flavor of these is given in Chapter 15, where it is shown that a spatial approach can be of considerable assistance in resolving potential prisoner's dilemmas.

2   Other sources of demand heterogeneity can, of course, be analyzed. Variation in incomes is the most obvious, but the analysis applies no matter the cause of demand heterogeneity.

Chapter 14

1   The European Court has ruled as illegal all attempts by manufacturers to refuse to deliver right-hand-drive vehicles to consumers wishing to take delivery on mainland Europe.

2   The authors wish to thank the editors of *Econometrica* for allowing the use of materials set forth in the article "Spatial Pricing in the U.S.A., West Germany, and Japan" (Greenhut 1981).

3   The interested reader is referred to Greenhut et al. (1980) for a more detailed discussion of spatial pricing by firms in the U.S. sample.

4   The summation $j = 2, \ldots, 5$ results because each respondent was asked to report prices in five markets (see questionnaire).

Chapter 15

1   Early contributions in location theory may also be found among many economists, including Launhardt, Smith, Ricardo, Mill, and Marshall.

2   This figure is adapted from Greenhut (1956, p. 254).

3   Reference should also be made to the closely related work of Christaller (1966).

4   It has been argued by Mills and Lav (1964) that the hexagonal arrangement of market areas need not arise. Greenhut (1970), Greenhut and Ohta (1973), and

Stern (1972) indicate, however, that the Mills-Lav result is founded on an implicit erroneous assumption.

5 In Lösch's view, "The real duty of the economist is not to explain our sorry reality but to improve on it. The question of the best location is far more dignified than determination of the actual one" (Lösch 1954, p. 4).

6 In the Löschian model (in contrast to Christaller) it is quite feasible for one production center to contain both intermediate and final production processes, but for another to contain only the intermediate-product process or only the final-product process (Parr 1973).

7 This figure and Figure 15.11 are taken from Greenhut (1970, Figure 12-3).

8 The savings in freight costs at Q_1 and Q_3 for each firm *may* more than offset the higher production cost. The opposite, of course, may hold.

9 See also Florence (1938, 1962).

10 This is consistent with the evidence in the United Kingdom, for example, of a migration of service firms out of London only in response to very sharp rises in office costs and significant changes in office technology. Even then, however, the pattern of relocation tends to be very constrained – generally moving west along the major communications network.

11 The brief hints given here will be expanded in later chapters.

Chapter 16

1 Second-order conditions are assumed to hold. They relate in the main to familiar convexity constraints on the demand function.

2 Attention is confined to cases in which demand and/or delivery-cost functions are everywhere concave, linear, or convex. Mixed functions would give rise to totally indeterminate results.

3 The reader can easily work through the corresponding argument for the case in which both functions are convex.

4 See Greenhut, Mai, and Norman (1986) for fuller details of these results and the results of the next section.

5 This assumption is, in fact, just the Hotelling-Smithies (or Bertrand-Nash) assumption noted in previous chapters.

6 The equivalence is, of course, dependent on the linearity assumptions.

Chapter 17

1 In order to avoid the complications considered by Gronberg and Meyer (Chapter 10), it is assumed that the consumer faces the same costs in customizing the product as does the producer.

2 It has been argued that entry to many airline markets is relatively easy (Bailey, Kaplan, and Sibley 1983).

3 Estimates over the years based on American data point to an annual loss in the rail industry of nearly $2.5 billion (Fiedlander and Spadt 1981).

4 See Schmalensee (1978) and Panzer (1979) along this line.

Chapter 18

1   Given the one possible limitation that there is no price undercutting.

2   This statement emphasizes the method by which propositions are proved in oligopoly theory. Proof requires merely demonstration of *existence*. If positive pure profit *can exist,* circumstances can be expected to arise in which it *does exist.*

3   This will be necessary, for example, if there is patent protection to existing goods, and it takes us back to Demsetz's remarks. Patents tend to be granted only when the patentable features of a commodity can be well defined. "Relocating" a patented product probably will require a new patent.

4   It may be worth restating that UPCV is equivalent to the Löschian price conjectural variation.

5   We confine x to be positive in view of the problems that arise in a computer simulation with $x < 0$. Note, however, that we are still able to contrast convex demand $(x < 1)$ with concave demand $(x > 0)$.

6   Rather than disrupt the text, a mathematical specification of the model is given in the Mathematical Appendix to this chapter.

7   Consumer density appears in the ratio $F/2D$. We can therefore assume $D = 1$ with no loss of generality.

8   This can be contrasted with the work of Eaton (1976), in which M tends to 1.7.

9   Other sources of pure profit have been suggested, but these relate in the main to bounded markets. It should be (trivially) clear that in bounded markets, an integer problem can arise. A market may be capable of sustaining N firms, but not $N + 1$. The N firms may then make positive pure profit.

Chapter 19

1   Note that "imperfect competition" encompasses the Chamberlinian approach; see also Harrod (1952, p. 140).

2   This efficiency extends from production to allocation and long-run price equality with marginal and average costs.

3   It is assumed that the individual is able to determine his alternatives rationally. Thus, a prospective economist who happens to be small in stature would tend to weigh lightly his alternative of becoming a professional basketball player. His lost-opportunity cost in basketball would tend to be "low."

4   For an early discussion of the nature of the firm and of the entrepreneur, see Coase (1937). A more recent analysis is to be found in Casson (1982).

5   Even though businessmen operate in a vastly different, more complicated system than the world of classical economics, we shall see that stability requires the same free entry and exit of firms as it does in the purely competitive economy. In effect, the stability requirement will also imply a long-run uniformity among viable firms for all concerned with evaluating profit-maximizing inputs and output.

6   This approach receives support from the duality theorem of linear programming and the related condition that if among $i + 1$ functional factors used in a production process only i are individually used most efficiently, while the remaining factor is used to an inefficient extent, the combination is inefficient, *ceteris paribus.*

All inefficient combinations yield greater costs than the lowest possible average costs. (Note that the inefficiently utilized factor of production could be any of land, labor, capital, or entrepreneurial resources.) It is worth noting, however, that the analysis is left unaltered if imputed rents are ascribed as fixed costs.

7   Again, it is worth emphasizing that a variable-cost ascription could be made with no change to the analysis. Diagrammatic presentation is eased by using the fixed-cost approach.

8   The reader may care to note that the diagrams used in this and subsequent sections are similar to those of Professor Demsetz. Demsetz (1968, p. 147) sets forth two AC curves, an APC (production) curve, and the ATC curve that includes ascriptions for selling costs on the top of production costs. The APC curve corresponds to what we have referred to in the text as the classical AC curve AC_c. Our second curve AC_u differs from the classical AC_c curve only by its inclusions of uncertainties. Demsetz's all-inclusive AC curve differs from his lower-level AC curve by the imputation of selling costs; our all-inclusive AC_u curve differs from the classical AC_c curve by including the (differential) uncertainty earnings required on optimal cost investment by the owners of imperfectly competitive firms. This higher-level AC curve, we shall also argue, is the same curve viewed by Chamberlin, except that he did not define the minimum amount of profit required by the particular activity.

9   Such a change in the behavior of firms in the industry and by potential producers will induce a change, of course, in the AR curve. We should also emphasize once more that the same conclusion would obtain if uncertainty were imputed as a variable cost.

10   The purist might find two possible exceptions to these comments: if demand functions are of negative-exponential form, or if the shape of the production function uniquely offsets the demand-curve effects. We would contend that neither of these effects is likely to be encountered in practice.

11   Ohta (1976) demonstrated for a competitive spatial economy (and thus heterogeneous oligopoly) that different demand-curve effects result when new competitive firms enter at a production center vis-à-vis at a distant location. He observed that "the invisible hand of competitive entry and exit signifies that tangency to the adjusted cost curve must sooner or later arise at a point nearer to the optimal one" (Ohta 1976, p. 1133).

12   This argument is also advanced by Greenhut (1974, chap. 4 and 8). To be sure, price is greater than MC in this theory, and hence it would appear that we have only technical (least-cost) efficiency, not allocative efficiency. However, the differential across industries is by the amount of uncertainty applicable to each industry. It is therefore not distortive of consumer wants, being predicated on an economic determinant that requires compensation.

13   If no selling costs are incurred, and only the quality of the product varies, the average product cost (APC) curve alone exists, not Demsetz's ATC curve. Any tangency between the AR curve applicable to a given quality of the good and the APC curve must occur at the downward-sloping portion of APC. Archibald further stressed that even if advertising is practiced and the ATC curve exists, the applicable MAR curve may not have a maximum, because increased output could

push price upward or downward depending on the effectiveness of the increased advertising.

14 Demsetz argued that there is no reason to exclude the possibility of cost optimization resulting from selected promotional activity, or from alternative qualities of good and/or plant locations. The MAR curve, he argued, does exist, and if the curve has a maximum point, free entry could shift it to a tangency position at the lowest point of the average total-cost curve. Demsetz further contended that variations in selling cost, location, and/or quality would generate a MAR curve with a maximum point.

15 Contrary to Demsetz, Barzel contends that no matter what mix of quantity and quality may be demanded by consumers, a fixed set of quantity-quality units must be conceived. At the point of tangency between average revenue and average cost (correctly measured), slopes must be negative. His complicated statement, but elementary (if not issue-avoiding) framework, can be specified as follows:

Let quality be included in the Demsetz model (e.g., in the form of the impact of advertising on the buyer's evaluation of the product). Then the firm's demand function can be written as

$$p^* = D(Q, R/Q)$$

where p^* is the real price of the quantity-quality package viewed by the consumer, with Q and R respectively reflecting the quantity and quality of the product. Because the consumer will purchase a larger quantity (or package) only if its real price per unit is falling, we have

$$\frac{\delta p^*}{\delta Q} < 0 \quad \text{and} \quad \frac{\delta p^*}{\delta (R/Q)} < 0$$

The average-cost function is, accordingly, definable as

$$AC^* = F(Q, R/Q)$$

Equilibrium requires

$$p^* = AC^*$$

and, of course,

$$\frac{\delta p^*}{\delta Q} = \frac{\delta AC^*}{\delta Q} < 0; \qquad \frac{\delta p^*}{\delta (R/Q)} = \frac{\delta AC^*}{\delta (R/Q)} < 0$$

It follows that both demand and cost curves must slope downward in equilibrium. Therefore, excess capacity must exist.

16 Schmalensee observed that the slopes of ATC and AR are equal under the tangency requirement; hence, $ATC_q = P_q$. But because $ATC_q = ATC_p P_q$, simple substitution indicates that ATC_p is unity and, in turn, that $ATC_q < 0$. Schmalensee, therefore, concluded that excess capacity must exist. However, Demsetz's MAR, in effect, was obtained from $dP/dq = (\delta p/\delta R)(dR/dq) + \delta p/\delta q$, where $(\delta p/\delta R)(dR/dq) > 0$, with $\delta p/\delta q < 0$, whereas in Schmalensee's system, dR/dq

was not defined to exist. Schmalensee thus conceives only of the price locus dp/dq, and this locus cannot be tangent to ATC at the lowest-cost point of ATC. He obtains his result, therefore, by assertion (i.e., without requisite justification), his critique of Demsetz thus being based on his use of different assumptions.

Chapter 20

1 This section of the chapter draws freely from "Estimates of Fixed Costs and the Sizes of Market Areas in the United States" (Greenhut and Hwang 1979). We would like to thank the editors of *Environment and Planning* and Professor Hwang for permission to reuse selected materials in that paper.

2 It should go without saying that Benson's analysis can be applied to any imperfectly competitive world in which there is a separation between consumers and producers.

3 Treating the market as the circumference of a circle avoids endpoint problems discussed by, for example, Salop (1979, p. 142).

4 Note that these comparative statics, particularly with respect to the mill price, are affected by the linearity assumptions.

5 It is assumed that the individual firms are sufficiently mobile to generate a zero-profit symmetric equilibrium – see Chapter 18.

Chapter 21

1 *Standard Oil Co.* v. *United States,* 221 U.S. 1 (1911).

2 47 *Cong. Rec.* 1225 (1911).

3 51 *Cong. Rec.* 12936 (1914).

4 Many cases have held that "unfair methods of competition" has a broader meaning than "unfair competition." Among those most prominently cited are *FTC* v. *R. F. Keppel & Bro. Inc.,* 291 U.S. 304 (1934), and *FTC* v. *Raladam Co.,* 283 U.S. 643 (1931).

5 *Atlantic Refining Co.* v. *FTC,* 381, U.S. 357, 367 (1965).

6 333 U.S. 683 (1948).

7 333 U.S. 690 (1948).

8 *Fashion Originators Guild* v. *FTC,* 312 U.S. 457, 466 (1941).

9 Senator Newlands, 51 *Cong. Rec.* 12030 (1914).

10 168 F.2d 175 (7th Cir. 1948).

11 See in particular Greenhut (1974), Chapter 7 on the basing point and Chapter 14, where the system [as in Greenhut (1956, 4th printing 1983, chap. 3)] is shown to be a form of *organized oligopoly,* hence equivalent to a monopoly.

12 384 U.S. 316, 322 (1966).

13 300 F.2d 92 (2d Cir. 1962).

14 142 F.2d 511, 517 (6th Cir. 1944).

15 Rivals' actions and reactions are fundamental to the operation of the spatial economy and imperfect competition, as indicated throughout this book.

16 257 U.S. 441 (1922).

17 333 U.S. 683 (1948).

18 *Beatrice Foods Co.*, 67 FTC 473 (1965); *Dean Foods Co.*, 70 FTC 1146 (1966); *US* v. *American Building Maintenance Industries*, 422 U.S. 271 (1975).

19 253 U.S. 421 (1920).

20 291 U.S. 309 (1934).

21 405 U.S. 233, 244 (1972).

22 Chapter 19 stressed this condition and analytically established the supposition that duopolistic equilibrium is identical, in terms of economic values, with a multifirm, intraindustry equilibrium.

23 In *FTC* v. *Sperry and Hutchinson Co.*, 405 U.S. 233, 244 (1972), the court held that, like a court of equity, the commission could consider "public values" beyond simply those empowered in the letter or encompassed in the spirit of the antitrust laws.

24 This section is derived from a study by Benson and Greenhut (1986).

25 Hence, our reason for proposing the circle market, not a hexagonal market.

26 *Price Flexibility and Consumer Satisfaction: Rate Deregulation Works* (Washington, D.C.: National Cablevision Association, 1984), cited in Lee (1984).

27 For example, the FCC under the Carter administration decided to alter the "1928" rule of a minimum 10 kHz for an AM broadcasting channel by allowing it to be reduced to 9 kHz, as in most countries in Europe. It shortly reneged on that change, thus limiting entry by government fiat.

Bibliography

Alonso, W. 1964. "Location Theory," Chapter 4 in J. Friedmann and W. Alonso, eds., *Regional Development and Planning,* pp. 78–106. Cambridge: M.I.T. Press.

Anderson, R. K., D. House, and M. B. Ormiston. 1981. "A Theory of Physician Behavior with Supplier-Induced Demand." *Southern Economic Journal* 48: 124–33.

Anderson, R. K., and M. B. Ormiston. 1983. "A Full-Pricing Analysis of the Owner-Managed Firm." *Southern Economic Journal* 50:57–70.

Archibald, G. C. 1962. "Chamberlin versus Chicago." *Review of Economic Studies* 29:2–28.

—— 1967. "Monopolistic Competition and Return to Scale." *Economic Journal* 77: 405–17.

Averitt, N. W. 1980. "The Meaning of 'Unfair Methods of Competition' in Section 5 of the Federal Trade Commission Act." *Boston College Law Review* 21:227–300.

Bailey, E. E., D. P. Kaplan, and D. S. Siblev. 1983. "On the Contestability of Airline Markets: Some Further Evidence," in J. Finsinger, ed., *Economic Analysis of Regulated Markets,* pp. 48–66. London: Macmillan.

Bain, J. S. 1956. *Barriers to New Competition.* Cambridge: Harvard University Press.

Barnett, S. 1975. *Introduction to Mathematical Control Theory.* Oxford: Clarendon Press.

Barzel, Y. 1970. "Excess Capacity in Monopolistic Competition." *Journal of Political Economy* 78:1142–9.

Baumol, W. J. 1982. "Contestable Markets: An Uprising in the Theory of Industry Structure." *American Economic Review* 72:1–15.

Baumol, W. J., J. C. Panzar, and R. P. Willig. 1982. *Contestable Markets and the Theory of Industrial Structure.* San Diego: Harcourt Brace Jovanovich.

Baxter, W. F. 1979. "The Political Economy of Antitrust," in Robert D. Tollison, ed., *The Political Economy of Antitrust.* Lexington, Mass.: Lexington Books.

Beckmann, M. 1968. *Location Theory.* New York: Harper & Brothers.

—— 1976. "Spatial Price Policies Revisited." *Bell Journal of Economics* 7:619–30.

Beckmann, M., and C. A. Ingene. 1976. "The Profit Equivalence of Mill and Uniform Pricing Policies." *Regional Science and Urban Economics* 6:327–9.

Benson, B. 1980a. "Löschian Competition Under Alternative Demand Conditions." *American Economic Review* 70:1098–105.

1980b. "The Impact of Entry at a Distance on Market Demand." *Review of Regional Studies* 10:62–8.

1981a. "The Optimal Size and Number of Market Areas." *Southern Economic Journal* 47:1080–5.

1981b. "Why Are Congressional Committees Dominated by 'High Demand' Legislators?" *Southern Economic Journal* 48:68–77.

1984. "Spatial Competition with Free Entry, Chamberlinian Tangencies, and Social Efficiency." *Journal of Urban Economics* 15:270–86.

Benson, B., and M. L. Greenhut. 1986. "Special Interests, Bureaucrats, and Antitrust: An Explanation of the Antitrust Paradox," In R. Grieson, ed., *Regulation and Antitrust,* pp. 53–90. New York: Wiley.

Berry, B. J., and W. L. Garrison. 1958. "A Note on Central Place Theory and the Range of a Good." *Economic Geography* 34:304–11.

Böhme, H. 1983. "Current Issues and Progress in European Shipping Policy." *World Economy* 6:325–52.

Bollabas, B., and N. Stern. 1972. "The Optimal Structure of Market Areas." *Journal of Economic Theory* 4:174–9.

Bork, Robert H. 1978. *The Antitrust Paradox: A Policy at War with Itself.* New York: Basic Books.

Brander, J. A. 1981. "Intra Industry Trade in Identical Commodities." *Journal of International Economics* 11:2–14.

Buckley, P. J., and M. C. Casson. 1976. *The Future of the Multinational Enterprise.* London: Macmillan.

1981. "The Optimal Timing of a Foreign Direct Investment." *Economic Journal* 91:75–87.

Capozza, D. R., and R. Van Order. 1978. "A Generalized Model of Spatial Competition." *American Economic Review* 68:896–908.

1980. "Unique Equilibria, Pure Profits, and Efficiency in Location Models." *American Economic Review* 70:1046–53.

Casson, M. C. 1982. *The Entrepreneur: An Economic Theory.* Oxford: Martin Robertson.

Casson, M. C., and G. Norman. 1983. "Pricing and Sourcing Strategies in a Multinational Oligopoly," in M. C. Casson, ed., *The Growth of International Business,* pp. 63–83. London: Allen & Unwin.

Chamberlin, E. H. 1933. *Theory of Monopolistic Competition,* 1st ed. Cambridge: Harvard University Press.

1956. *Theory of Monopolistic Competition,* 6th ed. Cambridge: Harvard University Press.

Christaller, W. 1966. *Central Places in Southern Germany,* trans. by C. W. Baskin. Englewood Cliffs, N.J.: Prentice-Hall. [First published as *Die zentralen Orte in Suddeutschland,* 1933.]

Clarkson, K. W., and T. J. Murio. 1982. "Letting Competition Serve Consumers," in Robert W. Poole, ed., *Instead of Regulation: Alternatives to Federal Regulatory Agencies,* pp. 135–68. Lexington, Mass.: Lexington Books.

Coase, R. H. 1937. "The Nature of the Firm." *Economica* 4:386–405.

1959. "The Federal Communications Commission." *Journal of Law and Economics* 2:1–40.

Cox, E. F., R. C. Fellmeth, and J. E. Schultz. 1969. *The Nader Report on the Federal Trade Commission,* New York: Barron Press.

d'Aspremont, C., J. Gabszewicz, and J. F. Thisse. 1979. "On Hotelling's Stability in Competition." *Econometrica* 47:1145–50.

Demsetz, H. 1959. "The Nature of Equilibrium in Monopolistic Competition." *Journal of Political Economy* 67:21–30.

1964. "The Welfare Implications of Monopolistic Competition." *Economic Journal* 74:623–41.

1967. "Monopolistic Competition: A Reply." *Economic Journal* 77:412–20.

1968. "Do Competition and Monopolistic Competition Differ?" *Journal of Political Economy* 76:146–8.

1972. "The Inconsistencies in Monopolistic Competition: A Reply." *Journal of Political Economy* 80:592–7.

DeVany, A. S. 1976. "Uncertainty, Waiting Time, and Capacity Utilization: A Stochastic Theory of Product Quality." *Journal of Political Economy* 84:523–41.

DeVany, A. S., W. L. Gramm, T. R. Saving, and C. W. Smithson. 1983. "Production in a Service Industry Using Customer Inputs: A Stochastic Model." *Review of Economics and Statistics* 65:149–53.

DeVany, A. S., and T. R. Saving. 1977. "Product Quality, Uncertainty, and Regulation: The Trucking Industry." *American Economic Review* 67:583–94.

Dixit, A. 1979. "A Model of Duopoly Suggesting a Theory of Entry Barriers." *Bell Journal of Economics* 10:20–32.

Dixit, A., and J. E. Stiglitz. 1977. "Monopolistic Competition and Optimum Product Diversity." *American Economic Review* 67:297–308.

Downs, A. 1957. *An Economic Theory of Democracy.* New York: Harper & Row.

Drum, D. 1976. "MBHC's Evidence After Two Decades of Regulation." *Federal Reserve Bank of Chicago, Business Conditions* (Dec. 1976):3–15.

Dunning, J. 1977. "Trade, Location of Economic Activity, and the Multinational Enterprise: A Search for an Eclectic Approach," in B. Ohlin, P. O. Hesselborn, and P. J. Wiskman, eds., *The International Allocation of Economic Activity,* pp. 395–418. London: Macmillan.

Dyckman, Z. Y. 1978. *A Study of Physicians' Fees.* Washington, D.C.: Council on Wage and Price Stability.

Eaton, B. C. 1972. "Spatial Competition Revisited." *Canadian Journal of Economics* 5:268–79.

1976. "Free Entry in One-Dimensional Models: Pure Profits and Multiple Equilibria." *Journal of Regional Science* 16:21–33.

Eaton, B. C., and R. G. Lipsey. 1975. "The Principle of Minimum Differentiation Reconsidered: Some New Developments in the Theory of Spatial Competition." *Review of Economic Studies* 42:27–49.

1976. "The Nonuniqueness of Equilibrium in the Löschian Model." *American Economic Review* 66:77–93.

1978. "Freedom of Entry and Existence of Pure Profit." *Economic Journal* 88:455–69.

Edwards, H. R. 1955. "Price Formation in Manufacturing Industry and Excess Capacity." *Oxford Economic Papers* 7:95–118.

Elzinga, K., and T. Hogarty. 1973. "The Problem of Geographic Market Delineation in Antimerger Suits." *Antitrust Bulletin* 18:45–81.

Evans, R. G. 1974. "Supplier-Induced Demand: Some Empirical Evidence and Implications," in M. Perlman, ed., *Economics of Health and Medical Care,* pp. 162–73. New York: Wiley.

Evans, R. G., E. M. A. Parish, and F. Sully. 1973. "Medical Productivity, Scale Effects, and Demand Creation." *Canadian Journal of Economics* 6:376–93.

Feldman, E., F. A. Lehrer, and T. L. Ray. 1966. "Warehouse Locations Under Continuous Economies of Scale." *Management Science* 12:670–84.

Feldstein, M. S. 1970. "The Rising Price of Physicians' Services." *Review of Economics and Statistics* 52:121–33.

Ferguson, C. E., and S. G. Maurice. 1978. *Economic Analysis – Theory and Application,* 3rd ed., Homewood, Ill.: Irwin.

Florence, P. S. 1938. *Investment Location and Size of Plant.* National Institute of Economic and Social Research, Study VII. Cambridge University Press.
   1962. *Post-War Investment, Location, and Size of Plant.* Cambridge University Press.

Fratrik, M. 1981. *Spatial Discriminatory Pricing With a General Cost Function.* Dissertation, Texas A&M Univesity.

Frech, H. E., III, and P. B. Ginsburg. 1975. "Imposed Health Insurance in Monopolistic Markets: A Theoretical Analysis." *Economic Inquiry* 13:55–70.

Friedman, J. 1983. *Oligopoly Theory.* Cambridge University Press.

Friedrich, C. J. (trans.) 1929. *Alfred Weber's Theory of the Location of Industries.* University of Chicago Press.

Fuchs, V. R. 1978. "The Supply of Surgeons and the Demand for Surgical Operations." *Journal of Human Resources* (Supplement) 13:35–56.

Fuchs, V. R., and M. J. Kramer. 1972. *Determinants of Expenditures for Physicians' Services in the United States 1948-60.* NBER Occasional Paper 117. Washington, D.C.: Department of Health, Education, and Welfare.

Gaskins, D. W. 1971. "Dynamic Limit Pricing: Optimal Pricing Under Threat of Entry." *Journal of Economic Theory* 3:306–22.

Gellhorn, E. 1984. "Baxter in the Pantheon of Antitrust." *Wall Street Journal* (Jan. 6), p. 16.

Gellman, A. 1971. "Surface Freight Transportation," in W. M. Capron, ed., *Technological Change in Regulated Industries,* pp. 166–96. Washington, D.C.: The Brookings Institution.

Gilman, S. 1983. *The Competitive Dynamics of Container Shipping.* Aldershot, England: Gower Publishing.

Grace, H. S. 1970. "Professor Samuelson on Free Enterprise and Economic Efficiency: A Comment." *Quarterly Journal of Economics* 84:337–40.

Green, J. 1978. "Physician-Induced Demand for Medical Care." *Journal of Human Resources* 13:21–34.

Greenhut, J. 1977. "On the Economic Advantages of Spatially Discriminatory Prices Compared with F.O.B. Prices." *Southern Economic Journal* 44:161–5.

Greenhut, J., and M. L. Greenhut. 1975. "Spatial Price Discrimination, Competition and Location Effects." *Economica* 42:401–19.

1977. "Nonlinearity of Delivered Price Schedules and Predatory Pricing." *Econometrica* 45:1871–5.

Greenhut, J., M. L. Greenhut, and W. H. Kelly. 1977. "A Spatial-Theoretical Perspective for Bank Merger Regulations," in *1977 Proceedings, Bank Structure and Competition, Federal Reserve Bank of Chicago.*

Greenhut, J., M. L. Greenhut, and S. Y. Li. 1980. "Spatial Pricing Patterns in the United States." *Quarterly Journal of Economics* 94:329–50.

Greenhut, M. L. 1956. *Plant Location in Theory and Practice.* Chapel Hill: U. of N.C. Press. 4th prtg., Westport, Conn.: Greenwood Press, 1982.

1966. "The Decision Process and Entrepreneurial Returns." *Manchester School* 34:247–67.

1970. "The Theory of the Spatial and Nonspatial firm." *Weltwirtschaftliches Archiv* 106:87–113.

1974. *A Theory of the Firm in Economic Space.* Austin: Lone Star Publishing. [First published New York: Appleton-Century-Crofts, 1970.]

1978. "Impact of Distance on Microeconomic Theory." *Manchester School of Economic Social Studies* 46:17–40.

1981. "Spatial Pricing in the U.S.A., West Germany, and Japan." *Economica* 48:79–86.

Greenhut, M. L., C. S. Hung, and G. Norman. 1986. "A General Theory of Spatial Competition and F.O.B. Pricing." Working Paper, University of Reading, Reading, England.

Greenhut, M. L., C. S. Hung, G. Norman, and C. Smithson. 1985. "An Anomaly in the Service Industry: The Effect of Entry on Fees." *Economic Journal* 95:169–77.

Greenhut, M. L., and M. Hwang. 1979. "Estimates of Fixed Costs and the Sizes of Market Areas in the United States." *Environment and Planning* 11:993–1009.

Greenhut, M. L., M. Hwang, and H. Ohta. 1975. "Observations on the Shape and Relevance of Spatial Demand Function." *Econometrica* 43:699–782.

Greenhut, M. L., and C. C. Mai. 1980. "Towards a General Theory of Public and Private Facility Location." *Annals of Regional Science* 14:1–11.

Greenhut, M. L., C. C. Mai, and G. Norman. 1986. "Impacts on Optimum Location of Different Pricing Strategies, Market Structure and Customer Distributions over Space." *Regional Science and Urban Economics* 16.

Greenhut, M. L., and H. Ohta. 1972. "Monopoly Output Under Alternative Spatial Pricing Techniques." *American Economic Review* 62:705–13.

1973. "Spatial Configurations and Competitive Equilibrium." *Weltwirtschaftliches Archiv* 109:87–104.

1975a. "Discriminatory and Nondiscriminatory Spatial Prices and Outputs Under Varying Market Conditions." *Weltwirtschaftliches Archiv* 111:310–31.

1975b. "A Theoretical Mapping From Perfect Competition to Imperfect Competition." *Southern Economic Journal* 42:177–92.

1975c. *Theory of Spatial Pricing and Market Areas.* Durham: Duke University Press.

1978. "Related Market Conditions and Interindustrial Mergers: Reply." *American Economic Review* 68:228–30.

Greenhut, M. L., H. Ohta, and J. Scheidell. 1972. "A Model of Market Areas Under Discriminatory Pricing." *Western Economic Journal* 10:402–13.

Gronberg, T., and J. Meyer. 1981a. "Competitive Equilibria in Uniform Delivered Pricing Models." *American Economic Review* 71:758–63.

1981b. "Transport Inefficiency and the Choice of Spatial Pricing Mode." *Journal of Regional Science* 21:541–9.

Grossman, G. E., and C. Shapiro. 1984. "Informative Advertising with Differentiated Products." *Review of Economic Studies* 51:63–81.

Grubel, H. G., and P. J. Lloyd. 1975. *Intra-Industry Trade.* London: Macmillan.

Hadley, G., and M. C. Kemp. 1971. *Variational Methods in Economics.* Amsterdam: North Holland.

Harbeson, R. W. 1969. "Toward Better Resource Allocation in Transport." *J. Law Econ.* 12:321–38.

Harrod, R. 1934. "Doctrines of Imperfect Competition." *Quarterly Journal of Economics* 48:442–70.

1952. *Economic Essays.* New York: Harcourt Brace.

Hart, O. D. 1980. "Perfect Competition and Optimal Product Differentiation." *Journal of Economic Theory* 22:279–312.

Hayek, F. 1973. *Law, Legislation and Liberty, Vol. 1, Rules and Order.* University of Chicago Press.

Holahan, W. L. 1975. "The Welfare Effects of Spatial Price Discrimination." *American Economic Review* 65:498–503.

1978. "Spatial Monopolistic Competition versus Spatial Monopoly." *Journal of Economic Theory* 18:156–70.

Hoover, E. M. 1937. "Spatial Price Discrimination." *Review of Economic Studies* 4:182–91.

1948. *The Location of Economic Activity.* New York: McGraw-Hill.

Horst, T. 1971. "The Theory of the Multinational Firm: Optimal Behaviour Under Different Tariff and Tax Rules." *Journal of Political Economy* 79: 1059–72.

1973. "The Simple Analytics of Multinational Firm Behavior," in M. B. Connolly and A. K. Swoboda, eds., *International Trade and Money,* pp. 72–84. London: Allen & Unwin.

Horvitz, P. and B. Shull. 1964. "The Impact of Branch Banking on Bank Performance." *National Banking Review* 2:143–88.

Hotelling, H. 1929. "Stability in Competition." *Economic Journal* 39:41–57.

Hotson, A. C., and K. L. Gardiner, 1983. "Trade in Manufactures." Bank of England Discussion Papers, Technical Series, No. 5.

Hwang, M. J. 1979. "A Model of Spatial Price Discrimination for the Price Schedule of Coal." *Journal of Regional Science* 19:231–44.

Isard, W. 1956. *Location and Space Economy.* Cambridge: M.I.T. Press.

Kaldor, N. 1935. "Market Imperfections and Excess Capacity." *Economica* 2: 35–50.

1938. "Professor Chamberlain on Monopolistic and Imperfect Competition." *Journal of Political Economy* 52:513–38.

Kamien, M. I., and N. L. Schwartz. 1981. *Dynamic Optimization.* Amsterdam: North Holland.

Kierzkowski, H., ed. 1984. *Monopolistic Competition and International Trade.* Oxford University Press.

Knickerbocker, F. T. 1973. *Oligopolistic Reaction and Multinational Enterprise.* Cambridge: Harvard University Press.

Knight, F. M. 1921. *Risk, Uncertainty and Profit.* Boston: Houghton Mifflin.

Kohlberg, E., and W. Novshek. 1982. "Equilibrium in a Simple Price-Location Model." *Economics Letters* 9:7–15.

Koopmans, T. C., and M. Beckmann. 1957. "Assignment Problems and the Location of Economic Activity." *Econometrica* 25:53–76.

Koutsoyiannis, A. 1975. *Modern Microeconomics.* London: Macmillan.

Kramer, G. H. 1977. "A Dynamic Model of Political Equilibrium." *Journal of Economic Theory* 16:310–34.

Lancaster, K. 1966. "A New Approach to Consumer Theory." *Journal of Political Economy* 74:132–57.

1975. "Socially Optimal Product Differentiation." *American Economic Review* 65:567–85.

1979. *Variety, Equity and Efficiency.* New York: Columbia University Press.

Lardner, D. 1850. *Railway Economy.* New York: Harper & Brothers.

Lee, W. E. 1984. "The First Amendment Versus Municipal Regulation of Cable Television." *Policy Analysis* no. 40. Washington, D.C.: Cato Institute.

Lerner, A. P., and H. W. Singer. 1937. "Some Notes on Duopoly and Spatial Competition." *Journal of Political Economy* 45:145–86.

Levine, M. 1965. "Is Regulation Necessary: California Air Transportation and National Regulatory Policy." *Yale Law Journal* 75:1416–47.

Linder, S. B. 1961. *An Essay on Trade and Transformation.* Uppsala: Almqvist & Wiksell.

Lösch, A. 1938. "The Nature of Economic Regions." *Southern Economic Journal* 5:71–8.

1954. *The Economics of Location.* New Haven: Yale University Press.

Lovell, M. C. 1970. "Product Differentiation and Market Structure." *Western Economic Journal* 8:120–43.

Luce, R. D., and H. Raiffa. 1957. *Games and Decisions.* New York: Wiley.

MacAvoy, P., and Sloss, J. 1967. *Regulation of Transport Innovation: The ICC and Unit Coal Trains to the East Cost.* New York: Random House.

MacLeod, W. B., G. Norman, and J. F. Thisse. 1984. "Competition, Collusion and Free Entry in Spatial or Differentiated Product Markets." CORE Discussion Paper No. 8436, Louvain-la-Neuve, Belgium: Center for Operations Research and Econometrics.

Machlup, F. 1952. *The Economics of Seller's Competition, Model Analysis of Seller's Conduct.* Baltimore: Johns Hopkins Press.

Magee, S. P. 1977. "Technology and the Appropriability Theory of the Multinational Corporation," in J. Bhagwati, ed., *The New International Economic Order: The North–South Debate.* Cambridge: M.I.T. Press.

1981. "The Appropriability Theory of Multinational Corporation Behaviour." University of Reading Papers in International Investment and Business Studies, No. 51.

Mansfield, E. 1962. "Entry, Gibrat's Law, Innovation, and the Growth of Firms." *American Economic Review* 52:1031–4.

Marshall, A. 1923. *Principles of Economics,* 8th ed. London: Macmillan.

Massam, B. 1975. *Location and Space in Social Administration.* London: Edward Arnold.

Meyer, J. R., et al. 1981. *Airline Deregulation: The Early Experience.* Boston: Auburn House.

Mills, E. S. 1972. *Urban Economics.* Glenview, Ill.: Scott, Foresman.

Mills, E. S., and M. Lav. 1964. "A Model of Market Areas with Free Entry." *Journal of Political Economy* 72:278–88.

Muth, R. F. 1967. "Urban Residential and Housing Markets," in H. Perloff and L. Wingo, Jr., eds., *Issues in Urban Economics,* pp. 285–333. Baltimore: Johns Hopkins Press.

Mueller, M. 1982. "Property Rights in Radio Communication: The Key to the Reform of Telecommunications Regulation," in *Policy Analysis.* Washington, D.C.: The Cato Institute.

Neale, A. D. 1970. *The Antitrust Laws of the U.S.A.* Cambridge University Press.
1976. *Antitrust Law: An Economic Perspective.* University of Chicago Press.

Needham, D. 1978. *The Economics of Industrial Structure, Conduct and Performance.* London: Holt, Reinhart & Winston.

Newhouse, J. P. 1970. "A Model of Physician Pricing." *Southern Economic Journal* 37:174–83.

Newhouse, J. P., A. P. Williams, B. W. Bennett, and W. B. Schwartz. 1982. "Does the Geographical Distribution of Physicians Reflect Market Failure?" *Bell Journal of Economics* 13:493–505.

Norman, G. 1979. "Economies of Scale in the Cement Industry." *Journal of Industrial Economics* 4:317–37.
1981a. "Uniform Pricing as an Optimal Spatial Pricing Policy." *Economica* 48: 87–91.
1981b. "Spatial Competition and Spatial Price Discrimination." *Review of Economic Studies* 48:97–111.
1981c. "Spatial Competition and Spatial Price Discrimination: An Extension." University of Reading Discussion Papers in Urban and Regional Economics, Series C, No. 7.
1983a. "Spatial Pricing with Differentiated Products." *Quarterly Journal of Economics* 98:291–310.
1983b. "A Geometric Note on Some Propositions in Spatial Pricing Policy." *Economics Letters* 12:341–7.
1986. "Market Strategy with Variable Entry Threats," in G. Norman, ed., *Spatial Pricing and Differentiated Markets.* London: Pion Press.

Norman, G., and J. H. Dunning. 1984. "Intra-industry Foreign Direct Investment: Its Rationale and Trade Effects." *Weltwirtschaftliches Archiv* 120: 522–40.

Norman, G., and N. K. Nichols. 1982. "Dynamic Market Strategy Under Threat of Competitive Entry: An Analysis of the Pricing and Production Policies Open to the Multinational Company." *Journal of Industrial Economics* 31: 153-74.

Novshek, W. 1980. "Equilibrium in Simple Spatial (or Differentiated Product) Models." *Journal of Economic Theory* 22:313-26.

Ohta, H. 1976. "On Efficiency of Production Under Conditions of Imperfect Competition." *Southern Economic Journal* 43:1124-35.

1977. "On the Excess Capacity Controversy." *Economic Inquiry* 15:153-65.

1980. "Spatial Competition Concentration, and Welfare." *Regional Science and Urban Economics* 10:3-16.

Osleeb, J. and R. Cromley. 1978. "The Location of Plants of the Uniform Delivered Price Manufacturer: A Case Study of Coca-Cola Ltd." *Economic Geography* 54:40-52.

Panzar, J. 1979. "Equilibrium and Welfare in Unregulated Airline Market." *American Economic Review* 69:92-95.

Parr, J. B. 1973. "Structure and Size in the Urban System of Lösch." *Economic Geography* 49:185-212.

Paul, M. E. 1954. "Notes and Excess Capacity." *Oxford Economic Papers* 6:33-54.

Pauly, M. V., and M. A. Satterthwaite. 1980. "The Effect of Provider Supply on Price," in *The Target Income Hypothesis and Related Issues in Health Manpower Policy*, U.S. Department of Health, Education, and Welfare Publication No. (HRA) 80-27, pp. 26-36.

1981. "The Pricing of Primary Care Physicians' Services: A Test of the Role of Consumer Information." *Bell Journal of Economics* 12:488-506.

Phlips, L. 1976. *Spatial Pricing and Competition*. Studies Competition – Approximation of Legislation Series, No. 29. Brussels: Commission of the European Communities.

1980. "Intertemporal Price Discrimination and Sticky Prices." *Quarterly Journal of Economics* 94:525-42.

1983. *The Economics of Price Discrimination*. Cambridge University Press.

Posner, R. 1976. *Antitrust Law: An Economic Perspective*. University of Chicago Press.

Pratten, C. F. 1971. *Economies of Scale in Manufacturing Industry*. Cambridge University Press.

Prescott, E. G., and M. Visscher. 1977. "Sequential Location Among Firms with Foresight." *Bell Journal of Economics* 8:378-93.

Price Commission. 1978a. *UG Glass Containers – Price of Glass Containers*. Price Commission Report No. 5, House of Commons 170. London: H.M.S.O.

1978b. *Metal Box Ltd. – Open Top Food and Beverage and Aerosol Cans*. Price Commission Report No. 3, House of Commons 135. London: H.M.S.O.

1978c. *Tate and Lyle Refineries Limited – Sugar and Syrup Products*. Price Commission Report No. 6, House of Commons 224. London: H.M.S.O.

1978d. *The Associated Portland Cement Manufacturers Limited – Increases in Cement Prices*. Price Commission Report No. 17, House of Commons 495. London: H.M.S.O.

Quinn, T. A. 1943. "The Hypothesis of Median Location." *American Sociological Review* 8:148–56.

Robinson, J. 1934. "Euler's Theorem and the Problem of Distribution." *Economic Journal* 44:398–414.

1971. *The Economics of Imperfect Competition.* London: Macmillan.

Rochdale Committee of Inquiry into Shipping. 1970. *Proceedings of the Rochdale Committee of Inquiry into Shipping.* London: Board of Trade, Cmnd. 4337, H.M.S.O.

Roche, G. 1983. *America by the Throat.* Greenwich, Conn.: Devin-Adair.

Rothschild, R. 1976. "A Note on the Effect of Sequential Entry on Choice of Location." *Journal of Industrial Economics* 24:313–20.

Rydell, C. P. 1967. "A Note on a Location Principle: Between the Median and the Mode." *Journal of Regional Science* 7:185–92.

1971. "A Note on the Principle of Median Location." *Journal of Regional Science* 11:395–6.

Salant, D. J. 1980. "Quality, Location Choice and Imperfect Competition." Doctoral Dissertation, University of Rochester.

Salop, S. C. 1979. "Monopolistic Competition with Outside Goods." *Bell Journal of Economics* 10:141–56.

Satterthwaite, M. A. 1979. "Consumer Information, Equilibrium Industry Price and the Number of Sellers." *Bell Journal of Economics* 10:483–502.

Saving, T. R. 1982. "Market Organization and Product Quality." *Southern Economic Journal* 49:855–67.

Scherer, F. M. 1975. *The Economics of Multi-Plant Operation.* Cambridge: Harvard University Press.

1980. *Industrial Market Structure and Economic Performance,* 2nd ed. Chicago: Rand McNally.

Schmalensee, R. 1972. "A Note on Monopolistic Competition and Excess Capacity." *Journal of Political Economy* 80:586–91.

1978. "A Model of Advertising and Product Quality." *Journal of Political Economy* 87:485–504.

Schwartz, M., and R. Reynolds. 1983. "Contestable Markets: An Uprising in the Theory of Industry Structure, Comment." *American Economic Review* 73:488–90.

Shephard, W. G. 1984. "'Contestability' vs. Competition." *American Economic Review* 74:572–87.

Shieh, Y. N., and I. Goldberg 1985. "Lardner's Law of Squares." *Economica* 52:509–12.

Shrieves, R. 1978. "Geographic Market Areas and Market Structure in the Bituminous Coal Industry." *Antitrust Bulletin* 23:589–625.

Shull, B. 1963. "Commercial Banks as Multiple-Produce Price-Discriminating Firms," in D. Carson, ed., *Banking and Monetary Studies.* Homewood, Ill.: Irwin.

Singer, H. W. 1937. "A Note on Spatial Price Discrimination." *Review of Economic Studies* 5:75–7.

Smith, D. M. 1971. *Industrial Location: An Economic Geographical Analysis.* New York: Wiley.

Smithies, A. 1939. "The Maximization of Profits Over Time with Changing Cost and Demand Functions." *Econometrica* 7:312–18.

1941. "Optimal Location in Spatial Competition." *Journal of Political Economy* 49:423–39.

Snyder, R. 1971. "A Note on the Principle of Median Location." *Journal of Regional Science* 11:391–3.

Södersten, B. 1980. *International Economics,* 2nd ed. London: Macmillan.

Sokolnikoff, I. S. 1939. *Advanced Calculus.* New York: McGraw-Hill.

Stackelberg, H. von. 1952. *The Theory of Market Economy,* trans. A. T. Peacock. London: William Hodge.

Stern, N. H. 1972. "The Optimal Size of Market Areas." *Journal of Economic Theory* 4:154–73.

Stevens, B. H., and C. P. Rydell. 1966. "Spatial Demand Theory and Monopoly Price Policy." *Papers, Regional Science Association* 17:195–204.

Stigler, G. 1971. "The Theory of Economic Regulation." *Bell Journal of Economics and Management Science* 2:3–21.

Sylos-Labini, P. C. 1968. *Oligopoly and Technical Progress,* rev. ed. Cambridge: Harvard University Press.

Takayama, A. 1974. *Mathematical Economics.* Hinsdale, Ill.: Dryden.

Tharakan, P. M. M. 1981. "The Economies of Intra-Industry Trade: A Survey." *Recherches Economiques de Louvain* 47:259–90.

Thisse, J. F., and H. G. Zoller (eds.) 1983. *Locational Analysis of Public Facilities.* Amsterdam: North Holland.

Ulph, D. 1983. "Rational Conjectures in the Theory of Oligopoly." *International Journal of Industrial Organisation* 1:131–54.

Vernon, R. 1979. "The Product Cycle Hypothesis in a New International Environment." *Oxford Bulletin of Economics and Statistics* 41:255–67.

Villegas, D. 1982. "Comparative Performance of Spatial Models of Economic Markets with Linear Household Demand." *Southern Economic Journal* 48: 893–908.

Weber, A. 1929. *Theory of the Location of Industry.* University of Chicago Press.

Weitzman, M. 1983. "Contestable Markets: An Uprising in the Theory of Industry Structure, Comment." *American Economic Review* 73:486–7.

Wenders, J. T. 1971. "Excess Capacity as a Barrier to Entry." *Journal of Industrial Economics* 20:14–19.

Williamson, O. E. 1968. "Economies as an Antitrust Defense: The Welfare Trade-offs." *American Economic Review* 58:18–36.

Winston, C. 1985. "Conceptual Developments in the Economics of Transportation: An Interpretative Survey." *Journal of Economic Literature* 23:57–94.

Author index

Alonso, W., 257, 258, 289
Anderson, R. K., 45, 46
Archibald, G. C., 320
Averitt, N. W., 368

Bailey, E. E., 383n2(ch.17)
Bain, J. S., 219
Barnett, S., 184
Barzel, Y., 320, 386n15(ch.19)
Baumol, W. J., 320
Baxter, W. F., 368
Beckmann, M., 121, 132, 175, 257, 278,
    282, 289, 378n3(ch.7), 378n4(ch.7)
Benson, B., 3, 21, 52, 58, 61, 344, 348,
    354, 355, 356, 358, 376n5(ch.4),
    388n24(ch.21)
Berry, B. J., 266
Böhme, H., 297
Bollobas, B., 265
Bork, Robert H., 359, 368, 370
Brander, J. A., 379n4(ch.9)
Buckley, P. J., 209, 220, 261

Capozza, D. R., 3, 20, 39, 50, 54, 90, 93,
    95, 128, 129, 130, 302, 311, 318, 330, 334,
    365, 375n7(ch.2)
Casson, H. C., 209, 220, 261, 379n4(ch.8),
    384n4(ch.19)
Chamberlin, E. H., 1, 31, 73, 263, 289,
    302, 319, 320, 323, 385n8(ch.19)
Christaller, W., 382n3(ch.15), 383n6(ch.15)
Clarkson, K. W., 370
Coase, R. H., 384n4(ch.19)
Cournot, 1, 281
Cromley, R., 238, 261

Demsetz, H., 303, 304, 305, 320, 385n8
    (ch.19), 385n14(ch.19), 386n14(ch.19),
    386n15(ch.19), 386n16(ch.19)
DeVany, A. S., 46, 351, 357
Dixit, A., 219, 222, 377n7(ch.5)
Downs, A., 262
Drum, D., 70
Dunning, J. H., 162, 209, 220
Dyckman, Z. Y., 45

Eaton, B. C., 93, 262, 279, 305, 306, 307,
    308, 309, 310, 311, 313, 314, 315, 319,
    330, 334, 375n1(ch.3), 384n8(ch.18)
Edgeworth, 1
Edwards, H. R., 319
Elzinga, K., 69
Evans, R. G., 45

Feldman, E., 261
Feldstein, M. S., 45
Ferguson, C. E., 31
Florence, P. S., 383n9(ch.15)
Fratrik, M., 380n1(ch.11)
Frech, H. E., III, 45
Friedman, J., 74, 75
Friedrich, C. J., 257
Fuchs, V. R., 45

Gardiner, K. L., 238
Garrison, W. L., 266
Gaskins, D. W., 199, 381n2(ch.12),
    382n6(ch.12)
Gellhorn, E., 368
Gilman, S., 296
Ginsburg, P. B., 45
Goldberg, I., 125, 376n10(ch.4)
Grace, H. S., 313
Green, J., 45
Greenhut, J., 3, 5, 20, 109, 110, 132, 135,
    157, 196, 241, 246, 344, 376n1(ch.4),
    376n2(ch.4), 377n14(ch.4), 379n1(ch.8)
Greenhut, M. L., 3, 5, 20, 52, 61, 71, 101,
    109, 110, 132, 135, 167, 172, 196, 217,
    218, 241, 246, 247, 249, 255, 261, 267,
    268, 271, 285, 290, 323, 331, 333, 345,
    346, 347, 356, 374n1(ch.2), 375n6(ch.3),
    376n1(ch.4), 376n2(ch.4), 376n6(ch.4),
    376n7(ch.4), 377n14(ch.4), 377n6(ch.5),
    377n6(ch.6), 378n7(ch.7), 379n1(ch.8),
    380n1(ch.10), 382n2(ch.14), 382n3(ch.14),
    382n2(ch.15), 382n4(ch.15), 383n7(ch.15),
    383n4(ch.16), 385n12(ch.19), 387n1
    (ch.20), 387n11(ch.21), 388n24(ch.21)
Gronberg, T., 127, 174, 175, 177, 179, 294,
    379n9(ch.7), 383n1(ch.17)

401

Subject index

ad valorem: and spatial price discrimination, 191–4; and transport cost, 189–91
agglomeration, economies of, 260
aggregate demand: convexity, 8, 23–6; elasticity of spatial, 7, 23, 24, 25, 26, 27, 29, 34, 36, 48, 49, 51, 56, 58, 61, 63, 64; individual demand curves and, 7–10; spatial firm's, 6–9, 13, 23, 30, 54, 71, 92; spatial vs. spaceless, 6–10; and varying net demands, 61–2
airlines services, 297, 298
antidumping legislation, 2, 6, 207, 284, 371
antimerger policy, 2, 68, 359
average costs: classical, 322, 325, 326, 329, 333, 345; explicit, 325, 346; including uncertainty, 325, 330

barriers to entry, 43
behavioral uncertainty, 315, 322, 323, 325, 326, 328, 330, 332, 333, 334, 352, 355, 356, 357, 358
Bertrand-Nash equilibrium, 20, 87, 90

capital immobility and positive pure profit, 315
capital indivisibility, 315, 334
ceiling price constraint and spatial pricing, 166–74
Celler-Kefauver Act, 68, 71
Chamberlin monopolistic competition: and excess capacity, 319, 340–3; and tangency equilibrium, 319, 340–3
characteristics approach, 74, 102, 147
Chow's test, 246
Clayton Act, 68, 362, 363, 364, 365, 366, 370
collusion and DPS: coincident location, 148–9; noncoincident location, 149–50
collusive oligopoly and nonzero conjectural variation, 148–50
commodity bundling, 233
competition effect, 30–1, 33, 34, 40, 43, 50, 51, 63, 353
competitive locations and spatial pricing policies, 274–88, 300

competitive price constraint, 166–74
competitive statics, 42–3, 86, 87, 88, 115, 129, 130, 197, 333, 387n4(ch.20)
conjectural variations, 14, 20, 22, 28, 29, 30, 39, 41, 49, 50, 51, 52, 54, 63, 104, 127, 129, 144, 148, 149, 150, 288, 290, 308, 313, 320, 333, 353, 356, 357, 358, 384n4(ch.18)
constant numbers equilibrium, 307, 308, 309, 314
control variable and delivered-price schedule (or trajectory), 183
cost-based theories: Von Thünen, 255; Weber, 255
Cournot-Nash equilibrium, 163, 325
cross-price elasticities, 148
cross-subsidization, 19
cumulative sales, 181
customer-supplied time, 47

delivered price and future price, 211
delivered price schedule: heterogeneous, 109; linear, 283; negatively-sloped, 139–41, 145–7; nonlinear, 169, 178; and price discrimination, 106, 167, 242; slope of, 104, 110, 113, 114, 138, 140, 143, 147, 148, 169, 170, 193, 241, 250, 377n6(ch.6), 381n10(ch.11)
delivery costs, 116, 237, 238, 258, 259, 275, 276, 277, 278, 279, 280, 285, 289, 290, 383n2(ch.16)
demand curve: actual, 30, 51; gross individual, 21, 22–7, 35, 63, 64; imagined, 31, 51
demand effect, 30, 31, 33, 34, 43, 50, 51, 70, 278
demand elasticity: and conjectural variations, 28–30, 32; and mill price, 23–4, 26–9
demand increasing effect of additional plants, 349
differentiated products, 295, 301, 304, 344, 350
diffusion rate of technology, 200, 202, 203, 206, 208, 209, 215

405